The
Carol J. Adams
Reader

At her file cabinets. Photograph by Matthew C. Halteman,
April 2015.

The Carol J. Adams Reader

Writings and Conversations
1995–2015

Edited by Carol J. Adams

Bloomsbury Academic
An imprint of Bloomsbury Publishing Inc

B L O O M S B U R Y
NEW YORK · LONDON · OXFORD · NEW DELHI · SYDNEY

Bloomsbury Academic

An imprint of Bloomsbury Publishing Inc

1385 Broadway	50 Bedford Square
New York	London
NY 10018	WC1B 3DP
USA	UK

www.bloomsbury.com

BLOOMSBURY and the Diana logo are trademarks of Bloomsbury Publishing Plc

Library of Congress Cataloging-in-Publication Data

A catalog record for this book is available from the Library of Congress.

ISBN: HB: 978-1-5013-2433-8
PB: 978-1-5013-2432-1
ePub: 978-1-5013-2434-5
ePDF: 978-1-5013-2435-2

Cover design: Catherine Wood
Cover image © Jo-Anne McArthur/The Unbound Project

Typeset by Deanta Global Publishing Services, Chennai, India
Printed and bound in the United States of America

Have a heart,

                I whisper over barbed wire.

What has struggled into life,

                       breathed through blizzards,

is more than bones on a plate.

                          Unwrite your lives

from that numbness.

                Find yourselves

spindly-legged in the cold.

        from "Calf" by Kathryn Kirkpatrick

Contents

Figures and tables

Tables

2A. MIRTH ASSESSMENT

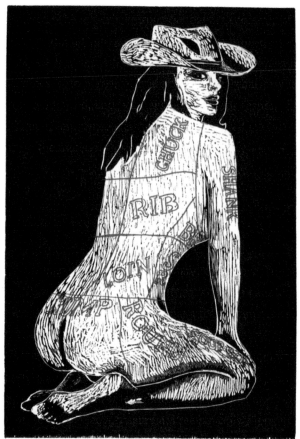

Findings: Between 65-70% of respondents
found the above image amusing; the remaining
were women who found it offensive. After
being told it was "kitsch", they conceded
there is no established relationship between
oppression of women and animals, and
that they should get a sense of humor about it.

Figure P.1 Melissa H. Potter, *2A. Mirth Assessment,* woodcut and
silkscreen, 1997.

Preface

For the past twenty years, I have written essays and participated in conversations and interviews that extend the theoretical work begun with my books, *The Sexual Politics of Meat* (1990) and *Neither Man nor Beast* (1994). After the publication in 2015 of the Bloomsbury Revelations (twenty-fifth anniversary) edition of *The Sexual Politics of Meat*, it was time to collect these writings.

I selected the thirteen essays and conversations in this book based on these criteria: Does it further our understanding of one of the central features of Western existence—the objectification and use of other beings? Does it introduce new ideas or expand on previous ones that continue to be important to the current conversation on animals, feminism, and interconnected oppressions? Does it provide insights into the relationship between theory and activism? Does it acknowledge how gender, race, and species interweave? Does it draw on what I have learned about how images work from showing *The Sexual Politics of Meat Slide Show* on numerous campuses? To answer those questions, I reviewed all my essays and interviews over the past twenty years, and identified the ones that I felt represented new interventions or elaborated in important ways on ideas in *The Sexual Politics of Meat* and *Neither Man nor Beast*.

The first chapter, "The War on Compassion" (2005), began to take shape when I was invited to give the Paul O'Neill lecture at

Transylvania University in Lexington, Kentucky. The lecture series invites scholars to discuss their new work. I had been haunted by the genocides that had occurred in my lifetime. Taking the statement "we were treated like animals," I explore the structural hierarchies that result both in this treatment (especially in its most genocidal forms) and the statement itself (comparing one's experience with that of animals). Why do individuals often fail to respond to violence against other peoples? Why do they fail to care?

"What Came Before *The Sexual Politics of Meat*: The Activist Roots of a Critical Theory" (2011) offers answers to several questions: "How is one an activist?" "How does one balance activism for those on the other side of the vigilantly-guarded species boundary with activism for those humans thrown and propelled toward that boundary by oppressive attitudes and actions?" Finally, "what does one learn from activism?" To answer these questions, and as a case study specific to writing *The Sexual Politics of Meat*, I describe a difficult activist experience from the 1980s.

"The Politics of Meat: The *Antennae Magazine* Interview with Annie Potts" (2010) explores how oppressive attitudes are expressed through popular culture and become embodied in representations. It defines *anthropornography* (the feminizing and sexualizing of animals and the animalizing of women). It considers specific ads, moving to a discussion about artists who use dead animals in their artwork and art and representations that resist objectification.

"Woman-Battering and Harm to Animals" (1995) was one of the earliest essays seeking to understand the theoretical aspects and implications of harm to animals as a part of battering. This essay shows how harm to animals furthers the control strategies of a batterer and proposes several feminist theoretical claims about the deliberateness of battering, the relationship between harm to animals and harm to children, and that harm to animals is violence in its own right while also showing how violence is interconnected.

In "Derrida and *The Sexual Politics of Meat:* A Conversation with Matthew Calarco" (2011), Matt and I discuss the relationship between Derrida's concept of carnophallogocentrism and my ideas in *The Sexual Politics of Meat.* In "Eating Well," Derrida suggests that the notion of the subject that is being critiqued in post-humanist thought should be understood not simply as a fully self-present, speaking, masculine subject but also as a quintessentially *human, animal-flesh-eating* subject. I suggest that the carnophallogocentric subject is the subject created by a culture with the foundational premise of the sexual politics of meat.

On March 20, 1996, the possible link between bovine spongiform encephalopathy, commonly called "mad cow disease," and Creutzfeldt–Jakob Disease, the fatal human equivalent, was announced. That a disease identified with cows since 1985 could possibly be spread to human beings by eating meat from infected animals prompted a crisis for the meat industry and consumers. In "'Mad Cow' Disease and the Animal Industrial Complex: An Ecofeminist Analysis" (1997), I explain why taking this crisis seriously is important to environmental and feminist theory. Most responses to this crisis represented a search for anthropocentric solutions to the problem: improve the meat supply rather than examine the practice of meat eating. This essay offers an ecofeminist methodology for approaching issues of meat production and the proliferation of zoonotic diseases (diseases from animals). Twenty years later, it is interesting how quickly "mad cow disease" faded from public consciousness. Like #piggate,[1] an event that exposes the key aspects of the sexual politics of meat constitutive of the culture cannot be placed before public scrutiny for long.

---

[1] A short-lived controversy in 2014 about whether, as an undergraduate at Oxford University, the British Prime Minister David Cameron simulated fellatio by placing "a private part of his anatomy" (the euphemism of the news reports) in a dead pig's mouth as another undergraduate held the head of the murdered pig on his lap.

Illuminating the dominant commitments of a culture too clearly, it must disappear.

In "Why a Pig? A Reclining Nude Reveals the Intersections of Race, Sex, Slavery, and Species" (2014), I examine an image that has haunted me for several decades: "Ursula Hamdress," an example of anthropornography. I propose the context for the photograph is the history of the "reclining nude" in art, and read a parallel construction of the body for consumption. Scholars concerned with race-making, representation, and the transition from modernity to postmodernity all gravitate to images that are the precursors of and motivators for the posing of a pig. Critical theory that investigates traditional Western depictions of women's beauty, specifically "the reclining nude," and follows these depictions into the late twentieth century, has failed to recognize specifically how this tradition has lept/fled/transcended human-centered figures to reinscribe retrograde and oppressive attitudes toward women upon domesticated animals. Delving past the species line in examining representations of female "beauty," or sexualized female bodies, exposes the structuring of consumption that is normalized and naturalized.

The *Critical Animal Studies* Interview with Lindgren Johnson and Susan Thomas (2013) explores the meaning of the feminist ethics of care, the attempts to spiritualize butchering, and includes a close look at a specific activism, the "kiss-in" at Chick-Fil-A that brought gays, lesbians, and their allies into Chick-Fil-A. This activism raised questions about how to do intersectional activism. The interview also considers whether animal slaughter can be an expression of care? (no), what I think constitutes care, what kinds of direct action are appropriate, and what traumatic knowledge is.

"Abortion and Animals: Keeping Women in the Equation" (1998) argues that the only proper context for discussing abortion is within the context of women's lives. There is no preexisting paradigm into which the question of abortion fits, because there is nothing equivalent to pregnancy. The human/animal dualism assumes a radical difference between humans and all other animals and is used to justify human's oppression of the other animals. It also undergirds the human-centeredness of antiabortionists. Eliminate that foundational dualism and the moral claims of antiabortionists—that human fetal life has an absolute claim upon us—is overthrown.

"After MacKinnon: Sexual Inequality in the Animal Movement" (2011) proposes that sexual inequality is one of the defining elements of the animal movement, effecting both the status of animals whose liberation is sought and the status of the women within the movement who seek the liberation of animals. I critique PETA's objectification of female bodies and identify several ways that sexual inequality operates to maintain oppression, including the use of animals as constituting a part of the definition of manhood. Sexual inequality inscribes a pornographic "femininity" on domesticated and defeated animals, and creates an atmosphere for structural inequality in the animal movement.

"An Animal Manifesto: Gender, Identity, and Vegan-Feminism in the Twenty-First Century. Conversation with Tom Tyler" (2006) identifies four main vegan-feminist claims, and argues that flesh eating and veganism should properly be defined as relationships with other animals, not personal decisions about food. It offers a critique of Donna Haraway's *Animal Manifesto* and finds in Derrida a more salutary approach. It argues that no matter the multiplicity of selves we each might constitute, and the academic concern for totalizing theories that consume slippery, ambiguous meanings and possibilities, eating as an act is something that is locatable.

I began thinking about the issues in "Post-Meateating" (2009) after keynoting at the 2000 Millennial Animals Conference in Sheffield, England. There was a clear divide between those citing continental philosophers and those drawing from feminist, antiracist, and activist theory in our talks. This prompted me to explore the potential of postmodern theory. I realized that the contemporary preoccupation with cultural representations ultimately undermines any challenge to the human exploitation of other creatures, as the *cultural* animal seems to have superseded the actual animal. In "Post-Meateating," I find certain binaries functioning, representing modern versus postmodern formulations of animals' lives and suggest that postmodernism may offer no particular relief to the proliferating of animal exploitation.

Through the interview with Marco Gilebbi, a brief history of ecofeminism, its "disappearance" and "resurgence" and the reasons for this are offered. The interview explores how the ecofeminist analysis of the environmental crisis would include examining patriarchal ideas of separation and autonomy. The ecofeminist articulation of "care" becomes both a radical critique of patriarchal privilege as it has been depoliticized, and becomes a remedy for responding to the crisis. The interview returns to a concern articulated in Chapter 3, the role of art in the midst of this environmental crisis.

I have not arranged these chapters chronologically but thematically, so that each essay or conversation extends or elaborates ideas that have preceded it. The chapters exist as conversations among each other, arranged to create movement through the ideas. When doing so did not impact the discussion at hand, I removed unnecessary repetitions. I wanted to protect the integrity of each chapter, but also allow them to be woven together, so that a reader could be propelled forward chapter by chapter and not be hampered by repetition. I provide page numbers indicating where the idea first appears.

There is also a movement in the images that appear in the following pages. Advertisements throw everyday phenomenon into relief. In presenting an advertisement, I seek to isolate it from its usual context (billboards, magazines, and restaurant posters) that helps to make it normative and unquestioned, and use it as an illustration of a dominant attitude about species, race, or gender. By changing its context, I hope to disempower it and expose its function as propaganda for dominance.

In *Neither Man nor Beast*, I began to include the work of artists in my books. In that book it was the work of Susan kae Grant. *The Pornography of Meat* contained the work of Nancy Hild, Penny Siopsis, Jo Spence, Sue Coe, Karen Finley, Leslie Dellios, and Eric Reinders. Now, in this book, the work of artists that resists the dominant way of seeing and being are threaded throughout the book and I give feminist artists the last word.

I celebrate that in 2013, artists Kathryn Eddy, Janell O'Rourke, and L. A. Watson co-founded ArtAnimalAffect, an artist coalition dedicated to bridging art and activism within the field of critical animal studies. Through artwork, research, and writing, their aim is to raise awareness of animal issues, as well as provide exhibit opportunities for contemporary artists who explore the social, political, and ethical dimensions of human-animal relationships. And I am honored that their first project, an exhibition inspired by *The Sexual Politics of Meat*, will open in Los Angeles, including the work found in *The Art of the Animal: Fourteen Women Artists Explore **The Sexual Politics of Meat*** published in 2015.

In my books, I identify how language supports but hides exploitation. To counter this, I coined new terms or wrenched terms from their usual environment to provide insights into accepted exploitative attitudes in the hopes of resisting them. These terms are introduced and used in the essays and conversations that follow. In her animation *Which Came First: An Interview with Carol J. Adams*, Suzy González captures this dynamic act of problematizing what we see as foods.

Figure P.2 Artist's statement: "Through my work, I search for what
might be named fourth wave feminist art by observing intersections of
identity, or more specifically, race, gender, and species. Reading feminist
theory has had an immense influence on my work. I wanted to dedicate
something to one of my favorite authors, Carol J. Adams, who has opened
my eyes to an ethics of veganism and its relationship to feminism. My
curiosity of how she came to realize these connections led me to ask her
'Which came first? Your feminism or your veganism?' I want to spread
awareness by sharing the messages of those who have had a profound
effect on my life, while creating messages of my own along the way."
Still from Suzy González's Animation, *Which Came First? An Interview with
Carol J. Adams.*

   Besides problematizing language, I struggle to find accurate words.
What do we call this movement against human supremacy? In the past
I have used the term "animal defense movement" (see Adams 1994b).
For Chapter 10, I chose a more generic term "animal movement" as I
believed it could also incorporate "animal studies" and "critical animal
studies." I use veg*n any time a reference could encompass vegans or
vegetarians. When appropriate to the meaning of the text, specific
references to vegetarians or vegans remain. The struggle for accurate
words was particularly challenging with Chapter 4. I am uncomfortable
with the term "battered woman," although it is one that the movement

against violence against women had itself adopted. I agree with Sarah Hoaglund (1988) that the term elides the agency of the batterer, while also ascribing an unchanging status to the victim. However, because it is the commonly adopted term, and is used by the scholars and activists from whom I draw my examples, I use the term in this essay.

In that chapter, I also use the conventional term "pet" to describe animals who are a part of a household. Those involved in the movement to free animals from human oppression prefer the term "companion animal." While I find this term helpful, the word "pet" was the word used most frequently by those describing their experiences. Thus, for consistency, I continue their usage.

My work has always been, in part, a meditation on care: When do we care? When don't we care? Why not? How do we transform our apathy to care?

Since 2002, I was immersed in what our culture views as the dyadic care relationship—caregiver to care receiver (described in Reiheld 2015). In Chapters 2 and 11, I refer briefly to those caregiving relationships: my mother's Alzheimer's and the amputation of a friend's leg. The friend was my mother-in-law who lived with us.

In my memory, this caregiving weaves through the chapters contained here. I remember arriving at my parents' house in May 2005, after giving the lecture that became "The War on Compassion" at Transylvania University. Caring in political and personal ways felt very fluid that week. The writing of "What Came Before *The Sexual Politics of Meat*" occurred during the last years of my mother's life; I shared caregiving of her with my sisters and my father as her Alzheimer's progressed. These caregiving trips home brought me back to the location of my activist roots. At first, the chapter was dedicated to my mother. By the time it was in proofs, it was dedicated to the memory of both my parents.

I remember being determined to finish the interview with Annie (Chapter 3). Though I did not understand the compulsion, I stayed up very late on a Saturday night in April 2010 to do so. The following afternoon, I was called to help with an emergency with my father. In 2005, I felt the same urgency to finish my work on "Robert Morris and a Lost 18th-Century Book: An Introduction to Morris's *A Reasonable Plea for the Animal Creation* (2005)." Again, I did not understand why I kept working on it on hot nights in July 2005, as my deadline was mid-August. I submitted it with relief and, a day later, my mother-in-law's amputation crisis began.

When scholars working on special editions of journals invited me to contribute, I often proposed conversations and interviews instead. These I could pick up and put down in between caregiving.

Caregiving changed me and my future writings will focus on this.[2] With the forthcoming appearance of "Towards a Philosophy of Care through Care" in *Critical Inquiry*, my next work integrating my personal experience of providing caregiving of elderly relatives with a feminist theory of care begins. Like my work of the past twenty years gathered here, it arises from and reflects living in community. We live in *and* learn from community. The chapters that follow incorporate my efforts to replace an instrumental ethic with a caring ethic and to widen our understanding of community in a way that protects all its members from harm.

---

[2]One has appeared: "Jane Austen's Guide to Alzheimer's," The *New York Times, Sunday Review,* December 20, 2015, p. 9.

Acknowledgments

I am grateful for the opportunity to engage with people thinking about resistance to oppression. I am thankful for all the invitations to speak at events and on campuses that ushered me into lively conversations around the world. While the content and importance of those conversations cannot be captured here, I hope the dynamic of the give and take of thoughts and questions found in Chapters 3, 5, 8, 11, and 13 gestures toward this. I thank my conversationalists: Matthew Calarco, Matteo Gilebbi, Lindgren Johnson, Annie Potts, Susan Thomas, and Tom Tyler. Vasile Stănescu suggested a project that became Chapter 5.

I am also fortunate that being the author of *The Sexual Politics of Meat* paved the way for me to meet so many wonderful scholars and activists, from whom I have learned so much and whose friendship I value. Particularly, I wish to acknowledge the following people who helped me with edits of various essays or in conversations that prompted new ideas represented in this book: Sarah Brown, Batya Bauman, Diana Blaine, the late Kathleen Carlin, Katie Carter, David L. Clark, Peter Cox, Karen Davis, Richard DeAngelis, Josephine Donovan, Erin Fairchild, Lisa Finlay, Marie Fortune, Bruce Friedrich, Jack Furlong, David Garvin, Lori Gruen, Eric Haapupuru, Leigh Nachman Hofheimer,

Nancy Howell, Mary Hunt, Mike Jackson, Susanne Kappeler, the late Marti Kheel, Gus Kaufman, Jr., Patrick Kwan, Jayne Loader, Brian Luke, Catharine MacKinnon, Randy Malamud, Leslie Mann, Jim Mason, Adrian Mellori, the late Bina Robinson, Holly Steward, Ken Shapiro, John Stoltenberg, Nancy Tuana, Karen Warren, Dave Wasser, and DeLora Wisemoon.

Thanks to the editors of volumes in which my writings or interviews first appeared: Giovanni Aloi, Marianne DeKoven, John Jermier, Mike Lundblad, Annie Potts, John Sanbonmastu, Kim Stallwood, and Tom Tyler. I have learned so much from my coauthors, Patti Breitman and Ginny Messina, and coeditors, Josephine Donovan, Marie Fortune, and Lori Gruen.

I appreciate the support of Wendy Lochner at Columbia University Press and Steve Cohn, the director of Duke University Press. My writings have benefited from all the copy editors of these essays, keen-eyed, with their finely honed skills at detecting unclear phrases, repetitions, misspellings, and poor grammatical choices.

Prefaces for other writers were wonderful opportunities to ponder ideas: Thank you to Steve Baker, Jesse Brooks, Kara Davis and Wendy Lee, Joan Dunayer, The E. G. Smith Collective, Gracia Fay Ellwood, Lisa Kemmemer, Jo Stepaniak, Will Tuttle, Kathryn Eddy, L. A. Watson and Abbie Rogers, Laura Wright, and Richard Alan Young for those invitations.

I acknowledge the great assistance of the interlibrary loan department of the Richardson Public Library.

I am grateful to my long time publishing buddies: Evander Lomke, Martin Rowe, and Gene Gollogy and The Bloomsbury team, from David Barker to Kevin Ohe, Mark Richardson and David Avital, and especially, for this book, the support of Haaris Naqvi and Mary

Al-Sayed, who embraced the vision for this book and helped it come into existence.

To all the photographers who sent me images, both those I used and those that are in my "sexual politics of meat" file. Thank you. Especially for this *Reader*: Kirsten Bayes, Reannon Branchesi, Alan Darer, Jacob Fry, Greta Gaard, Mitch Goldsmith, Matt Halteman, Matthew Jeanes, Hana Low, Jim Mason, Roger Yates/Vegan Information Project, Anne Zaccardelli. Deep appreciation to all of those readers who send me new examples of *The Sexual Politics of Meat* via snail mail, email, twitter, and Facebook, and specifically to Matteo Andreozzi, Lisa Robinson Bailey, Tanja Schwalm, and Paul Shapiro, for advertisements I used in this book. (Other examples can be found in the Bloomsbury Revelations edition of *The Sexual Politics of Meat*.)

A shout out to the work of Jo-Anne McArthur, weanimals.org whose courage and fortitude in placing herself in difficult situations and photographing the anguish of the life of animals, and then for sharing those photographs so that an author like myself can use them.

I thank Cynthia Brannum for the photograph of Darrell Plunkett's painting and Mike Itashiki for the photographs of Pamela Nelson's Mandalas.

Thanks to Burt Blackwood for sending me photographs and the information on the "Point of Reference" art exhibit. I am so grateful to the artists who shared their work with me for this book: Benjamin Buchanan, the late Robert Dunn, Kathryn Eddy, Suzy González, Vance Lehmkuhl, Pamela Nelson, Janell O'Rourke, Dan Piraro, Darrell Plunkett, Melissa Potter, Eric Reinders, Angela Singer, Cindy Tower, L. A. Watson, and Burt Blackwood and the Nashville Feminist Art Collective.

For the use of her poem, "Calf" and for a friendship in which we write and unwrite our lives, I thank Kathryn Kirkpatrick.

I thank those who have listened to these ideas for twenty (plus) years: my sisters Jane Adams and Nancy Adams Fry; my children, Benjamin and Douglas Buchanan; and especially Bruce A. Buchanan. I remember the love and support of Muriel Kathryn Stang Adams (1914–2009) and Lee Towne Adams (1922–2010).

Figure 1.1

1

The war on compassion

In our lifetime, what was not supposed to happen "ever again"—genocide—has instead happened again and again. As Samantha Power shows in *A Problem from Hell* (2002), her study of genocide in the twentieth century, the perception of genocide is all in the framing. Governments acting against a minority want the violence to be perceived as civil war or tribal strife, as quelling unrest and restoring order, as a private matter that does not spill over into the international community. Other governments weigh their own national interests against the needs of those being killed.

After watching the movie *Hotel Rwanda* and as I began reading *A Problem from Hell*, among the many disturbing questions that surfaced for me, besides the obvious one—How could we have let this happen?—was the question, How can we get people to care about animals when they do not even care when people are being killed?

But as this question came to mind, I realized that it was the wrong one because it accepts a hierarchy of caring that assumes that people first have to care about other people before they care about animals

"The War on Compassion," was first presented as The Paul O'Neill Lecture at Transylvania University, Lexington, Kentucky, May 2005. I thank the O'Neill Lecture Committee and the O'Neill family for inviting me to present new work under the auspices of the lectureship.

"The War on Compassion" was first published In *The Feminist Care Tradition in Animal Ethics: A Reader*, ed. Josephine Donovan and Carol J. Adams (New York City: Columbia University Press, 2007), 21–36. http://cup.columbia.edu/.

and that these caring acts are hostile to each other. In fact, violence against people and that against animals is interdependent. Caring about both is required.

While I could not read about genocide without thinking about the other animals and what humans do to them, I am sophisticated enough to know that this thought is experienced as an offense to the victims of genocide. However, I am motivated enough to want to ask more about the associations I was thinking about and sensing because *human* and *animal* are definitions that exist in tandem, each drawing its power from the other in a drama of circumscribing: the animal defining the human, the human defining the animal. As long as the definitions exist through negation (human is this, animal is not this, human is not that, animal is that—although what is defined as human or animal changes), the inscription of *human* on something, or the movement to be seen as human (for example, Feminism is the radical notion that women are human), assumes that there is something fixed about humanness that "humans" possess and, importantly, that animals do not possess. Without animals showing us otherwise, how do we know ourselves to be human?

Despite all the efforts to demarcate the human, the word *animal* encompasses human beings. We are human animals; they, those we view as not-us, are nonhuman animals.

Discrimination based on color of skin that occurs against those above the human–animal boundary is called *racism*; when it becomes unspeakably murderous, it is called genocide. Discrimination by humans that occurs against those below the human–animal boundary is called *speciesism*; when it becomes murderous, it is called meat eating and hunting, among other things. The latter is normalized violence. Is it possible that speciesism subsumes racism and genocide in the same way that the word *animal* includes humans? Is there not much to learn from the way normalized violence disowns compassion?

When the first response to animal advocacy is, How can we care about animals when humans are suffering? we encounter an argument that is self-enclosing: it re-erects the species barrier and places a boundary on compassion while enforcing a conservative economy of compassion; it splits caring at the human–animal border, presuming that there is not enough to go around. Ironically, it plays into the construction of the world that enables genocide by perpetuating the idea that what happens to human animals is unrelated to what happens to nonhuman animals. It also fosters a fallacy: that caring actually works this way.

Many of the arguments that separate caring into deserving/ undeserving or now/later or first those like us/then those unlike us constitute a politics of the dismissive. Being dismissive is inattention with an alibi. It asserts that "this does not require my attention" or "this offends my sensibility" (that is, "We are so different from animals, how can you introduce them into the discussion?"). Genocide, itself, benefits from the politics of the dismissive.

The difficulty that we face when trying to awaken our culture to care about the suffering of a group that is not acknowledged as having a suffering that matters is the same one that a meditation such as this faces: How do we make those whose suffering does not matter, matter?

False mass terms

All of us are fated to die. We share this fate with animals, but the finitude of domesticated animals is determined by us, by human beings. We know when they will die because we demand it. Their fate, to be eaten when dead, is the filter by which we experience their becoming "terminal animals."

The most efficient way to ensure that humans do not care about the lives of animals is to transform nonhuman subjects into nonhuman objects. This is what I have called the structure of the absent referent (Adams 2015: 21). Behind every meal of meat is an absence: the death of the nonhuman animal whose place the meat takes. The absent referent is that which separates the meat eater from the other animal and that animal from the end product. Humans do not regard meat eating as contact with another animal because it has been renamed as contact with *food*. Who is suffering? No one.

In our culture, *meat* functions as a mass term (Quine 1960: 99; Adams 1994b: 27), defining entire species of nonhumans. Mass terms refer to things like water or colors; no matter how much of it there is or what type of container it is in, water is still water. A bucket of water can be added to a pool of water without changing it. Objects referred to by mass terms have no individuality, no uniqueness, no specificity, and no particularity. When humans turn a nonhuman into "meat," someone who has a very particular, situated life, a unique being is converted into something that has no individuality, no uniqueness, and no specificity. When five pounds of meatballs are added to a plate of meatballs, it is more of the same thing; nothing is changed. But taking a living cow, then killing and butchering that cow, and finally grinding up her flesh does not add a mass term to a mass term and result in more of the same. It destroys an individual.

What is on the plate in front of us is not devoid of specificity. It is the dead flesh of what was once a living, feeling being. The crucial point here is that humans transform a unique being, and therefore not the appropriate referent of a mass term, into something that is the appropriate referent of a mass term.

False mass terms function as shorthand. *They* are not like *us*. Our compassion need not go there—to their situation, their experience— or, if it does, it may be diluted. Their "massification" allows our release from empathy. We cannot imagine ourselves in a situation where our

"I-ness" counts for nothing. We cannot imagine the "not-I" of life as a mass term.

To kill a large number of people efficiently, the killers succeed when they have made the people they are targeting into a mass term. Philip Gourevitch, writing of the genocide in Rwanda, explains, "What distinguishes genocide from murder, and even from acts of political murder that claim as many victims, is the intent. The crime is wanting to make a people extinct. The idea is the crime. No wonder it's so difficult to picture. To do so you must accept the principle of the exterminator, and see not people, but *a people*" (1998: 202).

Gourevitch says that "the idea is the crime." The victims are seen as a mass term by their oppressors: "not people, but *a people*." When a group is regarded as *a people*, not as being composed of individual people, certain conventions of thought and stereotypes take over. The claim is made that the people can be defined as a group, through racial, ethnic, or species characteristics: in Germany in the 1930s

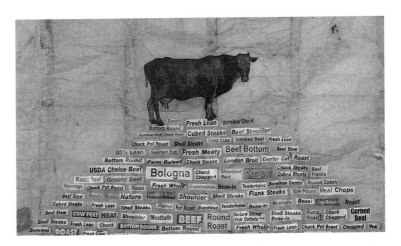

Figure 1.2 Artist statement: A dairy cow stands on top of a pyramid of "absent referents" cut out from supermarket circulars that reduce her to consumable body parts.
Janell O'Rourke, *Taken Apart*, 22″ × 30″, Collage, 2015.

and 1940s, what Jews are like and what Jews do; in Rwanda in the 1950s and forward, what Tutsis are like and what Tutsis do. These characteristics heighten the idea of their existence as being a threat to others or as being dirty. Then the false characteristics become fixed through their existence as a metaphor.

The presumptions and mistakes of racial biology reiterate similar presumptions and mistakes in "species" biology. Humans think they can know "cows" or "birds" and use adjectives drawn from this assumption: *cowlike, birdbrain*. Susanne Kappeler observes that

> Western theories of racism attained proper "scientific" status in the nineteenth and twentieth centuries in the guise of medicine, psychiatry, eugenics, anthropology, demography, and so forth. They stand in direct continuity with the theories that categorize nonhuman animals in species, and living beings into humans, animals, and plants—categories modeled on the paradigms of the natural sciences. These included attempts to establish classifications of "kinds" of people based on "typical" data—be it measurements of bodies and body parts, genetic data, or behavioral features. (1995: 327)

Gourevitch writes, "The idea is the crime," seeing *a people*, not people. One explanation for the appalling indifference of those of us who live in the United States and Great Britain to mass killings is that we, like their oppressors, may see the targeted victims as a mass term. When people are not experienced in their individuality their deaths may not feel immediate. During the genocide in Rwanda, one American officer explained the calculations they were doing: "one American casualty is worth about 85,000 Rwandan dead" (quoted in Power 2002: 381).

The "massification" of beings permits the dilution, the diminution of our attention. The more of a mass term they become, the less concern they need provoke. It is like an hourglass: the sands of our compassion drain into the bottom. How do we flip the hourglass? How do we revive or awaken compassion?

Mass terms are linked to subjects being diminished. In their diminishment, as I pointed out in *The Sexual Politics of Meat*, all that is left for them is to become metaphors for others.

According to Robert Pogue Harrison, in *The Dominion of the Dead*, what we do with our dead is what supposedly demarcates us as humans. We bury them. The dead influence us through the laws they bequeathed to us and the cultural and physical institutions we inherit from them. Everywhere we turn, we experience "the foundational authority of the predecessor" (2005: ix). For the moment, I will not argue with Harrison's presumption that humans are *necrocratic* and nonhumans are not. (Elephants' grieving processes are elaborate.) But, after genocides or fratricides like the Civil War, the survivors dig up the bodies buried in mass graves, as in Rwanda or Gettysburg, and try to reassert through separate burials each one's individuality against the annihilation of the mass term. We cannot undo the act of genocide—the dead are dead—but we can undo part of the idea that allows genocide, the use of mass terms, by asserting the individual and maintaining our ties to the dead as individuals.

And this is a basic difference; meat eaters bury animals in their own bodies. When nonhuman living beings are converted conceptually into false mass terms to enable their conversion into products, we come to believe that their deaths do not matter to themselves. Animals are killed because they are false mass terms, but they die as individuals—as a cow, not as beef; as a pig, not as pork. Each suffers his or her own death, and this death matters a great deal to the one who is dying.

"Treated like animals"

In the face of the knowledge that genocide has happened in our lifetime—not only once, but repeatedly—and that countries such as the United States and institutions such as the United Nations failed to respond—with Rwanda, the United States was reduced to parsing the difference between "acts of genocide" and genocide—the questions arise: Why didn't we respond? Why didn't we care?

Several forms of explanation have been offered, which Power details in *A Problem from Hell*. One important reason Power notes for peoples' apparent indifference, especially during the Holocaust,

Figure 1.3 *"When you go into hospital you don't want to be treated like me"* advertisement.

is disbelief: "The notion of getting attacked for being (rather than for doing) was too discomfiting and too foreign to process readily" (2002: 36).

Animals are killed daily for *being* rather than for *doing*; they may be killed because they are "just animals." Humans are not supposed to be killed because they are "a people." Moreover, it is humans who do the "doing" to animals. Human beings may be killed for doing (doing wrong, presumably, but not for doing wrong to animals). When humans are killed for being rather than for doing, the "beingness" attributed to them is often animal-like.

Many favorable descriptions of human beings emphasize doing rather than being. Humans use their intelligence; nonhumans are instinctive. Humans love; nonhumans mate. Humans cultivate friendships; nonhumans exhibit "affiliative behavior." Humans are humane, cultivated, and refined; nonhumans are beasts and brutal (Dunayer 2001). When someone says, "I was treated like an animal," they mean, "I was treated as though I had no feelings, as though I was not alive." We have created institutions that reinforce the contention that animals *are*, not that animals *do*. Karen Davis observes that "seeing animals in industrialized settings such as factory farms encourages the view that animals are inherently passive objects whose only role in life is to serve the human enterprise" (2005: 31). When someone says, "I was treated like an animal," they mean, "I was reduced to literal existence. I could not do; I was done to."

How are people made less human? Two of the most predictable ways are to define them as false mass terms and to view them as animals. Acts of violence that include animalizing language transform people into false mass terms, since animals already exist in that linguistic no-man's-land of lacking a recognizable individuality. When someone says, "I was treated like an animal," they mean, "I was treated as though I were not an individual." Conditions for violence flourish when the world is structured hierarchically, in a false Darwinian progression that places humans at the top:

Humans
Subhumans
Animals
Insects
"Material" nature; Earth, "dirt"

Figure 1.4

The farther down the great chain of being a creature is placed, the lower the barriers to violence. When someone says, "I was treated like an animal," they mean, "I was made vulnerable to violence by being moved down on the species ladder." This is reflected in the epigraph to the first book of Art Spiegelman's *Maus: A Survivor's Tale* (1986)—a quote from Adolf Hitler: "The Jews are undoubtedly a race, but they are not human".[1] Leo Kuper writes in *Genocide*: "The animal world has been a particularly fertile source of metaphors of dehumanization." People designated as animals "have often been hunted down like animals" (1983: 88). Or exterminated like insects.

When a group is deemed not human, oppressors have several options for establishing just who they see the group members as. For the hierarchy that places humans at the top is more complicated than the one I presented earlier:

Humans

Subhumans

The devil[2]

Primates other than humans

Mammals other than primates

   Predators

      Top carnivores[3]

      Carnivores

   Prey (herbivores: four-legged, two-legged)

   "Vermin" (rats, mice)

---

[1] Richard De Angelis pointed out Spiegelman's use of Hitler as he worked on his essay "Of Mice and Vermin: Animals as Absent Referent in Art Spiegelman's *Maus*."

[2] The devil (a human-animal being) walks upright, has the facial characteristics of a human, but has horns, hoofs, and a tail.

[3] Most carnivorous animals eat herbivores. The top carnivores are those who eat carnivores— for example, birds of prey (including eagles), lions and tigers, and white sharks.

Reptiles (snakes)

Insects ("pests")

   Spiders

   Cockroaches

   Ants

"Material" nature; Earth, "dirt"

Using propaganda campaigns, genocidal governments reinforce the idea of *being,* rather than of *doing:* Hitler considered the Jews to be subhuman and vermin; the Hutus in control in Rwanda regarded the Tutsis as cockroaches (*inyenzi*) or the devil. When genocidal governments rename humans as animals, they reinforce the ladder of human superiority by pushing some people off it. So when someone says, "I was treated like an animal," he or she is standing on the human ladder and looking down, to those who have never been on the top rung.

The original oppression

Human society takes from the oppression of animals its structures and treatment of people. Although we often fail to see the literal origins of human institutions, as Keith Thomas (1983) and Jim Mason (1993), among others, established decades ago, all forms of oppression can be traced to the treatment of animals by humans. Domestication became the pattern for social subordination; predation, the pattern for killing and extermination.

It is the nature of the burnt offering (the literal meaning of the word *holocaust*) of animals to disappear—whether consumed by fire or by human beings. The literal disappeared, but it became the form and function of an unequal human society's treatment of people.

When Theodor Adorno states, "Auschwitz begins wherever someone looks at a slaughterhouse and thinks: they're only animals" (quoted in Patterson 2002: 53), he is saying that the structure of human inequality begins in the abattoir. But some claim that there is a difference: domesticated/enslaved animals have been brought into existence by humans and have life so humans can take it, whereas people threatened by genocide already exist, and the genocidal impulse is to completely eliminate them. Nonexistence for human beings is their elimination as a specific group, ethnicity, or race; nonexistence for animals, according to this reasoning, is never being born in the first place. But the genocidal impulse, when considered, helps us see that this distinction is a fallacy. It assumes that speciesism is not an aspect of genocide and that racism is not a form of speciesism.

At least one writer believes that "the breeding of animals first produced the concepts of 'race' and of 'pure blood'" (Jean-Pierre Digard quoted in Sax 2000: 83). Speciesism has always been a tool of colonialism, creating a hierarchy of skin color and group characteristics. Kappeler observes that politics is zoology by another name: "the very point of categorization is to create discriminating *identities*, 'types' of people allegedly sharing the same (typical) feature(s), thus to justify their social and political roles . . . and invalidate their rights as individuals" (1995: 330).

The category "human being" is stratified:

Table 1 Race and "Evolutionary" continuum

Race continuum	"Evolutionary" continuum
Whites	Civilized "Beastlike" (peasants, farm workers)
Nonwhites	Primitive (pretechnological, indigenous, aboriginal) Hunters and herders Gatherers and farmers

European colonizers evaluated indigenous peoples according to their relationship with animals and the land. They assumed that those who controlled and killed animals were more advanced than those who tilled fields. One of the demarcations of the evolutionary status of a culture was whether it was dependent on animal protein. Thus a hierarchy descends from Western meat eaters to pretechnological hunters to gatherers.

Consider how the Belgians imposed a hierarchy in Rwanda. Gourevitch notes that whether Hutus and Tutsis were descended from different peoples, they "spoke the same language, followed the same religion, intermarried and lived intermingled, without territorial distinctions, on the same hills, sharing the same social and political culture in small chiefdoms" (1998: 47–48). But still there was a distinction. Tutsis were herders and Hutus were cultivators: "This was the original inequality: cattle are a more valuable asset than produce, and although some Hutus owned cows while some Tutsis tilled the soil, the word Tutsi became synonymous with a political and economic elite" (1998: 48).

Racism recapitulates speciesism. The category "human being" is stratified by speciesism; the hierarchy imposed by colonialism mirrors that of humans over nonhumans:

Table 2 *Race and species continuum*

Race continuum	Species continuum
Whites (civilized)	Humans/top carnivores imagery[4]

Primitive (pretechnological, indigenous, aboriginal, and targets of genocide)	Primates other than humans
	Mammals
	   Herbivores
	    "Vermin"
	Reptiles
	Insects

[4]Elite whites, colonizers, et al. reify their dominance through use of animal imagery from top carnivores, like eagles and lions.

The race continuum not only recapitulates the species continuum, but draws its strength in categorization from it.

Immigrants are also regarded, derogatorily, as animals. In an analysis of language used to discuss Latinos in newspapers, animal metaphors were found to be the predominant imagery. Researchers found metaphors of immigrants as animals that were lured, pitted, or baited; animals that can be attacked and hunted; animals that can be eaten; pack animals; and rabbits, needing to be ferreted out (Santa Ana 2002: 82–94). For example, American citizens give birth, but immigrants "drop their babies." Santa Ana writes, "The ontology of IMMIGRANT AS ANIMAL can be stated concisely: Immigrants correspond to citizens as animals correspond to humans" (86). Thus another hierarchy can be posed:

Human	Not human
Member of human society	Outsider or other
Citizen	Immigrant

According to Kappeler,

> Classification is neither neutral, being put to political use only "thereafter," nor is it objective: it is itself an act of social and political discrimination and thus the expression of the subjectivity of power. What is said to be a quality of the object is in fact a difference construed in relation to an implicit norm constituted in the classifying subject. Racism and sexism as political practices construct *another* race and *another* sex, a race of "others" and a sex of "others." (1995: 338)

The concept of "other" requires a normative someone or someones who are not other; who are the measure by which otherness is established; to whom otherness might move closer or farther away, but who do not themselves depart from the normative nature of their beingness. This "otherness" ratifies the primacy of those against whom otherness is defined.

Activist and scholar Karen Davis reminds us that from a chicken's experience, the human hand is the cruelest thing she will know (2005: 47). With Davis's insight in mind, consider this formative conversation in the history of genocide in the twentieth century: when Raphael Lemkin, who coined the word *genocide*, was studying linguistics, he asked his professor why Mehmed Talaat, the person responsible for "the killing by firing squad, bayoneting, bludgeoning, and starvation of nearly 1 million Armenians" (Power 2002: 1) was not prosecuted for what he had done. His professor told Lemkin there was no law under which Talaat could be arrested. The professor explained, "'Consider the case of a farmer who owns a flock of chickens,' he said, 'He kills them and this is his business. If you interfere, you are trespassing'" (Power 2002: 17). Perhaps one reason we did not respond to the genocides of the twentieth century is that we had learned to tolerate a hierarchical world in which killing is accepted.

I recently heard from feminist scholar Marguerite Regan who wrote

> I live 6 miles up the road from one of the largest slaughterhouses in the nation. Nobody in this little town blinks an eye as each day semi-trailer after semi-trailer crammed full of living entities streams down Main Street carrying cows to their brutal executions. Got behind one of these horrors the other day. The stench was overpowering, but what really got me was the bumper sticker: EAT BEEF: The West Wasn't Won on Salad.

The triumphalism of such contemporary declarations should remind us that when anxiety asserts itself about the place of animals in our hierarchical world, it is never asserting itself only about animals. In this case, it reinforces the United States' own genocidal treatment of Native American Nations and their lands.

Figure 1.5 Darrell Plunkett, *Chicken and Rooster*. Acrylic paint on canvas, 32″ × 17″. Photograph courtesy of Cynthia Brannum.

Why don't we care?

Jacques Derrida's "The Animal that Therefore I Am" identifies the most egregious actions humans have taken against other animals (including subsuming them all under the category "animal"): "Everybody knows what terrifying and intolerable pictures a realist painting could give to the industrial, mechanical, chemical, hormonal, and genetic violence to which man has been submitting animal life for the past two centuries" (2002: 395). He assumes that such a description may be "pathetic"—that is, evoking sympathy. Derrida argues that for the past few centuries, we have waged a campaign against compassion that allows factory farms and other horrors to continue. He calls it the "war on pity." Such a campaign instantiates objectification: both the objectification of the animals who become mass terms and the objectification of feelings, so they fail to be heeded in making decisions about the fate of terminal animals. If genocide requires the turning of humans into animals, the war on pity provides the institutional framework for not caring about what happens to someone labeled "animal."

Derrida says that

> no one can deny the *unprecedented* proportions of this subjection of the animal. . . . No one can deny seriously, or for very long, that men do all they can in order to dissimulate this cruelty or to hide it from themselves, in order to organize on a global scale the forgetting or misunderstanding of this violence that some would compare to the worst cases of genocide (there are also animal genocides: the number of species endangered because of man takes one's breath away). (2002: 394)

There, even he says it: what is happening to animals some "would compare to the worst cases of genocide." He adds,

> One should neither abuse the figure of genocide nor consider it explained away. For it gets more complicated here: the annihilation of certain species is indeed in process, but it is occurring through the organization and exploitation of an artificial, infernal, virtually interminable survival, in conditions

that previous generations would have judged monstrous, outside of every supposed norm of a life proper to animals that are thus exterminated by means of their continued existence or even their overpopulation. (2002: 394)

Samantha Power offers several explanations to begin the discussion of why apathy prevails over caring: we lack the imagination needed to reckon with evil, and it is hard to even imagine evil. It is assumed that people act rationally. American policy makers discovered that "rational people" can be gratuitously violent (with Derrida I might add, such a discovery was made by animal activists centuries ago). The failure to protest is interpreted as indifference, and those who do care do not have the political strength to change policy. The killing is reinterpreted, deflecting attention from the culprits. The national interest, or so it is thought, prevents intervention. Being attacked for *being* rather than *doing* seems unbelievable.

But now we can add to Power's list. The ability to objectify feelings, so they are placed outside the political realm, is another reason people have not cared. Submission to authority requires such objectification—indeed, rewards it. Not only do people learn that feelings do not matter, but even the awareness of feelings is lost within the objectifying mind-set. As a result, people may become afraid to care, which requires that they have the courage to break from the normalizing ideological screen that has posited that "it's okay if it's an *x*, but not a *y*."

The war on compassion has resulted in a desire to move away from many feelings, especially uncomfortable ones. As a result, fear, which is an understandable response to a new experience—say, that of encountering a snake or a spider—becomes the justification for killing a snake or a spider. If feelings were not objectified, we might have developed the ability to interact with the fear, to respect it and the beings who are causing it, rather than try to destroy both the feeling and the being.

The war on compassion has caused many people to think that it is futile to care. They are unable, imaginatively, to see how their caring will change anything. They experience a passivity inculcated by current political situations as well as by the media. They lack the imagination not to believe that something terrible might be done, but that the something terrible that is happening can be undone.

The war on compassion, further, has caused people to fear that beginning to care about what happens to animals will destroy them because the knowledge is so overwhelming. They prefer not to care rather than to face the fragility, at the least, or the annihilation of the caring self, at the most extreme, that they suspect arises from caring. But caring does not make people more fragile or annihilate them. In fact, through caring, individuals not only acquire new experiences and skills that accompany these experiences, but also discover that they are part of a network that can sustain them even when caring evolves into grief for what is happening.

Finally, the war on compassion has caused people to believe that they have to help humans first. As long as we treat animals as animals, as long as we accept that there is the category "animals," both the treatment and the concept will legitimize the treatment of humans as animals. Derrida hypothesized that the "war on pity" was passing through a critical phase. It may have begun when animal activists proclaimed that "if it's not okay for a y, it's not okay for an x," and in that proclamation began the process of overcoming the divisions between not only the x's (animals) and the y's (humans) but also compassion and the political realm.

2

What came before The Sexual Politics of Meat: *The activist roots of a critical theory*

In 1974, walking down a Cambridge, Massachusetts street, I suddenly realized that a deep and abiding connection existed between feminism and vegetarianism, between violence against women and violence against animals. I wrote my first paper on the subject in 1975. In 1976, I began writing a book about the patriarchal roots of meat eating. Within months, I was all set to see my small manuscript published. But it felt incomplete to me, lacking in a critical theory that organized and interpreted my ideas. I realized neither the "book" nor I was ready for its publication. I shelved the early draft.

I returned to Western New York, where I had grown up. I became a grassroots activist. What came before *The Sexual Politics of Meat* was the process by which I became the person who could write the book that finally appeared sixteen years after my first revelation. The activism of those intervening years was a crucible for developing the

"What Came Before *The Sexual Politics of Meat:* The Activist Roots of a Critical Theory" was first published in *Species Matters: Humane Advocacy and Cultural Theory*, ed. Marianne DeKoven and Michael Lundblad. (New York City: Columbia University Press, 2011), 103–38.

critical theory missing from my initial 1976 manuscript. But I did not become a rural activist because it would help me with my book. I became an activist because I believe strongly that injustice must be challenged. Indeed, through my activism I continually had to solve a basic issue: who comes first in activism, disenfranchised humans or animals? And the answer, the answer that transformed my early manuscript into *The Sexual Politics of Meat*, was that this is a false question. Divided loyalty (humans versus animals) is one of the issues my critical theory tries to overcome by identifying the interlocking, overlapping nature of disempowerment and oppression. Activism showed me how to think my way to the arguments that illuminate that insight.

This essay offers answers to several questions. How is one an activist? How does one balance activism for those on the other side of the vigilantly guarded species boundary with activism for those humans thrown and propelled toward that boundary by oppressive attitudes and actions? In other words, how does one integrate work for the other animals with work for disenfranchised humans (and vice versa)? And finally, what does one learn from activism?

To answer these questions and as a case study specific to writing *The Sexual Politics of Meat*, I explore a particularly difficult activist experience from the 1980s. It became a laboratory for recognizing intersecting oppressions and for learning how to be an activist. It began as a battle for fair housing and evolved into a fight for fairness in the media. It required that I learn how to research and write about these issues, providing an opportunity to learn how to write clearly and concisely. It took an enormous toll on me personally, and I draw on journal notes and dream summaries from that time to illustrate the process of inner education that activists experience. So profoundly did the experience stay with me that I continued to have dreams about it long after the confrontations and tensions of the times were over. On Christmas night, 1998, my dreaming self took me back to Dunkirk, New York, where we had lived until 1987: "I start to think about Dunkirk—the housing suit. How personal it all was. Bruce [my partner] calls out, 'don't make it sound easy.'" Then I awoke. My dreaming self had that right: It was not easy.

Rural ministry

In 1978, I was the executive director of the Chautauqua County Rural Ministry, an advocacy not-for-profit agency that worked predominantly with welfare recipients, farm workers, and resettled farm workers. It was based in Dunkirk, a small steel town experiencing the economic displacement of many of the larger steel cities such as Lackawanna, New York, and Pittsburgh, Pennsylvania. The Lackawanna steel plants were a shadow of their former selves. The Dunkirk steel plant hung by a thread, and other industries in western New York had shut down. In Dunkirk, the urban renewal program of the 1960s destroyed many beloved areas, but nothing had been built in their place. The sight of the empty lots around town inflamed the deeply conservative community's distrust of government. Yet, despite these strong antigovernment feelings, the city accepted federal monies for several years.

A 1975 study recommended that Dunkirk build one hundred units of low-to-moderate-income housing. That year, 811 people were shown to be living in substandard housing in the city of Dunkirk (population 16,000). In 1979, more than 60 percent of the city's rental units were found to have inadequate plumbing, heating, or sewer facilities. Overcrowding in the available apartments was another concern. Since 1975, the Department of Housing and

Urban Development gave the city of Dunkirk millions of dollars to upgrade homes, streets, lighting, and sewers in areas of concentrated deterioration, with the understanding that the city would also build the hundred units of needed housing.

But the city kept postponing a commitment to build the housing. Meanwhile, the millions of dollars that HUD gave Dunkirk were not spent in the area with the concentrated deterioration, known as the Core Area. Not surprisingly, the city had neglected the area where the largest number of minorities lived.

A low to moderate-income housing project slated to be built in a largely white part of town came before the City Council for approval. The white city government rejected it. I learned that whites had gone door to door in the area where the housing was to be built despicably arousing alarm by asking, "Do you want your daughter to be raped by a black man?" And so I found myself immersed in the "rub a dub dub of agitation" as Theodore Tilton called the activism of Susan B. Anthony and Elizabeth Cady Stanton.

Fair housing activism

A coalition of groups, including the Rural Ministry and the local branch of the National Association for the Advancement of Colored People (NAACP), began to educate people about why low- and moderate-income housing was necessary. Angry confrontations occurred at city meetings. Frightened by the opposition to the housing, the officials continued to reject any proposals for the desperately needed public housing.

Two interns from the local college, the State University of New York at Fredonia, were working with me to research the claims of the opponents. To respond to rumors generated by anti-housing forces we researched property values near the existing public housing project. We found that, contrary to rumor, the property values of these houses had not been affected by their proximity to a housing project. We researched what had happened to money that the Department of Housing and Urban Development had provided to the city for neighborhood improvement. Where had it gone since it had not gone to the Core Area? We compared what Dunkirk had promised to do with the money with what was actually done with it.

We discovered that in 1979, HUD had ranked Dunkirk two out of twenty-nine in terms of need for money from their Small Cities program. However, Dunkirk ranked twenty-eight out of twenty-nine in terms of feasibility of their program.

We researched the vacancy rate for apartments in Dunkirk. It was 1 percent. This meant that it was a landlord's market—the competition for available apartments was so great that low-income renters had to accept what was available, and what was available was substandard. The city was not enforcing the building code, and many of the apartment owners were absentee landlords. Twelve percent of the population of Dunkirk lived in substandard housing; factoring in race, 75 percent of minorities lived in substandard housing. (At my office, people would come to me with stories of their children waking up to find a rat staring at them.) Always earnest, I drafted several versions for what ultimately became a newspaper ad addressing the most frequently invoked anti-housing stances (See Figure 2.1).

Meanwhile, the city council was repeatedly turning down proposals for the building of new public housing units, though this meant a loss of other forms of HUD money. *This* money was finally going to target the substandard housing in the Core Area, but the council's vote against the housing meant that HUD withdrew the money for rehabilitating homes.

HOUSING AND THE CITY OF DUNKIRK

Rumor and Fact: What Do You Believe?

HAVE YOU HEARD CONVERSATIONS ABOUT THE PROPOSED SIXTY UNITS OF PUBLIC HOUSING FOR THE CITY OF DUNKIRK? DO YOU UNDERSTAND EVERYTHING THAT IS BEING SAID?

Which have you heard, rumor or fact?

RUMOR	FACT
WE DON'T NEED HUD (DEPARTMENT OF HOUSING AND URBAN DEVELOPMENT), AND WE DON'T NEED THEIR MONEY.	WRONG! HUD HAS HELPED DUNKIRK GREATLY BY FUNDING: ★ SEWER PROJECTS ★ REPAIRING SIDEWALKS ★ SITE IMPROVEMENTS ★ BUILDING BATH HOUSES ★ RECONSTRUCTING THE LAKEFRONT ★ THE SENIOR CITIZEN CENTER ★ THE HISTORICAL SOCIETY ★ DAYCARE ★ THE BOAT LAUNCH AND PIER ★ SOCIAL SERVICE PROGRAMS.
WHEN THIS HOUSING IS BUILT, POOR PEOPLE AND MINORITIES ARE GOING TO FLOOD INTO THE CITY.	WRONG! DUNKIRK CITIZENS THEMSELVES ARE IN NEED, AND WILL BENEFIT. DUNKIRK LOST 144 HOUSING UNITS TO URBAN RENEWAL. ELIGIBILITY FOR THE HOUSING IS BASED ON THE SIZE OF THE FAMILY AND INCOME. FAMILIES WITH AN INCOME OF UP TO $16,000 WOULD BE ELIGIBLE.
16 UNITS OF HOUSING ARE TO BE BUILT ON ONE BLOCK ALONE.	WRONG! NO STREET IS TARGETED FOR 16 UNITS. THE HOUSING AUTHORITY SPECIFIED A MAXIMUM OF ONLY 8 UNITS PER SITE.
OUR PROPERTY VALUE WILL DEPRECIATE BECAUSE THE UNITS WILL BECOME RUN DOWN.	WRONG! WHEN FEDERAL MONEY COMES INTO A CITY, THE CITY BENEFITS FROM INCREASED JOBS AND A RAISED STANDARD OF LIVING. THIS STIMULATION INCREASES PROPERTY VALUES. PEOPLE LIVING IN THESE UNITS WILL BE TAUGHT HOMEMAKING SKILLS.
DUNKIRK IS BEING PICKED ON BY HUD AND THE FEDERAL GOVERNMENT. AFTER ALL, WHY DUNKIRK, AND NOT FREDONIA?	IN 1975, DUNKIRK ASKED HUD FOR $3.1 MILLION. THEY RECEIVED IT. IN RETURN, THEY PROMISED TO BUILD 100 UNITS OF HOUSING. THEY NEVER BUILT THE UNITS. THEY BROKE THEIR PROMISE. WHAT HAPPENS NEXT WILL DETERMINE DUNKIRK'S FUTURE.
WE DON'T HAVE ANYTHING TO FEAR FROM THESE LAWSUITS, ANYWAY.	WRONG! OTHER CITIES HAVE BEEN SUED, AND THEY HAVE LOST. WITH EACH DELAY AND EVERY HARMFUL STATEMENT, THE PUNITIVE DAMAGES TO BE ASKED INCREASE. THINK OF OUR LAWYERS' FEES!
WE THE TAXPAYERS OF DUNKIRK ARE WILLING TO PAY THE ADDITIONAL TAXES TO KEEP HUD OUT OF DUNKIRK. IT'S WORTH IT.	LOOK AT HOW MUCH MONEY IS BEING TALKED ABOUT: ★ HUD COULD DEMAND THE RETURN OF $3.1 MILLION. ★ THE CONTRACTOR'S SUIT FOR $2.5 MILLION IS PENDING. IN ADDITION WE HAVE ALREADY LOST $689,000 for 1978/79. WE COULD LOSE $344,000 FOR 1979/80. DUNKIRK'S SMALL CITIES PROPOSAL FOR $1.6 MILLION WOULD NEVER BE FUNDED. FEDERAL REVENUE SHARING COULD BE LOST. THIS ALONE AMOUNTED TO $350,000 LAST YEAR. IF WE LOSE HUD'S SUPPORT OTHER FEDERAL AGENCIES WILL SOON FOLLOW. DUNKIRK NOW RAISES ONLY $2.22 MILLION WITH A TAX RATE OF $13.63 PER THOUSAND OF EVALUATION. THAT REPRESENTS A POSSIBLE MAXIMUM REVENUE LOSS OF MORE THAN $8.6 MILLION NOT INCLUDING ANY POSSIBLE FUTURE FUNDING THAT WOULD BE FORFEITED.

ALL OF DUNKIRK'S CITIZENS REGARDLESS OF AGE, RACE, or SEX, DESERVE GOOD DECENT HOUSING. ARE YOU HELPING THEM BY SPREADING RUMOR OR FACT? IF YOU WANT TO SEE DUNKIRK GROW, AND NOT BECOME A GHOST TOWN, LEARN THE FACTS! NO TOWN, CITY OR STATE CAN SURVIVE THE INFLATION OF THE 80's WITHOUT THE HELP OF THE FEDERAL GOVERNMENT. BY SPREADING RUMOR, YOU SAY "NO" TO THAT HELP FOR YOU AND YOUR CHILDREN!

PAID FOR BY DUNKIRK VOTERS FOR BETTER HOUSING.

Figure 2.1

A virulent anti-housing group, the Citizen's Action Board, acted as the channel for all the fear that people have about public housing, fanning the fires with racist discussion and taxpayers' rights rhetoric. In 1980, the *Buffalo Courier-Express* carried a front-page article on "Red-Hot Housing Debate is Costing Dunkirk Millions." The article included interviews with these anti-housing activists. They were motivated by many things—suspicion of the federal government, lingering fury over what urban renewal in the 1960s had done to the city, and the belief, as one person said, that "public housing discriminates against me, the middle class, the working people. We are paying the shot" (Haddad 1980: 1, D–13). One angry man

Figure 2.2 "RETREAT FROM DUNKIRK—N.Y., THAT IS!" Editorial Cartoon by Rob't Dunn. Published on the editorial page of *The Buffalo Courier-Express*, July 3, 1980. Original artwork presented to the author by the artist Robert Dunn, July 1980.

exclaimed, "I've taken the flag down in front of my house. And I will take the pole down soon. There is no freedom left in this country—it's making me sick." One of the individuals the reporter interviewed said, "Somebody is shipping minorities in here. I have nothing against them—but why us?"

I assumed the response to ignorance and fear is education. I believed that when two people or groups argued, each side would listen to each other, and would and could be open to the ideas of the opposing side. But ignorance and fear do not create receptive listeners.[1]

We attended meetings; we tried to speak. When the Citizen's Action Board complained that the government shouldn't be in the business of housing, I asked them how many had bought their own homes through Veteran's loans, a form of government subsidies. How many went to school on the GI bill? That was the federal government, too.

It was hard to be heard in the midst of the hostile crowd. As the local newspaper reported, "According to Ms. Adams, Dunkirk is in 'violation of the Fair Housing Act.' 'It's just not a matter of turning down HUD,' she said amid heckling and boos" (Lutz 1980a: 1, 4). One friend, and sister member of the NAACP, Mary Lee Williams (and wife of the minister of the Open Door of God in Christ Church), stood up and thundered, as only she could thunder, that in God's eyes we were all equal and no matter what happened on earth, in heaven we would be gathered together. She talked about equality before God and that when we go to meet our maker, no matter what kind of inequality there has been on earth, in heaven we will be equal. I watched as afterward, so many of the whites, those speaking out the loudest against the housing, rushed forward to talk with her. It was as though they wanted her assurance that they would get to heaven, despite the fact that they weren't changing their views on the housing.

---

[1] I drew on this insight in my book *Living Among Meat Eaters* (2001), when I offer advice for talking with meat eaters.

Heckling greeted most African Americans and whites who tried to speak in favor of public housing. Jesse Thomas, a former star athlete at Dunkirk High School, said to a crowd of 250 people gathered at one meeting, "You're saying we're not fit to live in Dunkirk." Someone shouted back, "You said it, we didn't" (Lutz 1980b: 1, 4).

The pro-housing forces realized that Dunkirk officials would not change without outside pressure, so we filed a class-action suit against the city of Dunkirk. But we also sued the Dunkirk Housing Authority, the Department of Housing and Urban Development, and a group of investors who purchased property planned as the site for the originally proposed but subsequently abandoned hundred units of housing. (They purchased it to prevent it from being developed for public housing.) The suit was filed on behalf of the Dunkirk-Fredonia branch of the NAACP, of which I was the chair of the Housing Committee, and individually named plaintiffs who represented low-income and minority renters deprived of access to housing, white homeowners deprived of the benefits of living in an integrated neighborhood, and black home-owners who lived in the Core Area who had been deprived of federally funded housing rehabilitation funds.

Former Speaker of the House Tip O'Neill famously said, "All politics is local." So, too, are attacks and hostility prompted by local politics: they affect your relationships with your neighbors and create a feeling of lack of safety. I was shocked by the fury of the anti-housing forces and dismayed by how they personalized their attacks. I was married to the local Presbyterian minister, Bruce Buchanan, who was also President of the Board of the Rural Ministry. (That is how we met.) Eggs were thrown at our house; anonymous letters encouraging the church to fire Bruce were sent to the church leadership. We felt overwhelmed. Neither of us was sleeping through the night. Both of us experienced increased nervousness and short tempers. My notes from that time include this: "the feeling of being exposed, being hated—when you feel you are basically a good person."

Dunkirk abuts the more affluent village of Fredonia, the home of a state university college. Many of the upper- and middle-level owners and managers of the Dunkirk steel plant lived in Fredonia or in the town of Dunkirk, but not in the city itself. The housing issue, according to the *New York Times* "became a magnet for blue-collar political discontent" (Lyons 1981: 61). Their anger had many sources. They felt "false promises" had been made to them; but in fact, the community money had gone to their neighborhoods. They felt a sense of loss of control of their environment signified by the empty lots around town from urban renewal. An increasing threat of foreign steel competing against their local product created job insecurity. They felt that the federal government was dictating to them. And on a very personal level, there was also a sense of betrayal that a white woman had turned against them. I was not only a white woman; I was the daughter of a well-known local judge.

After the inflammatory letter against us had been received by his congregation, Bruce and I talked with my parents, who lived nearby, about the implications of our activism. Recalling that discussion, I wrote:

> The tension between moving the community ahead—being progressive so that the ultimate [court] settlement is as favorable as possible—and being silent so that Bruce's and my safety are protected. I feel I have let my ideals down because I know I could have done and said more. [Activists: Be aware of your perfectionism!] Bruce and my father say you have already done enough—don't endanger yourself; don't hit your head against a brick wall. I accept the 2nd argument but not the 1st—to accept the 1st is to concede the point.

The way I make sense of my world is to read, read, read. Stunned by the virulence of the racism, I read books about the Dred Scott decision, histories of black women, histories of resistance during slavery, fair housing books, civil rights oral histories, books that explored the question *why does blackness matter so to whites?* (Toni Morrison's *Playing in the Dark*, not published until 1992, provides the most compelling answer; see also Olson, 2004.) I had never shelved the *idea* of the book on feminism and vegetarianism and continued to notice connections as I read my way through those histories, feminist literary criticism, books on attitudes toward animals, and mysteries and spy novels. (I needed some relief after all!) I was trying to figure out how dominance happens and what protects dominance once it has been established. Throughout the 1980s, as my activism led me into hostile situations, I would ask myself: *How does this relate to animals?* I was examining "animalizing" discourses, though I did not use those words then. This approach to multiple oppressions was very much a part of the radical feminist community I had lived in during the early 1970s.

Theoretically, my experiences were very stimulating. But one does not live one's life mainly on a theoretical level. Nothing prepared me for the virulent hatred that had been directed toward me. In October 1980, while on the island of Iona, a very sacred place in Scotland, I dreamt that *I was in City Hall and various anti-housing people threw small things at me—or swore at me. I became alarmed. Went to ask for protection from the police—the policemen left—ostensibly to get others—but never returned and watched from the other room as the crowd picked me up to beat me up. I woke up crying, "Help. Help."*

"What's Your Opinion?"

At the height of the housing confrontations, and after one of the emotional meetings at City Hall, someone remarked to me, "You can try to do all the good you can, but it is undone the next day on 'What's Your Opinion?'" I had never heard of "What's Your Opinion," a call-in radio show on a local radio station. The next day, on my way to work, I tuned into the station and was startled to hear the moderator of the show, Henry Serafin—a small town Rush Limbaugh—talking about me. He was complaining that "Carol Adams's Rural Ministry" was going to receive thirty thousand dollars in HUD monies if these funds were awarded to the city of Dunkirk. He also said, "We don't need any more minority housing," and pointed out that the funds would "benefit only the Core Area." I was infuriated that he was giving inaccurate information about the housing while also impugning my motives. Arriving at the church, I leapt out of my car, marched up the two flights of stairs to my corner office, and immediately dialed the station's telephone number. I was put on the air. I pointed out that "it's not minority housing; it's low- and moderate- income housing" and I reminded Serafin that since he was the chair of Dunkirk's Citizen's Advisory committee he should know better than to claim that any of those funds were coming to my organization. I asked him to correct the misinformation he was spreading. As for the funds for the Rural Ministry (it was three thousand not thirty thousand), they were earmarked for the Hotline for Battered Women, a resource Bruce and I had created two years earlier.

After I hung up, all hell seemed to break lose on the radio program. People could not stop talking about me. Not what I said, not any of the points I had made—but, and this floored me, whether I paid any income tax.

It turned out that "What's Your Opinion" had been providing an ongoing opportunity for the Citizen's Action Board, the anti-housing group, to stir up people's fears about public housing. Serafin, the moderator of the show and the owner of the station, was a member of the Citizen's Action Board, an owner of substandard apartments in Dunkirk, and one of the investors who bought up the property originally slated as the site for the hundred units of housing.

A year and a half later, the Dunkirk Police Chief, Edward Mulville, told the *New York Times:* "Serafin eggs people into saying things they wouldn't otherwise. He really is a detriment to the area. If I were driving through here for the first time and heard that show on the car radio. I'd change my plans to stop, step on the gas and keep right on going" (Lyons 1981: 61). But those of us in Dunkirk had no such choice.

I was invited to be the guest on "What's Your Opinion?" I agreed to appear with the understanding that Serafin would retract his statement that the Rural Ministry was to receive $30,000. Once we were on the air, he refused to do so. As I tried to describe the history of the Dunkirk housing controversy and help people understand why the money for home repair was going to go to the Core Area, he told me to "hurry up," to "cut it short." Then he said, "when are you going to start acting like a lady?"

Each successive program involved Serafin and his cohorts talking against the housing, the Rural Ministry, the mayor, me: who did I think I was, and so on. When I was introduced to someone in northern Chautauqua County, they would inquire if I were the same Carol Adams who was always being attacked on "What's Your Opinion?"

That June, a new twist in the personalization of the housing battle found its expression on the local airwaves. The *Buffalo Courier-Express* sent a reporter to research the controversy, and the resulting story appeared on the front page of the Sunday paper. Not understanding that I had kept my own name when I married, the reporter referred to me as "Mrs. Adams" (Haddad). The next day, "What's Your Opinion?" focused on the newspaper article and the question of my name: "Miss . . . or Ms. Adams, I don't know why she kept her maiden name.

Her husband's name is Buchanan. It sounds like a colored name, but it isn't."

As people learned of our efforts to get WBUZ to discuss the housing issue accurately, someone contacted us with this information: Serafin had accepted a placement of someone from the county's office of employment and training, but had refused the placement when the person turned out to be African American. He called the county and asked, "Don't you have any white girls to send me?" He complained the job applicant "would make charcoal look white." These comments had been recorded; we received copies.

Legal scholar Robert Cover refers to "the violence of the word" (in Matsuda 1993: 23). WBUZ was broadcasting the violence of the word—racist hate messages, slurs, and disparagements. WBUZ created an environment in which it was safe for whites to exhibit their racism. Mari Matsuda shows how racist speech is related to racist acts. "Gutter racism, parlor racism, corporate racism, and government racism work in coordination, reinforcing existing conditions of domination" (Matsuda 1993: 24). Racist speech on the radio and in the community tracked and reinforced the city's diversion of funds from the area in the city with the greatest number of substandard buildings and minorities and the city's failure to build needed housing.

Media advocacy and an informal objection

Through contacts in Washington, I learned about the Media Access Project and arranged to meet Andrew Schwartzman. From what he heard about WBUZ and the actions of its owner, Schwartzman felt there had been egregious violations. But, he warned us, it is hard to challenge licenses, it takes a long time, and the Fairness Doctrine, which requires that all sides of a controversy of local importance must be presented, was under assault in Congress. (The Fairness Doctrine was soon dismantled, paving the way for television stations like Fox News.) We needed to prove other violations, since the Fairness Doctrine violations, though egregious from our perspective, would not be seen as being so in Washington, D.C. So, we went to work to compile a case against WBUZ's license renewal. We investigated their license-renewal application and discovered serious misrepresentations to the Federal Communication Commission (FCC) regarding their local programming, their public surveys—as well as the apparent instance of racial discrimination.

On April 23, 1981, we filed *An Informal Objection to the License Renewal Application of WBUZ* with the FCC. The objectors were the Chautauqua County Rural Ministry, the Dunkirk-Fredonia League of Women Voters, and the Dunkirk-Fredonia Branch of the NAACP. Andrew Schwartzman of the Media Access Project in Washington, D. C., was our attorney. The *Informal Objection* is divided into two parts: 177 pages of recitation of information regarding areas where we believed WBUZ had violated FCC regulations, followed by over two hundred pages of Exhibits, including newspaper articles, information from WBUZ's public file, affidavits, and other material, that backed up our complaint. After we filed our *Informal Objection*, we received several anonymous calls about WBUZ. One person reported that WBUZ had run two on-air contests and then not given away the prizes. We checked into this and found it was true. This information was filed in an amendment to the *Informal Objection*.

That summer, Bruce and I were back in Scotland, where he was serving a Scottish church. One night, I dreamt one of the leading racists *threatens and attempts to rape me*. On the fourth of July, I dreamt, *a vague but plaguelike evil is spreading through Dunkirk, or at least, affecting some people in Dunkirk. I have a strange intuitive feeling that the deaths are being caused by men. Men who get possessed and murder their wives.*

We returned from Scotland in August and Bruce was appointed by the Dunkirk mayor to the Dunkirk Housing Authority and soon became its president. Our housing suits were settled out of court. The consent decree the Department of Housing and Urban Development signed committed them to fund the building of the housing. Thus, despite the fact that under President Reagan this housing program was eliminated nationwide, HUD still had to fund the units in Dunkirk because of the consent decree. As President of the Dunkirk Housing Authority, Bruce oversaw the bidding, contracting, and building of the housing. Those ninety-six units were the last units under that program built by HUD anywhere in the United States.

After the *New York Times* described the problems besetting Dunkirk, including the issues with WBUZ, the Justice Department's Community Relations Services offered to mediate between WBUZ and those of us challenging its license. We agreed to their mediating assistance to work with Serafin to solve our disagreements. We also tried to help him find a buyer for the radio station. He remained intransigent.

An administrative law judge held hearings in Jamestown to consider the information in the *Informal Objection*. He ruled that Serafin should lose his license to operate WBUZ. This decision was appealed to a three-person appeal board, which issued an interim opinion. In 1986, as the FCC was slowly moving through the process of considering whether to grant WBUZ a renewal of its license, "What's Your Opinion" program was abuzz with fury.

Caller: I don't think you can get a fair hearing from a Judge when Daddy is a judge.

(The WBUZ hearing was before an administrative law judge
from Washington not before any local judge.)

Serafin: Nobody ever gave me anything. I worked for everything I
have. These people want to take it all away.

Caller: I don't know what these people are doing. I wish they
would go south or something.

Serafin: The NAACP, I never had a problem with this group. I
understand, Carol Adams and her husband Bruce Buchanan
were members of it and on the Board of Directors of the NAACP.

Caller: One of the guys on the NAACP was hired as a guard for Al
Tech and he only came in once a week and was finally fired.

Caller: The Rural Ministry should change its name to
"hemorrhoid."

Caller: Carol Adams lives up on Pennsylvania Avenue. She lives in
a house owned by the church. I doubt that she pays any local
taxes. So she doesn't pay anything, except cause you trouble.

Caller: I don't know what's wrong with her.

Serafin: I have trouble figuring it out myself. . . . I think her
father—he's a nice guy—should tell her off. They ruined this
city by bringing in the money for those welfare people to come
and she doesn't pay any taxes. All she causes is trouble.

Caller: Her husband, who's supposed to be a minister, which I
have doubts of, he owns nothing here. He pays no taxes. He's
helping to tear the city apart with his wonderful wife here. I
don't know why he gets to be on the housing authority and
decide where the houses go. Why don't he stay in the pulpit
and preach good will? I think he should go to California with
his wife there—get on the first freight train and not get off 'til
they get to California.

Caller: I think that Carol Adams should mind her own business
and check her own backyard, too. They call themselves a holy

family. Let's get a branch of the KKK up here and run them
out of town. They've done nothing for no one here except the
colored people. Nobody likes them here, nobody wants them
here. Let's get them out of here. They only help minorities.

Caller: Why don't you bring charges of harassment against
Ms. Adams and that great minister but don't take them to
Mayville. Now I'm not against Judge Adams, he's a good friend
of mine, what do you think?

Serafin: Well, that's a thought.

When fighting racists, one forfeits not only privacy, but also privilege
and whatever class status has been achieved or inherited. Both Serafin
and the caller were anxious to distinguish between my father and me.
The caller was a retired policeman; this may be why he remained
deferential about my father's position.

Five more years transpired before our objection to the license
renewal of WBUZ was upheld: "The flagrant, egregious actions of this
licensee demonstrates that there is but one remedy: outright denial
of renewal of license" (Catoctin Broadcasting Corp., 2 FCC Rcd 2126
[Rev. Bd. 1987]. See also Turner 1986). It wasn't because WBUZ
had violated the Fairness Doctrine. WBUZ's other acts (specifically,
its employment discrimination, fraudulent on-air contests, and its
misrepresentations) turned out to be the compelling reasons it was
denied its license renewal. If Serafin had only given us a chance to
present the pro-housing viewpoint, those egregious violations would
never have been discovered.

In 1991, WBUZ went off the air. We had hoped that Serafin would
have agreed to sell before this happened, so that the local station could
continue to exist. But he refused. When interviewed by the local paper,
Serafin continued to deflect any blame, saying, "I think the mistake I
made was I dared to mess with Carol Adams" (Dill 1989).

Ours was the only community-based challenge to a radio-station license to prevail during the Reagan administration. The Media Access Project's Andrew Schwartzman observed that the importance of the case was not that we established new case law; we did not. Instead, we proved that blatant employment discrimination, conducting fraudulent contests, and misrepresentation under oath were sufficient bases for losing a license—even during the Reagan administration.

Feminist-vegetarian theory

In 1987, Bruce and I moved to Dallas. Bruce needed to continue his ministry in another context, the housing had been built, and I was going to finish writing my book on feminism and vegetarianism. During the three-day road trip, I read Margaret Homan's *Bearing the Word*, which introduced me to the concept of "the absent referent." Homans writes, "For the same reason that women are identified with nature and matter in any traditional thematics of gender (as when Milton calls the planet Earth 'great Mother'), women are also identified with the literal, the absent referent in our predominant myth of language . . . literal meaning cannot be present in a text; it is always elsewhere" (Homans 1986: 4). I stopped reading. *The absent referent . . .* isn't that what animals are too? Politicized, the term defined animals consumed as meat, and recognized the tension between presence/absence and living/dead. Without animals there would be no meat eating, yet they are absent from the act of eating meat because they have been transformed through violence into food. Behind every meal of "meat" is an absence: the death of the animal whose place the "meat" takes. The absent referent is that which separates the flesh eater from the animal and the animal from the end product. The function of the absent referent is to allow for the moral abandonment of a being while also emptying violence from the language. *Hamburger, pork loin, drumstick*—there is no "who" in these words, so how can there be a being who has been harmed?

The next morning, I realized that women, too, were absent referents in a patriarchal, meat eating culture. By the time we arrived at Dallas, I had the organizing theory for my feminist-vegetarian critical theory: a structure of overlapping but absent referents links violence against women and animals. I got to work writing the book as we unpacked and settled in. The following year, a friend nominated us for a ten-thousand dollar award for our creative use of law and legal institutions in a rural area where activism through the law had not been tried. We won the award and with some of the money I bought a computer upon which, in 1989, I finished writing *The Sexual Politics of Meat*.

The Sexual Politics of Meat argues that a process of objectification, fragmentation, and consumption enables the oppression of animals. Animals are rendered being-less through technology, language, and cultural representation. Objectification permits an oppressor to view another being as an object. The oppressor then violates this being by object-like treatment: for example, the rape of women that denies women freedom to say no, or the butchering of animals, which converts animals from living, breathing beings into dead objects. This process allows fragmentation, or brutal dismemberment, and finally consumption. Once fragmented, consumption happens: the consumption of a being, and the consumption of the meaning of that being's death, so that the referent point of meat changes. Consumption is the fulfillment of oppression, the annihilation of will, of separate identity. So too with language: a subject first is viewed, or objectified, through metaphor. Through fragmentation, the object is severed from its ontological meaning. Finally, consumed, it exists only through what it represents. The consumption of the referent reiterates its annihilation as a subject of importance in itself.

I found an overlap of cultural images of sexual violence against women and fragmentation and dismemberment of nature and the body in Western culture. I suggested that this cycle of objectification, fragmentation, and consumption linked butchering with both the representation and reality of sexual violence in Western culture, normalizing sexual consumption. While the occasional man may literally eat women, we all consume visual images of women all the time.

The interlocking oppression of women and animals could also be found in the use of a dominant and domineering language in which the meaning of the violent transformation of living to dead

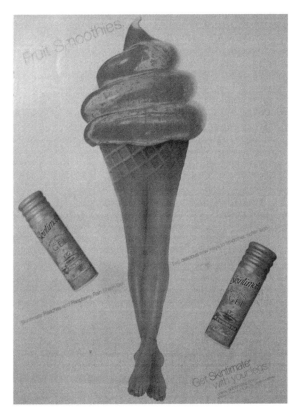

Figure 2.3

is consumed and negated as it is "lifted" into metaphor and applied to women. This structure of overlapping absent referents also moves in the other direction, in which women's objectification becomes the basis for cultural constructions about meat animals: women are animalized and animals are feminized and sexualized. These acts are interrelated and interconnected. In *Neither Man nor Beast: Feminism and the Defense of Animals* and *The Pornography of Meat* I extended my discussion of interconnected oppressions, arguing that the category of species in our culture carries gender associations. Even male domesticated animals are depicted as females in ads about turkey *breasts*, barbecues that portray pigs as buxom women wanting to be eaten, or "tasty chicks." Without the reproductive abuse of female animals, who are forced to manufacture "meat" for production through their *reproduction*, there would be no animal bodies to consume. Hostile terms for women such as *cow, chick, sow, old biddy,* and *hen* derive from female beings who have absolutely no control over their reproductive choices. Their ability to be exploited lowers their standing and gives a powerful, negative charge to the meaning of the slang arising from their exploitation. The category of gender in our culture carries species associations. Women are depicted as animals.

Why is the fate of domesticated animals so potently negative? In *Neither Man nor Beast*, I proposed that in our culture, "meat" operates as a mass term defining entire species of nonhumans (see discussion in Chapter 1, pp. 6–7).

How do you make a person less of a human? As I suggested in Chapter 1, two of the most predictable ways are to make a person or a group of people into (false) mass terms and to view them as animals. Acts of violence that include animalizing language create people as false mass terms, since animals already exist in that linguistic no-man's land of lacking a recognizable individuality. Disowning our animal connections is part of dominance. By definition in this dominant culture, the human transcends animality. Western philosophy defined humanness not only as *not animal*, but also as *not woman* and not "colored." In Western philosophy, the concept of manhood applied not just to adult men, but to the attributes of being human—rationality, autonomy, and unemotionality. Women's status is lowered by our being seen as animal-like; men's status is raised by being seen as the definition of what is human. (This is discussed further in Chapter 10.)

Reflections on interlocking oppressions

Running the Hotline for Battered Women during the late 1970s and early 1980s introduced me to shocking examples of interconnected oppressions. At one point, we were helping a woman who lived on a farm with her husband and her kids. She had called us; we had helped her get out, and find a safe place to live. One Sunday when her husband was returning his kids after his visitation with them, as they were about to get out of his pickup truck, the family dog appeared in the driveway. Her husband plunged the truck forward so that it ran over the dog; then he threw the truck in reverse and backed over the dog. He repeated this forward-backward motion many times. Then he got out of the truck, grabbed his shotgun, and in front of his devastated family, shot the dog several times. His violence was a form of controlling behavior. Harming or threatening to harm pets is often one of the most effective ways to exert control over another (see Chapter 4).

The traditional depictions of evolution, from "ape" to *Homo sapiens*, in which a lumbering bent-over creature eventually becomes bipedal, capture a prevailing myth of our culture—the natural progression of evolution to its zenith, the white human male. Any

First off, let's get one thing straight. We totally agree with Apple.* A truly powerful computer is measured in how often it's used.

IF YOU LISTEN TO APPLE, THIS IS THE MOST POWERFUL COMPUTER IN THE WORLD.

But while Apple has taken great strides in making the personal computer more useful, we've gone substantially farther.

Introducing the T2000SX notebook computer.

Quite simply, the T2000 SX is a more useful personal computer because it allows you to work how you want to work. When you want to work. And where you want to work.

Painstakingly engineered with you clearly in mind, the T2000SX will help you work more efficiently than ever before.

Virtually every feature you can find on a desktop computer, you will

Our technologically superior battery can be fully recharged in a mere ninety minutes.

find on the T2000SX: An 80386™SX processor with a math coprocessor socket, VGA compatible display, 1 MB (expandable to 9MB) of 80 nsec RAM, a 60 MB hard disk with 19 msec access time and 1.5 MB/sec data transfer rate.

The T2000SX has a 60MB hard disk with 19 msec access time.

But more important than the specs themselves, is the way the T2000SX lets you use them. Which is more often.

Our fluorescent side-lit screen provides even distribution of light. (Actual size.)

Because the T2000SX can fit easily into a briefcase (it weighs a scant 6.9 pounds), you can take it anywhere you go and use it in more ways than you can imagine.

Need to make revisions to a

© 1991 Toshiba America Information Systems, Inc. 386 is a trademark of Intel Corporation. *PC WEEK 2/25/91 issue. Apple is a registered trademark of Apple Computer Corporation.

Figure 2.4

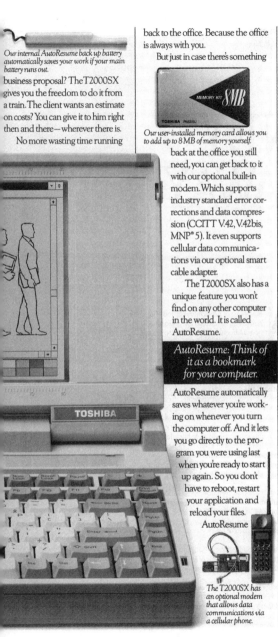

close examination of these depictions reveals that it is the white male human body that serves as the prototype. The evolutionary depictions reflect a series of cultural ideas, not only that humans are different from nonhumans but that men are different from women. Katherine Frith closely examined the way in which the traditional depictions of evolution were used in a computer ad. The final figure is not only standing erect but also holding a Toshiba computer, the symbol of technology. Frith finds that the ad not only depicts human dominion over animals but also a further example of dominance. The man holding the computer and representing evolutionary triumph is clothed as a white-collar worker. The invisible blue-collar worker is not the culmination of evolution; the suit-wearing, upper-middle class man is (Frith 1997: 1–14).

With the housing battle, I encountered interlocking oppressions up close and personal. I experienced the animalizing mythos behind the Toshiba ad that celebrated white, upper-middle class men's successes. It took me many years to think about it, but like many representations, it racializes *and* animalizes gender while engendering *and* animalizing race.

From the moment the anti-housing forces went from house to house asking, "Do you want your daughter to be raped by a black man?" they interwove racism, sexism, and speciesism. The archetypal rape scenario for racists—the specter of the black male rapist—had been used as an excuse for lynching black businessmen and other independent black men earlier in the century. In 1980, it was called into service to defeat needed low-to-moderate-income housing. It became the organizing, but rarely acknowledged, mythology of our community.

This scare tacit, of course, did not tell the truths about rapes: the most frequent form of rape is rape by acquaintances—husbands, ex-husbands, lovers, and boyfriends (Russell 1990). Women have the most to fear from the men they know, especially their sexual partners. The racist mythology makes black men the scapegoats of the dominant culture's refusal to acknowledge the actual source of women's lack of safety. The real danger in the community was not Black men, but the men to whom women were married. The force of the mythology of black-on-white rape in the United States often resulted in the neglect of the material, emotional, and spiritual needs of women of color who were raped. The *fear* of random black-on-white violence triumphs over the *fact* of interracial woman abuse and white-on-black rape as a form of racial terrorism (Harris 1991).

> When Black women were raped by white males, they were being raped not as women generally, but as Black women specifically: Their femaleness made them sexually vulnerable to racist domination, while their Blackness effectively denied them any protection. This white male power was reinforced by a judicial system in which the successful conviction of a white man for raping a Black woman was virtually unthinkable. (Crenshaw 1991: 42)

Rape laws, it is said, were written to protect only white women, not Black women, racializing womankind into two hierarchical groups— white property and Black whore.

When Susan Estrich was raped in 1974, she was asked by the Boston policemen, "was he a *crow?*" that is, someone who was black and not only black, but a stranger. In their books, that was *real rape* (Estrich 1987: 1).

Kate Clark analyzed reports about rape in the *Sun*, a tabloid with the largest circulation in the United Kingdom. The *Sun* uses subhuman terms for men who are strangers to their victims, (the "real rapists" in Ehrlich's terms) and if the victim fits their sense of respectable women (property). These attackers are called *fiend, beast, monster, maniac, "ripper"* (Clark 1998: 183–97).

In the United States, too, the "beast" language can be found. The rape and violent beating of a wealthy, white woman jogger in Central Park in 1989 provided the press with a field day for bestializing African American and Hispanic boys. They were *savage, a roving gang*, a *wolf pack*; she was their *prey*. (Only it turns out she wasn't. In 2002, DNA testing supposedly confirmed that she had been raped by someone other than these young men.)

Rapists aren't "beasts" or "animals." Generally, they plan their assaults. They target their victims. At the point at which humans are being the most deliberate in their actions, we call them "beasts." The "lower" animals are not bestial, that is, they are not ruthlessly violent. They are not beings lacking in dignity or altruism.

Paul Hock's *White Hero, Black Beast* asserts that "the threatened assault of the ever erect black buck on the chaste white lady has dominated the mythologies of the American south for more than three centuries" (1979: 44). The events unfolding in my town weren't in the American South; they were in a small, industrial city in upstate New York. Predictably, racist, sexist whites responded to my involvement in this antiracist work with venom. I asked an ally to sit in on one of the organizational meetings of whites who were opposed to the public housing. She came back and reported the white men discussing "Carol Adams and her big black bucks."

In 1915, D. W. Griffith's *The Birth of a Nation* created the film stereotype of the "pure Black buck." As the film historian Donald Bogle describes them, "Bucks are always big baadddd niggers, over-sexed and savage, violent and frenzied as they lust for white flesh." (2001: 13–14). Bucks originally were adult male deer, antelopes, or rabbits.

In the "black man rapes white woman scenario" the violation inherent in the alleged rape was against the white male, who had to assert his right to protect his property. "Do you want *your daughter*...?"

Historically in the United States, there were times when white men alleged rape to hide the fact that a white woman had *chosen* to have an African American man as her partner. Not just the white woman but the idea of her as pure, virginal, and sexless had to be protected. Like the threat of lynching in its effect on all blacks, the fear of rape helped to keep white woman subordinate, anxious, and dependent. It impugned black women by implying that black men preferred white women over them. And the idea of the black rapist also helped deflect attention from white men who, through rape, were sexually and racially terrorizing black women. The African American woman as victim became invisible.

By viewing African Americans as black beasts, European American men created two pornographic scenarios, one about rapacious black men lusting for white women and the other about lascivious black women available to anyone, man or beast. Both concepts interacted with the notion of white women as pure, virginal, and sexless: "Black womanhood was polarized against white womanhood in the structure of the metaphor system of female sexuality, particularly through the association of black women with overt sexuality and taboo sexual practices" (Carby 1987: 32). Black men were seen as beasts, sexually threatening white womanhood—a white womanhood defined to aggrandize the sense of white manhood. Black women were seen as sexed and as not able to be violated, because they would enjoy anything—including sex with animals. Kimberlé Crenshaw explains how "rape and other sexual abuses were justified by myths that black women were sexually voracious, that they were sexually indiscriminate, and that they readily copulated with animals, most frequently imagined to be apes and monkeys" (1992: 411). The historian Winthrop Jordan observes that "the sexual union of apes and Negroes was *always* conceived as involving *female Negroes* and *male apes!* Apes had intercourse with Negro *women*" (1969: 238).

These representations still animate racism. Crenshaw (1992) reports that into the 1990s, men who assaulted "black women were the least likely to receive jail time" (413).

George M. Fredrickson argues that "the only way to meet criticisms of the unspeakably revolting practice of lynching was to contest that many Negroes were literally wild beasts, with unconventional sexual passions and criminal natures stamped by heredity" (1971: 276). By animalizing blacks, the dehumanizing and destructive violence of lynching could be justified. And just so today, any racism that bestializes its victims enables its own self-justification.

The debate about why I had kept my maiden name upon marrying also highlighted the intersection of racism and sexism. The speculation that I had kept my maiden name because I was married to a black man illustrates racists' logic for why a white woman would disavow her husband's name. The dilemma I then faced was this: if I said, "no I am not married to a black man," this response would be interpreted as perpetuating a form of racism for it would appear that I was disavowing the idea that I might marry a black man. On the other hand, if I reacted by not dealing with it, by not responding to this salacious interest in my life, this nonresponse would allow it to remain a secret. As a secret, it would then feed their speculation about my motives. Either way, their concern was "what kind of man is she attached to?" Their desire was to place me within a male-identified environment while also looking for a way to discredit me.

Racists could only explain my activism by salaciously sexualizing both my black colleagues and me, seemingly confirming Joel Kovel's observation about racism being inherently sexualized. Citing the charges of rape against black men for touching, approaching, looking at, being imagined to have looked at, talking back to, etc., a white woman, Kovel reports, "a mountain of evidence has accumulated to document the basically sexualized nature of racist psychology"

(1971: 67). Neither the African American men nor I could be granted the notion of acting out of motives other than sexual ones. Because of my antiracist work, I could no longer be positioned as an innocent white girl, like those in the neighborhood who supposedly stood ready targets for the mythological rapacious black man. I was now, not virgin, but whore. But still, I, a white person, was given "possession" (through the possessive "her" in the reference to "her big black bucks") of the (now animalized) African American men in these white men's fantasies. I, a white woman, was granted greater individuality than the black men being referred to. Completely erased in these racists discourses were the black women, who were, in fact, the majority of the plaintiffs in the lawsuit.

A debate began in the community (from hairdresser parlors to factory lunchrooms) about the number of illegitimate children it was believed I had. (It ranged from one to six.) The ongoing interest in my supposed illegitimate children helped to forge a different image of me: not judge's daughter but poor white female trash. This language, too, has an animalizing subtext having to do with uncontrolled and indiscriminate sexuality. Recently, I have discovered how images of poor white female "trash" are applied to pigs depicted as willing victims of barbeques.

Interlocking oppressions are revealed through the animalizing of humans (through racism, genocide, sexism). The idea of "animal" exists to disempower targeted or vulnerable humans.

Retrograde humanism

After the publication of *The Sexual Politics of Meat*, I attended a meeting of the American Academy of Religion. A scholar who discovered my authorship asserted that she believed "the most important thing is to help humans. How can we talk about animals when the homeless need us?" This is a very typical—and predictable—response to animal advocates. "Why aren't you doing something important like feeding the homeless?" an angry male student asked me in 2002 at Marist College, when I invited questions from the audience after showing *The Sexual Politics of Meat Slide Show.*

This confrontational response to my work puts me in mind of my mother, who has dementia. When she looks at me, it is hard for her to recognize me as her daughter "Carol" because the "Carol" she remembers is fifteen years old, or thirty, but surely her daughter Carol can't be as old as this woman who appears before her. A few years ago, I took her along to help me pick out a new refrigerator for their house. We figured it would be something enjoyable for her. But she became furious when I told her what it cost. She said, "We've never paid that much for a refrigerator. You must tell them we don't want it." I suggested we talk about it outside, rather than in the hearing range of the salespeople. Sadly, I suggested this because I knew that when we got outside she would forget that she was angry, and what had just made her angry. My mother was angry because the price of the refrigerator was registered in her mind as though it were 1950s or 1960s or 1970s dollars, when, of course, they never would have paid that much for a refrigerator. I have heard this called "retrograde memory." Her memory pulls up information from before Alzheimer's set in. This memory tells her Carol is thirty and that refrigerators are not that expensive.

When people learn I am a vegan, or the author of *The Sexual Politics of Meat,* many react with such vehemence and accuse me of not caring for (1) abused children, (2) the homeless, (3) the hungry, (4) battered women (5) the environment, and (6) workers, among many other things. I guess I should be pleased that my veganism and/ or authorship of that book galvanizes people to demonstrate their concern for the disempowered; however, I am not sure that their awareness of the suffering of (1) abused children, (2) the homeless, (3) the hungry, (4) battered women, (5) the environment, (6) workers, and those other things lasts much longer than their conversation with me. Sometimes, I laughingly claim that my veganism has prompted more people to announce their concerns for human suffering than my activism ever did. I marvel at the desperation of meat eaters to hold onto the idea that they are more humane than I am—or than any vegan is (I am just a very convenient target). I believe we need a name for the reactions of people who start accusing animal activists of neglecting some form of human suffering when they learn we are vegan. I think this is "retrograde humanism."

Retrograde humanism is a kneejerk reaction, prompted by defensiveness. People want to believe they are good people. The structure of the absent referent, in which the animal disappears both literally and conceptually, allows them to believe that they are good people. Until they are among vegan or animal activists, the culture supports them in this belief. We animal activists restore the absent referent by talking about what animals experience. We are saying you are either harming animals or not. There is no neutral position here. Which side are you on? We might not even be saying this verbally; simply the mere presence of a vegan prompts some degree of soul searching in others.

When people say we care more for animals than for human beings, I think they mean:

Why aren't you caring for me? Why are you making me uncomfortable?

When I experience retrograde humanism, the first thing I notice is its vehemence. It is insistent and often angry. What it reminds me of are those heated moments in the Dunkirk City Hall when the anti-housing group was trying, desperately, to keep control of the debate.

Like me, many vegans and animal activists have worked in homeless shelters or domestic violence shelters; they're social workers, housing advocates, etc. The overwhelming majority of people who believe it is impossible to be both social activists in the conventional sense and animal activists are meat eaters, because they want to believe in its impossibility. Then they don't have to change.

Retrograde humanists clearly haven't figured out you can be doing both—working for social justice for human beings and for animals. Indeed, we could argue that in working for animals we are doing both, in that animal activists are including animals as a concern of social justice. We could argue this for many reasons, some of which end up reinforcing the human/animal division I would like to see eliminated. Slaughterhouses are deadly for animals, but they are also the most dangerous places for humans to work. Often undocumented workers are employed there and have few protections against an overly rapid line speed. People who live near factory farms often get ill from the effluvia. Concentrated animal farm operations cause water pollution. Eating vegan can lower one's chances of high blood pressure, heart disease, high cholesterol, and diabetes. It reduces the suffering that these illnesses can cause.

Human-centered thinkers want to provide a human-centered critique of a theory or practice that de-centers humans. They re-center humans by claiming that we have decided to *eliminate* humans from our realm of concern. They uphold the idea that humans must come first, all the while failing to recognize that incorporating animals into the dialogue and activism of social change doesn't eliminate humans from concern; it just reassembles the players by disempowering that human/animal boundary that enforces oppression. It refuses to view the world hierarchically.

People who may never have cared about the homeless before suddenly become possessed with indignation that I appear not to care about the homeless. I want to ask my interrogators, "Why are you so angry?" "Do *you* feed the homeless?" I want to point out that meat eaters tend to mention hungry children around the world when veg*ns talk about all the suffering animals go through—suffering that people are responsible for, given their choices to eat meat and eggs and drink cow's milk.

I still live in Dallas, where Bruce is the director of a homeless day shelter that provides about 1,400 meals a day. He has overseen the feeding of more than 6 million meals since we moved to Dallas. For many years, on a monthly basis, I picked up kung pao "chicken" donated by a vegan Chinese restaurant and delivered it to The Stewpot. So when I told my Dallas friends what happened at Marist College, the question "Why aren't you doing something important like feeding the homeless?" is very funny to them. They ask, "Well so you told him that that's what Bruce does, right?"

Or they wonder if I answer by describing how in the 1980s I oversaw the first "census" measuring rural homelessness; the resulting report on rural homelessness was the only one of its kind in the country at that time and was utilized by members of Congress in 1988 when drafting and passing the Stewart B. McKinney Homeless Housing Act. I started the "Friendly Kitchen" to provide meals for those who needed free meals (there *is* such a thing as a free lunch). I wrote a grant request for one million dollars to restore an old building, which would have two apartments for those who were currently homeless to get back on their feet. I also advocated for a housing committee within the New York Governor's Commission on Domestic Violence and then chaired it, creating relationships among not-for-profit housing advocates with skills in housing and domestic violence service providers who needed help with creating second-stage housing (housing after one left the shelter, to avoid homelessness).

"You told him all that, didn't you?" my friends ask.

And I say, "No, I did not."

This shocks them. They ask, "Wouldn't that have shown up that student?"

"Only by affirming the legitimacy of his question," I reply. To describe this activism would accept his dismissal of all I had just said as I talked about the ideas of *The Sexual Politics of Meat*. I wasn't going to do this. Which is why I don't answer, "What makes you think I haven't worked for humans?" I am not going to accept his dualistic view of the world (you can be working for animals *or* you can be working for human beings). Why would I accept his analysis that all I had just said was immaterial if I weren't feeding the homeless?

So, no, I did not say, "I *do* feed the homeless."

How does one answer the question without reinforcing its presumption—that human beings come first? Another possible response was, "Look at the human consequences of meat eating," and then to point out the environmental and health consequences of meat eating.

According her obituary in the *New York Times* (May 7, 2009), the late Dr. Carole C. Noon "was often asked why she spent so much time and energy caring for chimpanzees when children were going hungry. 'I'm always taken aback by the question because I don't view the world in two halves—eating chimps and starving children,' she said. She added, 'Except for a few percent of DNA, they're us.'" Even arguing the connections between the treatment of humans and animals—the argument from interlocking oppressions—carries the message that humans will benefit from animal advocacy. As indeed, they will. As long as the category of "animals" exists as a way of lowering and demeaning humans, disempowered humans will be victimized by speciesist attitudes.

But maybe the most important thing to say is that including the other animals within my social activism liberates me from calculations about being humane and what it means. I am charged by my critics as being somehow *less* humane because I include animals in my understanding of compassion. In that accusation, retrograde humanists reveal the human-inflected limitations to "humane" that haunt these discussions. Learning to feel compassion for animals enables one to approach the world, all of it, more compassionately. For me, it's not a restriction that closes up the heart and sends it in only one direction. Being alert to how animals experience their lives enriches my life, even when from that alertness I encounter overwhelming grief, sadness, and despair. I have learned that it is okay to feel grief; that grief may be inevitable in thinking about the lives of farmed animals, but that grief does not incapacitate me. It teaches me that we are connected and that my capacity for handling difficult emotions is much greater than I ever knew. (I wonder if, when it comes down to it, retrograde humanists are frightened by the overpowering sense of grief that they recognize will be experienced if they engage with the lives of animals.)

The irony isn't that retrograde humanists would approve of my past activism. I don't want to prove my legitimacy according to their human-centered standards. The irony is I had to overcome my own humanocentrism to write *The Sexual Politics of Meat*. I know the costs of holding such an all-or-nothing viewpoint: it caused me to postpone writing. After all, the original insight about the connections had come to me back in 1974, but *The Sexual Politics of Meat* only appeared in 1990. The intervening time between idea and completion, between the desire to write and success at writing, was one of conflicted purpose. Why could I pull all-nighters writing grants for services for battered women or for the million dollars that funded the building that would help homeless, or the *Informal Objection to the License Renewal of WBUZ?* Why could I sacrifice for these causes but not write my own book? I knew I had to honor the vision I had in 1974 regarding the connection. Yet there was illiteracy, poverty, discrimination, violence. Writing itself seemed a luxury in the face of urgent human needs. And then there was the topic: feminism *and* vegetarianism. Throughout the 1980s, the topic provided much entertainment for people. Especially painful were my meetings with battered women's advocates from across New York State. How could advocates against violence be eating a diet based on violence? But mine was a minority opinion.

I had to figure out how to be both an advocate and a writer. But more urgently, I had to figure out how to integrate my social justice concerns about illiteracy, poverty, discrimination, injustice, and violence with my fury about what was happening to the other animals. And in figuring this out, I became the person who could write *The Sexual Politics of Meat*.

Teleological fulfillment

On the other side of retrograde humanism is the ardent belief that some animal activists hold that animal rights activism is the teleological fulfillment of human rights activism. I think some of his readers—who then became animal activists after reading *Animal Liberation*—conclude that Peter Singer (1975) has made a teleological statement, in his preface. To wit: "There's been Black Liberation, Gay Liberation, Women's Liberation. Now let's talk about Animal Liberation." Reading this, some animal activists conclude, "Well Black Liberation, Gay Liberation, Women's Liberation—that's been done. I need only to focus on animals." Separating animal liberation away from feminism and other social justice issues promotes social injustice. Sexually exploitative vegan and animal activism can be traced from the 1980s to the present, including a short-lived vegan strip club. People for the

Ethical Treatment of Animals (PETA) often relies on different forms of human oppression as it seeks to release animals from oppression. PETA draws on all the pornographic conventions that advertisers draw upon. They exploit the association of women and death ("I'd rather be dead than wear fur"). They project adult male sexuality onto younger women (the Lolita model). They place women in cages, encouraging the human male to experience himself as superior. Not only is this wrong as it maintains the objectification of women, but as I argue in *The Pornography of Meat*, it is inappropriate activism because animals are marked by gender, as well as species.

Teleological fulfillment is simply the reverse of retrograde humanism. It results in evangelical-like activism rather than a movement that seeks to transform social relations among people as well as between people and the other animals. For instance, during the 1990s, animal advocates proposed that child offenders be tried as adults for animal cruelty. But this proposal failed to take into account any understanding of the prison-industrial complex in the United States. As Patrick Kwan points out, "Juveniles who are tried as adult are often held and sentenced to prison with adults, which make them prime targets for sexual and physical violence."[2] Such a sentence would appear to be a violation of international human rights law.

Over the years, numerous people have written me to say how *The Sexual Politics of Meat* changed their lives. I think one reason this book prompts such an intense response is because it gave voice to people's intuition that a connection existed between social justice issues and animal issues; that animal issues *are* social justice issues. They don't settle for either side of the retrograde humanism versus teleological fulfillment debate because they understand that multiple oppressions are at work. Intersectional oppressions call for intersectional activism.

---

[2]Patrick Kwan, personal communication, used with permission. May 2009.

I know *The Sexual Politics of Meat* gave new justifications for caring about animals. It provided a theory for an activist life committed to change, to challenging objectification, to challenging a culture built on killing and violence.

One way that I understand my activism is that it is an attempt to restore the absent referent. My writings are attempts to be faithful to the insight that the structure of the absent referent perpetuates violence. It means trying to keep the harm to individuals as a central point. The animals, like the rest of nature, are the raw materials upon which we construct our lives—literally—and upon which we construct our meanings of who we are human, *human and not animal*. For retrograde humanism, the issue is not really children starving. The issue is to keep the absent referent from being restored. What evangelical-like animal activist groups fail to acknowledge is that in a culture of oppression, there are multiple absent referents—both human and nonhuman animals. Equality, fairness, justice—these aren't ideas; they are a practice. We practice them when we don't treat other people or other animals as absent referents. We practice it when we ask, "What are you going through?" and understand that we ask the question because it matters to all of us what some are experiencing.

What I learned

Perhaps the greatest mistake I made in 1989 during the pre-publication process for *The Sexual Politics of Meat* was to agree to listing myself as an "adjunct professor" at Perkins School of Theology. It was true that I was a visiting lecturer—I had conceived of and taught their first course on "Sexual and Domestic Violence: Pastoral and Theological issues." But, since my graduation from Yale Divinity School in 1976, I had been an activist, not an academic.

When *The Sexual Politics of Meat* was published, this biographical information misled many groups of people, most dramatically, right-wing commentators. During the early 1990s, Rush Limbaugh feasted on *The Sexual Politics of Meat*, seeing it as the most egregious example of academic political correctness. But after my experience with Henry Serafin's comments about my life, Limbaugh seemed laughable.

I felt activists had been given the wrong message by the listing of me as a lecturer. I was an adjunct professor; my theory had been honed through my activism, and my activism defined me much more intimately than any temporary academic label. As I explain in the preface to the tenth anniversary edition, *The Sexual Politics of Meat* exists because of activism. It is engaged theory, theory that arises from anger at what is; theory that envisions what is possible. *Engaged theory makes change possible.*

One of my journal notes from the early 1980s says

Being an advocate in the pure sense of the word
is not being a legal technician though trying to line up legal
      expertise and guidance
is being willing to risk with people
is living on the raw edge of experience
being forced to be a filter
to let a variety of experiences filter, move through you.

Along Western New York one finds reminders of the former strength of steel plants. Just as steel is thrust into furnaces of three hundred to five hundred degrees Fahrenheit and becomes tempered, so too with me. Activism tempered me, strengthening me.

My activism enlarged my understanding of what courage is. I once heard my father telling someone about his World War II experience as a submariner. His captain had said, "Anyone can be brave during a depth charge; there's nothing else you can do but survive it." What is really courageous is to get back into a submarine knowing that at some point you are *going to be* depth charged.

I wasn't courageous in 1978 when I began advocating for fair housing because I assumed not only that I was right but that I could convince others. I was naïve and did not anticipate the consequences of challenging injustice.

I *was* courageous when I continued acting for what was right despite the consequences. In activism, no guarantee of outcome exists. You take the stance because you know the absent referent is not absent at all but awaiting acts of solidarity that transform the structures creating the absence.

Courage is not so much *an act* as a *commitment to a process*. All I needed in 1978 was the courage to take the next step. First, we tried education. When that failed, we pursued litigation. When there was a backlash, we consolidated. Then we went on the offensive and challenged the radio station. Each step became the self-evident one because of the previous step. We did not have a map for our path. We had conviction. Courage was my commitment to meet whatever happened as I took the next step. My inner self grew to meet the demands the activism required. You only have to have the courage to take the next step.

I learned activism can be very lonely. You do what you do because you believe it is important. Sometimes you are successful and sometimes you aren't. You can't measure the success of your activism by that outward measurement.

Another of my hastily scribbled notes from the early 1980s reads as follows:

Rules and Lessons of Organizing
Always use the facts—don't exaggerate them, you discredit your
  case at some later time

(statistics re: housing)
Don't allow pettiness to involve you
Don't waste your time anticipating the comments of the opposition
   (they will always think of something outrageous about you)
That which is most natural about you will be most feared.
Always allow locals to speak
Never lower yourself to your opponent's level.
Attempt at every chance for conciliation or mediation so that you can
   say when it's done we tried everything possible to work this out.
Don't waste your time defending yourself. Sometimes silence is the
   best choice; the art of embracing silence.
Learn to deal with your own anger.
Don't rush. Recognize that change takes time.

I did not know that the distance from the sudden revelation "there's a connection!" between meat eating and male dominance in the fall of 1974 and the publication of the book *The Sexual Politics of Meat* would be fifteen and a half years. In those years, I became the person who could write that book:

Focus/discipline/voice. My activism taught me *how* to write.
Connections/injustice/acknowledging harm/how privilege works.
   My activism taught me *perspective*—how to notice patterns of
   interlocking oppression in our culture.
Courage—my activism enlarged my ability to be courageous.

I needed all those to be the author of *The Sexual Politics of Meat.*

Annie Potts is an associate professor in cultural studies and human-animal studies at the University of Canterbury, where, along with Philip Armstrong, she also directs the New Zealand Centre for Human-Animal Studies. Annie is the author of *The Science/Fiction of Sex: Feminist Deconstruction and the Vocabularies of Heterosex* (Routledge 2002) *Chicken* (Reaktion 2012); co-author (with Philip Armstrong and Deidre Brown) of *A New Zealand Book of Beasts: Animals in our Culture, History and Everyday Life* (Auckland University Press 2013); (with Donelle Gadenne) of *Animals in Emergencies: Learning from the Christchurch Earthquakes* (Canterbury University Press 2014); and the editor of a special issue of the journal *Feminism & Psychology* on "Feminism, Psychology and Nonhuman Animals." She has served on the National Animal Welfare in Emergencies Management Advisory group, the New Zealand Companion Animal Council, and First Strike New Zealand. In 2014, she received a New Zealand Assisi Award for Services to Animal Welfare. She is the editor of the anthology *Meat Cultures* (Brill, 2016).

3

The politics of meat: The Antennae journal of nature in visual culture interview with Annie Potts

Annie Potts: Carol, what started your passionate political interrogation of the ways in which Western culture exploits nonhuman animals? And how did this impact on your work, life, and worldview?

If I could completely account for it, explain it, examine it, I could control it. And it isn't anything I actually control. Over the past thirty five years (!) whenever I start thinking I am done writing and engaging with animal issues—the minute I begin to imagine that I am going to work on a project that is ostensibly not animal-related—inevitably I read about something, or go for a walk and see something, and my mind starts generating all these responses and analyses and I know I have to just keep at it! Jane Goodall talks about repaying "some of the debt I owe the chimpanzees." For me, the debt to nonhuman animals is great, and I discover there are so many ways to repay the debt.

"The Politics of Carol J. Adams," with Annie Potts was first published in *Antennae*, 14 (Autumn 2010): 12–24. Used by permission.

My older sister says that as a child I was the least self-conscious person she ever knew. I engaged with the world without that patina of critical or suspicious awareness that characterizes more sophisticated or critically aware individuals. I was immersed in my world, and I loved my world—that world was a small village filled with critters— dog and cats, of course, but cows and horses, too. In my life I have always talked to and with the animals.

Having ponies and horses was probably transformative in many ways, but especially as a pre-adolescent girl; at that critical time in my life, I experienced my world widening rather than constricting: Riding bareback, lying on a horse's back as we both rested under a huge willow tree, playing hide and go seek with friends on horses in woods or towns or along a creek with friends. These experiences are written so deeply in my body.

Then, eight years after this time, I returned home from my first year at Yale Divinity School, just when Jimmy, a beloved pony, died. He was either shot by hunters or died of a heart attack after hearing

Figure 3.1 Still from Suzy González's animation, *Which Came First: An Interview with Carol J. Adams.*

the nearby guns. That evening, biting into a hamburger, I suddenly thought of Jimmy's dead body and asked myself, "Why am I eating a dead cow when I wouldn't eat my dead pony?" I encountered my own hypocrisy. The *fact* of the hamburger became a contradiction: "How can I, a feminist committed to stopping violence and working for liberation, eat dead animals?"

Within two months of becoming a vegetarian, I realized there was a connection between feminism and vegetarianism, and ever since then, I've had my work cut out for me! Whoever I was on the way to becoming before these experiences, well, who knows? I had to follow these ideas, and respect them, and live with them, and develop them. I recognized I had to become a vegan to be consistent with my philosophy. Then I had to learn how to write and figure out what I had to say and how to say it.

For the first fifteen years or so, (before *The Sexual Politics of Meat* was published), my ideas were often greeted with such disbelief, if not scorn, that I developed a good sense of humor. I think that has served me well.

The discovery of how our ethical framework is illegitimate because of its species-specific and species-centered nature completely and absolutely changed my life. I believe I am still being changed by it. I continually interrogate everything based on a nonviolent, species-inclusive ethic.

But most importantly, through all this—my childhood experience with animals and my adult experience with theory—I learned the art of attention. That is a priceless gift.

I now understand animals have touched me so deeply, I will never be "done" writing about animals.

In *The Sexual Politics of Meat* you outlined the basis for a feminist-vegetarian critical theory. What does this entail and why do you think it is important?

For twenty years I have struggled to find "sound bites" for *The Sexual Politics of Meat* and it's been very difficult to truncate the ideas. At "The Sexual Politics of Meat Slide Show," I've started giving out a handout with nine feminist-vegan points, which are:

1   Meat eating is associated with virility, masculinity. Meat eating societies gain male identification by their choice of food.

2   Animals are the absent referents in the consumption of meat. Behind every meat meal is the death of the animal whose

Figure 3.2 *Sausageness Baconness Manliness.* Photograph by Kirsten Bayes, Reading, England, 2015.

place the "meat" take. The function of the absent referent is to allow for the moral abandonment of a being.

3 A process of objectification/fragmentation/consumption connects women and animals in a patriarchal culture (they become overlapping absent referents). The visual "joke" that substitutes one fragmented object for another can be found throughout our culture. (Helmut Newton's *Saddle 1?*)

4 Feminist-vegan theory is ecofeminist, that is, environmental issues can't be understood without a feminist perspective and feminist issues can't be understood without an environmental perspective. I place animals into the middle of this insight. As an ecofeminist theory, it recognizes the environmental costs of animalizing protein. Meat production contributes to water pollution, climate change, habit fragmentation, and desertification of arable land. All protein is from plants; animalized protein requires that a living animal process the protein and then be killed.

5 Female animals are the absent referents in meat eating and in the consumption of dairy and eggs. There would be no meat eating if female animals weren't constantly made pregnant. Female animals are forced to produce feminized protein, (plant protein produced through the abuse of the reproductive cycle of female animals, i.e., dairy and eggs).

6 Women are animalized and animals are sexualized and feminized.

7 Anthropornography naturalizes sexual trafficking in and use of women. (See pp. 76–79, 238 and 252 for a discussion of anthropornography.)

8 In its analysis, *The Sexual Politics of Meat* intersects with "carnophallogocentrism." French theorist Derrida coined the

term in an attempt to name the primary social, linguistic, and material practices that go into becoming a subject within the West. Derrida was showing how explicit carnivorism lies at the heart of classical notions of subjectivity, especially male subjectivity. (See Chapter 5 for further exploration of this.)

9   I urge resistance to the ideological construction of living objects through adopting a feminist ethics of care. The feminist ethics of care is a political ethic: it understands that ideology influences how we choose whom to care about.

In the first edition of *The Sexual Politics of Meat* you state that butchering is the act that enables meat to be eaten; and as a paradigm, butchering provides an entry for understanding why a profusion of overlapping cultural images involving animals and women occurs. Can you explain this connection? Also, twenty years on, and now that a new edition of this book is about to be published, has the situation changed at all in your view? What progress—or lack of progress—do you feel has been made in the intervening years regarding our representation of, attitudes towards and treatment of nonhuman species?

Can I explain this connection? I can only do superficially here what the book is dedicated to doing. I find the intersection of overlapping cultural images and treatment of women and animals in a variety of places in Western culture—in metaphor, graphic and artistic depictions, men's description of their violence against women, women's description of their experience of sexual violence, the use of and harm to animals by batterers to create control over their sexual partner, and in advertisements and other discussions of meat as food.

I explain this connection in *The Sexual Politics of Meat* by suggesting that a cycle of objectification, fragmentation, and consumption links butchering and sexual violence in our culture, and that this cycle operates both literally and metaphorically. Consumption is the fulfillment of oppression, the annihilation of will, of separate identity. So too with language: a subject first is viewed, or objectified, through metaphor. Through fragmentation the object is severed from its ontological meaning. Finally, consumed, it exists only through what it represents. The consumption of the referent reiterates its annihilation as a subject of importance in itself. (I see this happening a lot in art, too.)

In terms of overlapping cultural images involving animals and women, things have gotten worse. Meat advertisements that sexualize and feminize animals have been around for more than thirty years, and during this time, they have become more widespread and more explicit. What *Hustler* pornographically imagined women as thirty-five years ago, Burger King, Carl's Jr., and many other dead animal purveyors recreate and suggest now. You can find *Hustler's* image of a woman going through a meat grinder image prettified in an ad for the HBO series *The Comeback* featuring Lisa Kudrow. Burger King takes the *Hustler* mentality—women as meat, as hamburger—and stylizes it for Super Bowl commercials. The 2009 *Sports Illustrated* swimsuit issue ("Bikinis or Nothing") includes an ad for Arby's with hands removing two hamburger buns as though they are taking off a bikini top.

Besides mainstreaming pornographic renderings of women as meat, another twenty-first-century enaction of the sexual politics of meat is the resurgence of the raw as "real." With the raw, there is always more of it. A photoshoot from a reality show called "America's Top Models" in 2008 required the contestants to pose in a meat locker wearing bras and underpants made from recently killed dead animals, that is, "raw meat."

Why raw meat? Raw meat may express a more immediate sense of violation of what once was, what once existed and only recently

Figure 3.3 Arby's full-page advertisement in the 2009 *Sports Illustrated* swimsuit issue.

lost their lives. With the raw, there is always more of it—more raw talent to compete in a realty show, more raw meat to be hung in lockers or worn as undergarments. Why raw meat? It is as though through the use of raw meat there's some sort of fantasy that one can experience life again as "raw, fresh, and tasty," that there remains some untouched, originary zone—connected to consuming dead flesh and naked women—that can be returned to, that dominant lives (assumed as male) that feel so constrained by trying to perform up to standards, those lives that are static can feel "fresh." Of course, the raw meat phenomenon also found a home at the Pierre Monard Gallery in the *Meat After Meat Joy* exhibit curated by Heide Hatry, where raw pieces of dead animals—instead of being molded into undergarments for supermodels—were staged/shaped/cut/sculpted into "art."

You ask, *What progress—or lack of progress—do you feel has been made in the intervening years regarding our representation of, attitudes towards and treatment of nonhuman species?* With animals, I think it's headed in opposite directions simultaneously. Vegan awareness and vegan food have grown exponentially, but so has a backlash. I think we have to understand, always, that a backlash against veganism is also the instantiation of a male-defined human subject (Derrida's carnophallogocentric subject, if you will.)

Here's the problem: the question in animal advocacy has become muddled about whether the issue is suffering or whether it is the death of the animal in itself that matters. Nonhuman animals matter because of who they are—individual beings—not because of a certain quality that obtains to them (their suffering). This isn't like parliamentary procedure where there has to be a second to the first (the "second" being "animals are suffering"). The minute we start arguing about suffering (for women or animals, or any one who is nondominant), we're already ceded their difference. As Catharine MacKinnon points out in "Of Mice and Men," white men did not have to prove they suffered for them to have rights. The focus on suffering creates a new category "humane meat" that helps people reduce the issue to "they aren't suffering, so it's okay to eat them." Of course, there is something insidious in the way the dominant culture incorporates critiques and makes them digestible (just decrease the suffering), but something else obtains here as well. We have to remember that some people get off on the suffering of others and that for others, their pleasure narcissistically outweighs any consideration of another's suffering.

Why, in the end, do we parse another's suffering and try to calibrate what is acceptable and what is not acceptable for them to experience on their way to becoming dead flesh? Why not stare what we actually are doing in the face—causing another's death for our own pleasure? Avoiding confronting this is symptomatic of one aspect of *The Sexual Politics of Meat*—it is hard to eliminate one's dependence on the instrumentality of another being.

In *The Pornography of Meat* (2003) you coined the term "anthropornography." What do you mean by this?

It was actually coined by a friend of mine, Amie Hamlin. I was showing the Sexual Politics of Meat Slide Show at the World Vegetarian Congress in Toronto in 2000, and remarked as I showed yet another photograph of a domesticated animal posed in a sexually inviting way so that the body wanting to be consumed was explicitly represented (probably the "turkey hooker"), I said, "This is not just an anthropomorphic image. It is a sexualized one, within a male dominant sexual economy. There needs to be a name for this." And without missing a beat, Amie called out, "anthropornography." *Anthropornography* means animals (usually species of animals presumed to be literally consumable) are presented as sexually consumable, in a way that upholds the sexual exploitation of women.

Discussing *Colored Pictures: Race and Representation*, Michael Harries identifies several patriarchal structures that obtain in the visual representations of the female nude: the assumption of a white male perspective as universal and an appropriation of female bodies for male prerogatives (Harris 2003: 126). These are present in anthropornography, as well. Animals in bondage, particularly farmed animals, are shown "free," free in the way that women are seen to be "free"—posed as sexually available as though their only desire is for the viewer to want their bodies. It makes animals' degradation and suffering fun by making animals' degradation sexy. Simultaneously, it makes women's degradation fun because to be

Figure 3.4 *Cackalack's*. Photograph by Mitch Goldsmith, Portland Oregon, 2015.

effective the advertisement requires the implicit reference to women's sexualized status as subordinate. For women, through pornography, their degradation is always already sexy. The sexualization of animals and the sexual objectification of women thus overlap and reinforce one another. The body parts of females, at times dead females, are subjects pornography has already sexualized. In a fluid move, these conventions are used to sell dead bodies.

Meat advertisements show us how pornographers do this: take a defeated being, in this case a dead animal, and pose him or her according to a pornographic convention, say, a restaurant that sells dead lobsters claiming "Nice tail;" barbecued pigs posed as young women (all pink, signifying whiteness), hanging on the arms of men; anorexic cows; chickens in high heels. In each case, she is dead and yet she wants it. Wants what? Wants sex; wants to be sexually used; wants to be consumed. And so violence has been made into sex. Meat advertisements do this to animals because pornographers do it to women. Pornographers do it to women because it works for them sexually. As MacKinnon explains, "To be a means to the end of the sexual pleasure of one more powerful is, empirically, a degraded status and the female position" (2005: 129). Which not only explains what pornography is doing and why, but why meat advertisements would gravitate to pornographic conventions to sell their dead products. They mix death with degradation. That equation has one

Figure 3.5 *A Better Class of Sushi.* Photograph by Greta Gaard, Minneapolis, Minnesota, 2013.

answer: the dead animal equals the female position. Pornographic conventions bleed into the bloodied animals that are shown wanting to be consumed, that is, wanting their own death.

As with pornography, anthropornography benefits from the way privilege is constructed. One aspect of privilege is that it disappears as privilege and appears as "what is." Pointing out how privilege works is very threatening to those who benefit from privilege because privilege allows itself to be unreasoned, unjustified, unexamined. It exists not to be examined. (One reason veg*ns make meat eaters uneasy is because the meat eater is triggered by the presence of a veg*n to begin examining the decision to eat dead animals.) Privilege isn't an idea; it's an experience. And generally, privilege grants pleasure. So, just as through pornography, as Catharine MacKinnon says, inequality is made sexy, through meat eating, inequality is made *tasty*. And in examples such as the curated exhibit, "Meat after Meat Joy" inequality has been made art.

Misery made sexy. That's anthropornography.

In a keynote address you made at the *Minding Animals* conference last year [2009] in Newcastle, Australia, you were dismayed at the contemporary proliferation of images depicting what you call called the "animalization of women" and the "feminization and sexualization of animals." How do you understand these forms of representation to function in popular culture and advertising?

They are working to maintain important aspects of consumer culture, to reinforce privilege by defining who is the consumer and who is the consumed, and to maintain the important fictions of essential differences between men and women and humans and nonhumans that enable power over the nondominant.

In *Staring: How We Look*, Rosemarie Garland-Thomson says "In late capitalism, the predominant form of looking, the mass exercise of ocularcentricity, is what we might call consumer vision" (2009: 29). Meat advertisements are at the heart of consumer vision, and animalizing women and feminizing animals is one of the ventricles in that heart. Garland-Thomson refers to Cohen's suggestion that "one central task of citizenship in our era is consuming" and continues by saying "the cultural call to be consumers primarily entails looking at commodities, not people." Animalizing women and feminizing animals helps in this process because it renders women and dead animals used as flesh as commodities.

In his discussion of *Silence of the Lambs*, Cary Wolfe proposes four categories: humanized human, animalized human, humanized animals and animalized animal. He sees the two ends of this continuum functioning more as fictions. But I would argue that in Western culture (and at the time of the Enlightenment and the writing of the American constitution) white-property owning men were the humanized human. The human was defined by male-identified characteristics of rationality. Even now, in terms of evolutionary depictions, the humanized human who emerges out of his primate ancestors is marked as white male. Casting individuals as animalized humans is usually influenced by race, sex, and class.

In Wolfe's analysis the animalized human is found in the movie in the young women being murdered by the serial killer; an example of the humanized animal is Precious, the dog.

I think Wolfe is onto something but I think it is more complex than this and I've tinkered with the formulation recognizing how femaleness is also a marker that has a definite impact on status.[1]

In *Silence of the Lambs* the serial killer is animalizing women—after all he is capturing them to cure their skins to make into a leather

---

[1] In the Bloomsbury Revelations edition of *The Sexual Politics of Meat* (2015), this is called "Sexual Politics of Meat Grid" so for consistency with that work, I have provided this name here.

Table 3 Sexual politics of meat grid

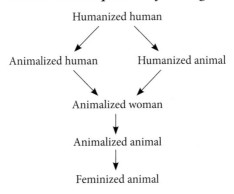

dress. And the lambs represent female victims—they are feminized animals. The feminized animal is the animal who is violable, able to be marked upon, the domesticated animals who become "meat." In meat eating, as I argue in *The Sexual Politics of Meat*, all animals become symbolically female. (And humane welfare laws often don't apply to animals used as meat.) Conventions include fragmentation ("are you a breast man or a leg man"?), consumable females (barbecued pigs as sexy females with thrusting hips and pendulous breasts), and strip teases (animals in various stages of disrobing), rendering all domesticated animals being consumed as female. Moreover, female animals are the ones who are the most abused in the production of meat which can only exist because female animals are enslaved reproductively to produce more "meat" for consumers (and artists).

Your examination of texts and images demonstrates how speciesism (and, in particular, the domination and killing of animals for meat) is linked not only to (hetero)sexism, but also to homophobia, racism, classism and other forms of marginalization. Can you give an example of this intersectionality in operation in visual culture in general—or in a specific ad or work of art?

First, let's acknowledge that whenever whiteness appears, it is a choice. Earlier I referred to the whiteness of the feminized pigs in the ads. That is a deliberate choice. Black women are often depicted as "wild" animals who have to be captured. Meanwhile in advertisements (and t-shirts, wall paintings, billboards, etc.) for barbecues, pigs are often depicted not just as white women, but as "slutty" white women, i.e., white trash. One part of the message is that these pigs wouldn't even charge for sex, that's how available they are. They are shown with large breasts, or fragmented, without a head. The white Christian man is always dominant over the imagined dead body of the ("lower-class" white) female-identified pig. (Implicitly Christian since "pork" is not tabooed for Christians.)

Lots of ads appealing to white, heterosexual man seem to be rebuilding what feminism and veganism have threatened. Heterosexual

Figure 3.6 *Pig Pickin' BBQ.* Photographed by Reannon Branchesi, Outer Banks, North Carolina, Spring 2003.

politics are also imbedded; the assumption is that woman is available as an orifice for men (and hamburgers/hot dogs). "Damelo" one Burger King ad has the woman say, "give it to me," a slang for sex. Her mouth is wide open. Antigay protests might refer to the killing of animals ("save the seals, club a faggot" as a t-shirt from the 1990s proclaimed), so that homophobia constituted itself in part through anthropocentrism. A specific ad may be help us recognize this. I am thinking of the Burger King parody of Helen Reddy's "I am woman hear me roar." In this case, it is men, uniting, to the clarion call that they are men, they need to eat meat, they won't eat "chick" food (quiche). The professional men pour out of restaurants and workplaces, the working class men leave their jobs on the street, all races come together, hopping out of cars, to join together in a march proclaiming their need and right to eat meat. In this video, meat eating unites all classes and races of men against women and symbols of women (the soccer Mom car). It can be both facetious and directly hit the spot: men want meat and that is what they should get.

In *The Sexual Politics of Meat Slide Show*, I began to trace an image from Titian's *Venus of Urbino* through Manet's Olympia (1863) to "Ursula Hamdress," from *Playboar: The Pig Farmer's Playboy*. All depict a healthy sexual being in a similar pose. Titian placed a dog at the nude's foot; Manet, both a black cat and an African woman servant. Manet's painting presents a colonialist, racist viewpoint. As Michael Harris explains, "In the nineteenth century, women of color were associated with nature, uncontrolled passion, and promiscuity. . . . Here within the privileged space of the white male gaze is a layered black subject who is at once socially inferior to a naked prostitute, for whom she is a servant, and yet a sexual signifier and a cipher; her mere presence is the equivalence of Olympia's nakedness" (Harris 2003: 126). David Harvey's *The Condition of Postmodernity* traces Titian's and Manet's inscribing meaning on a woman's body painting genealogically into modernity and postmodernity (Harris considers *Picasso's Les Demoiselles d'Avignon*, Harvey, Rauschenberg's postmodernist work *Persimmon*). But what Harvey recognizes is how the genealogy can be followed forward to an ad for Citizen Watch. So, too, with Ursula Hamdress. But, the way in which a pig is substituted for the woman reveals the interaction of overlapping absent referents that animalize and sexualize. Now the animalizing function has moved from margin to center: a dog at the feet of the "Venus" represented animality in Titian's painting. Manet placed an African servant to represent animal sexuality. With Ursula, the animalizing and sexualizing functions that are separate in Titian's and Manet's paintings are united in one being. This time, it both presumes and maintains the normativeness of meat eating while also sexualizing the killing and consuming of the nonhuman.

If the pig weren't white, there would be less of an anthropocentric hook not only because the genealogy of the pose is of white women, but also because African women and African-American women already bear such an association with "wild" sexuality, uncontrollable (again why they are often shown as wild animals), if a darker pig were used, it would have overwhelmed the anthropornographic staging of the photo. Because of the race hierarchy that still is inscribed so strongly in Western culture, a white pig was needed, so that the degradation being represented could be as strongly conveyed as possible (i.e., the whiteness associated with the pig, which normally would have provided a racial elevation, is contained/overwhelmed by the female and animal associations).[2]

One last example of intersections: in the famous Chick-fil-a advertisements that show a cow writing, the cow always misspells words. That animals can't spell inflects class associations because the unlettered class is rarely the professional, middle or upper class. Inability

---

[2]These ideas became the basis of my essay, "Why a Pig?" (see Chapter 7).

to control words and spellings is a marker of disempowerment. The cows in these ads have to be unlettered in terms of learning because they are not literally unlettered, that is unmarked with letters. It is the fate of the literal animal (the absent referent) to be written upon, truly, written over through the metaphoric figuration of the literal, and in many ways to be written upon, violated. Branding, docking, cutting off their beaks, snipping their tails, castrating them, cropping their ears, piercing them, the creation of trans-genic species, all these actions write upon the animal. So, of course, in visual culture, the animal cannot be lettered, that is, a wise and educated user of letters because the animal must bear letters.

Figures 3.7 and 3.8

U Wanna Peece of Me? Photograph by Carol J. Adams, Valley View Mall, Dallas, Texas.

The Marked Cow #0579. Photograph by Jo-Anne McArthur/We Animals, who spent a day at a small-scale dairy and veal farm. She writes, "Ears are clipped and tagged without anesthetic of painkillers."

Some contemporary artists use live animals—or the carcasses of slaughtered animals—in their art. In his glass tank works ostensibly examining "the processes of life and death," British artist Damien Hirst suspends dead and sometimes dissected animals (such as cows, sheep and sharks) in formaldehyde. Belgian artist Wim Delvoye has an "Artfarm" in China where live pigs are tattooed, their skins remaining "art works" after they are slaughtered. Turkish-born US-based Pinar Yolacan uses the heads, skins and feet of chickens as textiles and frills for garments worn by elderly women models in her "Perishable Art" exhibition. What is it about Western culture that applauds abject art involving the bodies of dead animals? And why do you think they receive acclaim from the contemporary art world?

Whatever else it is, art is the transmission of energy. Art that destroys someone else's energy to exist is bankrupt, derivative, and at some profound level, untrue. It's a sacrificial, substitutionary positioning of animal as victim who becomes "art." In experiencing "art," I don't mind being disturbed, upset, dismayed, or depressed, but I don't want to be the second hand beneficiary of violence, engaging in an act of viewing that can only exist because someone's death was willed, because someone's energy was the means to another's ends. There is another name for that which destroys—eliminating someone else's energy—and that name is murder.

It was said of the Chicago pork producers of the nineteenth century that they used everything of the pig's but the "oink." With art such as you mention, we experience the artist's oink. It is not an act of ventriloquizing (like the Chinese story teller I read about who could make the twelve different sounds of a pig being killed). It is the gaining of "voice" as an artist through the silencing of another's voice. Energy arising through the killing of animals makes the artist a butcher.

The act of killing animals (like the act of eating meat) is part of the project of constructing the carnophallogocentric subject. It is an act of self-definition as a privileged (male-identified) human, and it allows all other humans the access to that self-definition, too, as voyeurs and consumers. These artists can get away with murder because the law does not recognize animals as the subjects of their own lives; instead they are property. Artists, like butchers, are granted the right to take animate property and make it inanimate property.

The choices of these specific artists—whether it is suspending a dead animal in a vat, tattooing animals, or designing clothing around placentas—remind me of all the ways animals are treated as the literal, available as raw material for the consumption and use of humans. These are simply recent iterations of this. And I don't trust what they claim they are doing; because they use their language to lift their art into the metaphoric realm; so it is a double denial of the animals. For instance, Delvoye shows the human power over the literal not only by writing upon the pigs, but by making them absent referents, that is, extinguishing their literal existence. Yolacan, one of the artists in the *Meat after Meat Joy* exhibit, exclaimed to the *New York Times* back in 2004 when she was first discovered by them, "I've always been interested in the impermanence of *things*." (Horyn 2004) What *things* could that be?

Like Hirst and Delvoye, Yolacan actually creates, facilitates, and necessitates the impermanence of beings by their consuming of animals' bodies for their art. (Ignoring for the time her choice to use older women's bodies as vehicles for rotting flesh.)

In the catalog that accompanied *Meat after Meat Joy*, one of the prefatory articles introduced the idea that "Meat is the No Body." Thyrza Goodeve, exhibiting a slight anxiety about the entire venture, feels it is necessary to disassociate his artists from killing. He writes: "let us be clear—not one of the artists in this exhibition killed an animal in order to make his or her art. Meat is already dead. This does not mean it is not upsetting or offensive to see an art exhibition whose theme and source material is meat. But if killing is the question it has already been done" (Goodeve 2008: 10). Good god! To have to rationalize that "the animals were already dead anyway"—the typical answer from many meat eaters—is such an embarrassing and superficial way of exploring the legitimacy of using meat as a medium for artistic creation. (Goodeve, incomprehensibly, then goes on to say that this is why Victor Frankenstein got his material for the monster from *graves* instead of *slaughterhouses*. Sorry, Goodeve, Frankenstein also went to slaughterhouses. That the Monster actually refuses to eat meat does tell us something that *Meat After Meat Joy* seems to want to avoid—maybe there isn't any meat joy whatsoever? Maybe one cannot resist objectification through using objectification.)

Simultaneously, Goodeve shows us two things: an inadequate response to the question of killing animals for the creation of art and yet also the obvious necessity to assert an answer. Goodeve's answer suggests that something similar to what Timothy Bewes observes in *Reification or The Anxiety of Late Capitalism* is going on when it comes to using dead animals' bodies as the medium for "art." Bewes says that, "troubling feelings—in particular, the sense of anxiety toward reification—have become virtually universal in advanced capitalist societies" (2002: xii). Later he says, "Anxiety is the consciousness of reification; reification is the anxiety towards reification" (247). Anxiety comes with the territory of reification. Since meat eating is one aspect of the instantiation of reification (the creation of the absent referent), anxiety is one aspect of meat eaters' relationship to their activity. It will also be one aspect—even if it is well cloaked or hidden—in the relationship of artists to their (dead) medium. The difference between reification in Bewes's sense and meat eating is that the anxiety against reification contains within it the possibility of reversing reification, but an animal once dead cannot be restored to life. Thus art intercedes to make of this disaster (the death of the animal) something "redemptive" for humans—the ones who feel this anxiety (acknowledged or unacknowledged) about the animals' death, especially when they are the ones who caused the disaster that must be redeemed through their acts.

Many artists have shown us ways to explore violation without representing the act of violation or motivating the act of violation. (I recently saw the remarkable film of Beckett's dramatic monologue *Not I* at the Museum of Contemporary Art in Denver and it is absolutely riveting in representing the effects of violation without showing it.) I wonder if their works carry less markers of anxiety?

It would be naïve of me to argue this, but for the moment, grant me naiveté: If we are to acknowledge to the artist the power of imagination and this imagination is ostensibly so inviolable that we can't dictate the limits to which the artist can go in exploring that imagination, then why we can't we credit everybody with imagination and that imagination allows us to feel empathy and to imagine what violability feels like? In her book, *The Hemingses of Monticello: An American Family*, Annette Gordon-Reed says "History is to a great degree an imaginative enterprise; when writing it or reading it, we try to see the subject in time and space." Gordon-Reed acknowledges that both the writer and reader of history need imagination. All of us have to use our imagination all the time! It just turns out we're not supposed to use that imagination when it comes to animals' deaths; we're not supposed to place animals as subjects in time and space who, just before being killed and made permanently dead, would have chosen to continue living. I might say, "I imagine animals don't like to be killed. They don't like to be tattooed; they don't like to be represented as though they themselves aren't somebody." I'd like to claim that *that* imaginative response can stand alongside and have as much weight and claim to being a legitimate way of constructing the world and evaluating what's done in the world as any other perspective including the artists' own oink! The problem for me is that my viewpoint isn't the hegemonic one.

But, building on Bewes, let me suggest something else. If there is anxiety about our "thingly" quality (are we suspended between life and death by this?), perhaps such anxiety is allayed, in part, or at times, by reaffirming our power to make other beings into things (the impermanence of *things*). Of course, the resurgence of the raw fits in here, too—the newly made *thing* that once was alive. The fetishistic attachment to the dead animal in art will always create or motivate the creating of that object (the dead animal) but that motivating act will cause anxiety and that anxiety will leak out one way or another in connection with the art. No matter what the artist claims, a stuffed goat is never only a stuffed goat.

I'm reading *The Writing of the Disaster* at the moment, and Hirst seems to acknowledge implicitly Blanchot's idea that we can't address ultimately our own death. But current laws allow artists to manipulate and kill someone else if that someone else is a nonhuman. But isn't Hirst ultimately caught within Blanchot's contradictions too? I think Blanchot raises an issue I want to wrench from his context: How does one write about what doesn't exist (knowledge of your own death when [and after] you die)? Can one write about one's own death? ("[T]he experience that none experiences, the experience of death.") Does death not obliterate the difference between human and nonhuman animals? Or does death, by depriving humans of something uniquely human—the ability to write about it—highlight the difference? Is this where the unlettered status of animals leads us—the never-to-be-accomplished writing of the disaster? For if our death cannot be known, then we are like nonhuman animals.

You ask, *what is it about Western culture that applauds abject art involving the bodies of dead animals?* The short answer is people are afraid to be seen as against "art" for they will be accused of not being good consumers of art or of not getting it; they don't want to be illiterate consumers (unlettered) of the art; they want to be included, not excluded. To offer what will be viewed as a nonartistic critique renders one outside. Think of all the negative words for critics who address the medium the artist chooses (the dead animal). We are not supposed to join the conversation there. We are trying to say something *a priori* about the selected "medium" and there is no place for us to lodge our concerns aesthetically, and so we are expelled from the Eden of art (consumed or created). Because ours is labeled an "unlettered" critique, the labeling is meant to precipitate a different anxiety—not the one that the knowledge of the dead animal causes, but the one that being unlettered in a world of letters, uncultured in a world of culture causes. *Lord, don't let that be me: situated outside the pale; unregenerate; unable to be "cultured."* PETA's criticism of *Meat after Meat Joy* is critiqued in the catalog by John Wronoski of the Pierre Menard Gallery which hosted the exhibition. Wronoski doubts that "such responses bespeak thought occasioned by artwork," i.e., by not participating in relationship to the art itself, but criticizing the medium (the use of dead animals), PETA's criticism is somehow not valid.

I'm always concerned when there is some zone privileged and separate from everything else, that can't be judged like everything else, that the fiction about this untouched, originary zone—connected to art—can be returned to through the act of creation, that dominant lives (assumed as male) that feel so constrained by trying to perform up to standards, those lives that are static can feel "fresh" by experiencing the products of those who are able to (re)enter this (fictive) zone.

The zone of artistic privilege—why does it resemble the zone of privilege invoked by pornographers for free speech? The inviolability of the artistic work, the inviolability of the product of pornography is greater than the inviolability of the animal or the woman? (It could be argued that this is because, in fact, animals and women are not yet ceded to be inviolable as I discuss in *The Pornography of Meat*.) How that zone came into existence, what the conditions were that allowed such a zone to come into existence is really the question. Again, thinking about *The Hemingses of Monticello*, Gordon-Reid says what the law protected then, it continues to protect, now, even after the end of American slavery.

> People in history who, like John Wayles [the father of several children with an enslaved woman] were under the law's protection during life tend to remain under the law's protection—statutes, rules, presumptions, privileges, legal fictions, and all. People outside of the law's protection, like Elizabeth Hemings [the enslaved woman], generally remain outside, particularly when aspects of their lives do not comport with the law's strictures and fictions. (2008: 84)

She is showing that some sort of continuity of privilege obtains through the structures that were created to protect that privilege, that these structures create a longevity or a conceptual world (of dominance) without end. Even if the world of slavery ended, the conceptual world that co-existed with slavery and allowed slavery to exist, lives on. If that's the case, not surprisingly, then privilege protects itself, provides a way in perpetuity to keep itself... privileged. A species-specific privilege creates the space in which art that uses the abject bodies of dead animals exists and can be protected. When something—something specific like killing—has an ethics that stops at the species line, I want to know why, and the arguments "because they are animals" and "because they are artists" are insufficient as answers.

Let's also state another obvious point: the ability to be ironic about nonhuman animals (an acknowledged characteristic of postmodern art) is possible because one is *not* nonhuman. Irony arises from a position of power (at the minimum, human power) and has within it the power to critique all non-ironic responses to it for their lack of "getting it." The literal exists to be moved away from, to be ironized, even if the literal in some form is what is being encountered aesthetically.

Attention to the literal as literally of primary importance (the dead animal) is seen as a nonaesthetic response. It reminds me of a famous distinction feminists made between therapy and activism for battered women. Therapy said, "you have a foot on your neck, how do you feel about it?" Activism said, "let's take that foot of your neck." In this culturally privileging world, the artist's foot is hard to move.

Yet, Wronoski (again of *Meat after Meat Joy*) smugly says that though PETA's criticism was not occasioned by artwork "perhaps they do mean that art can still manage to stimulate the ordinarily insensate." Hmmm. So we are back to energy, but this time, it is not "meat," i.e., dead animals that are the insensate, when in fact they are truly insensate, they are, in fact the literal meaning of being a piece of meat—without feeling. Yet, in this triad of three subjects—the artists and gallery owners, the critics, and the (formerly living) material— the only ones who are credited with not being *ordinarily insensate* are the artists and their colleagues. How convenient! Those with their feet on the necks of the animals, those whose artistic oink sounds in the galleries of the Western world, are seen as the ones who are not *unfeeling*, i.e., insensate.

And why do you think they receive acclaim from the contemporary art world?

It's propaganda for speciesism. It is for human superiority what Leni Riefenstahl's *Triumph of the Will* was for Nazism. It may be exquisitely rendered, hypnotic even, but it's propaganda and it exists because humans view animals as property. Or as Marian Scholtmeijer says in *Animal Victims in Modern Fiction*, "we have a liking for the effect of animals upon our thoughts, as long as they do not challenge their instrumentality as mediators of culture" (1993: 5).

Art that reinscribes the denial of the animal through actively denying/depriving them of life—it's working at many levels. It simultaneously reassures our self-definitions as humans while also affirming human superiority. We not only get to watch what is happening to live and dead animals (and know this wouldn't happen to us), but the gaze, the act of experiencing art is something that we see as uniquely human. So by participating through spectating onto "art," we know we are human. We also can't disown the voyeuristic nature of it.

I believe people know at a deep level that they are connected to animals, that animals prefer to live rather than die, but we cover this through socialization and rationalization and a protected notion of humanness as constituting itself through the denial of the animals. But whenever I try to point it out, there's a preexisting hegemonic interpretive framework that means my pointing it out is called "strident" but the hegemonic interpretive framework is called acceptable, considered normative, considered even, artistically, avant-garde. The hegemonic is human-centered (and the human is defined by male qualities). It reassures and re-establishes human (male-identified) primacy at several levels simultaneously and because some of those levels are hidden or unacknowledged, it never has to expose itself for what it is. Art that is revolutionary but not revolutionary enough upholds the status quo.

Animal activist organizations such as People for the Ethical Treatment of Animals (PETA) also employ images of naked or scantily clad women in their campaigns against meat-eating and animal abuse. In *The Pornography of Meat* (2003) you show several examples of meat advertisements that have been appropriated by PETA for the purposes of animal activism: one such image is that of the "Cattle Queen" (which also appears as the cover image of *The Sexual Politics of Meat*, and was originally used at a 1968 feminist protest against the Miss America pageant and its portrayal of women's bodies as "meat"). The "Cattle Queen" picture shows a naked woman sitting with her back to the viewer, her body divided into sections labeled "rib," "rump," "loin," "chuck" and so on. PETA modifies this image in its anti-meat eating poster entitled "All Animals Have the Same Parts": again a naked woman's body is segmented and named according to different meat cuts. What is your perspective on the use of such imagery in animal activism?

First, it shows the functioning and strength of the structure of the absent referent. PETA admits visually through these and other examples that animals can't represent their own need to be liberated from human domination, otherwise they would be the ones shown in all their visual campaigns. Their absence tells us how powerfully the conceptual absenting of animals is. PETA seems to acknowledge that for many people the referent, animals, is gone. And they are trying to work with what is there, cultural consumption, by manipulating cultural images/issues. They are trying to get people to talk about veganism without having to address what has disappeared. It doesn't matter who they piss off. In fact, the more the better. Tastelessness is newsworthy; nonhuman farmed animals aren't.

Secondly, one of the implicit, if not explicit messages of such advertisements is, "Yes, you can become aware of animals' lives, but you don't have to give up your pornography." Thus, rather than challenging the inherent inequality of a culture structured around dominance and subordination, the ad instead tries to leverage sexual inequality on behalf of the other animals. It is an appeal to the carnophallogocentric subject, saying "really, you can still have objects in your life, you just can't have animals as objects." It naively believes that the "carno" can be taken out of the carnophallogocentric subject. It really doesn't understand how the human male subject is being constructed in Western culture. As I argue in *Neither Man nor Beast: Feminism and the Defense of Animals*, maleness and humanness are co-constructed, co-informing each other; the qualities most valued in humans are qualities associated with upper-class Western men.

In fact, every time PETA uses a naked or nearly naked woman to advertise animals' concerns it not only benefits from sexual inequality, it also unwittingly demonstrates the intransigence of species inequality. In this context, while some argue that PETA's ads using naked or nearly naked women are liberating, not only for animals but, in transgressive ways, for women too, such practices in fact only substitute one absent referent for another. The challenge for the animal movement is how to restore the absent referent to a dominant culture that refuses to acknowledge it. What must be borne in mind, however, is that the absent referent is a crucial point of intersection both for sexual inequality and species inequality. Logically, there can be no politically liberatory "substitution" of woman for animal, because what is being replaced carries its own marker of inequality. What appears superficially as substitution is actually the layering of one oppressive system on top of another.

Not only is this wrong as it maintains the objectification of women, but as I argue in *The Pornography of Meat*, it is inappropriate activism because animals are marked by gender, as well as species. As I have tried to show, one common way that sexual inequality is imposed on farmed animals is through advertisements that sexualize meat. Replacing animals with women is therefore not substitution or potentially liberating, because the original victim's fate is still there, present through reference.

What we in fact see is merely one debased subject being referenced within and by the other: the lowered status of the first (animal) is applied to the other (woman), who however already carries her own low status—marked as "female" in a world of sexual inequality. If animals are burdened by gender, by gendered associations, by the oppression that is gender, then clearly they can't be liberated through representations that demean women. PETA wants to lift the animalized and feminized animals up and out of their status as consumed and thinks this can be done while bypassing and actually using women's animalized status.

What are your thoughts on the employment of graphic imagery in campaigns against factory farming, meat-eating, and animal experimentation?

Do you mean the "bleeding Jesus" pictures, as one Catholic friend calls them, of damaged, injured animals? In these campaigns, the assumption seems to be "if we expose the structure of the absent referent in the destruction of a being (someone becoming something) we will get people to change, we will get people to care." I do know that people have been changed by watching videos like PETA's *Meet Your Meat,* and I know that some of these videos are so shocking that they do awaken an alarm or an awareness in some viewers. They are also helpful in legislative campaigns. But (and of course there is a but!) . . .

Whose duty is it to watch these? I receive emails all the time saying, "It is your duty to take three minutes and watch this graphic video." No, it isn't my duty. My retinas do not need those images sketched on their insides. The burden is often placed on women to re-inflict what I have called "traumatic knowledge" (see pp. 281–283). If we already know and have acted on this knowledge, it's okay not to watch. It is okay to set boundaries about what we take in visually and what we don't.

Moreover, a specific group of people exists who are voyeuristic and enjoy watching others suffer. I knew a filmmaker in New York City who used to show animal advocacy films on Sunday nights on the upper West Side. He told me he noticed that he was attracting a different clientele when he showed really graphic (i.e., more gory) films. He eventually stopped showing those kinds of films because he said he was creeped out by the men who came to watch.

I believe there is a place in campaigns for imagination. When I spoke at the University of Minneapolis, I went to The Frederick R. Weisman Art Museum. They had on loan an immense canvas (12' by 18') by Douglas Argue, "Untitled." It's a painting of chickens in cages in a factory farm. Because of the way the vanishing point extends way down the aisle of cages, it is as though we are standing in the midst of these captive chickens and their captivity goes on forever. As Derrida says in *The Animal that therefore I am (more to follow)* "Everybody knows what terrifying and intolerable pictures a realist painting could give to the industrial, mechanical, chemical, hormonal, and genetic violence to which man has been submitting animal life for the past two centuries." The painting isn't truly realistic in that the chickens themselves aren't bloodied or injured or as crowded as they are in true industrialized farming situations and yet the painting shows us another way to encounter what is happening to animals.

I'd also argue that graphic imagery isn't needed at all. Though Coetzee asserts we change because we got to know an animal, not because we read books, I would challenge him on this account. He says,

> We (participants in this dialogue) are where we are today not because once upon a time we read a book that convinced us that there was a flaw in the thinking underlying the way that we, collectively, treat nonhuman animals, but because in each of us there took place something like a conversion experience. . . . Our conversion experience as often as not centered on some other mute appeal of the kind that Levinas calls the look, in which the existential autonomy of the Other became irrefutable—irrefutable by any means, including rational argument. (Cavalieri 2009: 90)

Now I don't disagree with Coetzee that many people experience consciousness changing as a result of a relationship with an animal or animals (that is one aspect of the feminist care tradition in animal ethics that Josephine Donovan and I discuss in the anthology by that name and, of course, that is how I changed), but I know first hand that when people read books they can be changed. I hear from people almost daily about how reading *The Sexual Politics of Meat* changed their lives. And I suspect Coetzee, as an author himself, has heard similar attestations. There are multiple ways to change consciousness.

I would love to co-curate a show called "the sexual politics of meat" that gathered many of the negative images that I have collected as well as art like Sue Coe's and other's that resists the hegemonic world view, and in the space, create an environment for experiencing and reflecting on interconnected oppressions, and ways that we can resist it. Since I'm daydreaming here, I'd place it on the Turbine level of the

Tate Modern or at the Hammer Museum at University of California at Los Angeles.[3]

In your opinion, what does an effective visual campaign against animal exploitation involve?

I don't think there is any one way to come to consciousness about animals, which I presume is the usual motivation behind visual campaigns against animal exploitation.

I think the question is: How do we believe change happens? Do we need visual campaigns to succeed? Maybe our problem is that as a visual culture we are so hooked to visual solutions that we don't see other possibilities. In *Living Among Meat Eaters*, I propose that meat eaters are blocked veg*ns. (Whether this is actually true or not, acting as though it is true has changed how I relate and reach out to meat eaters.) Basically, people don't want to give up their privilege; after all inequality is tasty. I like addressing the "blocked" aspect of the situation. What's keeping you blocked? Confused notions of change? Confused notions of veganism? Realistically, here in the United States, if the United States government simply stopped subsidizing meat eating and dairy products, it would become exponentially so much more expensive that people would decide to consider veganism!

It seems PETA and other animal rights organizations assume we have to converse (often with great urgency) with the left-brain to bring about change. Often the approach is something like this: "Don't

---

[3]In 2013, I heard from the artist Kathryn Eddy, who, after reading this interview, contacted me. She wrote, "I have been reading back issues of *Antennae* magazine and ran across an old interview of yours from 2010 in which you mentioned a desire to co-curate a *Sexual Politics of Meat* exhibit and I would love to talk to you about it. I think we can make this happen, as I know several artists who have been influenced by your book and I know you do, too." In 2015, the book, *The Art of the Animal: Fourteen Women Artists Explore The Sexual Politics of Meat*, edited by Kathryn Eddy, L. A. Watson, and Janell O'Rourke was published. Their co-curated art exhibit featuring these fourteen artists will premiere at the National Museum of Animals and Society in 2017.

you know? Why can't you see! Do it now! This is urgent!" People resist being told what to do and they want to decide for themselves what is urgent. They automatically resist the message. I like to find ways around that resistance. I offer one-liners that keep people thinking, answers like "we don't eat anyone who had a mother," or "we don't eat anyone who has bowel movements." I also believe good vegan meals provided in non-stressful situations communicate a great deal on their own, and allow the person to incubate these ideas. I believe in the power of incubation and that we should structure campaigns that assume people can be reached through incubating ideas.

I had been resisting answering this interview for more than a month. Then I traveled out of town to show *The Sexual Politics of Meat Slide Show* and I did what I always do—the next day I went to the art galleries in the town. As always, it widened my sense of the world. And that's when I realized I hadn't been resisting, I had been incubating my answers!

Animal activist artists may also incorporate the bodies of dead animals in their politicized work. For example, New Zealand-based Singer performs what she terms "de-taxidermy" in her art; this process involves peeling back fur and skin on hunting trophies to expose where bullet holes have been deliberately hidden by a taxidermist. Singer's works overtly draw attention to the ways in which animals who have been shot or trapped suffer at the hands of hunters. She has also shown how possums, demonized as "pests" and killed without compassion in New Zealand, endure great pain when poisoned with toxins such as 1080; to this end, Singer places funereal beads on parts of a possum's body where a traumatic injury or disease process is obvious, again to highlight the intense suffering inherent in so-called "possum control" campaigns in New Zealand. Do you have any objection to art such as this? (If so, why? If not, why not?)

I've followed her career for a while and find it fascinating and important. (And I should acknowledge she used quotes from *The Sexual Politics of Meat* [as well as quotes from other writers] in her 2002 MFA Show *Wild-deer-ness*). I think she, like Beckett in *Not I*, creates ways to explore violation without motivating the act of violation. She also demonstrates how to engage with the issue of human-animal relations, and animality, without requiring any more deaths. Singer

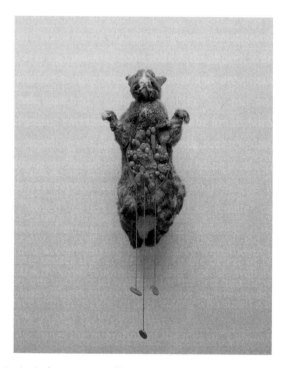

Figure 3.9 Artist's statement: "Working with the history of each particular animal I aim to recreate something of its death by hunt. Art works incorporating the look of hung or crucified taxidermy are inspired by the description from the hunter of the moment they hung the animal from a tree, cut it open and pulled the entrails out to drain the blood. I seek to uncover and expose the aggression inflicted on the animal by human hands."

Angela Singer, *Catch Caught* 2007. Vintage taxidermy rabbit, buttons, beads, zip, wool. 530 × 240 × 150 mm.

does not participate in what J. M. Coetzee's Elizabeth Costello calls "an enterprise without end, self-regenerating, bringing rabbits, rats, poultry, livestock, ceaselessly into the world for the purpose of killing them" (1999: 119). I like the way in which she creatively recycles the dead body to re-animate the issue of the structure of making an animal absent (bullet holes, what animals experience who have been shot or trapped) is one reason.[4]

Earlier I suggested that the difference between reification and consuming dead animals is that the anxiety against reification contains within it the possibility of reversing reification, but an animal once dead cannot be restored to life. Singer situates herself in such a way as to show us another way. As I have suggested, she provides ways to engage with animals' death without motivating the death. She takes the will to be dominant out of the equation. Earlier, I also quoted Scholtmeijer as saying "we have a liking for the effect of animals upon our thoughts, as long as they do not challenge their instrumentality as mediators of culture." Besides not motivating their death, Singer allows animals to challenge their instrumentality. I think she is doing something akin to what we see developing in and against vivisection: Technological advances have created alternative, non-animal methods, including "computerized modeling and predication systems . . ., genetically engineered cell lines, X-ray assays, batteries of human skin and tissue cultures, epidemiological studies of populations, and carefully controlled clinical trials" (Fano 1997: 136). There is no need to require new animal deaths. Artists have new mediums too, as technology continues to change (creating art on iPhones etc.), or by hunting through the trash (as Singer does), so when artists stick to imposing or requiring the death of an animal, it makes me curious. Why, now, participate in this regressive activity? What is being compensated for?

---

[4]Singer is one of the artists represented in *The Art of the Animal*. See note 3, p. 100.

Looking at Singer's work, she shows us a transpecies ethics—in which we encounter animals subject to subject.

In his research on the New Carnivore movement, New Zealand scholar Jovian Parry has shown how recent popular TV shows for "foodies"—such as Gordon Ramsay's *The F Word* and Jamie Oliver's *Fowl Dinners*—graphically flaunt the killing and consumption of pigs, calves and turkeys personally raised by and known to the celebrity chefs. Parry argues such shows seek to impress upon viewers that in order to be authentic consumers and true gastronomes they must know about, accept as "natural," and even actively participate in, the taking of lives for food. In your view, how does the New Carnivore movement—and its links to shows such as *The F Word*—impact on the notion of the "absent referent"? What worries you about this?

In the introduction to the twentieth anniversary edition of *The Sexual Politics of Meat,* I say, "When there is anxious masculinity, there will be manifestations of meat eating." The need to reassure masculinity is an unstated project of these televisions shows—a sort of desperate rebuilding of the carnophallogocentric subject. They want one sort of honesty (killing) and hide behind a greater dishonesty. The need to make the kill present is a hypermasculine reinscription of the sexual politics of meat.

Of course, everyone prefers to define "natural" according to what they wish to do. What, after all, makes the killing of animals "natural"? Plutarch points out that people do not have bodies equipped for eating flesh from a carcass, "no curved beak, no sharp talons and claws, no pointed teeth" (2003b: 47–48). In *The Sexual Politics of Meat* I quote Plutarch's taunt to his readers in "Essay on Flesh Eating": If you believe yourselves to be meat eaters, "then, to begin with, kill *yourself* what you wish to eat—but do it yourself with your own *natural* weapons, without the use of butcher's knife, or axe, or club" (2015: 30). We have no bodily agency for killing and dismembering the animals we eat; we require implements. The essence of butchering is to fragment the animal into pieces small enough for consumption. Implements are the simulated teeth that rip and claws that tear. Hannah Arendt claims that violence always needs implements.[5] So to begin with, the violence in these television remains implemental violence. Without implemental violence, would human beings be able to eat dead animals? They would be scavengers of dead flesh left by carnivores or consumers of insects—which is how scholars think human beings began as meat eaters. Is that, then, what is "natural"?

At this point, veganism has shown we can survive without animals and we can do it well; the food is good, etc. Vegans might claim this is what is "natural." But I think it is useless to play the game of staking a claim for the "natural" in a world so culturally overdetermined.

Implements remove the referent. For most eaters of dead animals, the structure of the absent referent means that the killing of the animals is off stage. But the structure of the absent referent does not require that the killing be off stage; it requires that the animal's life be subordinate to a human's desire. The structure of the absent referent renders the idea of individual animals as immaterial to anyone's selfish desires for consumption. In fact, looking at a living being as a disposable life initiates the process. Killing an animal onscreen or in your own kitchen participates in the structure of the absent referent because it makes the animal as an individual disappear. *Someone becomes something*—that could be one definition of the structure of the absent referent.

---

[5] "[V]iolence—as distinct from power, force, or strength—always needs *implements*" (Arendt 1970: 4).

In the taking of the animal's life these television chefs participate in the structure of the absent referent, especially if, after the killing, the animal's dead body is referred to by words that objectify and fragment the body, i.e., if after the death, the animal is now known only through body parts (wings, rack, breasts, hamburger, etc.). That is yet another aspect of the structure of the absent referent.

So, a sophisticated analysis might begin by saying "the structure of the absent referent is x, y, and z, (the literal death of the animal, the hiding of the facts of that death, and the lifting of the animal's death to a higher meaning through metaphor and consumption). With these television shows, we see "x" and "z" still functioning (the objectifying and the eating of a dead object) but "y" isn't absent; it has been made demonstrably present (the death isn't hidden). Why "y"? And the answer turns on the issue of the instantiation of the human male subject. I think this approach is helpful when we consider artists who use living or dead animals in their art, too. We then see that these activities—killing as spectacle, eating as spectacle, displaying dead bodies—are a human imperialism of the gaze.

If in another twenty years you are revising *The Sexual Politics of Meat* again, what would you hope to be able to add to that future edition?

Before I directly answer that question let me tell you about one way I became involved in an artist's envisioning of the future. In October 2008, I experienced the installation of *TH.2058* by Dominique Gonzales-Foerster. It was part of the Unilever Series at the Tate Modern, and had just opened. She imagined a future London where climate change (in this case, nonstop rain), has prompted the creation of an urban "ark" (my interpretation). Her explanation, "As well as erosion and rust, [urban sculptures] have started to grow like giant, thirsty tropical plants, to become even more monumental. In order to hold this organic growth in check, it has been decided to store them in the Turbine Hall, surrounded by hundreds of bunks that shelter—day and night—refugees from the rain." Among sculptures by Bourgeois (her famous *Maman*), Calder, Moore, etc., were the bed bunks, and on the bed bunks were books by Bradbury, Borges, LeGuin, Wells, etc. I haven't read all the books she included, but clearly they, like the installation, imagined a future world. She concludes her statement saying, "In the huge collective shelter that the Turbine Hall has become, a fantastical and heterogeneous montage develops, including sculpture, literature, music, cinema, sleeping figures and drops of rain."

At ground level, being among all this, the coherence of her piece was not so clear. Walking through it, people would stop and sit on the bunks and thumb through the books. During this trip to Scotland and England, when I visited a vegetarian restaurant, I would give them a copy of my book *Living Among Meat Eaters*. I had two copies left; one was going to be hand delivered the next day to Rootmaster (a vegan restaurant located in a double decker bus).

My partner, Bruce, came up to me and said, "Do you have copies of your book with you?"

"Yes," I replied.

"Well, leave it on one of these bunks that doesn't have a book."

I was astonished at the idea, but also intrigued. I headed toward the exit, where there was less light. My partner said, "No, not there. Put it up where there's light. Just sit down on one of the bunks." Bruce walked forward toward the center of the exhibit. As I wrote in my journal the next day, "I walked into the lighted area, but didn't have the ovaries to go into the heavily trafficked area. Book in hand, I sat down on one of the things and flipped through it. Then I put it down."

Meanwhile, Bruce was calling to me to come nearer. I shook my head. Thinking I had lost my nerve, Bruce came back to where I sat. I gestured to the book on the bench and then Bruce understood, I had already inserted my book into the exhibit.

As we walked out of the Tate Modern, Bruce reflected, "It's guerilla art. I bet they have a stack of books to put out if some of these walk away. You have more exposure here than you would at a veg restaurant."

Now I could rationalize this and say, "I imagine a different world, too, one without oppression." But neither my partner nor I truly grasped the dystopian situation Gonzales-Foerster was presenting. There were books on bed bunks, add another one. And so I did. But it, too, is a vision of a future, a future without meat eaters.

I know that the cultural transformations that we are working for will take longer than twenty years (unless a few more *e. coli* scares as well as a few scares from other zoonotic diseases linked to meat eating ["factory farm" influenzas] actually awaken self interested meat eaters to what they are doing). But to answer your question, what would I hope to add to a future edition of *The Sexual Politics of Meat*? I'm going to assume that a real transformation of our culture has occurred and our culture no longer confirms the claims I make in that book. I'd love to be able to say:

Look at how human subjects used to constitute themselves—through objectification of others. Consider how consumption used to work to confirm a certain kind of subject, a dominating one. I am heartened by the changes that have occurred in the past twenty years that have released animals and non-dominant humans, especially women (whose sexual servitude seemed to have been assimilated into a postmodern ethos with little disturbance) from their role as objects for the privileged human subject. What was all the fuss about anyway? Why was it always seen as a deprivation? Like equality, vegan food is great! Yes, it's hard to understand now how worked up people got at the idea they had to

Figure 3.10 Pamela Nelson, *Richardson*. Photograph by Mike Itashiki.

give up eating animals and animal products! Ultimately it wasn't about taste. It was always about their sense of self, their sense of entitlement and privilege. Taste changes easier than our self-definitions.

It isn't remarkable that artists were a part of this transformation, but let's take a moment and acknowledge that epochal moment when artists stopped using animals for their own artistic "oink."

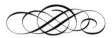

The chapter that follows contains some excruciating information. To relieve the intensity of reading about abuse and violence, I asked the artist Pamela Nelson if we might thread photographs of a few of her thirty mandalas through the chapter. Nelson makes mandalas out of plastic, beads, artificial stones, and other things that are of no value to our culture and get thrown away. She recycled them in a pattern that reproduces beauty. Nelson sees her mandalas as a feminist statement, because women are not valued enough in our culture; they, too, are discarded, dismissed, thrown away. Her artist's task was to answer the question, "How do you put the things that were thrown away together in a way that reflects beauty and order?" She answered,

> It is chaos when things are just thrown away, and to carefully rescue and give each piece that was tossed a place at the table, gives them order, purpose, a pattern, and beauty. It is showing life after being discarded.

After a trip to Ravenna, Italy, studying the ancient mosaics, Nelson was inspired to do assemblage with plastic instead of glass. Each piece starts out as acrylic on wood. A matrix of an epoxy resin holds it together. Nelson says,

> The circle evokes eternity in many cultures—world without end— but these mandalas represent more than the cycle of life and the feminine. They honor generations and traditions as well. Lubbock includes actual buttons from my grandmother's collection. My grandmother, an artist herself, influenced me in many ways, especially to become an artist.
>
> My mother was also an influence in aesthetics. I've incorporated her costume jewelry into the medallions, and Galveston acknowledges

Figure 4.1 Pamela Nelson, *Jefferson*. Photograph by Mike Itashiki.

Figure 4.2 Pamela Nelson, *Port O'Connor*. Photograph by Mike Itashiki.

her love of gaming and gambling. In their circles of life, my grandmother and mother loved and worked with beads and sequins and rhinestones—as I do—and our circles of art overlap and continue.

My circular mandalas assembled from bits of plastic and glass also remind me of the temporary nature of shiny costume culture. Placing these decorative items into a rhythmic composition is my way of making order out of the debris of life. As I work, my mind replays the Virginia Woolf quote: "Arrange whatever pieces that come your way."

That's what I've done, with pieces of my life—and my grandmother's and my mother's. I revere all women's handwork, for sewing, piecing, and embellishing to add joy in the world—not just the art world, the whole world.

Figure 4.3 Pamela Nelson, *Bryan*. Photograph by Mike Itashiki.

4

Woman-battering and harm to animals

A woman, a horse, and a hickory tree
The more you beat 'em the better they be

– FOLK PROVERB (CITED IN STRAUS 1977, 197)

Farmer John Wright lies dead. His wife has been arrested for suspicion of murder. At the secluded farmhouse where he died, the wives of the men investigating the crime begin to notice small signs that suggest a household in disorder: an odd quilt, an empty birdcage, a messy kitchen. These are unimportant concerns in their husbands' eyes, housewives' concerns, surely, but not those of men building a murder case. As the women survey the rooms, they discuss how Mrs. Wright had changed from a woman who enjoyed company and singing in a choir, to an isolated and dominated individual. They think of times when they ought to have visited, realizing how lonely she must have been. The birdcage is an apt symbol, for she, too, once free, was imprisoned behind bars, albeit invisible ones.

Upon discovering a dead canary with a broken neck in the sewing box, they realize that what could be considered the accidental hanging of John Wright was instead deliberate. He had apparently murdered her sole companion. The evidence was literally in their hands, and they decide to hide it. Thus, Mrs. Wright is judged and freed by *A Jury of Her Peers* (Glaspell 1927).

Susan Glaspell prophetically identified the problem of harm to animals by men who control and abuse their wives or female partners. *A Jury of Her Peers* documented many women's lives, and anticipated circumstances such as this one:

> [A woman] who had been sexually and physically abused over a long period of time, shot her batterer at the point where he was attempting to steal her prized exotic pet bird. This act of psychological abuse toward the woman, through the abuse of her pet, went beyond the point of tolerability (Dutton 1992: 27).

In fact, we now know that the murder of a pet often signals that the abuser's violence is becoming more life-threatening (see Browne 1987: 157).

Jean Baker Miller observed that until recently, the only understandings generally available to us were "mankind's," but now other perceptions are arising: "precisely those perceptions that men, because of their dominant position, could *not* perceive" (Miller 1976: 1). Susan Glaspell's short story *A Jury of Her Peers*, written eighty years ago, precisely portrays this insight. This essay plumbs the subject of Glaspell's short story as it is being experienced today by battered women and animals. It extends Miller's insights into the working of dominance and subordination in our culture in terms of species *and* gender. My concern is both for what happens to the harmed animal and what is accomplished for the batterer vis-à-vis his control of his woman partner. The killing of an animal as warning and to instill terror, or the sexual use of an animal and woman together results from and enacts male dominance. This is precisely what woman-battering, and, I will argue, violence against animals, is all about.

Woman-battering

Abusive men are the major source of injury to adult women in the United States.[1] According to U.S. Department of Justice's Bureau of Justice Statistics, "women are six times more likely than men to be the victim of a violent crime committed by an intimate" (Harlow 1991: 1). According to the U.S. Bureau of Justice National Crime Survey, in the United States a woman is beaten in her home every fifteen seconds (Harlow 1991). Testimony before the Senate Judiciary Committee indicates that as many as 4 million women are affected each year by woman-battering (see *Women and Violence* 1990). In the United States, a woman is more likely to be assaulted, injured, raped, or killed by her male partner than by any other assailant.

According to Anne Ganley battering is "assaultive behavior occurring in an intimate, sexual, theoretically peer, usually cohabiting relationship"; moreover, it is "a *pattern* of behavior, not isolated individual events. One form of battering builds on another and sets the stage for the next battering episode" (1989: 202). Battering is life-threatening behavior; a single attack can leave the victim dead or seriously injured.

When a man hits a woman, he has not lost control—he achieves and maintains control: *It is not so much what is done but what is*

---

[1]Much of the material in this section is taken from Adams (1994d: 11–21).

accomplished. Not only is he achieving and maintaining control, but he is reminding the woman of her subordinate status in the world:

> Battering may be done intentionally to inflict suffering. For example, the man may physically punish a victim for thinking/ behaving in a way that is contrary to the perpetrator's views. Or battering may be done simply to establish control in a conversation without intending harm. Regardless of the intent, the violence has the same impact on the victim and on the relationship. It establishes a system of coercive control. (Ganley 1989: 203)

Men who batter not only believe they have the right to use violence, but receive rewards for behaving in this manner—namely, obedience and loyalty. Battering guarantees that the man "wins" disputes, that the status quo in the relationship is maintained, and that the woman will not leave him (Stordeur and Stille 1989: 74). Battering erects an invisible cage: "Two key aspects of violence are threat and control. That is, the effects of battering are seen not only in the actual physical assaults, but in how fear of being hurt is used to manipulate and control a woman via threats" (Carlin n.d.: 1).

In response to battering, the victim changes something about herself in an effort to accommodate the perpetrator. Frequently, this involves restricting her free will, ending relationships with friends or family to whom he has objected (which is usually all of her friends and family, since they all pose a threat to his control), or even quitting work. Often his behavior limits her access to a car or her ability to even leave the house. Meanwhile, she attempts to soothe and please the controlling man, complying with his demands, agreeing with his opinions, denouncing his enemies. She accepts blame when things are not her fault and squelches any anger for fear of igniting his. She makes excuses for him. All to no avail. "When a woman tries to keep a partner calm by pleasing him, he gains exactly what he wants. He exercises his power over her and gets his way on a daily basis. It is ironic that she thinks she is 'managing' best when in fact she is most under his control" (Jones and Schechter 1992: 36).

Battering is a component or kind of sexual violation, since it occurs against one's sexual partner. Catharine MacKinnon's insights on this matter are helpful:

> [Battering] is sexually done to women. Not only in where it is done—over half of the incidents are in the bedroom. Or the surrounding events—precipitating sexual jealousy. . . . If women as gender female are defined as sexual beings, and violence is eroticized, then men violating women has a sexual component. (MacKinnon 1987: 92)

Or as another feminist has put it: "violence *is sex* to those who practice it as sex" (Annie McCombs, quoted in MacKinnon 1987a: 233, n. 23). Moreover, women are raped as a continuation of the beating, threatened with more violence if they fail to comply with their husband's sexual requests, forced to have sex with an animal, or forced to have sex to oblige the abuser's need to "make up" after a beating or the execution of an animal.

While MacKinnon's insight that battering is sexually done to women underscores that battering is an expression of male sexual dominance, one of the difficulties for a woman experiencing battering is identifying how it is that discrete aspects of her partner's behavior are abusive and represent his attempts at controlling her. Battering is a chronic situation marked by crisis events. But which moments, precisely, are a part of the chronic pattern?

Forms of battering

Anne Ganley, a psychologist who has pioneered in victim-based counseling for batterers, has identified—for assessment purposes— four forms of battering: (1) physical battering, (2) sexual battering, (3) psychological battering, and (4) the destruction of property and pets. She explains why she established these categories:

> Sexual battering overlaps with physical battering since both involve direct attacks on the victim's body. The destruction of property and pets overlaps with physical battering because both are physical acts against a person or object. However, the destruction of property and pets also overlaps with psychological battering since neither involves a direct attack on the victim's body. Too often sexual violence and the destruction of property/pets have been overlooked as part of the battering patterns. (Ganley 1985: 8).

Ganley perceptively discerns that in acts of destruction to property and pets, the batterer's goal is to affect the woman. It is not what is done but what is accomplished: "The offender's purpose in destroying the property/pets is the same as in his physically attacking his partner. He is simply attacking another object to accomplish his battering of her" (Ganley 1985: 15). But the destruction of property is qualitatively different from harm to animals or the execution of animals. Yes, for the batterer who threatens to injure or does injure animals, the animals' destruction may be like property destruction, that is, they are yet another object instrumentally used to represent the woman's fate. But, harming an animal inflicts physical damage, pain, and often annihilates someone—the animal. We cannot lose sight of *this* victim's perspective. What is so anguishing to the human victim about the injury of an animal is that it is a threat or actual destruction of a cherished relationship in which the animal has been seen as an individual. Thus it both inflicts psychological trauma on the woman and imposes a change in a valued relationship. Thus, I propose that this fourth form of battering be split into two separate categories: (4) destruction of property and (5) harm to animals.

The strength of these categories, as Ganley points out, is the identification as battering behavior of phenomena that are not ordinarily perceived as battering. This helps women recognize the interrelatedness of different kinds of behavior. As this essay argues, the establishment of a separate category for harm to animals is imperative for many reasons. When a batterer harms or executes an animal, he not only affects the woman, he also affects the animal.

Figure 4.4 Pamela Nelson, *Lubbock*. Photograph by Mike Itashiki.

The results of such double control and such power over two living beings necessitate closer attention.

How do batterers harm animals? Anecdotal evidence

We do not know how many batterers harm animals, nor, I would submit, do we need to quantify this form of battering to establish its import. It should be sufficient that those who work in battered women's shelters often know of batterers who threaten, harm, or murder animals or force sex between an animal and the woman.

These workers have reported to me personally that cats are more likely to be stabbed or disemboweled, dogs to be shot, both may be hung, though a choke chain leash enables a batterer to act quickly against a dog; sometimes the pet simply disappears or dies mysteriously. Batterers have chopped off the heads or legs of cats, stepped on and thus killed a Chihuahua puppy. Cats have been found nailed to the front porch. An activist in the battered women's movement recounted how her grandfather, when angry with his wife, would go to the barn and relentlessly and systematically whip her favorite horse. Another activist who works at a battered women's shelter described at least six situations she was acquainted with, in the first half of 1993 alone, in which pets were victimized by battering: two women did not leave the men who battered them because of fear for the pet; two women left but returned because of concern over their pets; and two pets were killed. Sometimes batterers have turned their trained "attack" dogs upon their partners (one man was convicted of murder for ordering his pit bull to attack his girlfriend; she was bitten more than one hundred times). Other times batterers have beaten their partners *with* an animal. In one instance, a four-month-old

Doberman-mix puppy was used to beat a woman; in another a man hit his wife with a frozen squirrel. *Time* magazine described a batterer, a violent man who was stalking his wife, who tried to flush a cat down the toilet (*Time*, June 29, 1994). My local paper described how one man slashed two pet cats to death and then threatened to turn the butcher knife on his wife and her dog.[2] In his Pulitzer prize-winning article "The Stalking of Kristin," George Lardner Jr. described the violent man—Michael Cartier—who eventually stalked and killed Lardner's daughter Kristin after she broke up with Cartier. In the wake of the first battering incident

> Cartier tried to make up with her. He gave her a kitten. "It was really cute—black with a little white triangle on its nose," Amber Lynch said. "It was teeny. It just wobbled around."
>
> It didn't last long. Over Kristin's protests, Cartier put the kitten on top of a door jamb. It fell off, landing on its head. She had to have it destroyed. (Lardner 1992)

In order to illuminate what transpires when a man who batters harms an animal, I will provide details from two painful incidents that are representative of injury to animals by batterers. These accounts are unsettling; reading them can be upsetting. Yet, to recognize the meaning of the injury or murder of pets by batterers, we have to have an understanding of what transpires.

> Hal came back with the rifle. He pressed it against her temple and clicked the hammer, then began ramming it into her stomach, yelling, "I'll kill you, goddamn it! I'll kill you this time" Finally, he laid the gun down and went outside. . . .
>
> When Hal left to get more beer, Karen fled, taking her small dog with her. Hal had nearly killed the dog several times when he was

---

[2]Reported in the *Dallas Times Herald*, June 15, 1991.

angry. She couldn't bear to leave it at home, knowing what would happen to it. (Browne 1987: 119)

She went to the police station and called a friend. The friend called Hal. Hal came to the police station and got her, and no one intervened.[3] He threatened her as he drove her home; she sheltered the dog.

> When they got to the house, Hal came around and jerked her door open. He yanked her out of the seat and onto the ground, then began kicking her in the ribs. Each blow knocked Karen farther across the driveway. . . . Finally, he stood over her, daring her to get up. Karen was afraid to move. The dog was still hiding in the truck; Hal carried it to the house and threw it against the concrete of the patio until he apparently thought he'd killed it. Then he made Karen go inside. (119–20)

Several days later, a friend helped Karen go to the emergency room of a local hospital. She had several broken ribs and her spleen had been damaged.

> She finally agreed to go to a local shelter and to receive outpatient care, but when they called to make arrangements they learned that the shelter wouldn't take dogs, Karen went home. The animal had survived, but it was badly hurt, and Karen felt responsible. She wanted to be there to take care of it; she knew Hal would kill it in retaliation if she left. (120)

Karen's inability to enter a shelter because they cannot take pets is confirmed by some battered women's shelter workers and volunteers, who told me that women were not leaving the abuser because they

---

[3] For a detailed analysis of the failings of law enforcement systems to protect battered women, see Jones (1994).

feared their pets would be killed.[4] Some who did leave would go back to the home within one to two days because of concern about the pet who had remained in the home. They would call to find out how the pet was and the husband would say, "I'm going to kill the animal." In the other detailed incident we will consider, the batterer killed the animal. It was described in the *Los Angeles Times*, and later quoted by Diana Russell in her important book, *Rape in Marriage:*

> The dawn of Michael Lowe's madness came on a sunny July day as he watched his shaggy white sheepdog chase playfully after a pet chicken in the family's rural Ramona yard. "Come here!" shouted Lowe to the dog. The animal, bought for Lowe's wife as a puppy, pranced over and sat at her master's feet. "I told you not to chase the chickens," Lowe said to the dog. "I told you not to chase the chickens."
>
> Lowe went inside the house and returned with a .357 magnum revolver. Cecilia Lowe knew what was about to happen, having become uncomfortable at that look, that tone of voice. She fell to her knees, pleading with Lowe not to harm the animal. She grabbed her husband around the legs and begged while the couple's 20-month-old son stood by crying.
>
> Lowe casually pumped a shot into the dog. The sheepdog ran under the family's truck, cowering in pain as Lowe went back into the house and returned with a .30-.30 Winchester rifle. He called to the animal and made her sit in front of him as he fired five more shots, killing the family pet. Three months later he did the same to his wife. Then he killed himself. (Russell 1990: 296)

---

[4]Battered women's shelters often cannot take pets because of Health Department regulations and the restrictions of their liability insurance. Since 1995—when this article was published—changes have occurred: some shelters have built kennels; others work with local vets to provide shelter, and animals are now included in order of protections.

The *Times* implies that Lowe's actions were "madness"; however, they were consistent with the deliberate, calculated behavior of a man who wants to establish or maintain control. Cecilia Lowe's discomfort with his look and his tone of voice also suggest a man who has used controlling behavior before, and who, with only a look or a specific tone of voice, can insure obedience.

Konrad Lorenz, in raising the issue of the morality of killing farm animals versus hunting nondomesticated animals, identifies the precise cruelty of a woman-batterer murdering a pet. While I do not agree with his confident assertion of the moral appropriateness of hunting, I do think he captures the cruel despotism that results through the institution of domestication:

> Morally it is much worse to wring the neck of a tame goose which approaches one confidently to take food from one's hand than it is, at the expense of some physical effort and a great deal of patience, to shoot a wild goose which is fully conscious of its danger and, moreover, has a good chance of eluding it. (Lorenz 1955: viii)

After being wounded by Lowe, the sheepdog still obediently came to him as he prepared to execute her. In this Lowe betrayed several relationships, not only with his wife and child, but also with the dog.

Psychological battering in the wake of harm to animals

Anne Ganley indicated that the execution of pets overlaps with psychological battering because it does not involve a direct attack on the primary victim's body. The psychological battering continues in the wake of harm to animals—especially the execution of a pet—by denying the woman the opportunity to express her reality, that is to mourn the loss of the pet. Part of the control that a batterer enacts is the doing of something that causes tremendous feelings and then not allowing the expression of those feelings. As Kathleen Carlin of Men Stopping Violence has observed, "It is a doubly powerful kind of sadistic control: 'I can hurt you so badly and then make it so that you cannot express it'."[5] Wanting to have sex after executing an animal would be a further way of denying her reality.

Consider Cecilia Lowe's situation after the killing of her dog by her husband. The dog was hers.[6] We do not know whether Michael gave her to Cecilia or not, though this again would conform with the controlling behavior of batterers. (Recall Michael Cartier who gave Kristin Lardner a kitten.) To whom could she turn with her grief over the loss of her dog and the serious threat her husband's behavior posed?

After an attack upon a pet in which the pet dies or she takes the pet to a pound, the woman experiences many feelings. She has lost a beloved friend, and thus feels profound grief. As with marital rape, she needs someone with whom to share her earth-shattering experience. Unfortunately, as with marital rape, the person to whom one would most logically turn for support and consolation is instead the cause of the pain. And the environment he is creating is one that punishes any initiative, that enforces a constricted and flat emotional life: "Prolonged captivity undermines or destroys the ordinary sense of a relatively safe sphere of initiative, in which there is some tolerance for trial and error. To the chronically traumatized person, any action [including grieving] has potentially dire consequences" (Herman 1992: 91).

---

[5]Conversation with author, October, 1994.
[6]Some would object to the notion of animals as property that this sentence countenances, but this was in fact the reality for the Lowes.

Mickie Gustafson's *Losing Your Dog* describes the range of feelings and reactions that occur upon the death of a pet:

- [A] dead animal is more than just a dead body. It represents happiness that has been lost and a bond that has been severed. Harmony is suddenly missing, and a wonderful source of happiness is no more. The resulting feeling of loneliness may feel overwhelming and almost unbearable. (1992: 14)

- Those who experience great grief share an overwhelming sense of desertion and loneliness, as well as a yearning for the deceased, which may become almost unbearable at times.

- Life appears unreal and meaningless to a grieving person, who may often become apathetic and deeply depressed. (21)

In these passages, Gustafson is describing the grief and emptiness in the wake of a pet's death from old age or from euthanasia. But the deaths that battered women mourn may be unexpected and sudden, or they may be expected—some women in fact may have been bracing themselves for such violence. In either case, the deaths occur within a context of violence and control. In addition to grieving, the woman may feel guilt, rage, hopelessness, for not being able to protect the animal from death at the hands of her partner:

The kitten was sitting in the yard. Billy got his rifle, walked up to it, and shot it. Then he hunted down the other two cats and shot them. Kim was hysterical—following him around, tugging on him, jumping up and down and screaming. She begged him not to kill the cats, and after he had, she begged him not to leave them there. So he picked them up and threw them over the fence. After Billy went to sleep that night, Kim crept out, found the cats, and buried them. Then she lay down in the field and cried. She blamed herself for their deaths. She should never have brought them to live around Billy. It seemed like all that was left was for Billy to kill her. Her diary for that day reads, "I wish I were dead. I wish I had been shot, too." (Browne 1987: 154)

If a battered woman realizes the life-threatening nature of the batterer's behavior toward the animal while the animal still lives, she may decide to take the animal to the pound in order to protect them. This will be equally devastating in terms of her relationship with the pet. She will still need to mourn the ending of the relationship even if she can console herself that at least the animal continues to live. (Of course, given the pet overpopulation problem, the shelter may euthanize the animal.) Gustafson describes the specific feelings one experiences in response to forced separation: "Having to choose between keeping your dog and something else may lead to feelings of anger and disappointment at being forced to make such a choice" (Gustafson 1992: 106).

Gustafson identifies "exaggerated anger and irritation" (20) as characteristics of the grieving person after the death (or loss to the pound) of a dog. But anger is one of those emotions that battered women are not supposed to express, constantly monitoring their emotions so that they will be flat in relationship to the controlling man. This is both a survival strategy and a coping mechanism. Ann Jones and Susan Schechter describe how many women "push down their angry feelings for fear that expressing anger may trigger even greater anger in the controlling partner" (Jones and Schechter 1992: 44–45). In the case of an animal's murder, the anger may be all the more legitimate, while necessarily being all the more denied. Thus psychological control continues after the death of the animal.

One final step remains that many batterers take before the woman is truly "broken." As Judith Herman describes it, "the final step in the psychological control of the victim is not completed until she has been forced to violate her own moral principles and to betray her basic human attachments. Psychologically, this is the most destructive of all coercive techniques. . . . In domestic battery, the violation of principles often involves sexual humiliation. Many battered women describe being coerced into sexual practices that they find immoral or disgusting" (Herman 1992: 83). For some batterers, sexual coercion involves forcing sex between a woman and an animal. Thus, a batterer forces her to violate her basic attachments to others—human *and* nonhuman.

Figure 4.5 Pamela Nelson, *Galveston*. Photograph by Mike Itashiki.

Forced sex with animals

A little-discussed form of battering involves the use of animals for humiliation and sexual exploitation by batterers and/or marital rapists. Batterers and marital rapists (and the two groups are neither mutually exclusive nor completely inclusive of each other) sometimes force sex between a woman and animal. For instance,

- "He would tie me up and force me to have intercourse with our family dog. . . . He would get on top of me, holding the dog, and he would like hump the dog, while the dog had its penis inside me." (Walker 1979: 120)

- One 25-year-old man raped his 16-year-old, menstruating, virgin girlfriend, by tying her spread eagled to the bed, and forcing his Doberman upon her. It took her eight years before she shared the story with anyone. (see McShane 1988: 73–75)

- Linda "Lovelace" reports that she was forced—under threat of death by her batterer—to allow a dog to mount her in the production of a pornographic movie. "From then on if I didn't do something he wanted, he'd bring me a pet, a dog." ("Lovelace" 105–13, also 206)

- In a California case in which a man was brought to trial for raping his third wife, his first wife "reported that her husband had purchased a large dog and trained it to have sex with her. Watching this occur enabled him to become sufficiently aroused to have intercourse with her." (Russell 1990: xii)

Pornography is often used when men force sex between a woman and an animal. It may be used as a desensitizing process. She is drawn into the process at first by him encouraging her to look at pornography with him—for instance, by watching videos together. This part she may like. But his goal is to raise her tolerance to the activities depicted so that she will duplicate them. Or, he consumes the pornography on his own and then wishes to reenact what he has seen.

> - He started taking me to sex shows where there were women and animals, esp. snakes. (*Pornography and Sexual Violence* 1988: 68, testimony by Ms. A)

> - This guy had seen a movie where a woman was being made love to [*sic*] by dogs. He suggested that some of his friends had a dog and we should have a party and set the dog loose on the women. He wanted me to put a muzzle on the dog and put some sort of stuff on my vagina so that the dog would lick there. (Russell 1984: 126)

> - One woman known to us related that her spouse always had a number of pornographic magazines around the house. The final episode that resulted in ending the marriage was his acting out a scene from one of the magazines. She was forcibly stripped, bound, and gagged. And with the help from her husband, she was raped by a German shepherd. (*Pornography and Sexual Violence* 1988: 104, testimony of Ms. Rice Vaugh)

Through pornography, dogs, snakes, and other animals help a man picture himself in the scene. They become stand-ins for the male phallus.[7] And this is true with watching forced sex between his female partner and an animal. Forced sex with animals is an indication of how abusive men extensively sexualize and objectify their relationships, including their relationships with other animals.

---

[7]Insight of John Stoltenberg, conversation with author, May 1993.

What does it mean in terms of the man's life-threatening behavior when he forces sex between a woman and an animal? I put this question to Kathleen Carlin of Men Stopping Violence. She replied,

> They represent different types of danger—whatever it is that the man uses, if there is a stand-in for him, it increases the sense of omnipotence of the man watching. It feeds the sense of him that merges his omnipotence and his use of her as an object, whether it is an animal or a machine. In one sense that increases the danger because it heightens the level of acceptable abuse. It merges his sense of omnipotence and her objectification. It intensifies her as an object. (Conversation with author, autumn 1993)

From the abuser's point of view, he is sexually using an animal as an object, just as others may use baseball bats or pop bottles. The animal's status as object is what is important in this instance. But, then, so is the woman's. Objects used for sex in this way, including animals and the women victims, are denied individuality, uniqueness, specificity, particularity. It is not who they are that matters as much as what can be accomplished through the use of them. Forcing sex between his human female partner and a nonhuman animal reveals the way that a batterer objectifies both of them so that they have become interchangeable objects. They become to him no different—and no less expendable—than a pop bottle. Ann Jones refers to instances such as these as pimping and categorizes forcible rape with an animal as torture (1994: 85, 93).[8] Surely, it is torture to the animal as well.

Forced sex with a pet animal may intensify the sense that a woman is betraying her basic attachments. Understandably, she will see

---

[8]"In fact, the batterer often is a pimp, forcing his wife to have sex with other men or with animals" (Jones 1994: 85).

this as immoral and disgusting. Coercive sex is always humiliating; coercive sex using an implement other than the man's body demonstrates how fully she, too, is an object without individuality, any particularity. When Linda Marchiano claimed her own name and her voice, she explained that forced sex with a dog made her feel "totally defeated. There were no greater humiliations left for me" ("Lovelace" 1980: 113).

Sexual coercion using an animal violates many women's moral, relationship principles. It is often the most unspeakable aspect of being a hostage to a violent man. For women political prisoners in Chile who had been raped by trained dogs,

> [t]his is evidently one of the most brutalizing and traumatic experiences suffered by women in prison. The survivors of this torment find it very difficult to report their exposure to this extreme sexual debasement. With sickening canniness, the torturers traumatize their victims into feeling shame for their own bodies. (Bunster-Bunalto 1993: 257)

Once safe, victims of sexual violence may move through a stage of remembrance and mourning in order to achieve healing. Through reconstruction of the story of the trauma, they transform "the traumatic memory, so that it can be integrated into the survivor's life story. . . . Because the truth is so difficult to face, survivors often vacillate in reconstructing their stories. Denial of reality makes them feel crazy, but acceptance of the full reality seems beyond what any human being can bear" (Herman 1992: 175, 181). Forced sex between an animal and a woman is so filled with shame and degradation that silence seems preferable to speaking. Because of the intensity of shame and silence in the wake of sexual attacks involving animals, healing from this victimization is rendered all the more difficult.

Forced sex with animals is an experience that needs to be told but is so horrifying it almost guarantees the silence. During the Renaissance, bestiality was referred to in law books euphemistically as "*offensa cujus nominatio crimen est* [the offense the very naming of which is a crime]" (Serpell 1986: 126). The unspeakability of these instances of coerced sex indicates how destructive is the psychological control of the victim by the abuser. Forced sex with animals merges sexual experiences with torture, and as one activist commented "breaks all the circuits." While the human victim is denied her own voice because of shame and disgust, the other victim is seen as voiceless because animals do not communicate in human language. Both victims experience the unspeakable and are made unspeakable as well.

Animals and batterers' strategies for control

Harming animals is in itself an act of violence against another living being. If the batterer executes the animal, he and everyone in his family perceive that matters of life and death are in his hands. Thus, he feels more powerful. Harming animals and/or using them sexually are also acts of instrumentalizing the animal to get to the woman.

The chart of coercion

After psychologist Alfred D. Biderman studied brainwashed American soldiers, his work was codified into a chart of coercion, which was published by Amnesty International. In her pathbreaking book, *Rape in Marriage,* Diana Russell demonstrated how Biderman's chart could also be used to understand the effects of torture on wives, as well as those who are seen ordinarily as "hostages." This chart of coercion is now used in battered women's shelters to help them identify the controlling tactics of their partner. Women can perceive numerous experiences that correspond with each general method of coercion.

In Table 4, I demonstrate how Biderman's chart can be used to reveal the variety of ways that animals are used coercively by batterers. Biderman's chart identifies the parallels between the experience of domestic captives, such as battered women, and political captives, and it depicts the way in which isolated cruel acts are actually interrelated. Table 4 establishes that anything that is coercive may and probably does include animals.

On the left side, Table 4 reproduces a modified chart of coercion (see Jones 1994: 90–91). On the right side are examples specific to woman-battering and harm to animals. Note that only one of these methods of harming an animal involves direct physical violence to the woman. Yet, all these methods generally occur in a situation in which a man has also used threats and bodily assaults against his partner. What these examples demonstrate is that harm to animals enacts a wide variety of coercive methods. Table 4 demonstrates the context of terror in which battered women live and through which animals are harmed.[9]

---

[9]In the past few years, some battered women's advocates have raised concerns about the use of Biderman's charts by shelters. They have focused their concern on several issues: (1) it cannot be seen as explaining woman-battering since it fails to contextualize the social structure of male dominance; (2) shelters should not see the chart as a codification of every form of psychological battering; thus, they should not assume that it is exhaustive in its identification of coercive controls; (3) it cannot be used as a tool to enable adovcates to assess the life-threatening nature of the batterer's actions, nor does it indicate order and predictability. This chart does not mean that the batterer is going to act out in the order in which items are listed. Thus, it is not a predictor of the safety of the woman. In other words, the chart functions best in offering an interpretive structure for women to understand the psychological battering she has experienced. When pressed into duty as a predictor of her safety or as a tool that explains *why* a man batters, it will lose its effectiveness. My purpose in reproducing it is to demonstrate just how fully insinuated within the coercive control of the batterer is his treatment of the animals in the household.

Table 4 Biderman's chart of coercion and examples of harm to animals as a form of woman-battering

Method of coercion	Examples
Isolation	
- Deprives victim of all social support for the ability to resist. - Develops an intense concern with self. - Makes victim dependent upon interrogator.	Killing a pet animal reinforces isolation, often depriving the woman of her last significant relationship, increasing her dependence on her batterer.
Monopolization of perception	
- Fixes attention upon immediate predicament; fosters introspection. - Eliminates stimuli competing with those controlled by captor. - Frustrates all actions not consistent with compliance.	Eliminates any competition from animals for attention by killing them; also eliminates the support a pet offers the victim.
Induced debility and exhaustion	
- Weakens mental and physical ability to resist.	Death or harm to animal induces physical reactions to grief (e.g., sleeplessness, headaches).
Threats	
- Cause her to live in terror.	Threatens to kill the pet; or kills the pet and says she is next.
Occasional indulgences	
- Insure compliance. [Indulgences may be accompanied by a lessening or cessation of violent acts, but a context of terror remains. Because of underlying threats, the occasional indulgences provide a false sense of safety: she is never safe.]	Gives her an animal. [He gives her an animal not because he has really changed, but to maintain control over her.]

(Continued)

Table 4 (Continued)

Method of coercion	Examples
Demonstrating "Omnipotence"	
- Suggests futility of resistance.	Killing an animal in the presence of her and the children. [Separation assault: attacking her animal when she leaves him.]
Degradation	
- Makes cost of resistance appear more damaging to self-esteem than capitulation.	Raping her with an animal, sexually exploiting the animal as well.
- Reduces prisoner to "animal level" concerns.	Making her eat or drink from the animal's dishes.
Enforcing trivial demands	
- Develops a forced habit of compliance in the prisoner.	Refusing to allow her to feed an animal or let the animal in or out at a certain time.

Sources: Ann Jones, *Next Time She'll Be Dead* (Boston: Beacon Press, 1994: 90–91, and Amnesty International, *Report on Torture* (1973), as adapted by the women's shelter of Northampton, Massachusetts. All examples and bracketed additions are by the author.

Control strategies and harm to animals

When we examine the *reasons* a man may harm an animal as part of battering, we can perceive his deliberate attempts at controlling her. These are the strategies.

1   He harms an animal to *demonstrate his power*. Making someone watch the torture of another is ultimate mastery, saying through these actions "this is what I can do and there is nothing you can do to stop me." She may wish to protect the animal, but she realizes she is unable to. She may feel she

let the pet down, or she may be hurt trying to protect the pet, and discover she cannot protect herself or the pet. Sometimes efforts to protect a pet may result in increased violence toward the woman (see, for instance, Dutton 1992: 27). In harming an animal, the man who batters simultaneously demonstrates his omnipotence and her complete loss of control.

2 He harms an animal to *teach submission*. Ann Jones describes the experience of one woman, whose husband decided to "teach submission" by forcing her to watch him "dig her grave, kill the family cat, and decapitate a pet horse" (Jones 1980: 298). Inconsistent and unpredictable outbursts of violence such as harming animals are meant to convince the victim "that resistance is futile, and that her life depends upon winning his indulgence through absolute compliance," the perpetrator's goal is to instill both fear of death and "gratitude for being allowed to live" (Herman 1992: 77).

3 He executes a pet to *isolate her from a network of support and relationship*. Her relationship with her pet may have been the last meaningful relationship she had been allowed to have. One way a man controls his partner is by severely limiting her social network, restricting her access to friends and families. In this way, he actively destroys her sense of self in relation to others (Herman 1992: 77). Murdering an animal severs a meaningful relationship. It also destroys the woman's sense of self, which was validated through that relationship. If this was the last remaining relationship she was allowed to have, in the loss of the pet she will see the loss of herself. Furthermore, the pet's presence may have helped her avoid adopting the batterer's point of view. It may also isolate her from friends who have pets, or make her feel dehumanized and hence

alienated from other humans. She may be fearful around other people who have pets, feeling bad because she has lost her pet, and also feeling that, although she was not the perpetrator, the other animals may not be safe because her own animals are dead. Because she may feel uncomfortable watching other people with animals, or may fear for these animals, she will restrict her contact with other people who have pets.[10]

4   He hurts pets *because he is enraged when he sees self-determined action on the part of women and children.* He wishes to control their actions; their self-determined responses to others, including other animals, infuriate him. Allowed a self-indulgent rage by society, he expresses it with impunity.

5   He harms an animal to *perpetuate the context of terror,* so he may not need to do anything else. As Judith Herman observes, "It is not necessary to use violence often to keep the victim in a constant state of fear. The threat of death or serious harm is much more frequent than the actual resort to violence. Threats against others are often as effective as direct threats against the victim" (1992: 77). Furthermore, making someone watch torture is a particular form of terror:

> Torture or destruction of a loved pet may be an even more powerful abuse than personal abuse. One woman witnessed a succession of 12 kittens tortured and eventually killed by her batterer. (Dutton 1992: 27)

6   He harms a pet as a *preemptive strike against her leaving him, as a form of separation violence.* If harm to animals occurs during a time that the woman is considering leaving the man

---

[10]Insight of Mike Jackson, conversation with author, spring 1994.

who batters, *it works as a strong incentive to stay.* Often, just as a woman is getting ready to leave, a batterer may perform a careless act that endangers the animal(s). For instance, one man spilled bleach on the kitchen table and it "accidentally" poured into the cat's water dish. The message was quite clear: if she is not there, the animals are not safe. She is held hostage by threats to the pet.[11]

7   He *punishes and terrorizes her for leaving by stalking her and executing an animal.* She comes back to her current residence and finds the family pet dead—for instance, a dog shot and left on the doorstep, a cat hanging in the kitchen—she knows that he's been there, that she has been invaded, that there is nowhere where she can be safe.

8   He may *force her to be involved in the animals' abuse,* making her feel that she is a traitor to animals. She is in the position where she thinks animals should not trust her, because she is not going to protect them.

9   He harms animals to *confirm his power.* The act of harming or killing an animal may contain its own gratification.

Each of these reasons for harming a pet reveals motives of aggrandizing or regaining one's power. Yet, often harm to animals,

---

[11]Martha R. Mahoney proposes that the term "separation assault" be used to identify the struggle to control that occurs when a woman decides to separate or begins to prepare to separate. "Separation attacks," she argues, should be used to designate the "varied violent and coercive moves in the process of separation assault." Mahoney maintains, "*Separation assault* is the attack on the woman's body and volition in which her partner seeks to prevent her from leaving, retaliate for the separation, or force her to return. It aims at overbearing her will as to where and with whom she will live, and coercing her in order to enforce connection in a relationship. It is an attempt to gain, retain, or regain power in a relationship, or to punish the woman for ending the relationship" (Mahoney 1991: 65–66). This and the following example need to be seen as separation attacks, constitutive parts of separation assault.

rather than being perceived as deliberate acts of control, are seen, as in the case of Michael Lowe, as madness. The control inherent to the act is seen instead as loss of control. Thus harm to animals perpetuates his plan to make himself appear crazy, ruthless, cold, uncontrollable, invulnerable, and not responsible. That is what batterers want to do—they want people, especially their partners, to think of them as crazy, because it makes them more dangerous in their partner's eyes. When she sees him harm or execute an animal, she may think, "there must be something wrong with him, he must be mentally ill, emotionally ill, or he must have some serious unresolved conflict with his childhood, and how sad or shameful." She may also think, "this guy is really crazy and he scares the hell out

Figure 4.6 Pamela Nelson, *Corpus Christi*. Photograph by Mike Itashiki.

of me, he could do anything."[12] That is the purpose of psychological abuse: to baffle and confound her. This is his goal, as it successfully obfuscates his purposes.

Harm to animals, woman-battering, and feminist theory

Harming an animal is a form of sexual mastery, the instantiation of dominance. It announces and reinforces the man's powerfulness, though it is cloaked in the deceptiveness of "madness." Several important reasons exist for recognizing harm to animals as a distinctive form of woman-battering.

1 Harm to animals exposes the deliberateness of battering

The first reason to acknowledge harm to animals as a separate category of woman-battering is because *it exposes the deliberateness of battering, its control rather than loss of control.*

In talking with individuals who work with batterers, and especially those who run batterers' groups, I learned two seemingly incongruous facts: though each of them knew of instances in which a batterer had injured or killed an animal, disclosure of harm to animals rarely occurred in batterers' groups. Why was this phenomenon omitted when batterers acknowledged other forms of violence? Was it shame? Was it that there simply was not sufficient time in these groups to cover all atrocities, and a de facto triage effect excluded discussion of harm to animals?

---

[12]Insight of Mike Jackson, conversation with author, spring 1994.

I asked this question of Mike Jackson of the Domestic Violence Institute of Michigan. Jackson argued that it was a purposeful concealment for the men's own advantages. He found that men were more willing to talk about physical abuse than sexual abuse, and more willing to talk about sexual abuse than animal abuse. Jackson based his answer both on his subjective experience and on how many times these three items were discussed. Shame, he argued, was too simplistic a reason, an acceptance of the batterers' tactics. In fact, Jackson argued, batterers do not want people to know how purposeful, willful, and deliberate their actions are. Batterers can obfuscate why they batter when it is physical violence (claiming "I lost control and punched her"), and they can confuse the issue of sexual assault (asserting "she was teasing me and said she wanted it"), but loss of control in a relationship with an animal is harder to defend because the deliberateness of the violence is exposed in the description ("I 'lost' control and then cut the dog's head off and then nailed it to the porch"). Jackson contends that there is not much leeway for a man to say he tortured animals and it was out of his control. Talking about these specific acts of violence reveal their willfulness and purposefulness. Harm to animals is a conscious, deliberate, planned strategy. A facilitator in a batterers' group upon hearing of the torture and/or killing of an animal, would be able to pick up on that and show precisely how purposeful the battering behavior is. It would become a point that refocuses on the agency of the batterer—that is, that he makes choices to be violent, and if he so chose, he could stop being violent.

Recall Michael Lowe's deliberateness: He calls to the animal, announces to the dog her infraction, walks into the house and returns with a revolver, ignores the pleas of his wife, the crying of his son, and shoots the dog. Lowe reenters the house, returns with a powerful firearm, calls to the animal, and then shoots her five more times.

Were Lowe to have reported that to a batterers' group, how could he possibly have claimed he lost control? Each step of the way, his deliberateness is evident.

Confirmation of Jackson's insight can be found in an all-male environment in which hostile expressions toward women are not merely condoned but encouraged. In such an environment where one's goal of humiliation and control can be openly acknowledged, harm to animals can be proudly described rather than silenced. And such bragging about these acts exposes how deliberate they actually are.

Consider the brutal male culture of the Citadel, the male military academy that endeavored to prevent the enrollment of Shannon Faulkner. Susan Faludi, in a *New Yorker* profile, evoking the violent, deliberately cruel environment of the Citadel, described how a common practice for Citadel students is bragging about humiliating ex-girlfriends. One cadet told how he had tacked a live hamster to a young woman's door. Another cadet "boasted widely that, as vengeance against an uncooperative young woman, he smashed the head of her cat against a window as she watched in horror." The cat story was his "calling card" (Faludi 1994: 72). Batterers, on the other hand, do not want to disclose their calling card—their deliberate decision to be violent.

2 Harm to animals and harm to children are closely related[13]

Pet-keeping, according to Yi-Fu Tuan, is dominance combined with affection. So, too, is child-rearing. Proposing a fifth form of battering, harm to animals, of necessity indicates yet one more: harm to children.

---

[13]This section arose from conversations with Mike Jackson. I thank him for his close reading of a previous version, and his discussions with me about this issue. Jackson articulated clearly the need to identify parallels in the treatment of animals and children.

It is beyond the scope of this essay to argue this, but it may be helpful to highlight the connections between harming animals and harming children.

Harming animals is a way of controlling/threatening children or consolidating control of the children. Sometimes the children are warned that their pet will be harmed if they leave with their mother; one father threatened to disembowel the cat. His child was present when his father Michael Lowe killed the dog. When a batterer kills an animal, *the children, mother, and the batterer all see that there are few if any repercussions for killing a (nonhuman) member of the family.*

Forcing her to neglect or abuse the animal, or forcing her to force the children to abuse or neglect the animals, or forcing her to neglect her children exist within the same continuum of coercive control. "Shut that animal up" may be the command or "make that dog learn by making it stand outside in the cold." Whatever they then have to do to shut the animal up will be done. This dynamic is sadly similar to "shut that kid up" or "make that child learn by. . . ."

The batterer may influence the children to be abusive with the pets. Not only must the mother witness the children being coerced or willful in hurting animals, but she cannot intervene with them to stop the abuse, because if she stops them, she is going to "get it" or they are going to "get it." Again we see how closely intertwined are physical violence and psychological abuse.

Harm to animals, like harm to children, may be the act that convinces a woman of the necessity of separating from her partner. Just as injury to a child may convince women to leave, because their tolerance about what is acceptable toward the children has been violated, so the killing of pets often was the final sign that convinced a battered woman that her partner was capable of murder ("these incidents often seemed to the women a representation of their own death" [Browne 1987: 157]).

An estimated 90 percent of the children in families where there is battering are aware of the battering that occurs there. Yet a terrible denial pervades the household, as though the children do not know and thus are not harmed, and this occurs when an animal is killed as well. In the wake of an animal's death, the mother must model how to handle grief for her children, but recall the constricted environment in which she can express herself. Children need to vent their worries and be greeted with honesty in response to their feelings of despair. Instead they may find an atmosphere of silence, because it is not safe to express feelings in the presence of a controlling man. In addition, children may be concerned about themselves. According to Gustafson,

> The death of the dog will give rise to many questions in children, among them questions about their own death and how the parents would react to it. If the parents appear—in the eyes of the child—not to mourn a much loved animal, how would they then mourn the child if the child were to die? (1992: 96, sexist language changed)

Harming animals forces denial upon women and children in many ways. She has to protect everybody—animal, children, herself. So, if a child approaches her and says "Mom, Sparky has a cut on his head," she may sit there and say, "No he doesn't." She does this because the batterer is also sitting there. She has to cut her feeling off for the animal. Strategically she learns denial as a survival mechanism. Purposefully denying that it matters to protect the cat, she must betray the cat. She has to demonstrate to the batterer that it does not matter, because she has learned that he hurts only the things she cares about, so she will pretend not to care about the animal. But to the children, not understanding this dynamic, they see their father hurt a dog or cat and think that their mother does not care. How do they interpret this?

Those 90 percent of children who are aware of battering behavior by their mother's partner may witness beatings, rapes, or injury to animals, thereby experiencing their mother's powerlessness. Even though they want to protect their mother or a pet, they usually are unable to do so and feel guilty about their inability to intervene. If they do attempt to protect their mother or the animal, they themselves may be injured. They may feel the mother's powerlessness as her fault and feel enraged with her, not the batterer.

The degree to which she or the children have an intense, respectful relationship with an animal is the extent to which he can harm her by harming the animal. And the degree to which she cares about her children is, similarly, the degree to which he can harm her by harming the children. He harms the animals or the children

Figure 4.7 Pamela Nelson, *Houston*. Photograph by Mike Itashiki.

knowing he will harm her. As is the case with battering, it is his choice to be violent.

3 There are multiple forms of violence against women; harm to animals is consistently present

Battering is one of several forms of male-dominant behavior over women, along with rape, sexual harassment, and sexual abuse of children. Liz Kelly, for instance, in *Surviving Sexual Violence*, documents how "specific forms of sexual violence are connected to more common, everyday aspects of male behaviour. . . . The basic common character underlying the many different forms of violence is the *abuse, intimidation, coercion, intrusion, threat and force men use to control women*" (Kelly 1988: 75–76). So, too, injury to animals and the use of animals to sexually abuse a woman are methods of control. The threat or actual use of a pet to intimidate, coerce, control, or violate a woman is a form of sexual control or mastery over women by men and occurs in many instances of physically controlling behavior.

In 1993, in what became known as the "condom rape" trial (because the victim had requested that her assailant use a condom), the raped woman broke down only once when testifying: when recounting how the rapist had threatened to kill her dog, who was whimpering in the bedroom closet. The testimony of survivors of child sexual abuse reveal that threats and abuse of their pets were often used to establish control over them, while also ensuring their silence, by forcing them to decide between their own victimization or the pet's death. Sexual harassment often includes pornographic material involving explicit depictions of human-animal sexual activity or reference to this material. (See Adams 1994a for a more in-depth discussion.)

An abortion clinic staff member found her beheaded cat on her doorstep; later, when she arrived at the clinic, she was confronted with signs that read, "What happened to your cat?" (Blanchard and Prewitt 1993: 259). Leaving a dead animal can be a warning, as two lesbians attempting to set up a retreat center for women in the South discovered in 1993 when they found a dog, dead, draped over their mailbox, with Kotex napkins taped to the body (Minkowski 1994: 73). One sex-specific form of torturing women political prisoners in Latin America was introducing mice into their vaginas. And, as noted, in Chile, female political prisoners were raped by trained dogs (see Bunster-Bunalto 1993).

Harm to animals is a strategic expression of masculine power and can be found throughout male controls over women.[14]

4 There are multiple forms of violence against animals; harm to animals in woman-battering must be placed here as well

Just as battering is one form of male dominance, so harm to animals through woman-battering is one form of animal abuse in which animals are objectified, ontologized as useable, and viewed instrumentally. Just as the status of women and children within

---

[14]Using an animal to harm a woman is a way of exerting control; this explains why there are instances of lesbian attacks on their partner's pet. While human male violence is responsible for most of the damage to women and the other animals in cases of battering, a patriarchal, hierarchical culture will find expressions of this form of violence in some women's same-sex relationships. Where there is an acceptance of a patriarchal value hierarchy, some lesbians will wish to establish control (and be on top in terms of the hierarchy) through violence. "38 percent of the [abused lesbian] respondents who had pets reported that their partners had abused the animals" (Renzetti 1992: 21). These acts of battering are considered violent and coercive behavior (see Hart 1986: 188). The battered lesbian whose partner injures or destroys a pet faces a double burden: overcoming the invisibility or trivializing of lesbian battering and the invisitibility or trivializing of abuse to animals.

the household is related to the cultural, economic, and ideological status of women in a patriarchal culture, so the status of animals in households is related to the cultural, economic, and ideological status of animals in a patriarchal, humanocentric culture: the violability of what are generally regarded as high-status animals in the home, such as pets, is related to animals' low status in culture in general.

Battering exposes how contingent is the status of women and animals in patriarchal culture: one moment "pet" or "beloved," the next injured or dead. Battering eliminates the status that the culture had granted to specific animals; it levels "companion animals" to the violable status of most animals in our culture.

Feminist commitments to end violence err if they stop at the species barrier. A commitment to stop violence can succeed only when all forms of oppression are included within our analysis, and all forms of violence exposed and then challenged.

5 Harm to animals is violence in its own right and shows how violence is interconnected

It was once thought that battering involved a series of discrete episodes: a slap here on this day, a hit there on that day. Such cataloging of separate events ignored the context of coercive control that the first slap initiated. It also often began its charting with "what did you do to provoke him?" The assumption was that A led to B, and that there were then C, D, etc. A linear analysis that maintained the separateness of each event was inadequate in establishing how battering behavior actually works. By identifying forms of battering, Anne Ganley aided the contextualization of battering; discrete actions, including how one speaks (batterers often linguistically objectify their partners), were interrelated. Similarly the chart of coercion provided a way of recognizing how a climate of terror is established by a violent man.

(Indeed, it could be argued that when battered women's shelters attempt to impose linearity upon the chart of coercion—that is, this will happen first, then that—that they too are misreading a nonlinear phenomenon.) Neither of these tools could be linear in their analysis because battering is nonlinear, establishing an *environment* of control and fear. (Recall, it is not what is done but what is accomplished.)

Once theory is freed from a distorted and distorting dependence on linearity, then we are closer to understanding the dynamics of male control through battering against an individual woman and also its connection with other forms of (largely unchallenged) male control in our culture. The movement from a linear analysis to a recognition of interconnected forms of violence within the home (connections between physical and psychological battering in the home) and without (connections between battering and other forms of male violence) continues when we identify what happens to animals both within the home (harm to animals as a form of battering) and without (a male-dominant culture that with impunity eats, experiments upon, and wears animals).

In *The Sexual Politics of Meat*, I argued that violence against animals cannot be understood without a feminist analysis, because this violence is one aspect of patriarchal culture—arising within and receiving legitimation from the way male sexual identity is constituted as dominance. Gender is an unequal distribution of power; interconnected forms of violence result from and continue this inequality. In a patriarchy, animal victims, too, become feminized. A hierarchy in which men have power over women and humans have power over animals, is actually more appropriately understood as a hierarchy in which men have power over women, (feminized) men, *and* (feminized) animals.

Animals have been largely absent from battering theory, as much as women have been absent from conventional animal rights theory.

But the way our culture countenances the construction of human male identity through control of others and the impunity with which women and animals are harmed reveals the errors of such linear approaches. Recognizing harm to animals as interconnected to controlling behavior by violent men is one aspect of recognizing the interrelatedness of all violence in a gender hierarchical world. The challenge now, as it has been for quite some time, is to stop it.

Matthew Calarco is an associate professor of philosophy at California State University, Fullerton. He works in the fields of animal philosophy, environmental philosophy, and Continental philosophy. He is the author of *Zoographies: The Question of the Animal from Heidegger to Derrida* (Columbia University Press). His most recent book is titled *Thinking through Animals: Identity, Difference, Indistinction* (Stanford).

5

Derrida and The Sexual Politics of Meat: *Conversation with Matthew Calarco*

What sorts of intersections, associations, or refusals might be found between Jacques Derrida's work and *The Sexual Politics of Meat*? Matt and I decided that a discussion format might enable us to explore answers to this question. What follows represents a part of that larger conversation. While my work in decoding the sexual politics of meat stretches over more than thirty years, expanding into close consideration of the functioning of representations, Derrida's elaboration on his neologism *carnophallogocentrism* remained largely suggestive and deferred. Matt and I recognize that this difference, among many other reasons, means that our goal never was to compare and contrast but to create a dialogue and exploration. We thank Vasile Stănescu for suggesting that we explore this topic together.

"Derrida and *The Sexual Politics of Meat*" a conversation with Matthew Calarco was published in *Meat Culture*, ed. Annie Potts (Leiden and Boston: Brill, 2016). Used by permission.

Matt Calarco   One of the more evident points of contact between your work and Derrida's writings on animals can be found in (1) your overarching project of critically examining and contesting the sexual politics of meat, and (2) Derrida's occasional attempts to think through the connections between subjectivity, sexism, and eating meat by way of his concept of *carnophallogocentrism*. In order to explore this overlap between the sexual politics of meat and carnophallogocentrism, it might be useful for me to lay out a few of Derrida's ideas in a bit more detail and suggest some points at which your and his project overlap and diverge.

It is important to note that Derrida's work on carnophallogocentrism (and animals more generally) was, despite his occasional protestations to the contrary, never in the foreground in the same manner that the sexual politics of meat is in your work. That Derrida nearly always deferred attention from questions concerning carnophallogocentrism and animals is indicative of both a certain caution and also (I would suggest) a lack of a sense of urgency in his writings. He always found time to write on other pressing socio-political issues and develop his positions in great detail on many of those issues; but when issues concerning animals and other nonhuman beings arose, he most often held any careful analysis of such matters in abeyance. There can be little doubt that Derrida was cautious when approaching issues surrounding animals and nonhuman life primarily because of the sheer difficulty and magnitude required for a full treatment of the topic. But his tendency to hold questions about animals in abeyance was perhaps not just a symptom of this caution and hyper-prudence. It is also clear—or at least, nearly everything in his writings and political activity would suggest—that the transformation of the living conditions of many animals as well as the transformation of human relationships with animals simply was not one of his over-arching priorities in the same way it is for your work or mine.

So, allow me to start off with a basic discussion of the concept of carnophallogocentrism and how it fits into Derrida's work. He mentions this concept in several of his writings, but his most sustained examination of it occurs in a 1988 interview with Jean-Luc Nancy entitled "'Eating Well,' or the Calculation of the Subject" (1991: 113–14). The interview is Derrida's contribution to Jean-Luc Nancy's attempt to take stock of recent work in so-called post-humanist thought (that is, thinking that proceeds from the critical interrogation of "humanism," or what it means to be a human "self" or "subject" in the Western philosophical tradition). Throughout the interview, Derrida repeatedly makes the point that, despite the seemingly radical and thoroughgoing critique of selfhood and subjectivity in recent Continental philosophy (and in Heideggerian and Levinasian thought in particular), insufficient attention has been paid both to the anthropocentric nature of dominant Western philosophical conceptions of subjectivity and also to the lingering anthropocentrism in the more cutting-edge, post-humanist critiques of subjectivity. In other words, he detects a certain dogmatic adherence to anthropocentrism even among his more sophisticated fellow post-humanist critics. It is in this context that Derrida tries to distance himself from dogmatic anthropocentrism by calling attention to the carnophallogocentric constitution of human subjectivity in the Western philosophical and cultural traditions.

Derrida's earliest writings aimed to expose the *logo*centric assumptions of these traditions (logocentrism here denoting the privileges and priorities granted by Western philosophy to the rational, self-aware, self-present, speaking subject [see especially Derrida 1976, part 1). And, when his attention turned to issues dealing more directly with sexuality and gender, he tried to demonstrate the inextricable linkages between logocentrism and *phallo*-centrism (phallocentrism here denoting the quintessentially virile and masculine aspects of

Western social institutions and conceptions of subjectivity), leading him to use the neologism *phallogocentrism* to denote these joint phenomena.[1] In "'Eating Well,'" Derrida suggests that *carno* should be added to *phallogocentrism* in order to emphasize that the notion of the subject that is being critiqued in post-humanist thought should be understood not simply as a fully self-present, speaking, masculine subject but also as a quintessentially *human, animal-flesh-eating* subject.

By the late 1980s, then, Derrida is arguing that the critical deconstruction of subjectivity should be seen as a critical deconstruction of carnophallogocentrism. This project calls for an intersectional analysis of at least three coordinates or registers in the constitution of subjectivity:

- self-presence (the *logos* of self-mastery, reason, speech, and transparent, unmediated access to one's inner mental life);

- masculinity (the manner in which virile and masculine ideals are infused throughout and dominate the socio-cultural order); and

- carnivorism (the requirement of the literal and symbolic consumption of flesh, a commitment to anthropocentrism, the hierarchical ranking of human subjects over nonhuman animals)

While there are significant differences between the sexual politics of meat and the deconstructive analysis of carnophallogocentrism as I have initially explained it here, I wonder if we might first turn to a discussion of how your project has certain *positive* affinities with Derrida's work.

---

[1] The "indissociability" of logocentrism and phallocentrism are discussed most lucidly by Derrida in "'This Strange Institution Called Literature': An Interview with Jacques Derrida," (1992: 57–60).

Figure 5.1 *Hey Rod, Do you think I'm Sexy?* Photograph by Jacob Fry, Gateway Center, Newark, New Jersey, 2014.

Carol Adams   I have a sense that in its analysis, *The Sexual Politics of Meat* intersects with "carnophallogocentrism" in several ways. Derrida was attempting to name the primary social, linguistic, and material practices that go into becoming a subject within the West and how explicit carnivorism lies at the heart of classical notions of subjectivity, especially male subjectivity. Similarly, I have been trying to show how a feminist analysis that decenters male subjectivity and challenges a violence long associated with human male behavior is impelled to include a critique of carnivorism, too. I argue that a challenge to the male-defined Western subject needs to include challenging the foods that are assumed to be "his" foods. In this, I make clear that I am not talking just about "men" but how everyone in the West is implicated by the sexual politics of meat.

I want to suggest that the carnophallogocentric subject is the subject created by a culture with the foundational premise of the sexual politics of meat. In other words, the sexual politics of meat is constituting this carnophallogocentric subject at many levels. I am not claiming this is the only force at work; I am asserting its influence is not negligible and needs to be recognized.

Matt, you identify three coordinates or registers in the construction of subjectivity that constitute, in a sense, the carnophallogocentric subject. Similarly, I propose several aspects to *The Sexual Politics of Meat*. It is not one "thing," one quality, one "fact," it is, rather, kaleidoscopic and shifting in how we experience it, but at the minimum contains these parts:

- The association of virility and meat eating
- The functioning of the structure of the absent referent
- Women and animals positioned as overlapping absent referents in a patriarchal culture

Virility and meat eating

In *The Sexual Politics of Meat*, I argue that a link exists between meat eating and notions of masculinity and virility in the Western world. Meat eating societies gain human male identification by their choice of food, creating and recreating an experience of male bonding in various male-identified locations, such as steak houses, fraternities, strip clubs, or (domesticated) at a barbecue.

Meat eating bestows an idea of masculinity on the individual consumer. Popular culture manifestations of the sexual politics of meat can be found imbricated throughout various media and in personal behavior. Generally, they imply that a man needs meat and that a woman should feed him meat. From French commercials to newspaper advertisements for Father's Day, the theme is reiterated. Meat eating is an act of self-definition as a privileged (male-identified) human.

A belief exists that strength (male-identified) comes from eating "strong animals" (for instance, "beef"), and that vegetables represent passivity. Thus, conventionally, veg*nism was considered appropriate for women and anyone associated with women. These ideas appear in the first chapter of *The Sexual Politics of Meat* and seem to resonate with Derrida's idea of "carnivorous virility." A bumper sticker like "Eat Beef. The West Wasn't Won on Salad" exemplifies this attitude. In one statement, it is putting down foods associated with women, elevating animal foods, and at its heart, celebrating the genocide of Native Americans.

The issue is not only human exceptionalism in the myriad ways it is recuperated to justify eating animals; it is how the human is conceived, as male-identified, with a male-identified diet. A 2006 Hummer advertisement features a man buying tofu in a supermarket. Next to him a man is buying gobs of raw meat. The tofu-buying man notices this and becomes alert to and anxious about his virility, apparently compromised by his tofu-buying. He hurries from the grocery store and heads straight to a Hummer dealership. He buys a new Hummer and is shown happily driving away, munching on carrot. The original tag line for the ad was "Restore your manhood" (Stevenson 2006). (It was changed to "restore the balance"). The implication that the Hummer acts as compensation for the veg*n man's failure to eat manly protein suggests that one aspect of culture committed to carnophallogocentric subjectivity is the belief in the logic of the sexual politics of meat.

Figure 5.2 *Manplatters chicken platters.* Photograph by Alan Darer, Pennsylvania Gas Station, 2015.

Since *The Sexual Politics of Meat* was published, I have noticed that many popular culture appeals to men (especially white, heterosexual men as in the Hummer ad) seem to be rebuilding what feminism and veganism have threatened. In terms of *The Sexual Politics of Meat*, we see several recuperative responses that seek to reinstate manhood, meat eating, and both interactively. From unsophisticated wall paintings on restaurants to slick Superbowl commercials, the message that meat's meaning is expressed through sexual politics is constantly recreated. The ads that I examine in *The Sexual Politics of Meat Slide Show* appeal to, reassure, flatter, massage, reinforce the carnophallogocentric subject Derrida espied.

The absent referent

Behind the *carno* in carnophallogocentrism is the absent referent. Through butchering, animals become absent referents. Animals in name and body are made absent *as animals* for meat to exist. Animals' lives precede and enable the existence of meat. If animals are alive they cannot be meat. Thus a dead body replaces the live animal. Without animals there would be no meat eating, yet they are absent from the act of eating meat because they have been transformed into food.

The function of the absent referent is to allow for the moral abandonment of a being. In many quotidian ways, the absent referent functions to cloak the violence inherent to meat eating, to protect the conscience of the meat eater, and to render the idea of individual animals as immaterial in the face of someone's specific and selfish desires to consume them.

Implicit in Derrida's use of *carno* is sacrifice; but *explicit* in his use is "*carn*ivorism," in other words, flesh eating. What the concept of the absent referent uncovers is both the fact that animals die individually, and that we wish to keep hidden what we are doing to animals. We cannot lose track of the fact that flesh eating occurs through an act of violence that the "carnist," in Melanie Joy's (2010) terms, accomplishes through an activity of consumption.

The act of killing animals (like the act of eating meat) is part of the project of constructing carnophallogocentric subjectivity. Isn't the violence underlying the act an important aspect of both "sacrifice" in Derrida's term and in associating the act with phallogocentrism? In Chapter 3, describing the "neocarn" movement, I argue that the need to make the kill present is a hypermasculine reinscription of the sexual politics of meat. The reiterative nature of the sexual politics of meat (finding new ways of reinforcing "carnivorous virility") suggests how fundamental it is to the operation of Western culture.

Women and animals as overlapping absent referents

In *The Sexual Politics of Meat*, I argue that women and animals are overlapping absent referents. This is tied to another aspect of the absent referent, when a dominant and domineering language consumes and negates the violent transformation of living to dead and "lifts" that experience into metaphor. Then it is applied to vulnerable or otherwise disenfranchised beings.

This structure of overlapping absent referents also moves in the other direction as well, in which women's objectification becomes the basis for cultural constructions about meat animals.

Figures 5.3 and 5.4 "Rosie the Organic Chicken" reassures the carnophallogocentric subject of the objects that give pleasure. "Eat me," she invites. "Wish this was made from tofu said no one ever" suggests the perceived dead end of veganism for a subject constituted by having objects. Where in tofu is the object to confirm the consumer's subjectivity? In contrast, BBQs function to assure the male-identified eater (depicted in the right hand corner) by providing an object. In a hierarchical world, tofu creates "no ones."

Rosie the Organic Chicken. Photograph by Hana Low, Oregon, 2015. *Wish this was made from tofu said no one ever.* Photograph by Roger Yates/Vegan Information Project. Dublin, Ireland, 2014.

It was difficult to find a sound bite for this theory, but by the time I wrote *The Pornography of Meat* I had one: in a patriarchal, meat eating world animals are feminized and sexualized; women are animalized. In *The Sexual Politics of Meat*, I say that the connections between women and animals that I am drawing are contingent and historical. But I argue that theoretically speaking, politically speaking, these contingent historical overlaps (in which the animal substitutes for the woman, and the woman, or part of a woman, substitutes for a dead animal) are relevant conjunctions to make.

I propose that in general women are visually consumed; animals literally consumed. Then, I push on just *who* we are consuming. This may be one place where I make explicit something that may be only implicit in Derrida. If the carnophallogocentric subject knows "himself" to be a subject through the inflection of meat eating and male-centeredness, then implicitly there are objects in "his" life that contribute to the creation of "his" subjectivity.

I am interested in those *objects*, and who our culture allows to become those objects, and how the process of objectification is working. In my work, I found an overlap of cultural images of sexual violence against women and fragmentation and dismemberment of nature and the body. I believe this aspect of my work—in which I propose how a cycle of objectification, fragmentation, and consumption normalizes sexual consumption by linking it with butchering—ties in with Derrida's concern about "commonly accredited oppositional limits" (2009: 36). If I can appropriate Derrida's term to explicate my ideas, carnophallogocentric subjectivity is invested in the oppositional framework of Western culture, and benefits from the lowering/debasing of some beings that accompanies this oppositional framework. But what I try to show is how the oppositional points (human/animal, man/woman for instance) are intensified by linking two parts of the negated side—female and animal. I do not believe these points are fixed, nor do I necessarily simply valorize the side that has been lowered. I am concerned with the dynamics of linking that occur on both sides.

This linking is important, because the carnophallogocentric subject is constituted, in part, through the power to objectify living beings, to make other subjects into objects. This subject whose qualities of self-mastery, reason, speech, etc., feel inherent—is not one way that this subject *knows* his (or her) self-mastery, reason, speech etc. precisely through the objectification of other beings?

I remember when O. J. Simpson was first suspected of murdering his wife. Often, the comments that I heard were that he was such a "charismatic" person. No one seemed to stop and think perhaps there was a link between his *charisma* and his battering behavior. He could behave the way he did in public because of what he was doing, controlling another person, in private. Similarly, is not one aspect of the construction of the carnophallogocentric subject the "consumption" or "sacrifice" (forced, imposed, not selected) of other beings to their needs or wants?

One of the things *The Sexual Politics of Meat* was trying to do was to capture the dynamics of this.

Calarco   Your remarks here on the contingent and historical aspects of the sexual politics of meat serve as an excellent starting point to carry our discussion forward. I would like to use those remarks to press on the question of whether this kind of attention to the sexual politics of meat in your work and carnophallogocentrism in Derrida's work is itself in need of a supplement.

Carnophallogocentrism as *the* dominant schema of subjectivity

When Derrida turns in the late 1980s to a discussion of carnophallogocentrism, this turn is the direct result of his earlier efforts to pinpoint both the dominant tendency of metaphysics and its unthought ground. The dominant tendency of metaphysics for Derrida is to elaborate and privilege a certain thought of presence and identity understood most often as a self-present, self-conscious subject. In this gesture, he is quite close to Heidegger. But where Derrida critically and importantly departs from Heidegger is in his characterization of subjectivity as specifically involving *human*, *masculine*, and *carnivorous* dimensions. These dimensions were not a point of focus for Heidegger, nor are they for most neo-Heideggerians. That Derrida takes these specific dimensions seriously is very much to his credit, as he is one of the very few Continental philosophers who have noticed not just the phallocentric aspects of metaphysical notions of subjectivity but also the anthropocentric and carnivorous tendencies of that tradition.

But I think Derrida also overplays his hand a bit on this point. Although his remarks on carnophallogocentrism are in no way programmatic, they are nevertheless intended to capture the deep structure, the "dominant schema" of subjectivity of Western metaphysics. And it is precisely here, in the attempt to name definitively the dominant and quintessential form of subjectivity that I think he overreaches. Although I would readily and enthusiastically agree that the concept of carnophallogocentrism brings together important and significant trends in so-called Western metaphysics, I doubt that it captures *the* dominant schema of metaphysical subjectivity. Are there not other important trends and tendencies to add to this hyphenated list? Why limit our analysis to logocentrism, phallogocentrism, and carnivorism? Why do these three registers have priority?

The point here is not that this list should be extended to 4+n registers in order to be made accurate and complete. The list of forces and relations that constitute us as subjects can obviously never be made complete. Instead, I am wondering whether we should subscribe to this neo-Heideggerian logic of dominant schemas in the first place. Is there really something called "Western metaphysics" whose dominant schema can be uncovered? And even if we were to arrive at such knowledge about the inner workings of Western metaphysics, what is the ultimate wager or hope behind this approach? What are the critical and transformative implications for uncovering carnophallogocentrism as the dominant schema of Western metaphysics? We might also ask: How would this kind of neo-Heideggerian approach relate to other critical analyses of Western culture that differ substantially in their focus and strategies (I am thinking, for example, of indigenist or Marxist critical approaches that often have very different premises and critical aims from those of deconstruction).

By setting up things in this neo-Heideggerian way (the search for dominant schemas, definitive limits of metaphysics, and so on), Derrida ends up (whether intentionally or not) framing the philosophical and critical task in such a way as to foreclose other analyses and to cut off linkages with other approaches. By contrast with Derrida, I would much prefer to understand the discussion of carnophallogocentrism and the sexual politics of meat as but one way to uncover a force that is (to use your words) "not negligible and needs to be recognized." If we begin from this space and in this kind of modest theoretical spirit, it creates the possibility for additional linkages between critical analyses and for allowing such analyses to mutually inform one another in a critical and progressive manner.

Ultimately, the problem I have with Derrida's analysis of carnophallogocentrism is that it remains at bottom almost entirely intra-philosophical and intra-theoretical. To explain this point further: What I find important about the concept of carnophallogocentrism is that it is, among other things, useful for (1) capturing important tendencies in our culture surrounding the constitution of "properly" human subjects, and (2) suggesting possible linkages among various critical perspectives and movements for social transformation (in this case, feminism and movements on behalf of animals). But the latter considerations are, at best, secondary for Derrida and always deferred in favor of his primary interest. His primary interest seems to lie in a careful philosophical analysis of the deep structures of metaphysics (we find hundreds upon hundreds of pages dedicated to careful readings of Heidegger, Levinas, Lacan, Descartes, Kant, and so on)— and not in creating alliances across radical and critical practices.

This point should not be taken to suggest that Derrida is entirely uninterested in radical politics and social transformation; but it is hard to resist the conclusion that such interests remain in the background. Any bridge that might be built between his preferred method of patient philosophical analysis and radical political transformation is almost always deferred in his work, much like "the question of the animal" is often deferred. And when he is pressed on the connections between deconstruction and social transformation, he most often dodges the question by implying that such questions are driven by those who expect a political "program" from him. But it is not the case that I or others expect or desire a program from him (I doubt anyone who is involved in this discussion or reads this material finds political programs desirable); instead, the question that is at issue here is how this kind of critical work informs or is informed by alternative modes of practice and movements for social transformation. For me thought and philosophy *begin* there, in the context of the disruption of the status quo, in the desire for radical and transformative practices; and the schemas, ontologies, and frameworks that are produced by philosophy in that context serve as responses to limits in practice or serve to create the space for unheard-of and presently unimagined practices.

Of course, a very generous reading of Derrida might seek to have us understand his work as suggesting much the same point, but it is clear that his political engagements (especially concerning animals) have a very different status in his work than such engagements might have for you and me. After reading through Derrida's remarks on carnophallogocentrism and animals more generally, one can only be left wondering how such concepts and discourse relate to existing practices aimed at transforming our thought and practices concerning animals. If we are seeking to critique ideologies and prejudices while building connections across movements for social transformation, then carnophallogocentrism might be a very helpful concept for such projects—or it might not; we would have to construct and develop the concept and then put it to work within specific contexts. We would have to ask: Does this concept create linkages where none previously existed? Does it allow us to see connections among oppressions that would have gone otherwise overlooked? Does it open up new perspectives and practices? Does it transform and enrich life and thought? Such matters are far more important to me than whether a given concept accurately captures the dominant schema of metaphysics. To that end, I would suggest that the critique of *anthropocentrism* (understood very broadly) might actually do more philosophical, critical, and political work than carnophallogocentrism, as it has the potential (if understood in a very specific and refined manner) to tie together and mutually inform multiple critical analyses, frameworks, and movements for social change. But the main point I would make here is that the creation of concepts has everything to do with creating the space for resistance, transformation, and new ways of living and very little to do with an intra-philosophical, intra-theoretical analysis that hedges every time it is confronted with questions concerning practice and the invention of new forms of life.

Returning to your remarks above, these points about the critical limitations of carnophallogocentrism take on a very direct relevance when they are placed in the context of your comments on the bumper sticker: "Eat Beef. The West Wasn't Won on Salad." You suggest, rightly, that such a statement exemplifies the attitude of carnivorous virility and is simultaneously engaged in "putting down foods associated with women, elevating animal foods, and at its heart, celebrating the genocide of Native Americans." While the concept of carnophallogocentrism would do much to help us make sense of what is going on here, I wonder if it (or any of the other of the myriad discourses on animal ethics) can do full justice to questions concerning, for example, Native Americans and other indigenous peoples and how they figure not just in the constitution of the carnophallogocentric subject but how they figure in and alongside struggles for animal defense. The respective political strategies, epistemologies, and worldviews of the many indigenous struggles for justice and similar movements for animals do not always align, and it seems essential to me for animal theorists and activists to discuss these differences more carefully.

These questions take on a different but still very direct relevance when we think about Derrida's larger strategy in focusing on carnophallogocentrism and anthropocentrism. If these ideologies and practices constitute the dominant schema of metaphysics, then we can be prepared for Derrida to demonstrate how *différance* and other forms of non-presence (ex-propriation and so forth) figure at the very center of the carnophallogocentric subject (and this is what he is doing throughout much of his work on animals). For Derrida, it is in the exploration and thought of how *différance* is at work throughout life that we might begin to challenge the hegemony of presence and its quintessential figure: the carnophallogocentric subject. But the details, implications, and stakes of such a strategy are very rarely discussed by Derrida or his followers. Instead, there is a kind of unspoken faith among Derrideans that there is some direct line between: (1) uncovering and contesting the basic workings of metaphysics, (2) a thought and practice of *différance*, and (3) radical social transformation. To my mind, much more would need to be said here; and I am not all convinced that this kind of approach constitutes a good strategy or a viable ontology.

The absent referent

Now, I would like to turn to some of the more positive and fecund connections between your work and Derrida's work, starting with the issue of the absent referent. Your invention of this concept in the context of issues concerning animals has always struck me as a singularly important achievement. Standard philosophical discussions of animals, especially those deriving from analytic animal ethics, pay lip service (at best) to the ways in which the unique lives of animals and the violence that many animals undergo at our hands is kept from out of sight for certain populations. And yet, there can be little doubt that it is by way of a profound relationship to singular, irreplaceable animals and the violence done to them that many people are moved to transform their lives with regard to animals. Far too little attention is paid to such connections in analytic animal ethics, where a premium is placed on the supposed transformative force of establishing formal, abstract similarities among "moral patients" and a concern for impersonal justice.

In paying attention to (1) the singularity of the animal beings we encounter and with whom we relate, and (2) to the hidden violence that characterizes the lives of many of those animals, you present an ethical approach that is extraordinarily close in spirit to the logic (if not the letter) of Emmanuel Levinas's ethical thinking and Derrida's appropriation and reworking of Levinas's ethics concerning animals in *The Animal That Therefore I Am*. Levinas argues (contra analytic approaches to ethics) that ethics has its origins in an unsettling, traumatic encounter with the "face" of the Other ("face" can be understood here, roughly, as any site wherein one encounters the Other's fundamental vulnerability). When I encounter the face of the Other, that Other presents her- or himself outside of the general category of "others" as a concrete, singular, irreplaceable Other. In such an encounter, I encounter *this* finite Other (as opposed to some abstract "other" with whom I have formal similarities), and I begin to catch sight of the hidden violence that my egoistic, unthinking existence often entails.

Although Levinas presents his general account of the ethical encounter within the context of inter-human ethics, it has been argued by many of Levinas's best readers that there is no legitimate reason for limiting the "logic" of this account to human beings alone. One could, in fact, read Derrida's work on animals as a subtle reworking of this Levinasian logic, as an attempt to stretch it and extend it beyond the particular anthro- and androcentric dogmas that plague Levinas's work. If one reads Derrida in this way, then what his work offers us is an attempt to attend to the singularity of animals in their lives and deaths, and joys and sufferings. That all of these things go missing in standard philosophical and metaphysical notions of animals and animality is evidence of the ways in which individual animals are reduced to absent referents in philosophical discourse.

The iterability of the carnophallogocentric subject

Another point of contact between your thought and Derrida's (as well as Judith Butler's) has to do with what you describe as the "reiterative nature of the sexual politics of meat." The carnophallogocentric subject, both in its form as an ideal subject position and as it becomes actualized in individual subjects, is never achieved once and for all. It must be repeatedly enacted, called into being in line with the conceptual-discursive-institutional ideal it invokes (this is what Judith Butler, in her reworking of certain aspects of speech theory, refers to as the performative nature of subjectivity). Thus, as you note, in order to achieve subjective stability it is necessary to find ever new methods and means for reinforcing this identity and shoring it up against that which would unravel it or challenge its dominance.

This notion of the reiterative nature of carnophallogocentric subjectivity has two important implications. On the one hand, it implies that there are the ever new ways of reinforcing carnivorous virility that we need to attend to. On the other hand, the very fact *that* carnophallogocentrism *has to be reiterated* means that it is unstable, structurally open to being challenged and contested, and that it has not fully determined or suffused the various systems of meaning and institutions that constitute individuals as subjects.

Adams The need to establish manliness through meat eating has always suggested an instability to masculinity. The difference between 1990 when my book first came out and now is this notion of re-upping or renewing one's "man card." This recent development shows just how unstable masculine identity is perceived to be. (An ad for beer that gives "man points" for putting together a barbecue but takes away more "man points" for cooking tofu on it.) Unlike my library card which does not have to be renewed, this "man card" apparently is constantly being depleted, exhausted, needing re-iteration. So, a strong and very powerful reality—masculine subjectivity—is continually being reinstated through both traditional and new means, while its instability is acknowledged.

Does the space open within its fissures to reconfigure it? In 2013, *Vanity Fair* carried an article ("Steak Shows Its Muscle") celebrating steak as "the butch foodie communion" not just for "flinty-eyed, Armani-suited leaner-than-thou businessmen, but for metrosexuals who wish to beef up their cultural testosterone." A. E. Hotchner continues: "What does steak say to us and about us? Well, it's manly. If food came with gender appellations, steak would definitely be at the top of the bloke column. Women can eat it, they can appreciate it, but it's like girls chugging pints of beer and then burping. It's a cross-gender impersonation" (2013). The space burps opens; the space closes.

The issue of agency in and against such reiterative moves also comes up in the way that some vegans who are men appear to accept the givenness of a culture invested in the sexual politics of meat. Trying to show that men are not "wimps," and instead can be "plant-strong," a few well-known "manly" vegans coined the term "hegans." Rather than pushing into the fissure and suggesting veganism liberates the gender binary, these vegan advocates appear to want veganism to fit into the humanist project, offering the assurance *you are not really changing as radically as you think you are if you become a vegan.* I see it as a conservative response to the threat to the carnophallogocentric subject posed by veganism. To me this seems like they are reassuring what Derrida called the phallogocentricism inherent in Western subjectivity.

It becomes necessary to track the various ways that the subject continues old kinds of exclusions, but has to create new alliances to do this. One of the aspects of these recent meat re-iterations is that they sweat with misogyny. Making connections between my first point ("men need meat") and my second (the function of the absent referent is to hide and promulgate violence), I have started calling some of the representations that have appeared *hate speech* as they celebrate the consuming of the full-bodied female body and position the female body in ways that announce she desires to be consumed. This hate speech normalizes violence.

The logic of logocentrism

Calarco   In order to explore further some of the limits characteristic of analytic ethical approaches to animal issues, I thought we might return for a moment to the theme of logocentrism. Above, I glossed Derrida's definition of logocentrism as "denoting the privileges and priorities granted by Western philosophy to the rational, self-aware, self-present, speaking subject." With that gloss in mind, we can note by implication that what gets subordinated by logocentrism are all of those "things" that fall outside of the *logos*, starting with "writing" (understood narrowly as written texts and broadly as those things that escape the full control of the sovereign, speaking subject), and extending to all of the other traits (for example, the emotions, passions) and beings (for example, animals, children, nature) that/ whom fall short of exemplifying full presence and full *logos*. In his early writings on logocentrism, Derrida sought primarily to make the point that all attempts at achieving logocentric closure and full presence are haunted by *différance*, writing, non-presence, and so on; and in his later writings on animals, he extends this analysis by showing the ways in which logocentrism subtly persists in certain forms of animal rights discourse and politics and produces a contradiction in the reinforcement of the very concept of rights and of the human it seeks to overthrow. I know that you have made related points in your critiques of analytic animal ethics.

Adams I like to think that understanding logocentrism helps illuminate why reactions to vegans and vegetarians are often so irate. They have threatened something thought to be *essential* to the subject. It also explains why the defensive flesh eater's response is to *argue*, to try to defeat through words/arguments the vegan/ vegetarian (who is demurring from a culture wordlessly through a dietary change). The non-speaking vegan's dissent must be lifted into the speaking world and there defeated. In *The Sexual Politics of Meat*, I propose, "At a dinner where meat is eaten, the vegetarian must lose control of the conversation. The function of the absent referent must be kept absent especially when incarnated on the platter at the table. The flesh and words about it must be kept separate" (2015: 75).

I devote two chapters of *Living Among Meat Eaters* to the problem of talking with meat eaters. I argue that veg*ns must learn how to stop the conversation, that is, they must refuse to be a speaking subject, refuse to engage at that level. In this, I disagree with the belief among activists (and the almost good-natured assumptions of the average veg*n) that we should always answer questions being posed to us. The presumption is that if we are "the best speaking subject," that is, if we can proffer forth the best arguments, we will win. I state that conversations "are functioning differently for meat eaters than for vegetarians." And that this logocentric interaction through words, through the speaking self, is "the most stubborn way that meat eaters hold on to their lifestyle" (2001: 91).

In believing they should respond with arguments and explanations of a veg*n diet, individual veg*ns recapitulate the premise and activities of many of the major animal activist organizations. These presumptions include:

1   It is by argument that people change.

2   A debate has a hierarchy, and your goal is to be on the top.

3   If we have the right "speech" we will prevail. The best arguments will win.

4   The other animals have no voice in human discussions. We must be "the voice of the animals."

5   So, the speaking subjects speaking on behalf of the "voiceless" have to prove themselves to be the best speaking persons or else we have betrayed the non-speaking animals.

Analytic philosophers like Tom Regan, Peter Singer, Steve Best, and Gary Francione accept the logocentric world view, too. They presume the same kind of space, the same kind of subject, the one who has control, the one who is more "reasonable." This worldview presumes that change happens this way. As I suggest in "Post-Meateating," the animal rights movement is a modernist movement in a postmodern time. As you have said, it is all *part of the legalistic and moralist approach to animals.*

Calarco   The issues you raise here concerning the defense of vegetarianism/veganism are important ones to consider; and, like you, I would suggest that standard philosophical arguments have (at best) a derivative and secondary role to play in this area. After speaking with countless meat eaters about vegetarianism/veganism over the past two decades, and after teaching standard philosophical material on vegetarianism/veganism to thousands of students over the past several years, I am more convinced than ever that philosophical arguments nearly always arrive on the scene too late to have the force that most animal ethicists wish them to have. And even when the arguments are considered rationally persuasive by readers, they rarely seem to have the transformative force with nonvegetarians/non-vegans that philosophers claim. I would suggest that for philosophical arguments to carry any persuasive force on these matters there must *already* be in place a certain set of dispositions, relations, and experiences that attune one to animals and their lives. So, even if one wished to retain a space for philosophical argumentation concerning vegetarianism (and I am not entirely opposed to maintaining such a space), it would seem that the space needs to be reinscribed elsewhere than at the foundations of vegetarianism (which is where philosophers would like to place it).

Likewise, when vegetarians/vegans play the role of the rationally persuasive subject in discussions over eating meat, not only does such a gesture place the speaker back into the very logocentric space of mastery that needs to be called into question; it also problematically reinforces the idea that what is at issue here lies in the domain of reason and argumentation (rather than, say, in the domain of what Levinas calls "the face," or emotions, relations, ethical interruptions, and so on). Arguments with meat eaters about vegetarianism/veganism are fairly easy to have, and perhaps even fairly easy to "win" for the masterful subject, but they rarely bring the discussion into the space where it needs to be in order to get at the heart of the matter—which is, namely, to rethink in a fundamental manner the way one relates and is related to other animals (oneself included).

Another pernicious, but often overlooked, consequence of this subtle reinforcement of logocentrism can be seen in the way that analytic ethics and argumentation map onto larger legal and political strategies for transformation. Given the premium placed on the rational, speaking subject within our logocentric culture, it comes as little surprise that the nonhuman beings animal rightists/welfarists seek to bring into the legal and political sphere most often resemble that same logocentric subject. Animals who can communicate in ways "we" can understand are more valued than those who cannot; animals who demonstrate "superior" (which is to say, anthropomorphic) intelligence are considered paradigm examples of animals with moral standing; animals who lack reflexive consciousness, language, familial relations, who are aesthetically disgusting to "us," or are culturally unpopular are consistently given less attention in political and legal struggles for animal justice.

In a related vein, and following the same logocentric logic, many legally—and philosophically inclined animal rightists seek to distance themselves from environmental struggles for justice for nonanimal beings, systems, and regions. It is assumed by nearly every mainstream philosophical and legal theorist for animal rights/welfare that the nonanimal natural world is owed no direct consideration and always and everywhere counts less than humans and animals. And the reasons given for the priority granted to animals are almost always logocentric in nature. Steven Wise's *Drawing the Line* is a prime example of this kind of tendency to exalt logocentric-type animals at the expense of less logocentric-type animals and the rest of the natural world. One of the primary motivations I have for entering standard philosophical and legal debates over animal ethics is to contest these kinds of logocentric consequences; and when I refer to the need for a deconstruction of vegetarianism/veganism (Calarco 2004) and its associated mainstream practitioners, it is precisely these kinds of logocentric limits and blindspots that I believe are in urgent need of deconstruction.

The power of phallogocentrism

Adams Animal activism not only incorporates the dominant presumptions about the speaking subject, it also operates largely from a *phallo*gocentric position (see Chapter 10). Both analytic philosophy that argues on behalf of animals and activism prefer the rational, reasonable male speaking voice. The disowning of the female speaking subject has a long history in the West. But it is one thing to encounter Mrs. Slipslop in Fielding, Mrs. Malaprop in Sheridan, or Tabitha Bramble in Smollett (Gilbert and Gubar 1979: 30–31). It is another to recognize that animal activism not only privileges the male speaking voice but actively disowns the female speaking subject. I gesture toward the issue of the speaking subject in the second section of *The Sexual Politics of Meat* ("From the Belly of Zeus") which is framed by the story of Zeus's swallowing of Metis, and Zeus's claim that she "gave him counsel from inside his belly" (Adams 2015: 81).

What does animal activism do with women's speaking voice? Their moves are not literally as anthropophagic as Zeus's, but symbolically, they are equally devastating, they announce the animal movement is no longer "just little old ladies in tennis shoes."[2] This comment has been around for decades, but most recently could be found in a profile of Wayne Pacelle head of the Humane Society of the United States, in the *New York Times Magazine*. "'We aren't a bunch of little old ladies in tennis shoes,' Pacelle says, paraphrasing his mentor Cleveland Amory, an animal rights activist. 'We have cleats on'" (Jones 2008). "Don't look at the aging bodies of women activists," they seem to be

---

[2]It might be interesting to think for a moment about why "little old ladies" have been wearing tennis shoes for so many years. Tennis shoes are certainly better for one's spine than heels; pregnancy often results in the widening of the feet; tennis shoes are very comfortable.

telling us. This posturing of the animal activist movement tries to fill the cultural space once occupied by the little old ladies (though it still needs them to do the work but hide the fact that they are doing it and that they are "old" and female).[3]

Several assumptions operate here:

- They assume they are speaking to the dominant subjectivity in the West, the carnophallogocentric subject.
- They assume this subjectivity has trouble/resistance to hearing little old ladies.
- They think they have to accept the limitations in perspective imposed by this subject.
- They have to "save" animal activism from the threat of empowered little old ladies.
- They have to reiterate their rationality over against the stereotype of the emotionally laden, female-identified body.
- They believe that the *carn* can be excised from the carnophallogocentric subject, plucked out, removed, ruptured, while leaving the phallogocentric subject intact.

Perhaps they believe all this, because this has worked for them.

---

[3]Animal studies has been challenged for making this same sort of move resulting in the disappearance of feminist writers who pioneered intersectional theory that included animals and offered early analyses of animal oppression. Susan Fraiman analyzes the disappearance of women in the story of the birth of Animal Studies (2012: 89–115). I appreciate her role in asserting the historical and theoretical importance of books like *The Sexual Politics of Meat* and those of my feminist colleagues. The important move is not to accept the either/or assumption presented by some of the gatekeepers of Animals Studies: either English-speaking feminist writers *or* Continental philosophy. This accepts the gatekeepers' formulations by reversal. I believe our conversation shows another way, as does *The Feminist Care Tradition in Animal Ethics*, in which Josephine Donovan and I placed Derrida within the feminist care tradition (2007: 14–15).

Figure 5.5 Vance Lehmkuhl, *Putting Her Foot Down,* 2009.

Certainly the animal activist organizations that display nude and nearly nude photographs of women in their outreach on behalf of animals enact these assumptions. Derrida's concept provides a tool for explaining just why women's naked bodies are so important to some animal campaigns. They think by assuaging phallogocentric subjectivity they can convince him (they clearly are appealing to heterosexual men in much of this) to stop eating meat. They want to remove the *carn* but leave the phallogocentric subject undisturbed. Derrida says in an interview included in *Acts of Literature*, "although phallocentrism and logocentrism are indissociable, the stresses can lie more here or there according to the case; the force and the trajectory of the mediations can be different . . . [a] radical dissociation between the two motifs cannot be made in all rigor. Phallocentrism is one single thing, even if it is an articulated thing which calls for different strategies" (Derrida 2009: 59-60). Once he appended *carno* to his idea of the subject, did he not also recognize its indissociability from the other parts?

Strategies that assume a culture invested in the carnophallogocentric subject requires the strengthening of the phallogocentric subject as we eliminate the "carno" aspect (meat eating) like some feminist discourse in Derrida's perspective, "risks reproducing very crudely the very thing which it purports to be criticizing" (Derrida 2009: 60).

Calarco The quotation from Pacelle is a particularly illustrative example of the standard logic of phallogocentrism that dominates leading forms of animal rights/welfare today. The privileged, "proper" forms of activism are those carried out by cool, level-headed, rational subjects who believe in the power of arguments and legislation. Women can certainly accede to this privileged space on occasion, but they do so only inasmuch as they renounce all non-logocentric traits, strategies, and considerations. My own experiences with fellow animal activists have suggested to me that precisely the opposite is often the case, that "little old ladies" are among some of the most important, inventive, and remarkable activists in animal defense circles. And the same holds true for the role of both older and younger women in several kinds of related struggles for social justice, ranging from environmental justice to queer politics to indigenous politics. Women, young and old, employing tactics that fall well outside the logics of logo- and phallogocentrism, have advanced these struggles in unprecedented and vitally important ways.

Returning to the specific context of animal defense politics, I want to underscore that this kind of phallogocentrism also functions to exclude a wide range of additional strategies and activists beyond those just mentioned. We should note, for instance, how a large number of mainstream philosophical and legal animal rightists routinely denigrate direct-action groups like the A.L.F. (and it is significant that younger and older women play a leading role in many of these actions). Such direct-action strategies and tactics that seek to short-circuit the long-term, incremental process of legislating our way to animal rights are often dismissed by mainstream animal rights activists for being not just ineffective (which is a questionable criticism, given the general ineffectiveness of nearly all proposed strategies to date) but also for being driven by many of logocentrism's "others" (blind emotions, irrational spontaneism, misguided fanaticism, and so on). This kind of dismissal occurs despite the fact that direct-action activists and theorists have developed an extraordinarily insightful series of strategies, practices, analyses, and alternative ways of living in view of animal justice, even as mainstream organizations and theorists leave largely unchallenged the hegemony of phallogocentrism, capitalism, and consumerism in our culture (as your remarks above make clear).

One of the helpful aspects of Derrida's concept of carnophallogo-centrism and your notion of the sexual politics of meat are that they help us to attend to these often invisible constraints that guide and limit thought and practice. Did Derrida notice the indissociability of carnivorism with phallogocentrism? Based on his scattered remarks on the issue, one can only conclude in the affirmative. He seems to want to make this series of centrisms not only indissociable but also central to understanding the dominant modes of constituting subjectivity.

This returns us, though, to the question of whether this series (carno-, phallo-, and logocentrism) is meant to be descriptively exhaustive or only partial, contingent, and strategic. And even if we decide that carnophallogocentrism only functions in the latter sense and does not seek closure over and against other critical analyses of subjectivity, this does not put an end to a whole series of very difficult questions that might arise here. To tease out a bit more one of the issues I raised above: What are we to make of decolonial struggles for social justice that make heavy use of the rhetoric and political strategies of humanism, human rights, and human dignity? How do we link our struggles with theirs when the respective strategies, rhetoric, and histories might conflict? I do not think there are any easy answers to such questions, but I should note here that it is at least clear to me that the resources for working through these matters are *not* to be found in animal defense circles that rely on traditional phallogocentric concepts and practices.

Adams   Yes, I agree with you completely. It is as though there is a tendency to an anthropomorphic notion of political change.

I like the term *carnophallogocentrism* precisely for what it accomplishes: the linking of carnivorous virility with the speaking subject, and the linking of the Western subject with meat eating.

The carnophallogocentric subject is granted privilege, and this privilege is experienced as pleasure. When this happens the privilege disappears as a social construction and is seen as something private, something personal: "This is your choice, not to eat meat, and my choice is to eat meat." At the minimum, the carnophallogocentric subject is the subject for whom this privilege is working.

So, I find the concept important as it helps to get at the problem of the person who admits to "carnivorous virility" but who does not want to believe "he" needs to change. And often the "virility" part is hidden, it is the naked "carnivorousness" that is claimed, but it is claimed in an implicitly virile way. The medium becomes a part of the message.

People often respond to *The Sexual Politics of Meat* by suggesting that the phenomenon I am examining is something that is out "there," just advertisements, as though they are not implicated in and by it. (*The Sexual Politics of Meat Slide Show* in a sense defeats a part of my purpose because it causes people to think my analysis is about images not attitudes.) Or the response is that *The Sexual Politics of Meat* is critiquing something that has passed (recent advertisements and attitudes notwithstanding). Or that my analysis of images is wrong because how images work has changed. And here is Derrida, in coining the term *carnophallogocentrism,* saying it is about the kind of subject we are, and my point is that this subject is constructed and inflected by a culture heavily committed to the sexual politics of meat.

Calf

Kathryn Kirkpatrick

Curled like a comma,
                 the new calf
survives February snow
                    without shelter,
just a few bald tree trunks,
                    and a lean-to
over bales of hay. His mother,
                   formidable
as a paragraph,
              has known a man's hand
at her backside
              up to his elbow with his iron limb,
his cache of bull semen
                 an interstitial, artificial
jerking off,
            and I am angry at the cattlemen
for rushing these calves
                 into snow,
for harnessing mother love
                    to their money machine.
Have a heart,
             I whisper over barbed wire.
What has struggled into life,
                    breathed through blizzards,
is more than bones on a plate.
                    Unwrite your lives
from that numbness.
              Find yourselves
spindly-legged in the cold.

6

"Mad cow" disease and the animal industrial complex: An ecofeminist analysis

On March 20, 1996, British Health Secretary Stephen Dorrell announced the possible link between bovine spongiform encephalopathy (BSE, commonly called "mad cow disease") and Creutzfeldt-Jakob Disease (CJD), the fatal human equivalent. The disclosure that BSE might have "jumped species" from cows to human beings through the consumption of infected meat caused shockwaves in the economy and affected the emotions of many people in Western countries, especially those in Great Britain. The announcement was a startling about face after years in which the British government had assured the public that British beef was safe to consume.

An initial exploration of this topic was possible thanks to the invitation of Nancy Howell at Pacific Lutheran University to explore the issue of ecofeminism and spirituality.

"'Mad Cow' Disease and the Animal Industrial Complex: An Ecofeminist Analysis" was first published in *Organization and Environment*, vol. 10, no. 1 (March 1997): 26–51. © 1997 Sage Publications, Inc.

An encepalopathy is any degenerative illness of the brain, and in these cases, it attacks the brain and gives a sponge-like consistency to it as the nerve cells are destroyed. It is a debilitating, fatal disease that afflicts many species. Until recently the most well known form of it was its manifestation in sheep, where it is called "scrapie."

Until 1979, the International Classification of Diseases, a system used to codify causes of death, did not include a specific category for CJD. CJD is a disease in which the time between infection and commencement of first symptoms can be very long, perhaps as much as thirty-five years. It is a debilitating disease, and reports of its progression can make chilling reading: "A year after becoming ill, [the patient] developed progressive intellectual deterioration and unstable gait. . . . After 17 months, the patient had swallowing difficulties, dystonic extensor posturing of the back, and had become progressively comatose with erratic eye movements" (Chazot et al. 1996: 1181).

CJD has been a difficult disease to diagnose and those stricken have often been misdiagnosed; doctors thought they had psychiatric disorders (Will et al. 1996: 921–25). In the case of transmissible spongiform encephalopathy (TSE), the body does not provoke immune reactions. Thus there is no practical test for identifying its presence in possibly infected but healthy humans or animals. Consequently there is no TSE counterpart to being HIV positive (at this time at least), thus no way of identifying how many people will succumb to it. Moreover, there is no way of knowing how many have died from it who were buried without accurate diagnosis, which requires an autopsy and the use of special chemical stains to examine brain tissue under a microscope. The agents that cause spongiform diseases, prions, have "prodigious resistance to heat, ultraviolet light, radiation, and many chemical disinfectants" (Altman 1996b).

CJD generally strikes elderly people. The cases of CJD that have stimulated the 1996 controversy were very different from the textbook cases. Not only did CJD attack young people, but, upon being autopsied, their brain tissue looked different, more like that of Alzheimer's sufferers than the classic "Swiss cheese" appearance associated with traditional cases of CJD.

The shockwaves that reverberated with the March 1996 announcement were due in part to the fact that the British government had, only a few years earlier, argued against the possibility that they were now admitting—that a possible link existed between these two diseases, BSE and CJD. Since the incubation period for CJD is anywhere from ten to forty years, many formerly happy beefeaters now worry that there is a time bomb ticking in their systems that they are powerless to stop.

On April 1, 1996, an official looking statement that appeared to be from United States Speaker of the House Newt Gingrich's office announced that he was becoming a vegetarian because he was afraid of mad cow disease. What is notable about this April Fool's joke is that "Mr. Gingrich's office took the trouble to announce that the news release reporting the Speaker's switch to vegetarianism was somebody's prank, that the 'release' did not come from his office" (Stout 1996: A10). Clearly someone in his office recognized that becoming a vegetarian in response to the crisis could be greeted as a reasonable response.

That same week, the *New York Times* proposed in its Week in Review section that the beef eating crisis represented a larger cultural phenomenon—people no longer trust what is put into their food. They have "free-floating anxieties over unknown hormones, additives, and food processing techniques performed out of public sight" (Darnton 1996c: 1). Perhaps the anxiety cultural commentators observe is not anxiety about what goes into food, but about what is food (i.e., should animal flesh be seen as food?).

In countries such as the United States and Great Britain, meat eating is protected because it functions simultaneously on so many levels, fulfilling, for instance, both an invaluable economic role and an unexamined appetitive drive. In this essay, I survey the social roots and consequences of a specific environmental problem, the eating of animals. Ecofeminist theory provides the analytical approach for this exploration.

Ecofeminism posits that the domination of the rest of nature is linked to the domination of women and that both dominations must be eradicated. To the issues of sexism, racism, classism, and heterosexism that concern feminists, ecofeminists add naturism—the oppression of the rest of nature. Many ecofeminist writers have demonstrated how animal exploitation is an aspect of naturism, incorporating specific attention to the status of animals into a larger critique of the maltreatment of the natural world.

Drawing on the four minimal claims of ecofeminism identified by ecofeminist philosopher Karen Warren, I will argue that from an ecofeminist perspective, the true madness exposed by the "mad cow crisis" is that people continue to eat meat. Warren stated that *ecofeminism* is a position based on the following claims:

i there are important connections between the oppression of women and the oppression of nature;

ii understanding the nature of these connections is necessary to any adequate understanding of the oppression of women and the oppression of nature;

iii feminist theory and practice must include an ecological perspective; and

iv solutions to ecological problems must include a feminist perspective. (1987: 4–5)

What Warren labeled as *minimal claims*, I will refer to as *basic claims*, a meaning that I believe inheres in her article.

Although there has been an enormous flowering of ecofeminist theory since Warren's 1987 classic article, I focus on that article and a 1990 article because they provide a clear philosophical framework for ecofeminist analysis. These two essays were extremely effective and influential in defining an ecofeminist perspective. Although, at this point, ecofeminism means several different things, Warren's basic definitional statement is helpful because it provides a solid foundation of ecofeminist insights that can be applied to an analysis of mad cow disease and the animal industrial complex implicated by this disease. Warren has not theorized, nor could she, all the problems susceptible to an ecofeminist analysis, including this one. My desire is to bring her framework forward. My contributions to Warren's classic statement of ecofeminism are twofold. First, I demonstrate how understanding the crisis in British beef eating benefits from an ecofeminist approach. Thus, I am analyzing a specific problem—the mad cow crisis—using ecofeminist theory and research. Second, by focusing explicitly on the crisis as it affects attitudes toward meat eating, I continue the work of extending ecofeminist theory to the lives and status of terminal animals (animals raised to become food for human beings).

An ecofeminist analysis demonstrates the importance to environmental and feminist theory of taking the beef eating crisis seriously. Unlike most reporting and analyses of the beef eating crisis, this essay critically stands outside the presumed norm of meat eating. In doing so, I build on the work I began in *The Sexual Politics of Meat* and "Ecofeminism and the Eating of Animals" (1991), where I reframe meat eating as a political act rather than as a nutritional one. This is also another reason for drawing on Warren's work. She identified how a conceptual framework functions to maintain oppressive systems. Her analysis is extremely helpful for viewing an oppressive system that is sanctioned and commonplace, such as meat eating.

Part of the motivation for writing this essay was the anger and horror I felt in response to the entire crisis as it unfolded after March 20. The mad cow crisis highlighted for me the glaring indifference to the lives of other animals who have been ontologized as usable. What was new in the mad cow crisis was not this ontology, but the unquestioning adherence to it, which most commentators and reporters evidenced. The beef eating crisis provides an opportunity to consider that which is usually veiled and kept from consciousness, the eating of animals; and that which enables it, the animal industrial complex.

Most responses to this crisis represent a search for anthropocentric solutions to an anthropocentric problem. Maintaining the instrumental use of nature has clearly been the underlying goal in this crisis: improve the meat supply rather than stop eating meat. Ecofeminism not only resists such anthropocentricity but clearly underscores the practical application of environmental principles.

The beef eating crisis is an excellent vehicle for illustrating an ecofeminist critique because it is a crisis created by a confluence of social enterprises with various interests and political agendas, all of which need to be exposed and critiqued. What follows therefore, is a critical reading of the beef eating crisis within the cultural milieu of capitalist patriarchy. I submit that mad cow disease is only the tip of the iceberg in terms of problematic practices associated with the production of animal protein. The beef eating crisis, however important in its own right, represents a deeper and more sinister set of institutional forces, cultural practices, and corporate machinations that support meat production and consumption.

Until beef eating came under close scrutiny, it often languished as an issue solely of personal habit. In fact, British beef eating influences and is influenced by economics, nationalism, and personal traditions, among other things. Ecofeminism offers a position from which to perceive the variety of forces that obtain when an economic mainstay, a cultural and national archetype, and a highly individual action—all actually different facets of one kaleidoscopic view—are thrown into turmoil. My ecofeminist analysis draws on several current oppositional positions, such as Marxism, philosophical vegetarianism, environmental theory, and feminism.

The essay is organized into four sections; each section builds on a basic claim of ecofeminism identified by Warren (1987, 1990). I extend this basic claim to explore different aspects of the beef eating crisis. The first section establishes some of the connections between the oppression of women and the oppression of terminal animals. The connections I discuss include the male identification of meat eating, and especially, beef eating, and how British national identity is connected to images of male beefeaters. I also explore the sexual politics of dairy, that is, the exploitation of the cow's reproductive labor, and the role this has played in the BSE crisis.

The second section expands upon Warren's analysis of the three main features of a patriarchal worldview (dualistic thinking, value-hierarchical, or up-down, thinking, and a logic of domination). I establish how these features of an oppressive worldview operate to facilitate meat eating by deontologizing terminal animals through viewing them as mass terms and making of them absent referents. Then I identify specifically how these features of a patriarchal worldview have been exhibited in the current beef eating crisis.

In the third section, using a socialist-feminist approach, I identify the environmental issues associated with meat eating in general, and their relationship to the beef eating crisis in specific. At the center of this relationship is the rendering business, the life-support system of the animal industrial complex. The feminist solutions section concludes this essay. It is tied to Warren's fourth claim that solutions to ecological problems must include a feminist perspective. It draws upon feminist standpoint theory to propose thinking from the viewpoints of cows, and argues (contra the prevailing Marxist viewpoint) for seeing terminal animals as alienated laborers. I submit that this is the inevitable conclusion to which the beef eating crisis leads us, with its references to cows' "working lives." I conclude with three recommendations for repudiating the patriarchal worldview, and offer some suggestions for further ecofeminist analysis.

Important connections exist between the oppression of women and the oppression of nature

Warren's first basic claim is that there are important connections between the oppression of women and the oppression of nature. In *The Sexual Politics of Meat* and subsequent writings, I argued specifically

Figure 6.1 Activist and photojournalist Jo-Anne McArthur spent a full day at a small-scale dairy and veal farm. She explains that her group "witnessed the milk line production, artificial insemination and the birth of a calf who was taken away from her mother not 15 minutes after she was born. In this photograph, dairy cows who have had their babies removed from them so that we can drink their milk, watch the new mother bond with her calf."

Mother with her new-born calf. Photograph by Jo-Anne McArthur/We Animals.

that important connections exist between the oppression of women and the oppression of animals, especially terminal animals. These connections include the sexualizing of meat consumption, so that it is associated with heterosexual male-identified sexual conventions. For example, menus and advertisements appeal to heterosexual male consumers by announcing the serving of the "best breasts and thighs," and by using conventions from pornography and prostitution to advertise meat. Meanwhile, women are "animalized"—often depicted on all fours, or in other ways that proclaim women to be closer to animals or animal-like. When the *New York Times* featured an article on a low fat hamburger recipe, it used the representation of a bipedal cow, shaped like an anorexic adolescent girl.

The sexual politics of beef

Beef eating in particular often crystallizes the sexual politics of meat. A *New York Times* story (Hochswender 1990) about the opening of a new men's store, proclaimed, "In keeping with the masculine spirit of the evening, the hors d'oeuvres were beefy. Roast beef on toast. Chunk chicken in pastry shells. Salmon and saucisson. None of that asparagus and cucumber fluff here" (B2). *New Woman* magazine announced in a gushing article on "love, sex, and flank steak" (Sheraton 1996) that what men want is

> *great sex and a great steak*—and not necessarily in that order. . . .
> Both are closely related, as muscular, full-bodied pleasures of the flesh, and each ignites desires for the other. A hot, juicy, blood-red steak or a succulently thick hamburger induces an overall sense of well-being and a surge of self-assurance that is sure to make him feel good about himself and, by association, you. That is especially true in this country, where beef is the quintessential macho fare. (108)

The colonial, male-identified politics of meat

To the configuration of maleness and meat eating identified previously in my writings, one could add the specific identity associated with beef eating in Great Britain. As Schama suggested in *The New Yorker*, beef eating represents "an entire gastronomic constitution, the marrow of political freedom" (1996: 61). The beefeater identity there is distinctly male; male identity is intertwined with national identity. Spencer explained in the *New York Times* that "beef has always summoned up images of the red blood and muscle power that created Britannia, ruled the waves and put the fire in John Bull's belly" (1996: 19). John Bull, the beefeater on gin bottles, the muscle power—maleness drips from each reference.

The beef eating metaphor was a metaphor for Britain's emerging status as a world power. In the nineteenth century, one American medical advisor attributed British success at being a colonial power to its population's meat consumption:

> The rice-eating Hindoo and Chinese and the potato-eating Irish peasant are kept in subjection by the well-fed English. Of the various causes that contributed to the defeat of Napoleon at Waterloo, one of the chief was that for the first time he was brought face to face with the nation of beef-eaters, who stood still until they were killed. (Beard 1898/1972: 272).

Even the phraseology regarding British beef reeks of nativism. Newspaper reports inform us that for the first time in 150 years, the Co-op, a major British retailer, was considering stocking its 3,000 stores with "foreign" beef (Darnton 1996a: 3).

Given the intimate connection between beef eating and national identity, minimal precautions rather than cautious actions were taken until March 1996. The British government handled this crisis in an understandable way, with the defensive mechanisms of understating, underestimating, and underfunding. Something so closely associated with identity may result in a response as intense as to something alien and tabooed. When AIDS in the United States was thought to afflict the "despised" individuals in terms of a racist and homophobic culture (addicts, Haitians, gay men), the response by the government and its agencies was halfhearted and underfunded.

In responding to a disease, reverence and revilement may be flip sides of the same coin of inadequate intervention. Not the hostility of homophobia, but the reverence of beef eating; not the tabooed act, but the sacred national act may provoke a similar government reaction of protecting the dominant interests.

The sexual politics of dairy

Why is it specifically "mad cows" that have threatened to destabilize consumption practices? To understand this, we need to understand the sexual politics of dairy.

The existence of dairy products and eggs requires the specific exploitation of female bodies. In *The Sexual Politics of Meat,* I coined the term *feminized protein* to denote eggs and dairy. With this term I wished to call attention to the use of female animals' reproductive cycles to produce food. Their labor is reproduction.

The exploitation of the cow's reproductive labor

It is precisely the sphere of reproduction for the cow that has been exploited. In fact, for the cow the sphere of production and the sphere of reproduction are the same:

> While for the male home and work are separate, and for the female work is in the home as well, animal "workers" cannot "go home"

Figure 6.2 As the calf takes her first steps, the cows watch the humans warily.

Calf take first steps. Photograph by Jo-Anne McArthur/We Animals.

at all. The modern animal industry does not allow them to "go home"—they are exploited 24 hours a day. In the case of animals the "home" itself has been brought under factory control. . . . Indeed, it is often the sphere of reproduction (mating, breeding, the laying of eggs), which the capitalist seeks to exploit. (Noske 1989: 17)

Without the life span of the "working" cow in Great Britain the infectious agent would not have an opportunity to manifest itself. The average terminal animal does not live long enough to manifest the symptoms of the disease. It is only because dairy cows have a functional purpose when alive that they live long enough to manifest the symptoms. Animals are raised for a specific purpose and their lives are cut short because their purpose relates not to their living but to their dying. It could be that the infectious agent is in other animals but they simply do not live long enough to manifest the symptoms. They are kept alive only the amount of time needed for them to become meat-bearing animals.

Since the average incubation period in animals, at minimum, is four to five years (Bradley and Wilesmith 1993), and can be eight to ten years, and the life of the average terminal animal is at the most two to three years (cattle, two to three years; pigs five to six months; sheep less than two years; see Lacey and Dealler 1991: 118), symptoms of the disease will not manifest by the time the animals are killed. For instance, in describing the problem of scrapie in sheep, neurologists explain:

> An animal may not develop clinically recognized scrapie until an age which far exceeds its commercial life span. Sheep harboring the scrapie agent may thus be sent for slaughter and marketed for human consumption. (Davanipour et al. 1985: 241)

The dairy cow is the only terminal animal who consistently lives long enough to manifest the symptoms. The cow's lifespan, unlike that of other terminal animals, is longer because the cow is exploited twice: first when alive, reproductively for her milk and offspring; and only then, after death, for her body. Because the cow is allowed to live longer due to her usefulness when alive, the disease symptoms have had the opportunity to fully develop. Thus, the demographics for infection will be known for dairy cows; they will remain less identifiable for all other terminal animals whose deaths precede the manifestation of the symptoms of the infection.

The devalued cow

This essay does not trace the devaluation of the cow in Western culture (see Rifkin 1992: 79–80 for an overview). Alternative ways of conceptualizing, and therefore relating to, cows are possible. For instance, a Hindu group has offered shelter for British cows threatened with slaughter. Think about what the term *cow* conveys.

As a term for a woman, *cow* is, in anthropologist John Haverson's words, "thoroughly derogatory," (1976: 515), characterizing the woman as fat and dull. . . . Exploitation of the cow for her milk has created a gender-specific image. Kept perpetually pregnant and/or lactating, with swollen belly or swollen udder, the "dairy cow" is seen as fat. Confined to a stall, denied the active role of nurturing and protecting a calf—so that milking becomes something done *to* her rather than *by* her—she is seen as passive and dull. The cow then becomes emblematic of these traits, which metaphor can attach to women. (Dunayer 1995: 13)

This view of the cow is ratified in images appearing in discussions of the beef eating crisis. Consider an image in the *New York Times* with the caption: "Terry Perkins milked some of his 130 cows" (caption to Altman 1996a: A4). In fact, machines were milking his cows, and he is shown attaching a contraption to a cow's udder; moreover milking is presented as something done to the cow rather than by her.

Whereas at some times and some places, cows have been held sacred, now they are "mad" and those so labeled have been or will be incinerated. The cow's degraded status was illustrated by the numerous "humorous" solutions for "disposing" of the infected cows. Among them was the proposal to ship the cows to Cambodia to detonate the dangerous and plentiful land mines that dot the countryside there.

MacKinnon (1989) demonstrates how women's devalued status becomes proof of our devaluation. As one commentator explained,

"The degradation of women stigmatizes women to the point where that degradation is taken as evidence that there was nothing of value to which harm could be done; a raped or pornographed person is damaged goods hardly worth the respect a recognition of her harm would bring" (Bartlett 1987, 1562). As a result of such circular reasoning, harm to a now-degraded individual does not require our attention. This appears to be the exact problem of dairy cows today: They are so degraded that their further degradation by the disease—and the popular title given the disease—functions as confirmation of their degraded status. Meanwhile, the cultural presentation of cows is of contented cows: happy herbivores, lucky and/or docile producers of a human commodity.

The oppression of women and the oppression of nature (e.g., cows) are intimately connected. The appetite pandered to is male identified. The exploitation is of female reproductive labor. Indeed, the term "mad cow" is yet another in a long lineage of hysterical-female metaphors that populate our cultural iconography. This phrase points out the oppositions between the hysterical female and a nationalist male beefeater identity: the uncontrollable and violable female, the controlling and powerful beefeater. They do not exist independently. There can be no beef eating without cows; cows enable the identity that necessarily negates their own existence. To understand this we must turn to Warren's second basic condition of ecofeminism.

Understanding the nature of these connections is necessary to any adequate understanding of the oppression of women and the oppression of nature

Historically, men positioned themselves as being morally superior to women and a male-identified humanity similarly positioned itself as

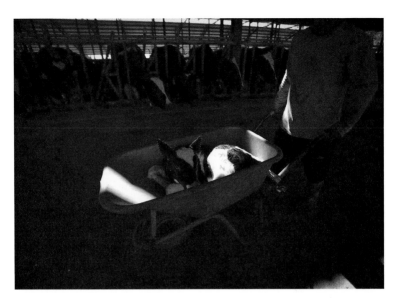

Figure 6.3 The calf is dumped in a barrow and wheeled to her home, a veal crate.

Calf in wheelbarrow. Photograph by Jo-Anne McArthur/We Animals.

being morally superior to nonhumans (with whom women were often equated). As Warren explains, "Women are identified with nature and the realm of the physical; men are identified with the 'human' and the realm of the mental . . . whatever is identified with nature and the realm of the physical is inferior to ('below') whatever is identified with the 'human' and the realm of the mental" (1990: 130).

To understand the nature of these connections between the oppression of women and the oppression of nature, Warren identifies a form of everyday thinking, resistant to analysis because of its pervasive and quotidian nature. Warren labeled this an "oppressive conceptual framework." Its function is that it "explains, justifies, and maintains relationships of domination and subordination." Specifically, a *patriarchal conceptual framework* "explains, justifies, and maintains the subordination of women" (1990: 127).

Warren identifies three significant features of an oppressive or patriarchal conceptual framework: *dualistic thinking, value-hierarchical thinking*, and "the glue that holds it all together" (Warren, personal communication, 1993), a *logic of domination*. I will briefly describe each feature, and then offer an extended analysis of how these features undergird meat eating. After this is established, we can recognize how these three basic features are evident in the beef eating crisis.

a   "Up-down" or "value-hierarchical thinking" places higher value, status, or prestige on what is up rather than what is down. Men are "up," women are "down"; humans are "up," animals are "down"; culture is "up," nature is "down"; beefeaters are "up," cows are "down."

b   Dualistic thinking is

[p]atriarchal value-hierarchical thinking [that] supports the sort of "either-or" thinking which generates *normative dualisms*, i.e., thinking in which the disjunctive terms (or sides of the dualism) are seen as exclusive (rather than inclusive) and oppositional (rather than complementary), and where higher value or superiority is attributed to one disjunct (or, side of the dualism) than the other. (Warren 1987: 6)

c   Value-hierarchical thinking gives rise to a "*logic of domination* which explains, justifies, and maintains the subordination of an 'inferior' group by a 'superior' group on the grounds of the (alleged) inferiority or superiority of the respective group" (Warren 1987: 6). So superiority justifies subordination.

Value-hierarchical thinking, dualistic thinking, and the logic of domination are the features of the encompassing ideology that Warren labeled the patriarchal conceptual framework. In this essay, I will refer to this dominating pattern of everyday thought as the patriarchal worldview.[1] What is so insidious about this form of thinking is that it functions simultaneously as both a legitimating *and* distancing device. Hartsock observes that ruling-class ideas "give an incorrect account of reality, an account only of appearances" (1983: 9). To achieve an appearance-based account, the animal industrial complex "de-animalizes" (Noske's term 1989: 8) terminal animals. When alive the body and the bodily functions of the terminal animals are "put to use in one capacity only . . . the *total* animal is being subordinated to this one activity" (Noske 1989: 19). We encounter terminal animals only when they have been further de-animalized in the appearance-based operations of the meat market where they are presented, for instance, as T-bone, lamb chops, hamburger, and "fresh" but dead chickens. This patriarchal worldview of appearances establishes meat eating as the default setting, the customary, the normal, the ordinary. To defer from it, requires going beyond appearances, an awareness that one has accepted the default setting and that alternatives to this setting exist. Let us look closer at the ruling-class ideas that undergird meat eating.

Dualistic thinking: Human-animal, meat eater-meat, subject-object

Dualisms reduce diversity to two categories: A or not A. They convey the impression that everything can then be appropriately categorized: Either it is A or not A. Val Plumwood calls these dualisms "the logic of colonisation" (1993: 41–68). Disjunctive pairs such as human-animal, male-female, adult-child, and White-non-White are seen as

---

[1] I will not argue for this in the following pages, but it could be argued that feminist epistemologies—which seek to undo dualistic (subject-object) relationships, and which emphasize relational epistemologies—are an important aspect of the feminist project of challenging the patriarchal worldview. For my discussion of this see Adams (1994b/2015: 151–61, 178–98).

oppositional rather than as complementary, and exclusive rather than inclusive.

The human-animal dualism often operates as a subsidiary of the subject-object dualism. Basically, meat eating involves a subject consuming an object. To adhere to this formulation requires the deontologization of the animals. This deontologization involves what could be called the massification of terminal animals. The patriarchal worldview is so successful that when it comes to meat eating, it is not often while sitting at a table and eating "meat" that one thinks, "I am now interacting with an *animal.*" We do not see our own personal meat eating as contact with animals because it has been renamed as contact with food. In our culture, "meat" operates as a (false) mass term (see pp. 6–7). By removing any associations that might make it difficult to accept the activity of rendering a unique individual into a consumable thing, we make the subject into an object. Not wanting to be aware of this activity, we accept this disassociation, this distancing device of the mass term "meat." For instance, newspapers report that Britain exported 240,000 tons of beef in 1995 (Darnton 1996a: 3). In fact, the British exported the flesh of at least 924,000 cows.[2]

The existence of meat as a mass term deontologizes animals. We can identify this process at work: The idea "someone kills animals so that I can eat their corpses as meat" becomes "animals are killed to be eaten as meat" then "animals are meat" and finally "meat animals," thus "meat." Something people do to animals has become represented as an agentless act involving only an object: meat. (This argument is indebted to Hoaglund's analysis of the term "battered woman.") From the human-animal, subject-object dualisms evolves another

---

[2]To calculate this I estimated that each cow weighed 1,000 pounds, and because somewhere between 48 percent to 62 percent of the cow becomes "beef," I used the figure of 52 percent.

one: meat eater-meat. Consciousness of the possible connections between these dualisms (and especially human-animal and meat eater-meat) is asymmetrical. People identify themselves as meat eaters, but acknowledgment that animals are the source of the food "meat" is uneasy at best. The problem is not only that the human-animal dualism keeps us from identifying with the victims of meat eating, because they are other than human; the problem is that meat functions in our culture loosed from its referent animals.

We interact with individual animals daily if we eat them. However, this statement and its implications are repositioned through the structure of the absent referent so that the animal disappears and it is said that we are interacting with a form of food that has been named meat. The animal used for meat eating disappears both literally and figuratively. The roast on the plate is disembodied from the cow who she once was. Dualistic thinking impedes acknowledging a noninstrumental ontology for animals.

Value-hierarchical thinking and the logic of domination

The patriarchal worldview provides an explanation for meat consumption intertwining dualistic thinking, value-hierarchical thinking, and the logic of domination: Human beings are different from animals; human beings are superior to animals; by virtue of that difference and concomitant superiority, we have the right to eat animals. But to reduce any guilt (or other potent feelings; see Luke 1992, 1995) that might exist about eating animals, we are also assured that because we are a kind and caring species, the animals live comfortable lives until they are humanely slaughtered. In a sense, meat eaters think they are doing what veg*ns are doing—eating ethically—without actually doing what veg*ns are doing—not eating animals. On March 20, 1996 this contradiction began to surface: The dualistic view of the de-animalized animal now competed with images of embodied, and at times, suffering, cows.

As a result of the patriarchal worldview that ontologizes animals as edible, no objective stance exists from which to survey the beef eating crisis. No matter what our individual actions are, the place from which we stand to survey the eating of animals is overwhelmed by the norm of "meat." Another value hierarchy thus is in operation, one that values certain attitudes over others. Meat eaters' views are "up"; veg*ns' views are "down." Although no disinterested observer or impartial semantic space exists for discussing the issue, veg*ns, from our "down" position are seen as the biased ones with inflamed opinions. In a flesh-eating culture, conflicts in meaning are resolved in favor of the beef eating culture. As Fraser explains, "since both domestic and official economic institutions support relations of dominance and subordination, the specific interpretations they naturalize tend, on the whole, to advantage dominant groups and individuals and to disadvantage their subordinates" (1989: 168).

The difficulty of introducing meaning for which there is no conceptual space has been theorized by anthropologist Edwin Ardener as a problem of dominance and muteness, and applied by Spender to understanding women's experience with "man-made language." As Spender explained, "Difficulty arises when one group holds a monopoly on naming and is able to enforce its own particular bias on everyone, including those who do not share its view of the world. . . . The dominant reality remains the reference point even for those of us who seek to transform it" (1980: 164, 229). As a consequence, the information veg*ns have about meat production practices has nowhere to go.

The contamination of the discursive space in which we might discuss the matter of cross-species consumption is further aggravated by ignorance. This is one of the results of being in the "up" position; it discourages close examination, for then the logic of domination (humans are better than animals, humans can eat animals, but will do so humanely, being human), would come under scrutiny.

Although veg*ns know a great deal more about the material conditions that enable eating animals than do "corpse eaters," discursive power, however, resides with the latter, not the former. When former President Reagan (who did not know French) met Francois Mitterrand (who knew both English and French) what language do you think they spoke? (Sedgwick 1990). In the dominant culture, bilingual veg*ns must always speak English. Lacking specific information regarding the topic, people with the most ignorance are able to set the limits of the discussion. As Sedgwick observed, "The simple, stubborn fact or pretense of ignorance. . . can sometimes be enough to enforce discursive power" (1990: 6). Because of the discursive control exercised by the dominant flesh-eating culture, it is when veg*ns attempt to speak "French" (i.e., reporting on slaughterhouses, factory farms, the threat of CJD from eating dead bodies) that they are accused of being "deeply undemocratic food faddists." (quoted in Frankel 1990); this was the charge in 1990 by Britain's Minister of Agriculture, John Gummer who also denounced vegetarianism as being "wholly unnatural" and appeared in public with his four-year-old daughter, Cordelia; both of them were eating hamburgers as assurance of the safety of British beef.

The how's and the who's and the when's of meat production are the French that our culture usually does not speak. Part of the problem that the beef eating crisis provoked is that suddenly people must learn this "foreign language" in order to understand how cows got BSE and why human beings might get CJD. Thus, the current crisis is in part an epistemological crisis. Do we want to learn a new language or not? Do we want to know how animals become meat or not? A frequently reiterated response has been, "I had no idea that this is how meat was produced." The unstated implication suggests how profoundly disturbing this information is: "Now that I know this, what does that mean about who I am, who I thought I was, what our culture does, and what our culture therefore is?" It prompts an examination of that which is usually unexamined: the logic of domination.

Whose crisis is it?

Having identified how the three aspects of an oppressive worldview function to legitimate meat eating, we can now recognize how they have functioned in response to the beef eating crisis itself.

Figure 6.4 Still wet from birth, the calf will be added to the rows of other calves and crates, and raised in this confinement.

Calf added to rows of calves. Photograph by Jo-Anne McArthur/We Animals.

Dualistic thinking

Dualistic thinking is clearly evident in the low status of the cows. In addition, it has operated in the conceptual splitting of humans from the other animals. Indeed, this conceptual disjunction may have contributed to the crisis because we did not see ourselves as mammals susceptible to a disease others mammals were manifesting.

It has been clear for at least a decade that the complex of diseases labeled TSE jumped species, and that mammals were especially susceptible. Cats were infected by pet food made from contaminated beef (Blakeslee 1994: B8). Mink farms in the United States have been sites of outbreaks of transmissible mink encephalopathy (see Robinson et al. 1994). The mink's diet consisted primarily of "downer cows" (cows unable to stand because of disease or injury). Researchers have reported that "BSE from brain tissues of infected animals has been transferred by injection or feeding to the following: cattle, pigs, marmosets, monkeys, goats, sheep, mice and mink" (Lacey and Dealler 1994: 1795, see also Table 4 in Dealler and Lacey 1991: 130). Peter Cox cites reports that the agent that causes kuru in humans (a scrapie-like disease thought to be caused by cannibalism) was experimentally inoculated into chimpanzees, marmosets, baboons, goats, cats, mice, hamsters, and gibbons (1992: 54).[3] Moreover, it has been known for some time that a primary form of transmission of TSE is through the oral route (i.e., consumption). If the animalness of human beings were not so actively denied by dualistic thinking, the recognition that TSE might "jump" to human beings due to their consumption of animals might have been granted more credence. We are mammals, too. Thus dualistic thinking prevented a

---

[3]Citing these instances does not mean that either Peter Cox or I endorse animal experimentation (for critiques of animal experimentation, see Adams 1994a/2015: 39–54; Langley 1989; Singer 1990: 25–94; Slicer 1991: 108–24).

conceptualization of ourselves as mammals, susceptible to a disease that strikes mammals.

Value-hierarchical thinking and the logic of domination

Value-hierarchical thinking is evidenced in the panic that is expressed when people realize that they may get the disease too, despite their superior standing in the species hierarchy. If cows were struck by a disease that was definitely not transmissible to humans, the problem would be greeted as an economic and veterinary one involving issues of animal disease and management. It would be addressed on a cost-benefit balance sheet that factored into the production costs a prediction that a certain percentage of animals would die from the disease. As with other diseases (such as porcine stress syndrome; see Mason and Singer 1980: 24), the stricken livestock might be viewed as an absorbable loss because of the gain from the increased production that the newly introduced practice enables.

The question of transmissibility, not the disease itself, has resulted in the panic. That is, the concern has been with what the disease may possibly do to human beings, not with the fate of the cows themselves. For instance, shortly after the March 20 announcement, a man walked into a McDonald's and requested a "Creutzfeldt-Jakob burger" (Darnton 1996a: 3). His reaction, like that of most of his contemporaries, reflected his concern about fate of people, not cows. This focus on the impact on human beings reveals the deontologized status of the cows. The value hierarchy is exhibited because it is those who are "up" (people) that matter.

The logic of domination is evident in the decision that the cows will continue to be exploited for their reproductive labors and only then will they be incinerated. The patriarchal worldview upholds the cow's deontologized status.

Feminist theory and practice must include an ecological perspective, and this perspective includes animals

The third of Warren's basic claims is that feminist theory and practice must include an ecological perspective. I submit that this perspective

Figure 6.5 While at the farm, Jo-Anne McArthur saw a sickly, fly-covered calf. Later that day, the calf was dead and being placed in a wheelbarrow to be wheeled away.

Dead calf wheeled away. Photograph by Jo-Anne McArthur/We Animals.

must include animals. Feminists, like many environmentalists, may not see a disease associated with cows, much less the consumption of cows, as an environmental issue. But that is because, as Noske argues, many environmentalists neglect that part of nature which is not "green" (1989: x). Domesticated animals (who now outnumber humans three to one; see Durning and Brough 1992: 66) long ago ceased being "fauna." As Davis observed, prejudices among environmentalists abound against "creatures whose lives appear too slavishly, too boringly, too stupidly female, too 'cowlike'" (1995: 196). The majority of animals dominated by humans have been so devalued that they no longer appear to be a part of nature. But this does not mean that we can exclude them from an environmental analysis. It simply makes our task more challenging. In examining the environmental consequences of meat eating, and exploring specifically the role of rendering, I bring a socialist-feminist perspective to this task because capitalism—"the pre-eminent culture and economics of self-interest" (King 1989: 116)—influences the anthropocentric decisions that have accompanied this current crisis.

Seager reminded her readers in *Earth Follies* of the "*mutual accommodation* of capitalism and patriarchy" (1993: 82). If patriarchy and capitalism accommodate each other, patriarchy, capitalism, and meat eating are consolidated. Without cattle, there would be no capital—at least etymologically speaking (the word cattle literally meant "wealth, property"; see Onions 1966: 154). As newspapers continually remind their readers, the TSE crisis affects a $15 billion business in the United Kingdom and hovers over a $36 billion business in the United States (though Gary Weber, a spokesman for the National Cattlemen's and Beef Association, put that figure at $160 billion, referring to "at least 1.5 million people in the cattle, feed, veterinary, pharmaceutical and veterinary industry"; Altman 1996d: 9).

Socialist feminism recognizes that, through capitalism, a rigid separation divides the political, economic, domestic, personal, and environmental, so that the reduction of a cow to a consumable commodity has been privatized. The result of this social division is that certain issues are banished to zones of discursive privacy rather than seen as foci of generalized contestation. Purchasing, preparing, and eating food is cast as a private/domestic matter. Issues involving the production of animal foods are depoliticized and economized— "cast as impersonal market imperatives or as 'private' ownership prerogatives" (Fraser 1989: 168)—such as when the rise of the animal industrial complex is attributed solely to the demands of the market, or when it is argued that we cannot interfere with the prerogatives of the animals' "owner." As feminism demonstrates, the divisions between politics, economics, and domestic issues are false.

The animal industrial complex

The beef eating crisis forces us to confront the invisible labor-social relations that go into the production of beef; it focuses our attention on the industry that brings us the burger.

After World War II the animal agriculture industry changed, becoming increasingly "mechanized, automated, and 'rationalized'" (Noske 1989: 14, see also Mason and Singer, 1980). This change created an animal industrial complex (Noske's term), which is the United States' second largest industry and its largest food industry. Currently 60 percent of American food comes from animals, both feminized protein and animal "corpses" or animalized protein. The animal industrial complex has "environmental side effects that stretch along the production line—from growing vast quantities of feed-grain to disposing of mountains of manure" (Durning and Brough 1992: 66).

The environmental impact of eating animals

One of ecofeminism's attributes is its concern with the consequences of the domination of the earth. The relationship between eating animals and environmental disaster is measurable: to feed a person following a vegan diet, one that relies neither on feminized or animalized protein, requires 300 gallons of water daily; to feed a person following a vegetarian diet that includes feminized protein requires 1,200 gallons; to feed a person following the standard U.S. diet of animalized and feminized protein requires 4,200 gallons (Robbins 1987: 367). Half of all water consumed in the United States is used in the crops fed to livestock (Lappé 1982: 10).

Animal agriculture is the major industrial polluter in the United States. A pound of animal flesh means that 100 pounds of livestock manure had to be disposed of, often in waterways. One cow produces as much waste as sixteen humans (Robbins 1987: 372). Eighty thousand dairy cattle produce 7.9 million pounds of manure a day ("Study to Examine," 1991: A15). Feedlots and slaughterhouses are responsible for more of the country's water pollution than all other industries and households combined. More than 50 percent of water pollution can be linked to wastes from the livestock industry (including manure, eroded soil, and synthetic pesticides and fertilizers). Slaughterhouse waste—fat, carcass waste, fecal matter—is several hundred times more concentrated than raw waste, yet it is dumped into rivers at the rate of more than two tons an hour. Robbins reports that 250,000 pounds of waste are produced every second by livestock in the United States; half of it comes from confinement operations and cannot be recycled (1987: 372).

Besides depleting water supplies, the animal industrial complex places demands on energy sources: 17,000 kilocalories of energy are burned to produce a kilogram of beef (Durning and Brough 1992: 70).

Millions of acres are deforested to convert land to grazing lands or crops to feed farm animals. Overgrazing or intensive cultivation causes these lands to become desert. Cattle are responsible for 85 percent of topsoil erosion—the loss of the organic soil layer that provides plants with nutrients and moisture (Robbins 1987: 358). Because of conversion of land to feed animals, wildlife are losing their habitats and are often crushed or wounded during the clearing operations.

Livestock account for "15–20 percent of global methane emissions—about 3 percent of global warming from all gases" (Durning and Brough 1992: 74). As the Worldwatch Institute Report on Progress Toward a Sustainable Society concludes: "All told, the price of meat might double or triple if the full ecological costs—including fossil fuel use, ground-water depletion, agricultural-chemical pollution, and methane and ammonia emissions—were included in the bill" (Durning and Brough 1992: 80).

Rendering, business as usual, and the environment

Seager illustrated how often in environmental crises the byword remains "business as usual" (1991: 70–108). She points out that it is convenient to use environmentally dubious practices because they often enhance industrial profitability. The "maximize profits" motive is evident in many aspects of the beef eating crisis, for as Noske observed, "present-day capitalism tends to eliminate anything in the animal which cannot be made productive" (1989: 20).

Animal waste poses an expensive environmental concern. The growth of the rendering business represents the "maximize profits" response to this environmental problem as it eliminates the burden of disposing of some of these costly wastes. Rendering makes money off of every part of the slaughtered cow but the moo. It appeared efficiently and profitably to dispose of parts of animal bodies that could not be sold as "meat" for human beings.

Rendering has been called a "garbage disposal service" (Cox 1992: 59). In fact, it might be called the life-support system of the animal industrial complex. The chairman of the rendering trade association remarked, "If there is no rendering industry, there is no meat industry" (quoted in Cox 1992: 59). Using the formerly-rejected pieces and parts of bodies from cows, sheep, and other animals, the rendering business produces fat products such as margarine and soap. To make more of a profit from this industry, the idea was conceived to produce feedstuff from rendered material rather than discard it as waste. Thus parts of dead sheep and dead cows were seen as potential sources of cheap protein for herbivorous animals, and so rendering began to produce protein products such as animal feed. The effects of turning herbivores into carnivores did not figure into the balance sheet.

Sheep have long been infected with scrapie, a form of TSE. Rendering recycled precisely the potentially infected material of an animal—the spinal cord, lymphoid tissues, intestines, and brains—back to other animals. In Great Britain during the 1980s, the process of preparing sheep parts for consumption by other domesticated animals changed. Also at this time, British farmers began to feed cows protein supplements that were derived from the bodies of other cows. These changes are thought to be the cause of BSE in cows.

In the 1980s, with cows dying of BSE, the British government offered 50 percent of the worth of the cow to farmers for "destroying" each infected cow. Because this price was so low, it is thought that many were not destroyed. The government valued the cows too little; some farmers valued them too much. If their cows appeared unaffected, they could choose to sell them at full price for meat. One butcher reported "Most people think that for every infected cow that was taken out of the herd, two infected cows got into the human food chain" (quoted in Katz 1996: 12A). Thus, we encounter the irony that eventually cows were not being fed to any mammals except human beings.

Rendering is not solely a British industry and problem. In the United States in 1995, 40.5 billion pounds of offal was processed; this equates to 10 billion pounds of animalized protein fed to terminal animals.[4] According to the United States Department of Agriculture (USDA), "14 percent (by weight) of the cow carcasses rendered in the U.S. are fed to other cattle" (Hager and Hosenball 1996: 59). A 1990 survey by the USDA of the 309 known rendering plants, "found that 13 percent processed adult sheep, usually simply mixing their remains with other rendered species. Eight percent included sheep heads. The techniques used—a continuous rendering process with no use of solvent—mirrored those used in Britain" (Physician's Committee for Responsible Medicine 1996: 3). Sheep and cattle remains are fed to cattle and chickens, and chicken's manure is then fed to cattle. Chickens are eating their own manure and parts of dead birds. Moreover, "chickens, pigs, and other animals are routinely fed animal remains, feces, even municipal wastes" (Physician's Committee for Responsible Medicine 1996: 3).

A proposal to ban sheep parts in animal feed in 1994 was not acted upon by the Food and Drug Administration. Opposition from some elements of the livestock industry derailed the proposal as did the "lack of inspectors to enforce such a ban" (Altman 1996d: 9). Not surprisingly, nine days after the March 20th announcement, the United States livestock industry and veterinary medical groups proposed a voluntary ban on the use of "ruminant parts in animal feed" (Altman 1996d: 9). However, there is no way to test a rendered

---

[4]This statistic was provided to me by Eric Haapapuru, of the Physician's Committee for Responsible Medicine, one of the researchers for their report, *Mad Cow Disease: The Risk to the U.S.*

product for sheep parts (Altman 1996c: A8), so there is no way for knowing if 100 percent compliance occurs.

To maintain current human consumption patterns in the Western world, herbivorous animals like cows were transformed into carnivores (fed sheep parts) and also to cannibals (fed other cows to consume). Tampering with herbivorous animals' diets is in and of itself an environmental issue, related to and contributing to the already identified environmental consequences of diverting food resources to animals rather than consuming them directly.

Garrett's (1994) *The Coming Plague* details the outbreak of numerous infectious diseases in Homo sapiens such as Ebola, HIV, and hantaviruses. Toward the end of the book, she links these outbreaks with environmental devastation. She sees a connection between the loss of original biodiversity and microbial opportunity, remarking on the consumption patterns that have encouraged this. "The extraordinary, rapid growth of the *Homo sapiens* population, coupled with its voracious appetite for planetary dominance and resource consumption, had put every measurable biological and chemical system on earth in a state of imbalance" (Garrett 1994: 550). This is true, too, of the imbalance that results from human manipulation of the internal environments of terminal animals that paved the way for the increase in TSEs.

Solutions to ecological problems must include a feminist perspective

In the previous section, I examined several of the most urgent environmental issues associated with the animal industrial complex. Warren's fourth basic claim is that solutions to environmental issues such as these must include a feminist perspective. Acknowledging the work of laborers whose bodies are the product that they must produce (that is, the cows themselves) evolves from bringing a feminist perspective to ecological issues.[5] Recognizing the perspective of the cows begins the process of reversing the degradation of the cow, as well as offering a place from which to theorize a solution.

As Haraway explains, "The standpoints of the subjugated are . . . preferred because in principle they are least likely to allow denial of the critical and interpretive core of all knowledge" (1988: 584). The patriarchal worldview has deontologized cows so that we fail to consider them laborers much less alienated ones. Drawing upon feminist standpoint theory we have the opportunity to think from the lives of the cow, the central females in this crisis (see Harding 1991: 105–37; Hartsock 1983: 231–51; Jaggar 1988: 369–89).

After all, where are the women in the beef eating crisis? The large majority of scientists, farmers, consumers, representatives of the animal industrial complex, government officials in England and other European countries, (except for an anonymous spokesperson for the Farmer's Union), and reporters reporting on these individuals are men.

---

[5]Space does not allow me to discuss the alienated labor of the worker who transforms animals into meat. Rosemary Ruether, author of *Gaia and God* (1991), reminds us that environmental exploitation takes place through social domination of the bodies of some people by other people. Owners and decision-makers maintain high profits for the few by passing on the costs to the many in the form of low wages, high prices, bad working conditions, and toxic side effects. The meat packing industry has one of the highest worker turnovers of all industries. One of the questions pursued in the TSE crisis is, What contact existed between victims of CJD and cows who had BSE? Jean Wake, who died in September 1995, had worked in a factory that put filling into beef pies (Darnton 1996b: A3). Another victim worked as a butcher from 1985 to 1987, and a third victim was a German woman who worked in a restaurant and came into contact with beef and veal. All the victims had eaten beef or beef products. These cases suggest there might also be a connection between those who worked with infected animals or their dead bodies, but whether an explicit cause and effect relationship exists is not at all established. Moreover, at the end of April, French researchers (Chazot et al. 1996: 1181) reported a case of CJD in a twenty-six-year-old man who was a mechanic, had no particular contacts with cattle, and had traveled abroad only once, to the south of Spain in 1990. However, at least one case of mad cow disease in a France was reported in March 1996, and we do not know how many cases previously went unreported (Darnton 1996e: A3).

We have encountered images of four-year-old Cordelia Gummer, the daughter of Britain's Minister of Agriculture, eating a hamburger with her dad in 1990. Margaret Thatcher provides a brooding counterpresence to Cordelia. Under Thatcher's reign, Great Britain underwent government deregulation, encouraged the attitude of "business as usual," and failed to provide sufficient funding for surveillance of the disease.

Between the powerless daddy's little girl and the powerful rightwing woman is the place where most women are located, but they are seldom found in this crisis. They are the women behind the male beefeaters, consuming meat themselves and often believing that their men need beef.

The most women I encountered in researching this subject were in an article written by a woman. "I'll never eat beef again," Sylvia Carswell averred, "I don't trust the Government an inch." Sophie Craven insisted, "I won't eat beef again for a long time, if ever again" (Strom 1996: A3). Of course, statements by only two women hardly constitute a reliable sample. But the fact remains that a male dominant world is the one represented in the media reports.

Lamentably there is one area where females greatly outnumber males: the afflicted animals are predominantly dairy cows. Only 20 percent of affected animals are beef cattle. Our task of bringing a feminist perspective to the environmental issues associated with the animal industrial complex must include these cows.

Can a Marxist analysis accommodate animals as laborers?

Clearly capitalist institutions view the cow as a commodity; but is it possible for us to recognize that the cow herself is an alienated laborer? It may be objected that to extend the status of alienated laborer to animals such as a cow is to misinterpret Marx. But the beef eating crisis with the reference to cows' "productive lives" offers an opportunity to recognize that it is time to reject the Marxist dualistic approach to human work and animal work.

The human ability to transform nature is a central feature of the Marxist conceptualization of what is distinct about human beings (see Schmidt 1971). The Marxist emphasis on production, reason, and (human) sociality is profoundly anthropocentric. It posits animalness as the antithesis of humanness and accepts a view of the deanimalized animal. From the Marxist point of view, animals can be neither social nor cultural, "they solely belong to the realm of necessity i.e., natural history, the laws of matter and motion. While humans are free agents, in making their own sociocultural history, animals are unfree in that their (natural) history is made *for* them" (Noske 1989/1997: 76). Braverman, in *Labor and Monopoly Capital*, argued that human work is conscious and purposive, directed by the power of conceptual thought. What we have in these dualistic formulations is the Marxist variation of the patriarchal viewpoint that de-animalizes the animals (for a detailed response to Marx, see Benton 1988, 1993).

Is it not possible that animals, too, gain and enact conscious intentionality through their interaction with the natural world, that is, through production (Ingold 1983)? Should production be the basis for differentiating human beings from the other species? Is it accurate to define production anthropocentrically? For instance, at one point tool use was seen as solely a human capacity, and that which catalyzed instrumental rationality. When it was discovered that some animals did indeed use tools, it was then argued that the uniquely human trait constituted using tools to make tools. Yet how does this equation of tool use, cognitive ability, and humanness account for the fact that some of the most intelligent animals, such as whales and dolphins, have no limbs and are sound-oriented rather than tool-users (Noske 1989/1997: 151)?

Animals: The paradigmatic alienated labor

The Marxist analysis of the worker being alienated from the fragmented product is epitomized in animals whose bodies are used for food. Noske draws parallels between factory animals and human industrial workers without simply equating them. She does so by using the four interrelated aspects of alienation Marx identified as functioning under the capitalist mode of production to illustrate her points.

1   Workers are "alienated from their product which embodies their own labour and of which they are dispossessed" (Noske 1989/1997: 13). What further alienation from a product can there be than becoming the product itself? Animals forced to specialize in becoming "meat" are alienated from their totality.

2   Workers are alienated from their own productive activity, which does not belong to them. "The term productivity pertains to one particular capacity in isolation (for example, milk production), whereas an animal's well-being concerns the whole animal" (Noske 1989/1997: 17). For instance, the dairy cow has been forced to specialize in the labor of milk production. When she no longer can labor, her "productive life" is over.

3   Workers are alienated from species life. Noske saw this operating in the isolation of humans from their integral relationship with nature, and with society. For animals, "capitalist industrial production has either removed the animals from their own societies or has grossly distorted these societies by crowding the animals in great numbers" (19).

4   Workers are alienated from surrounding nature. As Noske observed, "The animal's relationship to that part of nature

which is to be its food clearly shows the extent of its
alienation. Factory food is to a large extent alien and not
suited to the animal's digestive system" (19). Being fed other
animals through rendered protein products being perhaps the
most dramatic example of this.

Since March 20, 1996, newspapers have referred to the "productive
lives" of cows (Darnton 1996d: A1). As a spokeswoman for the
National Farmer's Union explained in March 1996, when the dairy
cow "comes to the natural end of its [*sic*] working life it [*sic*] would be
slaughtered" (quoted in Lyall 1996: A5). Thinking from the life of the
alienated laborer, the cow, we might wonder whether she views her
life—much less her body—as so divisible.[6]

The ecofeminist task

I have placed the beef eating crisis within an ecofeminist framework
that recognizes the specific exploitation of female animals, and
the environmental consequences of adhering to a patriarchal
worldview that deontologizes animals. I have argued for expanding
feminist standpoint theory to think from the life of the cow. I have
juxtaposed the cultural icon of the mad cow with the colonial
beefeater. Now, the task is to think ourselves out of "patriarchal
conceptual traps" (see Gray 1982) by "*reconceptualizing* ourselves

---

[6]I find it noteworthy that an example of thinking from the life of the cow can be found in
an interview with Art Garfunkel, in which he describes the reaction of cows to his loud
singing as he walks across America: "'Cows give me this amazed stare. I've passed fields
where seventy-five cows are frozen, every eye on me. I slow down and play games with
interspecies communication: what gestures read to them?' Garfunkel slowly semaphored
his arms, seeking the cow frequency. 'When I go to the bass range with long *moo* sounds, I
sense that I'm communicating. Taking them seriously makes them feel pregnant with a kind
of moment, a quivering existential happening'" (Friend 1993: 43–44).

Figure 6.6 Artist's Statement: *veal calf wheelbarrow* **was inspired from a photograph by Jo-Anne McArthur titled:** *Wet From Birth, Organic Dairy Farm, Near Madrid, Spain.* **I had been making collages and cut outs of factory farm cells. The artwork deconstructs the photograph by parceling out the body of a calf into a heap of words. Veal is a less offensive, generic "mass term" for what is in essence a baby male calf stolen from his mother to live out his short lonely life in a crate.**

Janell O'Rourke, *Veal calf wheelbarrow,* 3″ × 5″, cut rice paper and tea bags, 2015.

and our relations to the nonhuman natural world in nonpatriarchal ways" (see Warren 1987: 7). The conventional response to the beef eating crisis that has characterized business and governmental reactions arises from a patriarchal worldview that seeks to continue business as usual. If through ecofeminism we "recover ontology as the ground for ethics" (King 1989: 134), as King suggests, we will do so by repudiating the logic of domination. Here then are some suggestions for resistance:

1   *Knowledge crises offer positive opportunities.* Rather than managing a crisis, and riding out the knowledge crisis, a noninstrumental

way of knowing is possible, one that affirms relationships with other animals rather than de-ontologizing them.

2 *Restore the absent referent, not consumer confidence.* Seager observed that "environmental problems are often cast as failures of public relations; and by corollary, then, it is assumed that 'solutions' lie with aggressive public relations management"[7] (1993: 87) The issue becomes one of restoring consumer confidence—reassuring those who hold the dominant perspective—rather than restoring the absent referent and thus releasing terminal animals from their object status.

3 *End the practice, don't protect it.* In several senses, a meat diet already kills people in developed countries, as a minority of op-ed columnists proclaimed in the wake of the March 20th announcement (see Barnard 1996; McCarthy 1996). The healthfulness of a vegan diet in a first world context has been established (see Dwyer and Loew 1994: 87–110; Gruen and Gaard 1995: 230–41; Mangels and Havala 1994: 111–22; Pluhar 1992: 189–215; Varner 1994a, b). Meat eating has been linked to many of the life-shortening diseases that afflict individuals in developed countries (heart disease, cancer, high blood pressure, strokes, diabetes). Infection with salmonella, campylobacter, and E. coli O157:H7 among others is a serious problem. In fact, in the United States, the United States Department of Agriculture estimated that *Salmonella* and *Campylobacter* bacteria on meat and poultry "may together cause over 4 million illnesses and up to 3,000 deaths each year.

---

[7]It appears that this solution was having some success, as figures that were released in early May showed that British beef consumption had rebounded to 85 percent of its level before the March 20 announcement. Interestingly, nearly half of the teenagers surveyed indicated that they had stopped eating beef, and 4 percent had cut all animalized protein from their diets (Reuters North America 1996). (Half of the 10 British victims were teenagers.)

That translates into almost 11,000 illnesses and eight deaths each day" (DeWaal 1996: 1, emphasis in the original).

In announcing the results of a study that reported a relationship between red meat consumption and non-Hodgkin's lymphoma in women between the ages of fifty-five to sixty-nine years old, the *New York Times* also reiterated: "Red meat has previously been linked to colon cancer, and animal fat is believed to increase the risk of prostate cancer and heart disease" ("Research Links Cancer Risk," 1996: C19). Demonstrating the insidious nature of the animal industrial complex, on the same day that this new study was reported, President Clinton announced that the Agriculture Department would make beef purchases of up to $50 million for its school lunch program to help stabilize beef prices. In addition, he announced that the Agriculture Department would open "millions of acres of environmentally sensitive land for grazing" (Purdom 1996: A9).

In terms of the effects of contemporary meat production on the consumed animal, the human consumer, and the environment, the beef eating crisis is actually only a minor, but compelling, part of a much larger problem. My contribution to understanding this problem is to place it within an ecofeminist analysis. But more work remains. To begin, we might consider the status of chickens in the animal industrial complex. A patent has been applied for a substance called rectite, a superglue that would be applied to the birds' anuses in an attempt to prevent excrement from contaminating the birds' bodies. When I talked with Karen Davis (personal communication, March 1996), founder of United Poultry Concerns, she described their living situation:

These birds literally live in excrement. They are fed it, they're pooping it all the time, thousands of birds living in their own poop. Broiler chickens and turkeys, their droppings are huge. An abnormal amount of poop coming from abnormally large chickens. They have nothing to peck in but this litter and poop. They are literally pecking the poop, being fed it, and the poop as it is being decomposed is releasing ammonia. One of the great ironies—a world of manure—and people think they are eating a health food![8]

Besides applying an ecofeminist analysis to the status of other terminal animals in the animal industrial complex, tracking the progress of TSEs in North America will be important. On April 27, 1996 the equivalent of mad cow disease was discovered in a Saskatchewan game farm elk. I suspect reports like this will continue to surface. In addition, an ecofeminist analysis of the ongoing campaign against McDonalds by environmentalists and animal defenders is urgently needed (see McLibel 1996).

Individual acts need not be neglected. The patriarchal worldview lodges itself in each individual consumer. Can there be a place in ecofeminist ethics for the unsavory rendering business and other aspects of the animal industrial complex? I think not. Veganism is

---

[8]For more information on the status of chickens, see Davis (1996). In February 1996, Russia banned further American poultry sales. Russia claimed that "the ban was needed to protect consumers here [in Moscow] against infected poultry until the United States improved its standards" (Gordon 1996: 17). U.S. poultry producers argued that Russia was using the health issue as a smokescreem for protectionism, because Russian producers fear that American producers will destroy the industry. Thus, industry spokespeople in the United States viewed it as a trade issue, not an inspection or food safety issue (a surprising *third* of all American exports to Russia is poultry).

Russian specialists who conducted inspections of American poultry processing plants complained that "health and safety standards in the United States were wanting, citing the problem of bacteria and chemical residues in the meat" (Gordon 1996: 17). Although the *New York Times* article quotes representatives of chicken producers, it leaves unchallenged the imputing of hidden motives to the Russians. It never directly addresses whether the Russians are mistaken in their assessment of poultry inspection in the United States. Yet, according to the Center for Science in the Public Interest, "the poultry industry has maintained processing practices that actually increase the percent of contaminated products" (DeWaal 1996: i).

a possible model for enacting ecofeminist consciousness. No, it does not solve the problem for eaters of British beef in the 1980s, when exposure to BSE was the greatest. Indeed, one of the victims of CJD in England had been a strict vegetarian since 1991. But, the beef eating crisis ought to prompt more than a search for a way to make meat safe, and so protect human privilege. When viewed as an environmental issue, it is an opportunity to resist such human privilege.

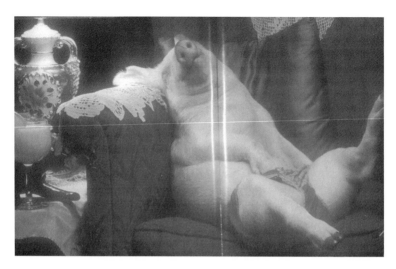

Figure 7.1 "Ursula Hamdress" from *Playboar.* This image appeared in *The Beast: The Magazine that Bites Back,* 10 (Summer 1981): 18–19. It was photographed by animal advocate Jim Mason at the Iowa State Fair where it appeared as a "pinup." More recent issues of *Playboar* have renamed "Ursula" "Taffy Lovely."

7

Why a pig? A reclining nude reveals the intersections of race, sex, slavery, and species

Several recent books of critical theory have included investigations of the traditional Western depiction of women's beauty or women's sexual availability especially as it has been captured in the "reclining nude" pose. Yet, as critical theory traces these depictions forward into the late twentieth century, it has failed to recognize specifically how this tradition has lept the human body. In this essay, I return to an image that has been vexing me for thirty years, and illuminate it as an example of the reclining nude as it was imposed on an other-than-human body. I argue that cultural theory must include consideration about species hierarchies and attitudes when examining racial and sexual representations. Otherwise it is impoverished. Attitudes about sex and race that continue to be imposed on an other-than-human body are permitted to be retrograde and oppressive, escaping the kind of scrutiny that would be brought to bear if the representation were imposed on a human body.

"Why a pig?" emerged from a keynote address given at the "Animals and Animality Graduate Student Conference" at Queen's University in Kingston, Ontario. June 2010.

"Why a Pig? A reclining nude reveals the intersections of race, sex, slavery, and species" first appeared in *Ecofeminism: Feminist Intersections with Other Animals and the Earth*, ed. Carol J. Adams and Lori Gruen (London: Bloomsbury, 2014), 206–24. Used by permission.

I seek to change this. In specific, I am concerned about the image of "Ursula Hamdress" (see Figure 7.1). I first encountered this image in the early 1980s. Jim Mason had been in the Midwest and decided to go to the March 1981 National Pork Producers' conference in Kansas City, Missouri. He wandered through the trade show, flush with 480 exhibitors and 15,000 visitors. The implements of contemporary hog raising are there: farrowing stalls (which imprison a sow who has just given birth), cages, pens, slatted floors, feeders, etc. "Here Hess and Clark, Pfizer, Dow Chemical, Elanco, American Cyanamid, etc. are exhibiting the myriad varieties of antibiotics, disinfectants, growth promotants, pre-mixes and other factory drugs and supplies." Jim, who by that point had many visits to factory farms under his belt, notices the absence of dust, manure smell, dank, acrid air, and "no shrieks of crowded pigs."

He heard a buzz and saw lots of people gathered around something; they were all staring at and talking about the picture of *Ursula Hamdress*: "a photograph of a pig in panties sprawled in a chair. I overhear one of the men explain how a veterinarian sedated the pig so that she would hold still for the picture" (1981: 68).

"Ursula" was named for actress Ursula Andress, a "sex symbol" (in the terminology of the 1960s) as a result of her role in an early James Bond film. In 1965, she posed for *Playboy*. "Ursula Hamdress" with her painted trotter nails and red Victoria Secret-like panties, was posed as a centerfold for the magazine *Playboar—the Pig Farmer's Playboy*.

In the early 1980s, I recognized that two "genealogies" had combined in Ursula Andress—the pornographic and the domesticated farm animal. In terms of the pornographic, "Ursula Hamdress" was posed as though she were the centerfold for a pornographic magazine. The accouterments in the photograph were staged in such a way to evoke a nineteenth-century brothel, but the being was distinctly different than the kind of being usually found in that setting or as a centerfold, a pig.

The other genealogy—that of the lives of farmed animals, from which "Ursula" had been elevated into a human-inspired environment—had its own setting and accouterments. Since the publication in 1980 of Jim Mason's and Peter Singer's *Animal Factories*, with its photographs and text, an animal activist who encountered the photo of "Ursula Hamdress" would recognize something distinctly different about her, too: she showed none of the signs of having lived the kind of life the majority of her sister sows endured. She was unblemished. No other sow had chewed on her, forced into a cannibalism through the stress of crowded conditions. She wasn't thirsty or hungry; hadn't been hauled in a transport truck for hours without water or food.

By the time the 1990s rolled around, Ursula Andress's iconic sex symbol status had faded. The "joke"—Ursula Andress in *Playboy*

Figure 7.2 *Pigs in a crowded transport truck.* Photograph by Jo-Anne McArthur/The Ghosts in Our Machine. Canada, 2012.

becomes "Ursula Hamdress" in *Playboar*, had lost its referent for most consumers. However the visual referent remained. *Playboar* circumvented this dated association by making just one change: They changed the name of the pig.

"Ursula Hamdress" became "Taffy Lovely." The sole updating they did for this magazine of barnyard-school, fraternity-humor—the humor derived from dominance—was to change the name of the sedated pig.

Otherwise, that issue of the magazine has stayed exactly the same. All of the other visual and verbal jokes and double entendres were left untouched and it seamlessly moved into the twenty-first century with the iconography of the twentieth. To the editors of *Playboar*, there was a sense of an unchanging set of consumers from the 1960s to the twenty-first century, and they weren't just pig farmers.

The genealogy of the reclining nude

Another genealogy exists into which Ursula Hamdress fits, a genealogy identified recently by several important cultural critics, but a genealogy that in their discussion does not include "Ursula." I will argue that it should.

The three works I will consider are David Harvey's *The Conditions of Postmodernity* (1997) which describes the movement from modernity with its emphasis on rights and a teleology of progress to postmodernism with its flowering of fluidity, multiplicity, plurality; Michael Harris's *Colored Pictures: Race and Visual Representation* (2003) which examines black artists' responses to racist imagery, and Nell Painter, who makes the invisible and the universal perspective associated with whiteness in Western culture visible and specific by providing *A History of White People* (2010). Each author devotes visual space to the evolution of the pose called "the reclining nude." Scholars concerned with race-making, representation, and the transition from modernity to postmodernity all gravitate to images that are the precursors of and motivators for the posing of a (possibly dead) pig. Placing this (possibly dead) pig within the larger cultural tradition they analyze is important.

David Harvey's *The Conditions of Postmodernity* (1997)

In Chapter 3 of *The Condition of Postmodernity*, David Harvey takes a big risk. He chooses five images that feature naked women without alluding to that specific fact. He begins by introducing a chart by Hassan that identifies the "Schematic differences between modernism and postmodernism" (43). It as though postmodern binaries do and don't exist; binaries are a remnant of the modern project; but these schematic differences can't be freighted with meanings of essentialism or universalism. Here are a sample of the binaries he and Hassan identify:

Modernism	Postmodernism
Form	antiform (disjunctive, open)
Design	chance
Hierarchy	anarchy
Distance	participation
Centring	dispersal
Semantics	rhetoric
Signified	signifier
Metaphysics	irony

Race, sex, and species are not "schematic differences" for Hassan. After twelve pages of discussion of these binaries among other things—twelve pages in which gender is neither theorized nor examined—one turns the page and finds David Salle's *Tight as Houses* (1980). Salle's is the only image that is allowed to take up the space of an entire page. It is difficult to "read" in its detail—there is a sketch (written upon the negative of a photograph?) that is imposed over a photograph of

Figure 7.3 While David Harvey finds "the collision and superimposition of different ontological worlds" a major characteristic of postmodern art, it also characterizes anthropornography, the sexualizing and feminizing of animals and the animalizing of women. Animals in bondage, particularly farmed animals, are shown "free," free in the way that "beautiful" women have been depicted as "free"—posed as sexually available as though their only desire is for the viewer to want their bodies. In *Quality Meats Store Front*, a steakhouse has superimposed a cow's head upon Titian's *Venus d'Urbino*, "one of the first reclining nudes in Western art" according to Harris. Maybe the message is that these are not different ontological worlds. Note the dog in the lower right corner.

Quality Meats Store Front. Photograph by Anne Zaccardelli, 2013.

a woman's well-rounded naked body. It seems to illustrate Harvey's statement that "the deconstructionist impulse is to look inside one text for another, dissolve one text into another, or build one text into another." In Harvey's words, "the collision and superimposition of different ontological worlds is a major characteristic of postmodern art" (51). The image is the site of collisions, of building a text upon another text. That this text is a woman's body is both obvious and untheorized.

Four pages later, naked women begin to appear more frequently. Titian's *Venus d'Urbino* greets us with her unabashed stare and her hand coyly covering her pubic area. This *Venus*, "one of the first reclining nudes in Western art" and originally called by its owner "*la donna nuda*—the naked woman" (Harris 2003: 128) has generated many successors, including, as Harvey notes (twice!), Manet's *Olympia*. Turning the page, there she is, assured, brash even, her eyes meeting ours, her hand laying on top of her right leg and thus, also, obscuring her pubic area.

Across from *Olympia*, Rauschenberg's *Persimmon* stares at her viewers through a mirror. Harvey remarks that "Rauschenberg's pioneering postmodernist work *Persimmon* (1964), collages many themes including direct reproduction of Ruben's *Venus at her toilet.*" Juxtaposed with *Olympia*, *Persimmon* appears to rework Manet and Titian as well—what faces out now faces in, but the mirror restores the gaze. According to Robert Hughes's *The Shock of the New*, Rauschenberg "was fond of embedding an ironic lechery in his images" (335).

In *his* choice of images, Harvey appears to have had some fun evoking an ironic lechery. At the end of the chapter, a naked young woman stares at us from an advertisement for Citizen Watches. She recalls *Persimmon*, with her backside facing frontward in the advertisement, naked except for a watch. As I noted in my use of images in *Pornography of Meat*, watches are a primary vehicle for inscribing dominant attitudes (2003a/2015: 57). In postmodern times, advertisement strategies influence art and art influences advertisements—superimposing images and creating referentiality across their once discrete fields.

Harvey's decision to use paintings that represented women's bodies to illustrate the evolution of art into postmodernity seemed to backfire on him. After the first edition of his book was published, Harvey's genealogy of images quickly came under critique. Tellingly, feminists found acts of both commission and omission.

One of the commentators was D. Massey whose "Flexible Sexism" was a stunning critique of the implicit sexism in his analysis that ignored any insights from feminist theory and the explicit sexism in the illustrations in Chapter 3.

She writes:

> His commentaries ponder the superimposition of ontologically different worlds, or the difference between Manet and Rauschenberg, but they are oblivious to what is being represented, how it is being represented and from whose point of view, and the political effects of such representations. David Salle's "Tight as houses" is the most evident case of this where Harvey gives no indication that he has grasped the simple pun of the title and its clearly sexist content. Whose gaze is this painting painted from and for? Who could get the "joke"? The painting is treated with dead seriousness by Harvey, who cites Taylor (1987) on how it is a collage bringing together "incompatible source materials as an alternative to choosing between them" (Harvey 1997: 49). My own response, as someone who was potentially *in* that picture, and who saw it with completely different eyes, was: "here we go, another pretentious male artist who still thinks naked women are naughty. . . ." The painting assumes a complicit male viewer. (1991: 44–45)

In a note to the paperback edition, at the end of that chapter, Harvey responds to critiques such as Massey's. He seems stung by the criticism. He writes:

> The illustrations used in this chapter have been criticized by some feminists of a postmodern persuasion. They were deliberately chosen because they allowed comparison across the supposed pre-modern, modern, and postmodern divides. The classical Titian nude is actively reworked in Manet's modernist Olympia. . . . All of the illustrations make use of a woman's body to inscribe their particular message. The additional point I sought to make is that the subordination of women, one of many "troublesome contradictions" in bourgeois Enlightenment practices, can expect no particular relief by appeal to postmodernism. (1997: 65)

Harvey failed to recognize that using images that objectify women and empower the privileged position of the presumed male spectator require explicit response. He also chose to represent only the work of white men (though the creators of Citizens Watch are anonymous). Resistance required either comment or intentional juxtaposition with more liberatory images.

Michael Harris's *Colored Pictures: Race and Representation*

Michael Harris's *Colored Pictures: Race and Representation* makes up for Harvey's silence. He is alert to racial and sexual representation as he updates the genealogy of reclining nudes for the twentieth century. He also explicitly examines race as it is inflected in the genealogy. Harris observes that "even in black communities, black was a negative signifier." He points out that "blackness, unlike Jewishness or Irishness, is primarily visual." He elaborates on this visual and negating nature of blackness: "Racial discourses, although they are discourses of power, ultimately rely on the visual in the sense that the visible body must be used by those in power to represent nonvisual realities that differentiate insiders from outsiders" (2).

Toni Morrison's *Playing in the Dark* brilliantly illustrates Harris's insight about blackness as a negative signifier. She describes how, in conceptualizing ideas like freedom, nineteenth-century American whites needed the "unfree" black person to represent the "not-me." She writes, "It was not simply that this slave population had a distinctive color; it was that this color 'meant' something" (49). This leads Morrison to a discussion of the ending of *Huckleberry Finn*, in which Jim is not freed. She observes the "parasitical nature of white freedom."

Does Manet's *Olympia* betray this parasitical nature? A prostitute replaces Titian's *Venus*. In place of a white servant in Titian, Manet places an African woman behind the white woman, helping her. The white woman looks out of the painting toward the viewer; the African woman looks at the white woman.

Because of the way Manet brings race into his painting, Harris's commentary fills in the gap that Harvey's "no comment" methodology left unsaid. Harris carefully interprets the genealogy Harvey visually presented. What Harvey trusted his readers to do, Harris does not leave to chance—or interpretation. Moreover, he explicitly identifies the racial hegemony being inscribed. His chapter, "Jezebel, *Olympia*, and the Sexualized Woman," describes how "During the nineteenth century, the black female body in art had become a signifier of sexuality, among other things, as myths of black lasciviousness became entwined with other sexist ideas" (126).

The black servant is not just a signifier of sexuality, but also for disease, an association that had been "part of the essentialist stereotyping of nonwhite women" (126). Further, "In the nineteenth century, women of color were associated with nature, uncontrolled passion, and promiscuity" (126).

Let's note that *not* just in the nineteenth century have women of color been associated with nature, uncontrolled passion, and promiscuity, often by presenting them as wild, rather than domesticated animals. Annette Gordon-Reed reminds us that "The portrayal of black female sexuality as inherently degraded is a product of slavery and white supremacy, and it lives on as one of slavery's chief legacies and as one of white supremacy's continuing projects" (319).

In *Olympia*, Harris argues, "within the privileged space of the white male gaze is a layered black subject who is at once socially inferior to a naked prostitute, for whom she is a servant, and yet a sexual signifier and cipher; her mere presence is the equivalence of Olympia's nakedness" (126). She is the "not-me" of the painting; her imputed degraded sexuality suggesting a different kind of "not-free" status.

In his discussion of the female nude, Harris moves backward in time from Manet's *Olympia* to Titian's *Venus*. He finds three recurring aspects in this popular classical subject in Western art that I mentioned in the *Antennae* interview (Chapter 3): evidence of patriarchal structures; the assumption of the universality of the white male perspective; the appropriation of female bodies (126). Harris finds these three characteristics of Western art functioning in Titian's painting, and then, moving forward, exposes it in various art works of the nineteenth century. He identifies compositional strategies that emphasize the visual availability of the woman being depicted, specifically a vertical line that thrusts downward to the vaginal area. Harris points out that this vertical line highlights the genital area of the nude woman. In fact, the composition of Titian's and Manet's paintings also includes a horizontal line made by the arm of the woman. That line, too, moves toward the pubic area of the white woman. Here is the place where the vertical and the horizontal intersect. (It is reproduced with "Ursula Hamdress," too.

As for the way Titian and Manet portray their subject's eyes: "The fact that each woman meets the viewer's gaze suggests that both women are complicit and compliant in the sexual arrangements" (129).

Harris then turns to the ways colonialism/imperialism inflected the image of the sexually-consumable woman. He considers Jean Ingres's *Odalisque with a Slave,* and how it depicts "primitive sexuality" to be found outside Europe. Harris says, "All the painted harem nudes are available for visual consumption by the viewer—who is implicitly a European male" (130).

Linda Nochlin notes how paintings such as Ingres's "body forth two ideological assumptions about power: one about men's power over women; the other about white men's superiority to, hence justifiable control over, inferior, darker races" (quoted in Chadwick 1990: 199).

Regarding the odalisques, what you see is what you get: both visual and literal sexual consumption in the service of and confirming the imperialist practices of the West. Harris writes, "All the nudes as paintings were available as artifacts for ownership and private consumption by male patrons, a fact that rehearsed or reiterated colonial and imperial adventure and its appropriation of land, resources, and people" (130).

Harris's genealogy then claims a place for Paul Gauguin's *Spirit of the Dead Watching.* Harris sees this as an inverted *Olympia,* "the black attendant and the reclining woman [now on her stomach] have become one" (131). The reclining woman is a pubescent girl. She is younger, more demure, less frank in her gaze, and fully submissive. The white bedclothes echo Titian's painting.

Pablo Picasso's *Les Demoiselles d' Avignon* (1907) is the next painting in Harris's genealogy. White prostitutes are depicted with African-themed masks, and though the white women are holding various poses, most of them standing, their poses suggest reclining nudes. By placing African masklike faces on several prostitutes, Picasso, merged "the primitivized white female and the imagined libidinous black woman into one body" (131). Picasso's painting creates a black invisibility: "The mask forms insinuated a black presence yet subordinated it to the white females whose sexual consumption was linked to the colonial physical consumption of Africa" (131).

Harris's genealogy of the reclining nude ends with a photograph: "A South Sea Siesta in a Midwinter Concession" that was displayed at the California Midwinter International Exposition in 1894.[1] The non-Anglo woman is shown reclining on a mat—her breasts are uncovered, though her genital area is covered. "The photo shows the woman in a pose from a male-dominated discourse, but she gives no evidence of a willing compliance" (132). That was her power as a photographed subject: to refuse. The subjects of the paintings and the Citizen's Watch ad, if they exercised such control in their gaze, could not control the representation of their gaze.

But, what if a photographed subject has no power to refuse? What if the photographed subject is an other-than-human animal either sedated or dead? Her eyes will be closed, yet there is no resistance in this act.

Harris helps us place the genealogy of the reclining nude within the context of oppressive attitudes regarding sex and race, and how these intersected. From Harris we can see how juxtaposition and superimposition function not only as artistic strategies, but as ways that complicate and confirm oppressive situations.

---

[1] Harris believes the photograph was shown; I wonder if the woman wasn't on display there. As this event was an echo of and re-presentation of some of the exhibits of the Chicago World's Columbian Exposition, it would seem that they would have arranged to have people from nondominant cultures on display, as they did in Chicago. Thus, it could be a photograph of a woman in the exhibit that was at the California Exposition.

Nell Painter's *History of White People*

Intersectionality is always happening. It is happening with whiteness, too. It's just that whiteness, having been under-theorized for so long, often needs something else to put a spotlight on it. I will argue that when *Playboar* positioned a pink pig in the classic reclining nude pose, this became the "something else" that can turn a spotlight toward how whiteness is (and is not) functioning.

Nell Painter, in her *History of White People*, explores the ways in which whiteness came to signify power, prestige, and beauty. Though its staying power is remarkable (Roediger), whiteness was never monolithic in its granting of power and prestige. Whiteness, Painter reveals, also had a component of the "not-me" and the "not-free." She discerns two kinds of slavery in the anthropological work of eighteenth-century "science of race" scholars. Enslaved peoples whose bodies were forced to perform brute labor, including Africans and Tartars, were represented as ugly. But, luxury slaves also existed: they were "valued for sex and gendered as female" and became representations of human beauty. Painter describes how the term *odalisque* (and accompanying terms) carry with them "the aura of physical attractiveness, submission and sexual availability—in a word, femininity. She cannot be free, for her captive status and harem location lie at the core of her identity."

Painter examines the migration of the idea of "Caucasian" beauty, and how it spread across the English Channel into Britain; the uncontested fact was that beauty resided in the enslaved. Georgian, Circassian, and Caucasian were all interchangeable names, so that in 1864 when P. T. Barnum asked his European agent "to find 'a beautiful Circassian girl' or girls" to exhibit in his New York Museum, Painter says, "In the American context, a notion of racial purity had clearly gotten mixed up with physical beauty." But when they arrived,

Barnum's "Circassian slave girls" had the appearance of light-skinned Negroes as they all had "white skin and very frizzy hair." These white-skinned, frizzy-haired women offered a way to reconcile "conflicting American notions of beauty (that is, whiteness) and slavery (that is, Negro)" (51).

The science of race and the evolution of white slavery as a beauty ideal migrated into an attractive subject for male artists. As Painter describes, "By the nineteenth century, 'odalisques,' or white slave women, often appear young, naked, beautiful, and sexually available throughout European and American art" (43).

One cannot ignore Ingres if discussing odalisques, so like Harris, Painter turns to his paintings. Ingres's work "was a sort of soft pornography, a naked young woman fair game for fine art voyeurs." Painter notes that while the "odalisque still plays her role as the nude in art history," her part "in the scientific history of white race has largely been forgotten" (43).

Jean-Léon Gérôme's *Slave Market* also comes under review. In this painting, a young naked girl is being exhibited for sale. Her stance recalls (or prefigures) that of Picasso's prostitutes. Her pelvis tilts or rolls (suggesting submission as well as availability [see Adams 2003a/2015: 106]).

Painter notes the existence of slavery today, an issue that Nicolas Kristof and Sheryl WuDunn tackle in the first chapter of their book, "Emancipating Twenty-First Century Slaves." Their conservative estimate is that there are three million women and girls (and a small number of boys) who are enslaved in the sex trade (10).

Like Harvey and Harris, Painter finds a genealogy of images that carry forward into modernism. Two recent books, Edward Said's *Orientalism* and Anne McClintock's *Imperial Leather*, used white slave iconography on their book covers, though neither book dwelt on white slavery. Regarding this, Painter concludes, "Late twentieth-century

American scholars seemed unable to escape Gérôme or confront slavery that was not quintessentially black" (56).

What else is a negative signifier beside blackness? Animality. Who else in contemporary society is enslaved besides women, girls and an unknown number of boys? Other animals; the largest number being farmed animals. And so, whether we follow Harris, Harvey, or Painter, we arrive at "Ursula" and confront a slavery that is neither black nor human.

I created a chart to track the genealogy of the "Reclining Nude."

All of Harvey's examples are of white women. Harris demonstrates the presentation of the reclining nude and what happens when one watches for the way racial and gender attitudes are inscribed together, so that African women represented animality.

Painter considers a specific kind of presentation: that of white beauty as it was related to the enslavement of white women. I am looking for the way gender and race leap over the species line and become represented in a "reclining nude" that has a pig posed in a way similar to Titian's *Venus d'Urbino* and her successors. Harris notes "a fluidity between popular culture and fine art that gains momentum in the mid-nineteenth century and is taken for granted at the beginning of the twenty-first century" (11). *Playboar* fits the bill.

Harvey's, Harris's, and Painter's critiques are important, but the mistake of their critiques (though whether Harvey's "no comment" is a critique or not is open to debate), is to believe that there is any sort of (human-based) closure to this genealogy.

Critical theory that investigates traditional Western depictions of women's beauty, specifically "the reclining nude," and follows these depictions into the late twentieth century, has failed to recognize specifically how this tradition has lept/fled/transcended human-centered notions to reinscribe retrograde and oppressive attitudes toward women and domesticated animals. My argument is that

Table 5 Genealogy of the "Reclining Nude" and cultural commentary on gender, race, and species

	Harvey	Harris	Painter	Adams
Salle's *Tight as Houses*	×(photo with etchings)			
Titian's *Venus*	×	×		×
Manet's *Olympia*	×	×		×
Ingres's *Odalisque*		× *with a slave* (1840)	× *Grand* (1819) × *Le Bain Turc* (1862)	×
Powers's *The Greek Slave*			× (sculpture)	
Gérôme's *Slave Market*			×	×
Gauguin's *Spirit of the Dead*		×		×
Picasso's *Les Demoiselles*		×		
South Sea Siesta		× (photo)		
Matisse's *Odalisque*			×	
Rauschenberg's *Persimmon*	×			
Citizen Watch	× (photo)			
Ursula/Taffy				× (photo)

any of these critical theorists who think that tracing this genealogy can succeed when it is looking only at depictions of homo sapiens, especially female homo sapiens, has missed an interesting and important aspect of the genealogy. This aspect reveals how delving past the species line in representation of female "beauty," or sexualized female bodies, exposes the structuring of consumption of not just women, but domesticated animals. It is normalizing and naturalizing this consumption because it has fled the human without discarding representational aspects of race, sex, and class. Nonanthropocentric cultural theory will acknowledge how the sexualizing and feminizing of bodies intensifies oppressions on all sides of the species boundary.

The function of animalizing and racializing: That's why a pig

The way in which "Ursula," a pig, is substituted for the woman reveals how overlapping absent referents that animalize, sexualize, racialize, and figure "youthfulness" interact.

In both Titian's and Manet's paintings we can find an animalizing function that exists parallel to the white woman at the center of the canvas: a little dog at Venus's feet in Titian, the African woman servant *and* a black cat in Manet.

When *Playboar* intervenes into this genealogy and places a female pig smack dab in the center of its staged photograph, the animalizing function has moved from margin to center. The animalizing and sexualizing functions which are separate in Titian's and Manet's paintings are united in one being.

With Harris and Painter providing foundational insights, we notice what we might not have noticed at first when we consider "Ursula": "Ursula" is marked as white. The white slave, the odalisque, available for sexual consumption has become the "white" enslaved female, available for literal consumption.

Once we notice how the pig's pink skin recalls white slavery, we realize why the pig's "racial" characteristics matter. Her whiteness is an anthropocentric anchor. As I discuss in *The Pornography of Meat*, if it were a "colored" pig (and after all, pigs can be many different colors), the nondominant associations (gender, species, *and* race) would have been so great, there would be no anthropocentric hook. Because of the race hierarchy that still is inscribed so strongly in Western culture, a white pig was needed, so that the degradation being represented could be as strongly conveyed as possible (i.e., the whiteness associated with the pig, which normally would have provided a racial elevation, is contained/overwhelmed by the female, animal, and enslavement associations). In addition, a "colored" pig would not have evoked the tradition of the *odalisque* and its figuration of whiteness. When we consider "Ursula Hamdress"—this popular culture manifestation of misogyny and objectification—we cannot ignore the racist figuring of white beauty that it is also drawing on while perverting it. The key here is that white beauty has a history tied to enslavement as well.

Harris's genealogy culminates in a photograph as does mine; his, the "siesta-taker," mine, "Ursula." Harris writes that the photograph suggests "a willingness by the photographer to contribute to the existing tradition of artistic nudes. Though this tradition was largely absent from American art, the nudity of a primitive nonwhite woman was more acceptable than that of a white woman" (132).

Why? Why was it more acceptable to photograph a primitive nonwhite woman? Harris suggests it is because it "offers a stage to play out white moral superiority." Visual consumption also provided distance from—yet enjoyment of—this dangerous, erotic-laden woman.

So, too, with a pig. The moral superiority is that of the human male; the visual consumption is of whiteness and (a farcical) "beauty;" the photograph offers the same distance and yet enjoyment of this very familiar, but now erotic-laden pig. And so the tradition moves whiteness to the nonhuman. With "Ursula," the photographer and all those who contributed to the creation and execution of the photograph express cynicism, while achieving detachment *and* enjoyment.

"Ursula Hamdress" is probably one of the founding images of anthropornography. Anthropornography is a neologism coined by Amie Hamlin and introduced in *The Pornography of Meat* to identify the specific sexualizing and feminizing of animals, especially domesticated animals consumed as food. Animals in bondage, particularly farmed animals, are shown "free," free in the way that "beautiful" women have been depicted as "free"—posed as sexually available as though their only desire is for the viewer to want their bodies (especially when such freedom was a lie). They become the "not-free free." *Playboar* puts a face on meat eating that encapsulates a heinous, deeply offensive history of enslavement, misogyny, and racism. Anthropornography opens another avenue for these freighted meanings and images to be disseminated in and through popular culture.

Harris concludes his examination of the reclining nude as presented by artists representing the dominant culture with a discussion of voyeurism. He draws on the work of David Lubin who argues that "gazing at women voyeuristically is a means by which men may experience, re-experience or experience in fantasy their virility and all the potency and social worth that implies. Voyeurism by any definition, suggests detachment, estrangement, viewing from a distance" (134).

Harris extends Lubin's insight: "Voyeuristic engagement with the black/primitive woman safely separates the viewer from her dangers and reinforces his position within acceptable boundaries. He is white and gazes at the spectacle and danger of nonwhiteness, and he has the option of making real but disaffected forays into this realm as an exercise of his male prerogatives and power. Using the nonwhite female body as a spectacle . . . offers a stage to play out white moral superiority because the exotic woman is a sign of the wanton sexual danger that white society has mastered" (134).

Which brings us back to the National Pork Producers meeting in Des Moines and the excited buzz around looking at "Ursula."

What was to be gained by the voyeuristic experience of encountering "Ursula"?

Several things:

The cues that the largely-male attendees were encountering were of a pornographed pig, so that in public they could do what, generally, with pornography, one did in private.

They would recognize that this pig had not endured life in one of their factory farms. So, for them the depiction of "Ursula" feeds on humor of the dominant culture about the one who "escapes." They would have possessed the cynical knowledge about how few pigs actually would have such unbruised skin as she did.

With "Ursula," there is the voyeurism not of the nonwhite (human) female body, but of the (ostensibly) white (nonhuman) female body.

"Ursula" would have been the real "pork producer;" her reproductive labor the necessary slavery for future piglets.

The human male exceptionalism that benefits from the positioning of Ursula/Taffy was further reinforced because *Playboar* was for sale at a public event (the National Pork Producers Council), and the participants could take the publication home and introduce it to their private space. The privileged male consumer knew that he was never going to be the enslaved consumed.

Harvey suggests that women's objectification is not resolved by postmodernism. The past forty years have also been a time in which meat eating has been regressively associated with masculinity.

 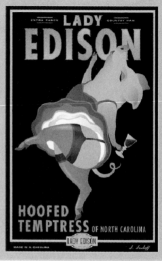

Figures 7.4 and 7.5   Ursula's "Daughters": the debased lifted up, the captive set free, the dead is alive, the female animal as sexualized being. Are they the new odalisques? Nell Painter showed how the term carried "the aura of physical attractiveness, submission and sexual availability—in a word, femininity. She cannot be free, for her captive status and harem location lie at the core of her identity." But for these images of pigs, their death *after* captivity and fate as BBQ lie at the heart of their sexualized identity. First captive, then dead, and *then* her new status as full-bodied female wanting to be consumed. The pig's nakedness is not represented; it might call attention to her pigness. The pig's flesh must be pink or else a racialized pig would call attention to her animalness. The story being told for voyeuristic consumption is not of a dead pig, but a sexually consumable plus-sized white female.

Best Butts. Photograph by Matthew Jeanes, Georgia, 2004.

The postmodern representation might or might not resist complicity with the three points of Harris's recognized oppressive framework (patriarchal attitudes, white male as normative viewer, appropriation of female body) though Harvey clearly indicates that he did not believe it did resist this, nor was the postmodern intervention going to provide any particular relief. However, anthropornography does not resist it; it is not only complicit in this oppressive approach toward representing women, it simultaneously hides and celebrates its complicity, simultaneously makes fun of itself and never truly resists the figuration—consumption it seems to say is consumption and the "carnivorous virility" (Derrida) that constitutes the Western subject is okay by them.

This is the status quo reinscribed: this is the status quo not just reinscribed, but extended, compelled to sink, compelled to register the lowering that "carnivorous virility" is causing, this doubled interactive lowering, and "carnivorousness" is at the heart of it. The message made explicit: "This being is consumable." Just who *this* being is is fudged slightly, fudged to delight the virile carnivorous viewer.

Perhaps no area of representation intersects race, sex, and species as much as barbecue images. In *Making Whiteness*, Grace Elizabeth Hale argues that the "New South" of the early twentieth constructed whiteness (and its enforcer Jim Crow laws) as an identity in response to the success of the Black middle class. Her work, like that of Harris and Painter, is concerned with racial making. Barbecues that use images of full-bodied white female sexual beings are a strange legacy of this constructed whiteness. With the images that advertise barbecues, what you see is what you get—visual and literal consumption of the full-bodied female body. They are "Ursula's" daughters and they share her fate.

Massey—who tackled Harvey's lack of critical consciousness— observes: "It is now a well-established argument from feminists but not only from feminists, that modernism both privileged vision over the other senses and established a way of seeing from the point of view of an authoritative, privileged, and male, position" (45). Massey continues: "The privileging of vision impoverishes us through deprivation of other forms of sensory perception." She then quotes Irigaray, "'In our culture, the predominance of the look over smell, taste, touch, hearing, has brought about an impoverishment of bodily relations . . . the moment the look dominates, the body loses its materiality' " (46).

Massey suggests something more is going on: "more important from the point of view of the argument here, the reasons for the privileging of vision is precisely its supposed detachment."

This is what the posing and photographing of Ursula finally achieves—detachment from a body for whom materiality was everything but emptied of all meaning, a body whose role was to grow bodies for consumption and then be consumed itself.

Harris too, recognizes the implications for his genealogy of the voyeurism of the viewer: the act of looking becomes "the equivalence of sexual action; he is able to give the nude woman an ocular caress" (129).

After those pork producers looked at and laughed about "Ursula," after the ocular caress, they went home and returned to pigs whom they could touch, artificially impregnate, kill, and consume.

Lindgren Johnson is a lecturer of English at the University of Virginia and the author of *Race Matters, Animal Matters: Fugitive Humanism in African America, 1838–1934* (forthcoming, Routledge).

Susan L. Thomas is an associate professor of gender and women's studies and political science at Hollins University. She is grateful to Carol J. Adams for making this interview possible.

8

The Critical Animal Studies *interview with Susan Thomas and Lindgren Johnson*

Lindgren Johnson and Susan Thomas: In your famous theorization of the absent referent in *The Sexual Politics of Meat* you discuss the various ways that western, patriarchal culture elides violence against animals. Nonetheless, you illustrate how there remains a tacit cultural acknowledgment, despite these elisions, of the pervasive violence that defines our relations with animals: that violence is the very means by which animal metaphors resonate and can help to express the *human* experience of violence, for instance.

Surprisingly, in recent protests of Chick-fil-A president's anti-gay marriage platform there seems to be very little acknowledgment, tacit or tactical, of the company's violence against the animals upon whom it depends and profits. While abstinence from meat is a medium of resistance in these protests it only amounts to boycotting Chick-fil-A and its signature "product" as a way to

The *Critical Animal Studies* Interview by Lindgren Johnson and Susan Thomas was first published in *Critical Animal Studies*, vol. 11, no. 1 (2013): 108–32.

Note: I have shortened a couple of answers when they covered material previously discussed in this *Reader.*

support gay and lesbian rights. The violence inherent in slaughter has not even been "used" as the means by which to articulate violence against gays and lesbians. Alongside this boycott, the other crucial element of the general protest has been public displays of love in the form of "kiss-ins" staged in front of Chick-fil-As across the country. It is, ironically, in the profession and display of human love that animals and their abuse get lost.

What are the dangers of human love, even love that consciously resists patriarchy (and heteronormativity), in the animal justice movement? Do these protests present a new articulation of the intersection of meat and sexuality that you explore in *SPM*, or is this a different iteration of the same thing?

This is a complex and thoughtful question. One of the images I saw from the time of the "kiss-in" was someone dressed as a cow with a sign that said: "Eat Hate-Free Chikin." That to me is an oxymoron—to eat the dead bodies of these animals who have been so badly treated in life and death is to participate in a hateful action; but because of the structure of the absent referent, individuals do not see their consumption of dead chickens as problematic.

Human love that consciously resists patriarchy is a love that would be vegan. My friend Dan Spencer, the author of *Gay and Gaia: Ethics, Ecology, and the Erotic*, writes that "the erotic energy that most deeply connects us with others can point to a deeper ecological connection with all of creation." He argues that "ecological ethics must become the grounding for all ethics, whether business ethics, biomedical ethics, sexual ethics, or international ethics" (1996: 9). This embodied love would involve a consciousness of the impact of our material practices on the earth, subordinated peoples, and all creatures.

But, building an activist community that is responsive to inter-connected oppressions is challenging and time-consuming, and the "kiss-in" illustrates the kinds of work that remain to be done. In answering your question I'll look at the issues of the sexual politics of meat that are implicit to Chick-fil-A, and which attached themselves to challenges to a heteronormative view of animals, and then at the issues for activism that is in solidarity with other oppressed groups.

Let's begin by saying what we know about Chick-fil-A. It was started in 1946, just as the United States was going in to what I have called "the fourth stage of meat eating" (meat from dead animals kept in industrial farming situations). Its base is the south, and its biggest growth is in the suburbs of southern cities. Its owner is a Southern Baptist.

Chick-fil-A's featured product is the dead bodies of chickens. Certainly, the chickens are absent referents whose deaths enable not only the consumption of their dead body parts, but the existence of the restaurant chain, and of the wealth of the Cathy family, which enables their "charitable arm," the Winshape Foundation, to support causes close to their Southern Baptist hearts like opposing marriage equality and promoting the wrongly labeled and harmful "ex-gay" therapy.

Perhaps we might also explore whether the argument that legalizing gay marriages doesn't destroy heterosexual marriage is accurate. The idea of a gay marriage that is between equals *does* challenge a heterosexual marriage based on inequality; it offers the idea that two subjects can be in relationship. Heterosexual marriages in which women are objects of consumption and not equal, that is an aspect of the sexual politics of meat. I still think that Andrea Dworkin's analysis in *Right Wing Women* is underappreciated. She wrote that right-wing women recognize the same issue as feminists (especially violence against women); they just have a different solution (marriage to a man who will ostensibly protect her).

Chick-fil-A sprang to greater attention when The Richards Group in 1995 created an advertising campaign around the idea that cows would, out of self-interest, encourage human consumers to "Eat Mor Chiken." The cows' inability to correctly spell words implicitly reinforced human superiority. (Even if cows could spell, they would not be able to spell correctly.)

Chick-fil-A discontinued its ad campaign at the height of the scare over "mad cow disease" a time when meat eaters reduced their consumption of meat from dead cows and began eating more dead chickens. The absent referent was made too present because of the cultural anxiety about what cows were eating; Chick-Fil-A apparently didn't want to appear to be taking advantage of that crisis. Their goal was never to disturb complacency about meat eating.

The "Eat Mor Chikin" campaign also encourages the idea that "horizontal hostility" (disagreements and arguments among disenfranchised groups) is funny. So it helps to feed the viewer's privilege in many ways. The irony is not lost on me that the "kiss-in" and the conflicted emotions this created—how to support gay marriage without supporting the eating of dead chickens—could have created an instance of horizontal hostility among social justice groups. The result is fragmented justice movements.

Chick-fil-A exemplifies some of the basic aspects of the sexual politics of meat. It often inflects gender in its advertising: Depicting a cow wearing a chicken mask holding a sign saying "Wanna a Piece of Me?" (p. 86); the "It's a Grill" Campaign featuring the color pink, and on the day of its kick off involved handing out pink balloons and cigars (p. 264). Chickens are never seen as in possession of their own body parts (their bodies reduced to and labeled "nuggets," "strips" etc.). Moreover, one of the machines that cuts up chickens' dead bodies is called the "Triple X-Stream Stripper" and is advertised through the metonymic association it presents with a woman's body (p. 264).

Figure 8.1 Eric Reinders, *Moo.*

Figures 8.2 and 8.3

It's a Grill. Photograph by Carol J. Adams, Dallas, Texas.
X-stream Stripper advertisement.

The chicken's body is eviscerated literally and conceptually. As a product of violence, it exists within a patriarchal ethical system, that the (violent) means justify the (consumer's) ends (see Davis 1996/2009 and Potts 2012).

Another aspect of the sexual politics of meat that is functioning in all this are the gendered associations of meat. At this point, sociologists and anthropologists have been publishing academic papers for years that confirm my basic argument in Chapter 1 of *The Sexual Politics of Meat*: meat eating is associated with manliness.

The sexual politics of meat includes the idea that healthy heterosexual men want and need to eat meat. Since *The Sexual Politics of Meat* was published, I have noticed that many popular culture appeals to men (especially white, heterosexual men), seem to be rebuilding what feminism and veganism have threatened. In terms of *The Sexual Politics of Meat*, we see several recuperative responses that seek to reinstate manhood, meat eating, and both interactively. Veganism is burdened by sexual politics, namely, the short lived coining of the term "hegan" for male vegans, in order to establish that "real men eat veggies."

Some advertisements show men "patrolling" other men for "effeminate behavior" (Kentucky Fried Chicken and Slim Jim among others have shown men ostracizing other men if they appear to be failing to conform to established heterosexual male norms.)

Heterosexual politics are embedded in other ways, too. Meat ads often articulate the assumption that a woman is available as an orifice for men. Recent examples have exploited homophobia in their formulation: that refusing meat raises questions about one's masculinity *and* sexuality. Or, that refusing meat answers the question about one's sexuality: you're gay. Recent examples of this basic formulation range from a German ad campaign that was proposed (but not pursued) that "tofu is gay meat" to "Gayboy" a vegetarian sandwich on a menu at a Brooklyn deli.

In his "A Queer Vegan Manifesto," Rasmus Rahbek Simonsen also discusses this point, "historically, deviating from eating meat has carefully been tied to the discursive production of masculinity—and not simply in terms of aberration or one's momentary preference for a certain food object—vegetarianism (and more apposite to my essay, veganism) comes to constitute a set of gendered acts that are linked to the whole of what signifies as male (and female), which certainly includes sexuality. . . . As a man, in this manner, refusing to partake in the proscribed consumption of meat disrupts the discourse on male sexuality and gender. In the way that different food items carry specifically gendered connotations (i.e. meat: masculine), we see how male vegans become a problem within heterosexual discourse" (2012: 52, 55).

What occurred in the summer of 2012 around boycotting Chick-fil-A and creating a "kiss-in" cannot be separated from the sexual politics of meat that enables and cushions establishments like Chick-fil-A. The issue of boycotting Chick-fil-A may have ended up vesting dead chickens as food with more patriarchal meaning, not less. I talked about advertisements that show the patrolling of male behavior which is seen as transgressive—eating vegetables or cooking with (or *like*) a woman is a synecdoche for someone who is refusing all forms of male privilege, including access to women. Last August, in Dallas, a policeman went to Chick-fil-A, bought someone to eat, and then ate her in front of two policewomen who were lesbians. That was the sexual politics of meat on so many levels.

I agree that not discussing the violence inherent in slaughter as the means by which to articulate violence against gays and lesbians was in general a missed opportunity, though I also understand why it was not fully addressed and some activists have raised this precise point. Jasmin Singer (2007), cofounder of *Our Hen House*, reported "Many people with whom I've spoken feel that having experienced oppression as a gay person makes them more likely to be compassionate toward animals." Singer's online magazine/website *Our Hen House* also did an interview with Nathan Runkle, the founder of Mercy for Animals, (and a victim of gay bashing) about his activism for animals as a gay man.

The failure to acknowledge the violence against animals in the production of food for Chick-fil-A is a reminder of the power of the structure of the absent referent of dead animals. It also points out the challenges of intersectional activism.

This was not a protest about the "product" of Chick-fil-A. In this it was unlike boycotts that say "your product is unethical"—like the grape boycott led by United Farm Workers in the 1960s, the Nestle infant formula product being dumped in Africa in the 1970s, and the non-fair trade chocolate and palm oil boycotts now.

Nor was it like other protests against companies whose owners support right-wing groups like Coors Beer, Carl's Jr., and Domino's Pizza. Once it was decided not only to boycott but to do the "kiss-in," then the issue became one of "space." The public displays of love in the form of "kiss-ins" staged in front of or inside Chick-fil-A's across the country changed the protest.

The "kiss" is an integral part of a marriage ceremony, so the "kiss-in" wasn't just normalizing what was being deemed as unnatural (gay love), but in a sense also sanctifying a space. They were simultaneously protesting and hallowing, saying "love can be found here."

I asked my friend, Sarah E. Brown, who blogs at http://queerveganfood.com/, what she had felt about the "kiss-in." She told me, "I was disappointed by the images that popped up on many social media outlets highlighting protest 'kiss-ins' that involved buying and eating the dead animal flesh from Chick-fil-A and posing next to it in mid-pucker, suggesting 'this meat is for us, too.'"

The message thus became: we kiss like you and love like you and *we eat like you.* But why wouldn't it be that message in a human exceptionalist culture? There are many reasons that the "kiss-ins" operated from within the framework of human exceptionalism; most social change movements do. You don't have to look far for stories from activists on their experiences trying to make connections among social justice causes: Hamburger fundraisers for rape crisis centers, or domestic violence shelters that accept "meat" from hunted animals, or an ad for "Take Your Daughter to Work Day" that highlighted the importance of the power lunch by saying "Mary Had a Little Lamb . . ." and showed a lunch consisting of dead lamb parts.

But the question, *How does one do activism from an intersectional perspective?* is a complex one, for which there is no one right answer. I felt it was important to bring in the voices of other activists to address this issue.

In discussing the challenges of getting social justice movements to stop promoting the eating of dead animals, one friend, Adrian Mellori reported to me, *I actually tried to confront this when a local lesbian was having an event at a place and was like "Be sure to buy the chicken sandwich! For everyone they sell a dollar goes to the HRC." I suggested calmly that people send the dollar directly to the HRC instead of allowing a business to profit from queer activism while also killing an animal to do so. As you can imagine, I was ostracized and laughed off the board.*

While intersectional theory has been expanding, we need to acknowledge that intersectional activism has many challenges inherent to it. Katie Carter who is with Feminist Agenda PDX—an online directory of feminist activism and networking in Portland, OR, wonders *how much and in what ways this kind of theoretical perspective can be practically implemented when it comes to more direct demonstrations of protesting oppression as in the case of Chick-fil-A "kiss-ins."*

Unquestionably, the issue of the violence inflicted on animals by Chick-fil-A as a company was completely ignored—but so were many other issues that intersect with issues of gay rights (e.g., the treatment of Chick-fil-A workers, the existence of giant chain restaurants and the impact they have on smaller, independent restaurants, the impact of chain restaurants on farming and natural resources, etc.). Theoretically, these issues are connected in important ways. But when it comes to practical implementation of these points, I think it becomes a lot harder to convey the connections. This is, in part, linked to the nature of protests—you have a very short amount of time to convey your message to people who are likely already somewhat hostile to you because of the fact that you are participating in a demonstration in the first place (based on the stigma attached to activists by many people). You also are very dependent on the media covering your protest and then accurately conveying your message, if you are to effectively reach a broader audience than those who might happen to be direct witnesses.

If the form of dissent against oppression that you are engaging in is a public protest, I think your demonstration of that issue has to be very direct and clear so that your message can be conveyed accurately. If there are too many messages coming across at once, the points of all the issues may be lost in the shuffle, which doesn't help anything. The connection between marriage equality and animal rights is not immediately apparent to most people, and the work that you would have to do to help people understand the connection would likely need to be more in-depth than could be conveyed at a visual protest like a "kiss-in." In my opinion, as activists we have to consider the practical effects of the means of protest we use—is this going to effectively convey our message and (hopefully) convince some people of the point we are going to make?

The question isn't just about *what is the message?* It is about how to create alliances. Adrian points out that it often hard to say, *"We all need to look at our shit. I contributed to the torture and death of nonhuman animals by shopping here in the first place, but didn't decide to make a move against them until my own life was at risk" while also saying "Chick-fil-A is a homophobic business."*

To acknowledge that Chick-fil-A is a homophobic business but not an animal abuse business removes personal responsibility from the activist. And often, oppressed groups have so much going on that it is difficult to imagine they also have shit to work on.

The best activism I have ever done, in my opinion, was being part of a white anti-racist organization in which we took 4 months first to look at ourselves, our own internalized white supremacy, and so on before attempting to go outward and fight racism and white supremacy around us. True activism involves evolving as people ourselves and stopping the oppressors that harm us and others. If we only attack them and do not look at ourselves, it is only part of the equation.

Katie picks up on this idea of how one builds solidarity for activism from an intersectional analysis:

A lot of alliance building would need to happen between these two movements that right now are relatively isolated from each other before a protest that engaged both of these issues would be effective. Having been a part of many protests in the past, it is often not appreciated by either side if one protest is "co-opted" by the agenda of another group— so in the interest of creating a more cohesive social justice movement it would be my opinion that a lot of work would have to be done ahead of time to enable these two groups to effectively engage in a protest that conveyed how their messages intersected, and weren't just two protests happening in parallel that had different agendas, messages, tactics, etc. I think we have a lot of work to do before the protests themselves to build a more cohesive movement in which we, as activists, understand one another, see the connections between our movements, and have discussed how best to work together to bring about a more just world.

I also invited comments from Erin Fairchild, an activist whom I met after she and other feminists staged a protest against PETA while they were in Portland following their hurtful and sexist "Save the Whales" campaign. *If I'd have participated in this protest, I might have made a sign that read "Animals and Humans Deserve to Live With Dignity and Respect," or "Homophobia and Factory Farmed Animals are Bad for Your Health." If I were leading with my heart, that's where I'd have gone. To Katie's points, however, I wonder if that message may have been too complicated or multi-layered for a direct action like the "kiss-in"? I also would not have expected my comrades in protest to agree with me, or feel called to this intersectionality. In other words, if I had participated in this protest, I would not have needed to know where others fell on the vegan to animal eating spectrum. Their political action has merit to me, regardless of individual views on animal rights.*

In fact, when we protested [PETA's "Save the Whales" campaign] the group of us protesting were banded together as feminists, in this instance focusing on the treatment of women (particularly fat women)—but we weren't all vegan identified, and some of the protesters were meat-eaters. We were asking PETA to offer women of all sizes ("women" within the socially constructed gender binary, "woman" as other to "man") the same level of dignity and respect that they hold for animals. In my mind, the objectification of women and animals, and subsequent violence against both, are absolutely connected and dependent upon each other. And, I don't need everyone I join in action with to share this perspective (unless, of course, we are deliberately taking on that intersection of violence in our activism).

I also believe that there's no "pure space" that any of us as feminists, activists or radicals can occupy that obscures us from the same critical lens through which we view oppressions like violence against women and animals. Liberation based consumer choices have, for example, become terribly difficult to make. I don't expect everyone I organize with to only purchase goods that were made with sustainable and equitable labor practices. I myself am not able to accomplish this—which does not make my lifetime commitment to violence prevention and trauma intervention less worthy. I can't be made immobile by the complex, interlocking system of oppressions that scaffold extreme capitalism.

I believe we should always ask questions, challenge ourselves to think deeper, to look for what we've missed and where we've fallen short. I also believe that upturning structural violence requires us to rely on unexpected allies, to be vulnerable in ways that are scary, and to search for the underlying good intentions of those who challenge us.

Many have argued that to acknowledge animal cruelty you must actually see animals in the process of being exploited. This visibility is the prerequisite change (hence the necessarily cloistered nature of slaughterhouses). Similarly, for an interview that you gave for *Satya* in 1995, you argue that because they insist on the visibility of the absent referent "vegetarians think more literally than others":

> **We are not seeing food; we're seeing a corpse, we're seeing dead animals. Because we think literally as well as metaphorically, our attempt to move the literal issue will arouse a certain degree of hostility and distress because our culture in general wants to move away from the literal. It wants to disengage.**

Recently, though, there seems to be a move *toward* the literal. Farmers' markets, for example, appeal to people because they can buy meat from a farmer who has had a personal relation with the killed animal, "knows where that meat came from," and can give the consumer that history. Similarly, upscale restaurants and even grocery stores (I'm thinking of the rise of salumerias, for example) advertise their food through the display of whole animal carcasses, allowing and profiting off carnivorist customers' ability to, quite

literally, "[see] a corpse," the very thing you say vegetarians "see."
The thinking here seems to be that if we make the entirety of the
(dead) animal visible, whether in the form of that animal's history
or that animal's body, then meat eating becomes more ethical,
pleasurable, and, of course, "respectful," a word that gets bandied
around a lot.

As long as the process is visible, these practices seem to say, it
is right. Can we assume, then, that heightened visibility of killing
and seeing the animal *as* animal is not the means to change? If so,
where do we go from here?

There is an aphorism that "if slaughterhouses had glass walls everyone
would be a vegetarian." But in fact, I don't believe that. As you indicate
later in the question, many people are aware of what is happening
to animals and still participate in eating them. I would argue that to
challenge animal cruelty, meat eating, dairy and egg consumption, it is
important to acknowledge the individuality of the animals. If people
look at animals as "mass terms" and not as individuals, then they still
may not care about what happens to them even if they learn about
animal cruelty. Also, some people get off on watching animal cruelty.

As I try to discuss in *The Sexual Politics of Meat Slide Show*,
the entire issue of how to transform a visual culture that inscribes
oppression through the visual is very complicated. So, first, there is
not a *similarly* here in what I am trying to discuss in that interview
about relationships between meat eaters and vegans and the idea of
watching animal cruelty. I actually don't think our retinas should
be burned with those images. The idea that "vegetarians [by which
I meant complete vegetarians or vegans] think more literally than
others" is that we know the literal facts about consumption and that
when we try to introduce these ideas into a conversation we will not
get the welcome we think we will get.

Figure 8.4 Dan Piraro, "Gelatin," *Bizarro.com*, 2016.

I expanded on this idea in my book *Living Among Meat Eaters* (which many vegans write to tell me they read yearly):

> Vegetarians have a tendency to speak literally; our culture avoids the literal. We say meat is muscle from a corpse or eggs are reproductive secretions. While literal thinking is important in understanding the world, especially when the issue is animal exploitation, literal thinking can also trip us up. As I point out in *The Sexual Politics of Meat* part of the battle of being heard as a vegetarian is being heard about literal matters in a society that favors symbolic thinking.

You are asked, "why are you a vegetarian?" And you say, "I just don't want to eat dead animals." Or, "I think of meat as an animal's corpse."

Suddenly, the nonvegetarians—thinking that they were engaging in nothing more than a pleasant "get to know you" question—find that the conversation has changed in intensity. By answering honestly about what you have learned about meat eating and dairy production/consumption—ostensibly factual information—you are prompting a connection in the nonvegetarian with something they have usually blocked out of their consciousness. Suddenly, somewhere in themselves, a part of them says, "Whoa! What's happening here? I don't want to hear this information! This makes me feel uncomfortable. Who is that person to make me feel uncomfortable? Oh, those emotional vegetarians."

Speaking literally is experienced emotionally.

You stated a literal truth or fact. It is experienced as an emotional statement because its content prompts feelings within the nonvegetarian. Feelings the nonvegetarian does not want to be aware of. You will very shortly thereafter be accused of being emotional. (Adams 2001/2009: 94)

I was trying to help vegans understand that when most meat eaters ask someone "why are you a vegan?" they don't really want to know the answer. In our tendency to be literal we believe in the sincerity of the interaction, when experience might suggest otherwise.

The locavore movement and other friendly slaughter assertions are *not* making *the entirety of the (dead) animal visible*. The animal's history is what is *not* available; it is not available to us to know exactly how she lived her life, nor how she experienced her death. What we have is the pretense and premise that sufficient information is available for us to conclude that eating her dead body is okay. It is all within a very anthropocentric setting about what is made visible.

What does it mean to say they see the animals *as* animal? Clearly, they see—they ontologize—the animal in question as an edible animal; unlike the way they might be ontologizing companion animals. The still hold an instrumentalized notion of the animal. In *Neither Man nor Beast*, I suggest, drawing on the work of Catharine MacKinnon, that the problem is more the epistemological stance that creates the knowledge/view that animals are edible, rather than the ontological status itself. The latter can be changed if we change the epistemological stance.

For many people, realizing that their "food" is from violence is sufficient knowledge to change their relationships with animals, for some people, that knowledge about violence is not sufficient.

One thing I think we can assume is that the visibility is a part of instantiating the sexual politics of meat. That the performative value of killing is working to communicate not just something about humans against domesticated animals but about gender.

The need to make "the kill" present through reference or in action is a hypermasculine reinscription of the sexual politics of meat. After the killing, the animal's dead body is probably referred to by words that objectify and fragment the body. So, if after the death, the animals are now known only through their body parts (wings, rack, breasts, hamburger, etc.), that is yet another aspect of the structure of the absent referent.

This trend that you are discussing, while getting a lot of attention, has not actually changed the number of animals being held in captivity. The majority of people are still getting their food from the animal industrial complex (*viz.* Chick-Fil-A). Moreover, many of the people who I have seen interviewed, while lifting up the oxymoron like "humane slaughter" and other considerations about the treatment of animals, continue to eat dead animals from the animal industrial complex when those "special treatment" animals aren't available to be consumed.[1]

The fetishistic attachment to the dead animal as food will always create or motivate the creating of that object (the dead animal) but that motivating act will cause anxiety and that anxiety will leak out and try to find new ways to insulate it from critique. These "Nouveau flesh eaters" are still eating meat from a dead body whose life had been emptied of meaning by the freedom to kill that being.

In *The Sexual Politics of Meat* I talk of the "nothingness of meat." I have often thought about what I am trying to say there. Because the animal who was alive was never "nothing," was always *someone* in relationship with other *someones*, but that another being, a human, can determine what happens to them in their lives and pick the time of their death, places them on the road to a "nothingness" that will be the site of fetishization.

Dead bodies deemed as edible become endowed with the quality of "edibleness." Lots of choices were available for what the dead body could become endowed with. It could have been aesthetic distaste or ethical refusal but out of all the options, it is this.

In "The War on Compassion," I wrote meat eaters bury animals in their own bodies. When nonhuman living beings are converted conceptually into false mass terms to enable their conversion into products, we come to believe that their deaths do not matter to themselves. Animals are killed because they are false mass terms, but they die as individuals. They die as a cow, not beef, as a pig, not pork.

---

[1]These paragraphs were shortened because they reprised the answer to Pott's question in Chapter 3 about celebrity chefs flaunting the killing of animals. In their celebration of butchering, the locavore movement, like the celebrity chefs, fetishize their killing of animals. As I try to show in Chapter 3, such fetishization, rather than refuting the structure of the absent referent participate in it (pp. 104–106).

Each suffers his or her own death, and this death matters a great deal to the one who is dying.

The instability of meat as a product (something in the process of decay that must be maintained as edible), seems to reproduce itself at the meaning level; it must constantly be rendered as not just edible but marketable, and this is the latest marketing approach.

In *Living Among Meat Eaters* I suggested that we should view people who still eat dead animals and their reproductive secretions as blocked vegans and that their actions and statements tell us what is blocking them. I am not saying they *are* blocked vegans, I am saying if we look at them in this way, what does it show us?

Your M.Div. is from Yale, and your approach to animal being is informed by Christianity and what you describe as a feminist care ethic, one that pays attention to and seeks to care for the vulnerabilities of the body. Yet popular culture seems to be swinging in the other direction, with the locavore movement and its promotion of the intimacy of slaughter gaining increasing popularity. More specifically, works by Temple Grandin and Michael Pollan, to name just a few, locate "spirituality" in intimate and "close" acts of killing. What do you make of this trend? How has animal slaughter become the ultimate expression of care, not violence?

Let's just clarify that when you say my approach to animal being is informed by Christianity that I am not comfortable with this characterization. I am dialogue in with Christianity, but my approach to animal being is compassion. I find the language and beliefs of Christianity as I understand them (not the dominant culture's understanding) helpful within a context where that matters.

Popular culture has *always* been in the other direction. The work for compassion is always uphill. That is what I was trying to say in my essay on "The War on Compassion."

The locavore movement's spiritualizing of the consumption of dead animals doesn't surprise me; it complies with basic parts of the sexual politics of meat. If we listed off all the oppressive things done in the name of spirituality we would have quite a tome! To see that yoga practitioners think being non-vegan is consistent with their yoga practice and beliefs, that Buddhists are able to integrate a diet that harms animals into their lives, that people who meditate leave their meditations and eat dead animals—well, the area of spirituality has always been chained by people's desire to continue to eat dead animals and egg and dairy.

Just because Pollan and Grandin assert that this is a spiritual act doesn't mean that it is a spiritual act. I notice how "sacrifice" gets spiritualized, but it is never *our* sacrifice that we are asked to consider or spiritualize, but someone else's. Spiritualizing of a situation often occurs to displace the political critique.

I think Vasile Stănescu has skewered Pollan on hunting; and of course Pollan's spiritualization of the hunt involves several aspects of the sexual politics of meat (male bonding over a slaughtered creature, the act of the hunt itself as constituting a fulfilling and important moment in male identity, etc.).

There is also the ripping off of and reductionism of certain Native American hunting practices that clearly enacts a form of cultural imperialism.

Animal slaughter is *not* the ultimate expression of care, it is merely claimed to be. I think it is a regressive expression of dominance. Out of all the choices they could make in describing it, why this one? What does it tell us?

It's a classic example of denial, reversal, false naming, and defensiveness: "an act is what I say it is." Such rhetoric is exploitative and false. In the feminist ethic-of-care tradition, killing of animals for food fails to do one important thing: ask the animals what they want and respect their answer.

In your recent work, *The Feminist Care Tradition in Animal Ethics,* you explain to the readers that there are several core principles that undergird the feminist ethic-of-care approach to animal ethics. One of these core principles is a person's "moral duty to oppose and expose those who are contributing to animal abuse" (4). Another contends that "human beings have a moral obligation to care for those animals who, for whatever reasons, are unable to adequately care for themselves. . . ." Do these principles you outline include direct action, which you have been reluctant to endorse, and which we would define as any explicitly public and political action (such as strikes, sit-ins, open rescues, and blockades) taken by an individual or a group to highlight a problem? More broadly speaking, what do you think constitutes "care"?

I have never been reluctant to endorse direct action. I have written prefaces to two books that include stories from women some of whom describe direct action (Kemmerer 2011a, b). For instance, I think Patty Mark's pioneering work with open rescues is remarkable, and I admire it. I *have* refused to endorse a certain form of direct action: picketing at homes. I have always clearly explained why I am opposed.

I know what it feels like to have your house targeted. Twice in my life I've had that happen. In the 1980s when my partner and I were involved in trying to bring integrated housing to a small city in upstate New York, our house was "egged." The anti-housing group, a racist group, picked the person who lived across from us as their president precisely so that they would have their meetings across the street from our house. They would gather early, stand outside, by their cars, just talking and talking and staring at our house, which had a large picture window in front. Then, as they left their meeting, they would do the same thing.

I remember one Saturday, bicycling back from a visit to one of the Black plaintiffs in the racism suit we had filed against the city, the U.S. Department of Housing and Urban Development (HUD), and the city's housing authority. (The Fair Housing law identified different classes of plaintiffs—for instance, middle class whites who were being deprived of the benefits of integration, and low income Blacks being deprived of decent housing.) She was a young woman and she was dying of lupus. But she had bravely added her name to the list of plaintiffs knowing that this would expose her to criticism and scrutiny. The day I bicycled back home, I felt so sad. She was in such pain, and so frail, and her kids were so little. I turned the corner onto my street and there were all the cars parked in front of our house. And the white men were coming out of the house, and staring at me.

Their goal was to scare and intimidate. That day, they succeeded.

We did not feel safe in our own home and that is a terrible feeling.

Elsewhere I have talked about traumatic knowledge (Adams 2003b). In her book, *The Gender of History*, Bonnie Smith used that term in describing how amateur history (the history associated with women) consists of "the writing of multiple traumas." She identifies the traumas that women historians of the early nineteenth century would have experienced: They were aware that their rights were eroding in the midst of a time when universal rights were being (supposedly) championed. They or family members had survived revolutions and wars, and at a personal level, had experienced the threat or actuality of rape, poverty, violence, abuse. Smith explains, "death, representing history's immanence, was always on hand" (Smith 1998: 21).

Traumatic knowledge is the knowledge of organized and/or persistent acts of violence. It is painful knowledge—knowledge about everyday practices and everyday sufferings. It feels relentless. It is a major challenge to any individual who experiences it and to any movement composed of individuals who bear its truths. It affects us personally, interpersonally, and strategically.

In my introduction to the new printing of Howard Williams' magnificent nineteenth-century historical survey of vegetarianism,

The Ethics of Diet, I applied Smith's idea of traumatic knowledge to the vegetarians who appear in Williams' volume (Adams 2003b: xviii). "The knowledge that other animals are being butchered to feed humans, even though other foods are available that require no such Butchery, is also a form of traumatic knowledge." For vegetarians, vegans, animal activists, traumatic experiences are re-encountered regularly. This adds to the trauma.

Cathy Caruth suggests that the traumatized "carry an impossible history within them, or they become themselves the symptom of a history that they cannot entirely possess" (1995: 5). Last October (2012), reflecting on activism and the law, as one of the keynoters at the Lewis and Clark twentieth Annual Animal Law Conference, I spoke publicly for the first time about those years in 1980s. I thought that given that I had now written about it (Chapter 2), I could speak about the experiences. But as though proving Caruth correct that we are symptoms of a history we cannot possess, I found myself crying in the midst of the talk as I remembered the experiences of those years.

Is targeting houses a way of spreading traumatic knowledge? We experience the traumatic knowledge of knowing what is happening to animals, so we decide we have the right to make other people feel traumatized because of their role in contributing to animal suffering. Not feeling safe in your home is a terrible feeling. I do not believe in furthering such an experience.

In the 1990s, in Dallas, where we now live, the church where my partner, Bruce, was one of the ministers, hosted a city-wide Planned Parenthood empowerment program for teens about how to say no. Over several years, Operation Rescue tried to get the church to stop hosting the event. They began by picketing the church will bull horns and very graphic signs; then they moved to interrupting a church service Bruce was leading, and then, the following year, they picketed our house.

This frightened our two young children. While we were busy talking to the police about the cadre of protestors outside—one of whom had come onto our property, battering our back door ferociously and all of whom were gathered in front of our house at that moment, with a bullhorn calling to us—unbeknownst to us, our two children were crouched behind a large chair. My older son, who was in elementary school, had grabbed his boy scout knife, to protect his three-year-old brother.

After the police left, we talked to the kids about what bullies were, compared Operation Rescue to bullies in elementary school, and we talked about abortion. I remember my older son asked if he could go tell the anti-abortionists that even rabbits abort.

Several weeks later, as my older son sat in his class, he suddenly felt like screaming, thinking about the protestors. During that time, my three-year-old scanned the environment—was Operation Rescue coming back?

This is why I am against direct action that targets home where children live. I do not find it theoretically or logistically justifiable. Nothing will convince me that picketing and targeting homes of vivisectors or others where kids live can be seen as legitimate. And what do the children learn? Their parents are probably explaining that those people outside are simply bullies.

I am curious to know how individuals in the animal justice movement decided this is the way to do it? What was the decision making process? Why would anyone want to participate in traumatizing children? Why would animal activists create traumatic experiences for others presuming that this is the way to end the originating trauma (what is happening to animals)?[2]

---

[2]Lori Gruen discusses home demos as part of her discussion of direct action in the first pages of her chapter on "Animal Protection," in *Ethics and Animals: An Introduction* (2011).

But I have a larger question, how we decide cause and effect in the animal justice movement and how we know what works, how do we measure success? How does one action (whatever that is) become the litmus test for activism? My question is how does the privilege granted to those who are dominant influences our actions, our methods and our campaigns? I discuss this in "After MacKinnon": Male militaristic language; we have to "rally" around leaders (some of whom have a history of sexual harassment), the methodologies of confrontation, claims that we are at war, that says we must, must, must, watch gory videos ("the animals experience this, the least we can do is watch this"). Who says? For instance, who decided street harassment of fur-wearing women was the appropriate way to challenge the fur industry? It certainly seamlessly mapped onto sexual harassment of women on the street and helped to sustain the experience that the public space is not the same for women as for men.

How do we come to believe any of these are the best methodologies for change and how do we know they are successful methodologies for change? Why is this the model we have to accept? Who has decided this is the way? I know that the idea of teaching people how to eat vegan is seen as a privatized solution—and yet every person who learns to trust that they can cook vegan and that vegan tastes good, is one less person we have to change. I know that the meat boycott of the early 1970s wasn't about animal justice issues, it was about prices, but it still had the effect that slaughterhouses had to stop slaughtering as many animals. I don't want to participate in this notion that "these kinds of actions have effects and those kinds don't." I think we don't know.

In an interview with ARZone in 2010, I said, "If the animal rights movement was stripped of its male rights language, its mainly male leaders and the sexist approach of some of the promotional material, what would we have? We would have to acknowledge that it is largely a movement of women who care about animals. Being a part of a movement that is overwhelmingly female identified is often not seen as positive. So I have always felt that the animal rights movement compensates for its basic female identification by lifting up "fathers" (Singer, Regan, Francione, etc.), but situating these fathers to debate each other, and by making sure that most of the spokespeople are men. When you add PETA and others sexist ads, you find a movement that is trying to talk to men about some of the objects in their lives."[3] What is wrong is the compensatory behavior that deflects attention from analyzing and acknowledging this.

I think Susan Fraiman's point about the hyper-rational writings of some in the field of critical animals studies raises some interesting questions that relate to the point I was trying to make (2012).

My definition of care is based on the writings of Simone Weil. She famously defined "attention." She wrote, all that our neighbors require of us is that we ask, "what are you going through?" and that we are willing and able to hear the answer. In the introduction to *The Feminist Care Tradition in Animal Ethics: A Reader*, Josephine Donovan and I identified several core principles:

1   It is wrong to harm sentient creatures unless overriding good will result *for them.*

2   It is wrong to kill such creatures unless in immediate self-defense of oneself or in defense of those for whom one is personally responsible.

3   Humans have a moral obligation to care for those animals who, for whatever reason, are unable to adequately care for themselves, in accordance with their needs and wishes, as best the caregivers can ascertain them and within the limits of caregivers' own capacities.

4   Finally, people have a moral duty to oppose and expose those who are contributing to animal abuse. (2007: 4)

---

[3]http://arzone.ning.com/profiles/blogs/carol-j-adams-live-chat.

Figures 9.1 and 9.2 When I was in my first year at Yale Divinity School, I participated in a march seeking to legalize abortion in Connecticut. I'm holding the left-side of the banner. In 1990, the first March on Washington for the Animals was held. Among the women holding this impressive banner in front of the Capitol are Batya Bauman (with hat), to her left, CJA with baby Benjamin, and to my left, the late Marti Kheel.

Abortion March. Photograph by David Moore, New Haven, Connecticut, October 1972. From *The Yale Daily News,* January 23, 1973. Copyright *Yale Daily News* Publishing Company, Inc. All rights reserved. Reprinted with Permission.

March on Washington. Photograph by Bruce A. Buchanan, Washington, D.C., 1990.

9

Abortion and animals: Keeping women in the equation (1998)

What does abortion have to do with animal defense? Nothing.

Nothing. The only proper context for discussing abortion is within the context of women's lives. There is no analogous moral situation to that of a woman who is carrying a fetus within her. Attempts to establish analogous situations will always be unsuccessful. There is no preexisting paradigm into which the question of abortion fits, because there is nothing equivalent to pregnancy.

A clear difference exists between human fetuses and nonhuman animals who have already been born. The fetus, as defined by German abortion rights activist Susanne von Paczensky, is "a human being to be created and grown by a woman if she chooses to do so"[1] (Paczensky 1990: 183). This definition clearly establishes the

---

[1]Paczensky is, I think, staking out the affirmative definition of pregnancy, a feminist ideal at the moment. Unfortunately, at this time, pregnancy requires no specific decision to continue once fertilization has occurred.

primacy of the pregnant woman in making the decision about the fetus. This does not render the fetus as a physical appendage, but situates the fetus within the context of a woman's life, growing within her body—and up until sometime in the weeks after the twentieth week—unable to grow anywhere else. A fetus's dependency upon the pregnant woman is not at all similar to the situation of the other animals, once born.

Yet there is much confusion about this. Although abortion has nothing to do with animal advocacy, the anti-abortion movement has shaped the debate so that we find ourselves succumbing to a certain logic of incrementalism, which goes something like this: If we care about sentient life, and the fetus is sentient life, then we need to care about what happens to the fetus. In addition, we fear that if we don't articulate an anti-abortion position, we will confirm in people's minds that as animal advocates we are anti-people. Antiabortionists contribute to this by asking, often with great hostility: "if you are for animals why aren't you for the unborn?"

This reasoning—"if animals, why not (some human cause)?"—is a basic formula in the arsenal of defenses of animal exploiters. Animals' lives are made secondary by being subsumed within a human-centered framework. We can only be seen as credible by asserting what we are doing to address some human-centered problem. But human-centeredness is precisely what we are challenging. The question about where animal advocates stand on abortion is often a way of denying legitimacy to animal advocacy on its own terms. People do not want to confront the violence that is constitutive of their lives, in the form of habituated meat eating, among others things. It is simpler to deflect the focus back to us, to transfer the defensiveness to the pro-animal movement.

Challenging humancenteredness

Most anti-abortion advocates are offended by the animal defense movement because we are the ultimate challenge to their extreme human-centeredness. They have a definition of life that is so broad it encompasses a newly fertilized egg, yet it is so narrow that it does not consider grown animals with well-developed nervous systems and social sensibilities. Then in the face of their absolute view of the human fetus, we relativize the human species within a worldview that respects other animals and the rest of nature.

Eliminate the human/animal dualism that assumes a radical difference between humans and all other animals and the moral claims of antiabortionists—that human fetal life has an absolute claim upon us—is overthrown. Instead, human fetal life is placed in a new context: legitimate concern for the rest of nature.

The decision to limit the number of human births is a decision for life, for the life of the global community. Each human birth from a developed country has an immense impact on animals and the rest of nature. Given this view it becomes more difficult to argue that every human fetus is equally or more important than the earth and its creatures.

It is seductive to see a progression from being for the animals to being for the unborn humans. I can understand its pull. But that progression often occurs because fetuses are presented to us as though they are miniature replicas of you and me, tiny humans floating in space and not dependent on a woman's body for sustenance. The logic of advocacy for the unborn arises only because the presence of the pregnant woman herself has been erased.

The battle over abortion isn't actually about sentience since close to 90 percent of abortions are performed in the first trimester. A twelve-week fetus has muscle reflexes but no developed nerve cell pathways in the brain's cortex that would enable it to experience pain. One pediatric neurologist observes, "Pain implies cognition. There is no brain to receive the information" (quoted in Kleiman 1985: 11). In 1984, the American College of Obstetricians and Gynecologists issued a statement on the pain of the fetus, which reads in part: "We know of no legitimate scientific information that supports the statement that a fetus experiences pain early in pregnancy. We do know that the cerebellum attains its final configuration in the seventh month and that myelinization (or covering) of the spinal cord and the brain begins between the twentieth and fortieth weeks of pregnancy. These, as well as other neurological developments, would have to be in place for the fetus to perceive pain" (quoted in Kleiman 1985: 11). Establishing that human's intrauterine brains cannot register information about pain in no way undercuts claims on behalf of the other animals' extrauterine brains to register pain.

Abortion within the context of women's decisions about their fertile years

Abortion in the first trimester is nine times safer than pregnancy. Legal abortion can save women's lives; before 1973, more than 5,000 U.S. women died and tens of thousands of others were seriously injured *each year* as a result of illegal abortions. Between 1973 and 1993 more than 300,000 women around the world have died *each year* as a result of illegal abortions. Women's lives are at stake when abortion is criminalized

It is estimated that worldwide, each woman experiences two unwanted pregnancies in her lifetime. Of the women under 45 in the United States, nearly half will have had abortions. Women we trust have confronted the problem of an unwanted pregnancy and made the decision to abort. Women who have worked ardently against abortion, upon discovering they are pregnant, have made the decision to abort. But most women who get abortions also keep quiet about it. Thus, an experience that is more widespread for women than getting a college diploma is wrapped in silence. In the cultural framing of the issue, just as the fetus is separated from the pregnant woman, the decision to abort is separated from a woman's entire life.

Abortion is discussed as if it were a discrete deed. But it should not be abstracted out of, nor is it irrelevant to, the way abortion arises in women's lives. Most women are fertile for about thirty years. This fertility, and what the woman wishes to do about it, is a part of her life plan. As ethicist Beverly Harrison argues, "From the standpoint of a woman's experience, a . . . basic . . . moral question operates: 'What am I to do about the procreative power that is mine by virtue of being born female?' The question of abortion arises only in this wider human context." Harrison argues that whatever intrinsic value is granted in the abortion debate, it must include granting intrinsic value to the well-being of a woman and the value of her life plan (1983: 9, 16).

Decisions about our procreative power are not made in an atmosphere of sexual understanding and support. Nor is it made in a culture where reliable birth control is available. Abortion and abstinence are the only forms of birth control that are 100 percent effective. Six out of 10 women having abortions do so because their contraception failed.

One cannot theorize from nonexistence

The animal advocacy movement actually helps us recognize a basic claim of the pro-choice movement: You can't hypothesize, much less regret, your own nonexistence. Animal exploiters protest, "Isn't it better that a cow was brought to life; was allowed to live, and then quickly dispatched, then never to have lived at all?" Their faulty assumption is that one can lament one's own nonexistence. But one cannot do that. A cow who never existed does not experience the deprivation of life, nor does an aborted fetus.

Many dedicated animal activists are strongly against abortion. I have talked with them across the country. I understand their vehemence; we can find no common ground on abortion. But I urge them to recognize how their activism is manipulated by an anti-abortion movement that cares nothing about animals. If you are against abortion, don't have one. Work on behalf of quality prenatal care for all pregnant women, as well as food, shelter, and health care for all children. Beware though of publicly announcing your position; by doing so you aid and abet the most vocal anti-abortion activists, a religious right wing determined to set back women's efforts at equality.

The question is not whether any one culture will have abortion or not; it will. The question is, what types of abortion will be available and for whom? Access to knowledge about abortion, and, if necessary, to a safe and legal abortion is one aspect of reproductive freedom. Reproductive freedom is central to women's freedom. Abortion is a woman's choice and should remain that. Let us resist confused logic that reduces it to something else.

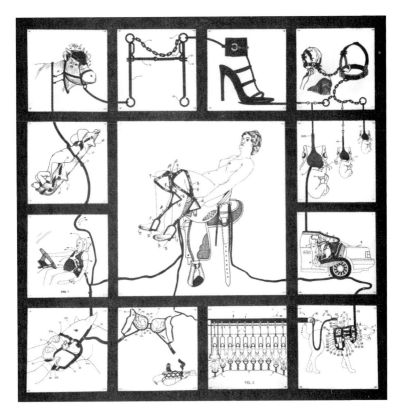

Figure 10.1 Artist's Statement: *Patent Pending* is an ongoing investigation of the female body (both human and non-human animal) as an object and target of patriarchal power. Patent inventions depicting various devices of restraint from the turn of the twentieth century through the present day are appropriated and digitally manipulated in order to critique the diverse modes of subjugation that occur at both the micro-level of individual bodies and at the macro-level of society. Devices of restraint such as dog collars, leashes, harnesses, ropes, and chains created to control the bodies of nonhuman animals, are not coincidentally used to discipline women's bodies as well in, "the bondage equipment of pornography," as Carol J. Adams has noted. Historical relationships between devices of animal restraint and women's fashion are also explored, such as Gucci's "horsebit" leather loafers, high heels, and jewelry, whose iconic gold and silver clasps are modeled after the mouth restraints used in horse riding.

L. A. Watson, *Patent Pending.* 35 in. × 35 in., installation of digital prints on Hahnemuhle paper, 2014.

10

After MacKinnon: Sexual inequality in the animal movement

"You become what you do not resist."

– CATHARINE MACKINNON

For the past thirty years, animal activists have challenged the interdependent nature of dominance and subordination vis-à-vis our relations with other species. At the same time, they have largely avoided the question of how the system of *human* dominance and *animal* subordination tracks, intersects with, and diverges from *men's* dominance and *women's* subordination. Despite the work of radical feminists to identify the linkages between the oppressions of women and animals, establishing the common patriarchal roots of both groups' subjugation, a feminist perspective has yet to be incorporated into the theory and practice of the mainstream animal movement. This is unfortunate, because sexual inequality is one of the defining elements of the animal movement, defining both the status of animals

"After MacKinnon: Sexual Inequality in the Animal Movement" was first published in *Animal Liberation and Critical Theory*, ed. John Sanbonmatsu (Lanham: Rowman & Littlefield, 2011), 257–76.

whose liberation is sought, and the status of the women within the movement who seek the liberation of animals.

As my title indicates, this essay was prompted by my reading and reflecting upon Catharine MacKinnon's "Of Mice and Men," and as a result by my sense that, because of the way the animal movement is structured, it could fail to hear MacKinnon's radical feminist insights in any substantive way that would induce it to change its tactics and approaches. Metaphorically, then, this essay might be considered a musical counterpoint, an exercise in contrapuntal themes, in which I focus on the interaction of MacKinnon's insights in that essay and her other writings with my own theories. My concern throughout is with both theory and activism. To understand why MacKinnon matters, or should matter, for movements to end the human oppression of other animals, we must first have an appreciation of her radical feminist critique both of male domination, and of *liberal* understandings of gender and sex.

The basic survival issues facing women arise because of sexual inequality: women experience the social reality of domination made into sex through rape, incest, pornography, sexual harassment, forced pregnancy, and captivity in the home. Patriarchy is a global system of systemic economic inequality; of sexual violence, intimidation, and killing by men,[1] and of the racializing of that

---

[1] At least once in their lives, 44 percent of women are victims of rape or attempted rape (MacKinnon 2005: 39). Women and children are considerably less safe in the home than are adult men. Battering is the major cause of injury to adult women. The World Health Organization, in the first comprehensive documentation of global violence released in October 2002, found that 40 to 70 percent of female murder victims in Australia, the United States, Canada, Israel and South Africa were killed by their husbands or boyfriends. Marital rape is among the most common kind of sexual assault there is. One in three American girls and one in seven boys are sexually abused. One-half of all rape victims are under eighteen years of age; 25 percent of rape victims are under twelve years of age. Woman battering is a major cause of homelessness for women and their children. At least 40 percent of homeless women became homeless after suffering abuse by male partners, and now face rape on the street rather than battering in the home (Golden 1992). Homeless women also face sexual harassment from landlords and building superintendents in seeking apartments. More than 90 percent of working women surveyed had been sexually harassed on the job.

sexual violence.[2] As such, sexual inequality affects *every* woman's life. As MacKinnon sums up the predicament of women in the United States and elsewhere, "women's situation is made up of unequal pay combined with allocation to disrespected work, sexual targeting for rape, domestic battering, sexual abuse as children, and systematic sexual harassment together with depersonalization, demeaned physical characteristics, use in denigrating entertainment, deprivation of reproductive control, and forced prostitution" (2005: 24).

For MacKinnon, sexual inequality therefore means that we can't take the "sex" out of sexism, because *gender reflects a systematic inequality of power, and sexuality is a form of its practice.* Sexuality is "a social construct of male power: defined by men, forced on women, and constitutive of the meaning of gender" (1989: 128). Thus, sexuality is predicated on the domination of women by men, and "this domination is sexual."

The liberal feminist critique, by contrast, holds that gender oppression can be uncoupled from sex: that the hierarchy of inequality has nothing to do with sexuality per se. This, however, only mystifies the material basis of inequality, which derives from men's sex right and

---

[2]Sexual inequality is racialized: "The combined influence of rape (or the threat of rape), domestic violence, and economic oppression is key to understanding the hidden motivations informing major social protest and migratory movements in Afro-American history" (Hine 1989: 913). "I believe that many Black women quit the South out of a desire to achieve personal autonomy and to escape both from sexual exploitation from inside and outside of their families and from the rape and threat of rape by white as well as Black males" (Hine 1989: 914). Sexual harassment and rape of domestics, mainly women of color has been well documented; Patricia Hill Collins refers to it as sexual extortion. Collins points out that according to statistics, Black women are more likely to be victimized than white women (Collins 1990: 178) and Angela Davis has demonstrated how sexual violence is central to the economic and political subordination of African Americans. Byllye Avery, founder of the Black Women's Health Network, argues that we must connect the issue of Black teenage pregnancy to incest. "When you talk to young people about being pregnant, you find out that most of these girls did not get pregnant by teengage boys. Most of them got pregnant by their mothers' boyfriends or their brothers or their daddies. We've been sitting on that. We can't just tell our daughters, 'Just say no'. We need to talk to our brothers. . . . We need men to stop giving consent, by their silence, to rape, to sexual abuse, to violence" (Avery 1990: 79–80).

the constitution of heterosexuality as such. MacKinnon writes: "To notice that these practices are done by men to women is to see these abuses as forming a system, a hierarchy of inequality" (1990: 13). In other words, the liberal conception of gender neutrality ignores what is distinctively *done to* women, as well as *who is doing it* to them (1990: 6).

In mainstream discourses about "animal rights," we find a similar (and similarly unexamined) assumption operating among activists and theorists: namely, that gender and sexuality have no bearing on the problem of speciesism as such. While taking radical positions against human domination of other species, many animal activists and theorists adopt an oddly *liberal* view when it comes to questions of gender. The domination of women by men, and the domination of animals by human beings are not only kept in separate accounts—they are seen as having nothing to do with one another. This lack of insight into the interconnections between speciesism and sexism, I want to suggest, seriously compromises the animal movement. So long as the movement fails to address the problem sex inequality poses, it remains in thrall to the dominant patriarchal culture, colluding in a regime of sexual hierarchy and domination that both hurts women and damages its own radically transformative potential. The animal movement—like other social movements and institutions in patriarchal society—both mirrors the inequalities of the larger culture, and constitutes itself through those same inequalities.

In what follows, I want to do two things. First, I want to examine some of the ways that ideologies of masculinity, male-centered definitions of reason and "the human," and female sexual subordination play themselves out in speciesist ideology and practice, in order to show why patriarchy and sexual inequality *matter* for the domination of animals by human beings. Second, I want to show how the animal movement itself, by ignoring or remaining insufficiently attentive to the connections between patriarchy and speciesism, ends up reproducing women's inequality in its structure, its focus, its arguments, its use of women's labor, and in the accessibility it provides to sexual exploiters.

Sexual inequality elevates "Rational Man" to represent the definition of "the Human"

Sexual inequality elevates men to represent the definition of "human"; women represent the not-man, and thus, the not-human. As MacKinnon puts it, women are "the animals of the human kingdom, the mice of men's world" (2005: 93). This definition of human as not woman, not animals can be traced back to Aristotle. As Wendy Brown details in her study of *Manhood and Politics*,

> It was precisely the sharpness of the Athenian conception of manhood that bore with it a necessary degradation of women, a denial of the status of "human" to women. To the extent that women were viewed as part of the human species, they would recall to men the species' animal or "natural" aspect. Alternatively, women could be denied fully human status and remain the somewhat less threatening repository of the "lower elements" of existence. (2002: 56)

In other words, manhood = humanhood: those who wish to be seen as worthy must try to show how they fit into this equation. As MacKinnon writes in "Of Mice and Men":

> Men's debates among themselves over what makes them distinctively human have long revolved around distinctions from women and animals. Can they think? Are they individuals? Are they capable of autonomous action? Are they inviolable? Do they have dignity? Are they made in the image of God? Men know

Figure 10.2 The fragmented, headless woman cannot be rational or have a speaking voice.

they are men, meaning human, it would seem, to the degree their answer to these questions is yes for them and no for animals and women. (2005: 94–95)

The question MacKinnon poses in this essay is why animals must first be shown to be similar to us (fit into our definition of the *human*) before they can be deemed worthy of our attention and our respect. Why do animals have to be like us (the common tack taken by analytical moral philosophers defending animal rights) to be free of human mistreatment of them? Just as women should not need to be "like" men to be accepted as fully human, so animals should not have to be seen as similar to humans to have their lives matter to us. In fact, the whole theoretical discussion of "similarity" is not really a discussion about animals at all, as MacKinnon points out, but about human power *over* animals.

The Western definition of the "man of reason" thus coincides with gendered notions about male behavior and masculinity. The idea of a rational person draws upon "men's gender-specific criteria" (Harding 1983: 48) and more highly valued activities identified as male or "masculine." To be a person is to be *rational* and to esteem autonomy over relationship—in other words, to be the antithesis of what is thought to be female. "[T]he feminine has been associated with what rational knowledge transcends, dominates or simply leaves behind" (Lloyd 1986: 2). Men's experience has been mistaken as representing human experience, while rationality has been mistaken as representing the highest attribute of humans. The central categories and habits of Western political thought—concern about rights, interests, the status of the individual over and against others, what constitutes being human, and so on—have all arisen on the basis of these two errors. Has not men's experience structured/delimited the threshold issues regarding the social contract and inclusion within the moral order, by fostering the presumption that we must prove how animals are like us? Why must we prove that animals suffer (and suffer in ways like humans) in order to have them recognized as beings worthy of better treatment? Men never had to prove they suffered to "have their existence validated and harm to them seen as real" (see MacKinnon 2007: 326). "Why is just existing alive not enough? Why do you have to hurt?"

As MacKinnon notes, the term *male* "has nothing whatever to do with inherency, preexistence, nature, inevitability, or body as such.

Because it is in the interest of men to be male in the system we live under (male being powerful as well as human), they seldom question its rewards or even see it as a status at all" (1987a: 264, n. 6). Being a powerful male is culturally constructed. It is demonstrated in part by one's use of animals. Specifically, by severing one's connection to one's feelings and by "being a man" who hunts, kills, and in other ways violates the other animals (as with scientific experimentation). Emotions are denigrated as untrustworthy and unreliable, as invalid sources of knowledge. Crucially, the emphasis on rationality precludes appealing to the one aspect of ourselves as human beings that might enable us to recognize the situation of animals and hence to respond to it: our capacity to care (on this see Donovan and Adams 2007). We experience this capacity through our bodies. The devaluation of the body and its emotions, and how both have been treated in philosophy, in history, in science, and in everyday life, thus has everything to do with its equation with women, nature, and animals, and the treatment

Figure 10.3 Blender advertisement.

of women, nature, the body, and animals has everything do with the elevation of men.

The elevation of "rational man" in Western thought, and its corresponding devaluation of the (female/animal) body has two immediate consequences for the animal movement. First, as feminist critics have pointed out, animal rights theorists themselves often appeal to humans to stop harming animals, in a way that bifurcates the human into "rational thinker" or "emotional reactor." In addressing the "rational thinker," rights theorists tacitly accept the prior ontological divisions and categories created by a world of sexual inequality. In positing its two primary texts as Peter Singer's *Animal Liberation* and Tom Regan's *The Case for Animal Rights*—texts that insist on their reasonableness—the animal movement reiterates a patriarchal disavowal of emotions as having a legitimate role in theory-making. Paradoxically, theorists articulate positions against animal suffering, while at the same time they maintain that our emotional responses to this suffering can never be appropriate sources of moral knowledge. The working assumption appears to be that emotional responses to suffering are not trustworthy as the foundation of theory.

Second, the fetish of a disembodied and abstract Reason in our society effectively obscures real structures of inequality and violence, by keeping the actual experiences of women and animals at arm's length. Just as women experience the social reality of domination made into sex through rape, incest, pornography, sexual harassment, forced pregnancy, and captivity in the home, animals experience the *material reality* of human oppression through a patriarchal matrix that renders them into objects of manipulation, scientific torture, mass annihilation, and consumption. What MacKinnon calls a neo-Cartesian mind game reduces the experiences of women, and of animals, to abstractions, rendering them *immaterial*. This mind game treats everything as ideas. To take one example: the common argument that corpse eaters offer to veg*ns that "plants have life too and so we can eat animals," is implicitly patriarchal. To draw lines where lines should not exist (i.e., by claiming that eating an animal is essentially different from eating a human being) does not mean that we cannot draw lines at all (i.e., distinguishing between eating a cow and eating a carrot). Questioning the appropriateness of drawing such lines is ironically an example of Cartesian doubt, which denies the validity of ideas rooted in lived reality. As MacKinnon points out, Cartesian doubt is a function of human male privilege. This privilege enables a standpoint that views everything as made out of ideas (1987a: 57–58). One might pose the "theoretical" question of whether carrots are being exploited. But once we situate ourselves within the lived, embodied reality we know as this world, we surely know that the eating of a cow, pig, or chicken is different from the eating of a carrot.

MacKinnon also sees this neo-Cartesian mind game functioning in the argument that pornography is an idea, a speech, rather than an act, a documentation of torture. Human male privilege can view everything as being made out of abstractions. But women (and animals) lack such luxury when someone else's privilege is hitting them in the face, calling them "cunt" as they walk in the street, sexually abusing them as children, sexually coercing them as adults, and sexually coming on to them as they volunteer as animal activists. MacKinnon writes:

> When something happens to women, it happens in social reality. . . . In other words, the harm of second-class human status does not pose an abstract reality question. In social life, there is little that is subtle about most rapes; there is nothing complex about a fist in your face; there is nothing nuanced about genocide—although

many nuanced questions no doubt can be raised about them. . . . It is the *denial* of their social reality that is complicated and raises difficult philosophical questions. Understand that the denial of the reality of such events has been a philosophical position about reality itself. Unless and until it is effectively challenged, only what power wants to see as real is granted reality status. (2006: 57)

Power, a function of human male privilege, enables a standpoint that controls what is designated "real" and considers everything as being made out of ideas, out of abstractions. For instance, when Linda Marchiano ("Linda Lovelace") testified that she was forced into the making of the pornographic film, *Deep Throat*, her statements about her experience of brutal sexual slavery while making that film (in *Ordeal*, her autobiography) became the subject of a libel suit. In other words, the film was seen as an "idea," hence as protected speech, rather than as a document of actual, physical torture and degradation. Her reality disappeared. Similarly, when corpse eaters invoke the baseless image of screaming, suffering carrots, lettuce, and tomatoes in order to justify eating animals, the animals' reality disappears. Because of the perspective arising from male privilege, the reality of *suffering* gets reduced to a debate about ideas, and whatever is an idea is protected as speech.

As MacKinnon points out, through pornography, women *become* men's speech. Thus does the mind triumph over the body, men over women, ideas over reality. And privilege remains undisturbed because abstractions ignore the context of power. When the working definition of "human" is what *manhood* is, and rationality is valued as one of the qualities of manhood, then women represent what is not valued—femaleness, and what femaleness is associated with: the body, emotions, and animals.

Figures 10.4 and 10.5

Gaslamp strip club. Photograph of matchbox cover by Carol J. Adams.
Real breast in plants. Photograph of Burgerfuel Restaurant poster by Sabine
Steinegg, Christchurch, New Zealand, 2016.

Sex inequality inscribes the use of animals as part of its definition of manhood

A popular Burger King advertisement in 2006 satirically appropriated
and subverted Helen Reddy's feminist song, "I Am Woman, Hear Me
Roar," turning it into a paean to masculinity and meat-eating. In the
ad, a man declares his right to eat meat because he is a man: "I am
man hear me roar . . . . I'm way too hungry to settle for chick food.
Yes I'm a guy . . . I will eat this meat. . . . I am man." Then the voice
over proclaims, "The Texas Double Whooper. Eat like a man, man."
The life and death power over animals that men have traditionally

had in the West establishes a part of the meaning of manhood. Species inequality is inscribed within the definition of manhood, a definition that grants men the right to act violently toward animals and women with impunity. Meat eating continues to be associated with male privilege, establishing meat eating as a virile, manly thing to do. Just as philosophers elevated the "man of reason" for whom mind conquers matter, and historians elevated a male idea of the professional historian who rejected the trivial, the domestic, the feminine, so too the everyday corpse eater recapitulates these gendered rejections of the body by consuming the bloody bodies of feminized animals.

The sexual politics of the hunt in contemporary hunting culture meanwhile celebrates man as hunter and life-taker. Both associations (virility in meat-eating, virility in hunting/killing) drip with power as well as blood (see Luke 2007 and Kheel 2007). Many of the recent school shootings in the U.S. involved gunmen targeting girls and women; and even when women and girls weren't the target, the shootings have all been done by men and boys. As Daniel Moshenberg observes, "Men and boys with guns are stalking and hunting women and girls in schools repeatedly. Until we see 'the gun problem' as equally a problem of violence against women, nothing will change" (2006). Men and boys thus stalk female human animals as well as nonhuman animals. Gender identity as a system leads directly to male violence and domination directed against both sets of subjects.

The question of "manhood," then, clearly enters into the politics of the animal movement at all sorts of levels. One more example that bears mentioning is the increasing vogue among men in the direct action wing of the movement to portray the struggle for animal liberation as a *war*. Learning about animal oppression provokes a variety of feelings—sadness, distress, anger, powerlessness, indignation, outrage, and horror among them. Men, however, are traditionally taught to perceive all negative emotions as anger. Those who feel only anger in response to animal suffering, rather than the complex of emotions that accompany anger, may experience animal activism as a battle rather than as a process. Naturally, if animal activism is seen as a war, men's feelings about the other animals can in this way be rendered comprehensible and even honorable. To be at war avoids being "unmanned" by caring about animals. But the referent is no longer the animals; it is the battle. This maintains a disengagement from feelings such as tenderness, empathy, and sympathy. And it provides a heroic, male-identified metaphorical framework for one's work to "save the animals."

Bonnie Smith, a feminist historian (describing Hayden White's critique of traditional tropes of history) writes that since "the past serves up accounts of violent events that are over . . . readers (including scholars) can let their violent fantasies roam freely when doing history" (1998: 9). This raises a disturbing question: Does learning about animal oppression provide a similar function in terms of allowing the roaming of violent (male) fantasies? Sometimes the focus on describing violence against the animals becomes a justification for violent actions, and frequently for the use of violent metaphors. We are told that we are engaged in a "new civil war," that violence against animal oppressors is acceptable, that our activism should be "by any means necessary." Women and men are encouraged to join this new civil war. The problem is that to be at war upholds gender dominance within the movement while it protects male activists' "manhood." It links the animal movement with extreme right and terrorist male groups who also use the discourse of the "warrior." Further, women are already experiencing a war, a war against them. Why should we join another? And why is it necessarily a war?

Bellicose language that celebrates armies fighting, warriors redeeming, soldiers marching (under orders) for the greater good ignore one of the basic feminist insights into animal oppression, which is that the ability to care and respond to animals exists within each of us. Though our empathic imagination is actively repressed through socialization, it can also be actively accessed. Moments of interaction between a human being and an animal being often open up the ability to respond to the situation of animals. But with warrior talk, not only is the warrior talk of other (right wing) movements legitimated, not only are the emotions of sympathy and empathy (for both animals and for one's own opponents) denied, but the traditional male response to threats against one's possessions and one's identity are reinforced: making war.

As this analysis suggests, one of the challenges for the animal movement is getting men to give up male-identified power over other beings. To be in the animal movement, the individual man must "refuse to be a man"—to use John Stoltenberg's term for the process of disowning the privilege that comes through sexual inequality. This undoubtedly goes some way toward explaining why there aren't more men in the animal movement. Logically, if the animal movement leaves the definition of "manhood" undisturbed it cannot accomplish its goals of liberating animals since, by definition, manhood involves use of and killing of animals, as well as the promotion of a "warrior" ethos that reproduces the values of aggression and masculine heroism of a patriarchal order.

Sexual inequality inscribes a pornographic "Femininity" on domesticated and defeated animals

MacKinnon's understanding of how "gender is a substantive process of inequality" "a material division of power" (1989: 58) is helpful in

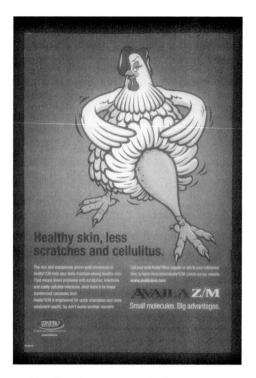

Figure 10.6 *Healthy skin* pharmaceutical advertisement.

understanding how femaleness becomes symbolically associated with
defeated animals:

> [T]o be victimized in certain ways may mean to be feminized,
> to partake of the low social status of the female, to be made into
> the girl regardless of biological sex. This does not mean that men
> experience or share the meaning of being a woman, because part
> of that meaning is that inferiority is indelible and total until it is
> changed for all women. It does mean that gender is an outcome
> of the social process of subordination that is only ascriptively tied
> to body and doesn't lose its particularity of meaning when it shifts
> embodied form. Femininity is a lowering that is imposed; it can
> be done to anybody and still be what feminine means. It is just
> women to whom it is considered natural. (1987a: 234, n. 26)

Sexual inequality makes the dominated animal "female" in reality or metaphorically. Cast as female, the animal becomes either immaterial or symbolic of the defeat (thus the mounting of dead animals' heads as trophies). Thus, species inequality is gendered.

Sexual inequality creates a hierarchy about animals: domesticated animals are seen as female, wild animals are seen as male—until, that is, the hunter kills the animal, at which point, as defeated prey, he or she is treated linguistically as female (see Adams 2015: 54). The victim of the hunt is a dominated power within a sexual system that is structured along lines of dominance and subordinance; ergo, the dominated animal becomes symbolically female. Karen Davis argues that the reason farmed animals have been neglected by the environmental movement is because they are "creatures whose lives appear too slavishly, too boringly, too stupidly female, too 'cowlike'" (1995: 196). Davis shows how both wild and domestic turkeys are subject to human sexual violence (2001). Similarly, Susan Davis and Margo DeMello challenge the social/sexual construction of rabbits:

Words about women and rabbits—like "dumb bunny" and "cunt"—belittle and degrade women and rabbits simultaneously. And the very success of the Playboy Bunny—a creature that is half rabbit and half woman, after all—reveals a male penchant for a very chilling notion of female sexuality: one that is bound in notions of prey, childishness and submissiveness, on the one hand, and unbridled lust, fertility and even witchery on the other (2003: 312).

Animal oppressive activities, including almost all forms of corpse-eating, "work" ideologically and materially by equating the individual animal with femaleness. Industrialized farming depends on domesticated female animals' reproductive labor. Consumption of domesticated animals cannot exist without the enslavement of female animals to reproductive labor. To control fertility one must have absolute access to the female of the species. Cows, sows, chickens, and female sheep are exploited in ways that merge their reproductive and productive labor. Their bodies must be reproduced so that there will be "meat" for humans, so that there will be cow's milk for humans, so that there will be eggs for humans. Female animals are not worthy of respect. Their importance is *what* they do—*reproduce*—rather than *who* they are—individual animals. They become a *what*. There is no *who*.

The status of the female of the species meanwhile establishes the status of the male domesticated animals. The slang use of species names such as *cow, sow, chick* demonstrates the unworthiness of that species and anyone to whom the name is appended. All domesticated animals carry the "taint" of this exploitation of female reproductivity; it is one reason that animals are seen as always already replaceable (there will always be more animals because of the slavery of female animals). Farmed animals' unworthiness becomes associated with their species as such, which in turn is associated with or defined through the demeaned status of its females. Deprived of any recognizably "human" (read male) characteristic, like reason, which might redeem them as subjects and lift them out of their lowly status, male domesticated animals become merged with femaleness.

How the movement trades in sexual objectification of women—and therefore of animals

How do animal oppressors change? How does someone become awakened to consciousness of individual responsibility for the death of animals? How does a culture learn to care about domesticated animals? As we have seen, one powerful structural barrier to caring about animals is the ideology by which domesticated species have been "lowered" through their equation with femaleness. So effective and total is this ideology that campaigns on behalf of animals believe that they cannot win over animal oppressors simply by showing the actual lives of domesticated animals. Farmed animals are inevitably seen as a nothingness, associated as they are with femaleness. To get around this problem, some campaigns on behalf of animals have ironically chosen to substitute a different subject for their campaigns, one who has *also* been desubjectified: the woman who lives in a state of perpetual undress. In doing so, however, they are only reinforcing the very system of sexual objectification that consigns *both* women and animals to perpetual domination.

While several organizations have promoted their causes using sexual images of women, People for the Ethical Treatment of Animals (PETA) is most notable for its choices to use women models, naked women, and to associate itself with pornographers like Hugh Hefner and *Playboy*. In a world in which sex is what women have to sell, PETA provides a way to "sell" their sex for a *cause*. A January 2007 example was PETA's "State of the Union Undress" (available at YouTube for anyone who verifies they are eighteen or older), a video in which a young woman is depicted (through the magic of video intercutting) addressing the US Congress on the subject of animal exploitation— as she slowly strips off all her clothing. One of the implicit, if not explicit, messages of such advertisements is, *Yes, we're asking you to give up animals as objects, but you can still have women as objects! You can become aware of animals' lives, but you don't have to give up your pornography.* Thus, rather than challenge the inherent inequality of a culture structured around dominance and subordination, the ad instead tries to leverage sexual inequality on behalf of the other animals. In fact, every time PETA uses *a naked* or nearly naked woman to advertise animals' concerns it not only benefits from sexual inequality, it also unwittingly demonstrates the intransigence of species inequality.

In its defense, PETA asserts that there is nothing wrong with nakedness; that feminists who object are puritanical and denying the beauty of the body; that these campaigns bring people to their website or prompt them to make phone calls to PETA where they do learn about issues relating to animals' lives. This of course is the liberal position on women's sexuality—that it can be freed from carrying the meaning of inequality. PETA's spokespeople further defend the choice of campaigns featuring women's naked or near-naked bodies by arguing that the women in their campaigns have consented to their participation. Such arguments are inherently problematic. In a world in which sex is what women have to sell, isn't the concept of consent emptied of much of its meaning? What does women's "no" to being used as a sex object actually look like in our culture? As MacKinnon has pointed out, of the debate about consent in rape cases: " . . . when force is a normalized part of sex, when no is taken to mean yes, when fear and despair produce acquiescence and acquiescence is taken to mean consent, consent is not a meaningful concept" (1990: 4). The problem of consent surfaces at other levels of animal movement organization as well. PETA, for instance, narrows its employment pool when it asks young women applying to certain positions at the organization if they would pose in a cage, for instance, or in other ways display themselves. If their employment at PETA is predicated on their willingness to perform certain acts of selling the message through their bodies, then de facto, those women unwilling to do so are not going to be hired (some remove themselves from consideration after being asked this question). If only those who say, "Yes I will participate," are being hired, it is again hard to know what a "no" really looks like.

In *The Sexual Politics of Meat*, I proposed that animals are "absent referents" in an animal oppressive world. They are made absent through interventions such as corpse eating, in which the animal disappears as animal to become food, through vivisection, in which the animal becomes the "object" of study, and is reduced to his or her body, and then reduced further to the symptoms that that body exhibits. In this context, while some argue that PETA's ads using naked or nearly naked women are liberating, not only for animals but, in transgressive ways, for women too, such practices in fact only substitute *one absent referent* for another. The challenge for the animal movement is how to restore the absent referent to a dominant culture that refuses to acknowledge it. What must be borne in mind, however, is that the absent referent is a crucial point of intersection *both* for sexual inequality and species inequality. Logically, there can be no politically liberatory *substitution* of woman for animal, because what is being replaced carries its own marker of inequality. What appears superficially as substitution is actually the layering of one oppressive system on top of another. (In another recent PETA campaign, a woman was posed as though cut up like a piece of meat, demonstrating both sexual and species inequality—the dead animal's fate was effectively layered upon the woman's fate as an object.)

Ironically, one common way that sexual inequality is imposed on farmed animals is through advertisements that sexualize meat. Conventions include fragmentation ("are you a breast man or a leg man"?), consumable females (barbecued pigs as sexy females with thrusting hips and pendulous breasts), and strip teases (animals in various stages of disrobing), rendering all domesticated animals being consumed as female. Replacing animals with women is therefore not *substitution* or potentially liberating, because the original victim's fate is still there, present through reference. A turkey posed as a prostitute, a turkey "hooker," refers not only to the turkey's fate but uncritically invokes, and thus reinforces, the debased status of the prostitute. The word "substitution" implies that the object is changed, and that substituting women for animals is somehow "transgressive" (e.g., women with udders in "Milk Gone Wild," a parody of the spring break beach parties, "Girls Gone Wild"). What we in fact see is merely one debased subject being substituted for the other: the lowered status of the first (animal) is applied to the other (woman), who however already carries her own low status—marked as "female" in a world of sexual inequality. If animals are burdened by gender, by gendered associations, by the oppression that is gender, then clearly they can't be liberated through representations that demean women. It isn't helping animals, and it certainly isn't helping men—to continue to believe that privilege is something to hold on to, to masturbate to. We live in the world pornography has made, and so do other animals.

Contemporary capitalist agriculture has developed into a multi-billion dollar industry that, like the porn industry, makes money off of the bodies of others, that controls female sexuality, is obsessed with nipples and pregnancy and uses vibrators (yes, these are all aspects of industrialized farming's treatment of female animals) in ways that blur the line between the pornographer's world and the world of industrialized farming. This is one meaning of the term "the pornography of meat." Another meaning to the term is found in the imposition of common conventions in pornography (rear-entry shots; sexualized poses; and language about sex) on animals, so that the message becomes that animals, too, *want* to be desired. Through such references, meat advertisements presume they are talking to users of pornography.

In *The Pornography of Meat*, I showed that animals in bondage, particularly farmed animals, are shown "free," free in the way that women are seen to be "free"—posed as sexually available as though their only desire is for the viewer to want their bodies. It makes animals' degradation and suffering fun by making animals' degradation sexy. Simultaneously, it makes women's degradation fun because to be effective the advertisement requires the implicit reference to women's sexualized status as subordinate. For women, through pornography, their degradation is always already sexy. The *sexualization* of animals and *the sexual objectification of women* thus overlap and reinforce one another. The body parts of females, at times dead females, are subjects pornography has already sexualized. In a fluid move, these conventions are used to sell dead bodies.

As MacKinnon and other radical feminists have argued, pornography is a central factor in women's subordination. "Pornography makes sex into a violation and makes rape and torture and intrusion into sex" (2005: 303). Pornography is a multibillion dollar industry—larger than all regular media combined.

> Because the profit from these mass violations counts and women do not, because these materials are valued and women are not, because the pornographers have credibility and rights and powerful friends to front for their interests and women do not, the products of these acts are protected and women are not. So these things are done so that pornography can be made of them. Everyone who has been looking high and low for a "direct casual link" between pornography and harm might consider this one: it takes harming women to make it (2005: 302).

Meat advertisements show us how pornographers do this: take a defeated being, in this case a dead animal, and pose him or her according to a pornographic convention, say, a restaurant that sells dead lobsters claiming "Nice tail;" barbecued pigs posed as young women (all pink, signifying whiteness), hanging on the arms of men; anorexic cows; chickens in high heels. In each case: She is dead and yet she wants it. Wants what? Wants sex; wants to be sexually used; wants to be consumed. And so violence has been made into sex. Meat advertisements do this to animals because pornographers do it to women. Pornographers do it to women because it works for them sexually. It works for them, because *sexual inequality* is sexy. As MacKinnon explains, "To be a means to the end of the sexual pleasure of one more powerful is, empirically, a degraded status and the female position" (2005: 129). Which not only explains what pornography is doing and why, but why meat advertisements would gravitate to pornographic conventions to sell their dead products. They mix death with degradation. That equation has one answer: the dead animal equals the female position. "Pornography creates an accessible sexual object, the possession and consumption of which is male sexuality, to be possessed and consumed as which is female sexuality. This is not because pornography depicts objectified sex, but because it creates the experience of a sexuality which is itself objectified" (1989: 140–41).

Meat advertisements that sexualize and feminize animals have been around for more than thirty years, and during this time, they have become more widespread and more explicit. Pornographic conventions bleed into the bloodied animals that are shown wanting to be consumed, that is, wanting their own death. Similarly, pornography makes of actual women's experience, an absent referent. As MacKinnon explains, "abused women become a pornographer's 'thought' or 'emotion'. . . . Once the women abused in it and through it are elided this way . . . pornography is . . . conceived in terms of what it says . . . rather than in terms of what it does" (1993:11). Not only is species gendered through the feminizing of animals, as gender subordination but gender is in turn animalized. This animalization is one aspect of sexual inequality (see Adams 2003a). The animalizing of women and the sexualizing of animals is the point at which the structure of the absent referent overlaps, interlocks, and intersects. The creation of the woman as absent referent through the sexualizing of her body and then the use of it in pornography, prostitution, rape and battering, melds with the creation of animals as absent referents by negating their individuality as living beings and by using/abusing their bodies through slaughtering, milking, experimenting upon, and hunting. There is one road, not two: a road of objectification, fragmentation, and consumption that requires and enacts the structure of the absent referent in relationship to nondominant others, whom it posits not just as objects but similar, metaphorically-overlapping objects providing sexual pleasure. I have called this the *sex-species system.*

The *sex-species system* insures that men have access to feminized animal bodies and animalized women's bodies. Another Burger King

Figure 10.7

ad demonstrates this. The "Whopperettes" shows women dancers, who suddenly, upon command from the "Burger King"—"Ladies, build your whopper!"—begin to throw themselves down upon each other in a pattern that creates a huge hamburger. While "have it your way" sounds in the background, one can also hear the "oofs" as women supposedly land on top of another. That *Hustler's* "Last All-Meat Issue" featured a woman on a hamburger bun back in 1978 shows how completely hard-core pornographic conventions have now bled into popular culture. (The Burger King ad was shown during Super Bowl 2006.)

It may be that the more veg*ns make meat eaters uneasy, the more meat will be sexualized. People don't know what to do with uneasiness. But they do know what to do with sexualized messages: ignore what has actually happened to the being who has been reduced into a consumable object of representation, *her* experiences, and just get it on. Sexualizing domesticated animals through advertisements for cultural consumption restabilizes assumptions about their literal consumability. When the animal movement engages in the same representational strategy, it merely recycles the terms of an order that oppresses both animals and women.

Sexual inequality creates an atmosphere for structural inequality in the animal movement

In making veganism a political decision, animal activists rightly draw attention to the relationship between the personal and the political. However, the movement has remained extraordinarily indifferent to the ways in which the seemingly impersonal structures of patriarchy introduce patterns of sexual dominance and submission within the movement itself, patterns which inevitably play out in workplace conditions and interpersonal relations. The aforementioned PETA campaign depicting women as meat, for example, could be cited as an example of the creation of a hostile work environment for women working at PETA. A judge in one recent court case (unrelated to PETA) ruled that an image displayed at a plaintiff's workplace depicting women as meat helped create a hostile work environment, forming a context in which acts of sexual harassment occurred.) But sexual politics plays out in more subtle ways within the movement as well.

In the animal movement, men still predominate as leaders and speakers, women as the grassroots workers doing the day-to-day work. Just as the Gross National Product does not measure housework, it does not measure volunteer hours. Unpaid labor is more likely to be provided by women than men, whether in the animal movement or at home. Without it, the movement could not survive. In addition, the glass ceiling for employees exists in animal organizations just as it does anywhere else in our society. Meanwhile, because of sexual inequality, women are doing work for animals instead of feminist work, or feminist-animal work. While some women come to the work for animals from the feminist movement, and see animal oppression as a part of women's oppression (on this see Gaarder [2011] who found some women activists expressed empathy to animals based on shared inequities), many women may become activists for animals in order to protect themselves from recognizing their own oppression. In other words, it may be easier to work on behalf of others who are suffering rather than to confront one's own situation.[3]

Why do women make this choice? MacKinnon suggests a reason: "People feel more dignity in being part of any group that includes men

---

[3]Andrea Dworkin was the first to suggest this to me.

than in being part of a group that includes that ultimate reduction of the notion of oppression" (2005: 30). Though it has more women than men, the animal movement has more men than the feminist movement. Meanwhile, if women want to challenge women's oppression, we hear, let them join the feminist movement. If the animal movement challenged women's oppression, the fact that women outnumber men so greatly in the movement would be more apparent and the animal movement would more explicitly experience the lowering that comes from being associated with women. The animal movement cannot afford to do this, or so it seems to believe. Among other reasons, this may be why there is such an emphasis on the fact that no one else is doing *this* work—the work for animals—whereas someone else is doing the work for women (i.e., feminists). The claim that *we must do this work because no one else is!* helps to keep everyone distracted from just *who it is* that is doing most of that work. And so, a dualism about those who experience inequality evolves: those who can speak for themselves and those who cannot. Thus, animal activists are told we are the "voice for animals" or the "voice for the voiceless." The decision that couches advocacy as *speaking for those who cannot speak* contributes to the difficulty of seeing sexual inequality and perhaps, as well, species inequality. This decision communicates that it is equally or more important to speak for those who can't speak than to speak for oneself. This often leads to the conclusion that if you can speak for yourself you are not as oppressed as those who can't. For instance, after the Michael Vick arrest for being a major part of a dog-fighting ring, a discussion occurred on the nationally-syndicated Diane Rehm talk show that went something like this: *Why all this attention to dog fighting when there are women being beaten? At least women being beaten can speak for themselves.*[4]

---

[4]Diane Rehm Show, August 2007 (as reported to the author by a listener).

In fact, there are times when women being beaten cannot speak up for themselves, for in doing so they may risk their lives or the lives of their children or companion animals. By emphasizing *speaking for another*, however, we send the message that as long as we are speaking for those who cannot we therefore do not have to attend to other issues regarding those who can speak for themselves. For example, we might come to believe that battered women, because they can speak for themselves, already have sufficient power to change their lives.

Moreover, when the ability to speak on behalf of animals is lifted up as the more important act, how then do we see that animals are already communicating with us in a variety of ways? Or that it shouldn't take speech (and our ability to "hear" it) to provide the proof that animals should not be oppressed? Animals protest their treatment in many ways—they escape, they turn away, they growl, snarl, hiss, bray, or bark, they resist, they flail, they flatten their ears or bite, they kick, they swish their tails, they paw the ground or the doors, they scratch, and in other ways documented by animal behaviorists exhibit displeasure, dislike, and rejection. If we bring attention to our interactions with animals, no human voice is needed to articulate what they need. As Josephine Donovan has said, "if we listen, we can hear them" (2007: 76). By setting itself up as "the voice of the voiceless," the animal movement vaunts human language while trying to create some grounds for equality of treatment for those who don't use it (the voiceless) and ignoring the social reality of those with human voices who cannot speak about their oppression. Thus it fosters a double misimpression: about who is the "speaker" and who are the speechless. Women who speak on behalf of animals are identifying themselves as self-sacrificing, perhaps because of the tacit recognition that women continue to hold a position of subordination both within and without the animal movement.[5] Meanwhile, and ironically, because of sexual inequality and the gendered nature of speech in Western culture, men who speak are constituting themselves as men (the status quo) often through male-identified logocentric, rational narrative (anatomized in Donovan and Adams 2007).

There is a further way, though, that the personal and the political merge in the animal movement: sexual inequality creates an atmosphere for the outright sexual exploitation of women in the movement by men. The animal movement is thought of as a movement of compassion for animals. Because of this, women activists may believe that the men they meet in the movement will be compassionate and that they won't be insensitive. Thinking they will find gentle men in the movement, women lower their defenses and—guess what? They find themselves as sexualized in the animal movement as they are out of it. Indeed, they are victimized by sexual exploitation in the movement. I have received numerous personal reports from victimized animal activist women. Sexual exploitation can take place in many arenas, but one popular, and confusing one, is the conference circuit. Feminists in the animal movement have discussed the inappropriateness of calling serial sexual exploiters *predators*. To use the term *predator* for such male behavior applies a negative meaning to actual predatory animals. Serial sexual exploiters are not acting as "nature" would have it but in a socially constructed way, and they could change. Basically they are refusing to act justly toward women. Child sexual abusers chose professions that give them access to children (the church, the educational system, scouting activities); perhaps some men

---

[5]MacKinnon identifies yet another issue: "How to avoid reducing animal rights to the rights of some people to speak for animals against the rights of other people to speak for the same animals needs further thought."

choose the animal movement because it gives them access to so many women.

Serial sexual exploiters in the movement adhere to certain forms of "grooming behavior" to lower their target's defenses. "Grooming behavior" was first identified as the deliberate ways child molesters choose to acclimate children to their sexual advances (having them sit on their laps, talking sexually, showing them pornography, touching first in a "safe" place, then moving their hands). Child sexual abusers benefit from an age difference; serial sexual exploiters benefit from the lowered defenses of women in the animal movement who anticipate *humane* men.

Serial sexual exploiters in the animal movement may begin with being flirtatious in public. The grassroots woman activist may feel flattered; someone is actually noticing the work that is often unnoticed. The next step is for the serial sexual exploiter to find an environment that is private (*Can you give me a ride?*—perhaps because he's from out of town and doesn't have a car, or perhaps because they are going to a protest together). Within the private environment, he sexualizes the talk in a general way (say, discussing topics such PETA's "State of Undress" or other ways of directly discussing something having to do with sex to see if the language and the topic is tolerated). In this private environment, he tests out the boundaries further by sexualizing the conversation in a more personal manner. He might seize on some personal information that is revealed and up the ante: discussing how she looks, for example, or the energy he feels being near her. The grooming behavior continues by the selection of an environment that is supportive of the continual erosion of the target's boundaries. For instance, he might suggest going to a bar. Then, he talks about how there is *an attraction between them*. Unlike routine dating behavior, the time frame for these interactions is often accelerated (indeed this may all occur in one night). And unlike routine dating behavior, the sexual exploiter is not looking for an ongoing relationship; indeed, the behavior he exhibits is specifically to disarm the woman quickly so that he can use her and move on. He is persistent; he won't take no for an answer. She worries about being rude. There may be some threatening, *I won't work with you. You led me on.* And when the night is over, the sexual conquest achieved, suddenly the *attraction* was only a *flirtation.* When the victim protests, verbally threatening behavior occurs: "Who will believe you?" "I will accuse you." "You will hurt the movement." Traumatized, by what has happened the victim may not be able to think clearly or linearly.

Meanwhile, once again assured of his dominance through this sexual conquest, the serial sexual exploiter benefits from her traumatized state. His life is not shattered by the experience; it is enhanced. He can continue to behave as always while the victim is putting the pieces back together and trying to maintain her work on behalf of animals. Not wanting to put the movement at risk by attempting to hold him accountable, she remains silent and he moves on to his next target. Since individual women aren't seen as "the movement" per se, this sexually abusive behavior is not perceived as putting the movement at risk. It would be her speaking up that would be seen as hurting the movement. If the serial sexual exploiter is a visitor, a well-known activist, or scholar, he benefits from moving on, and choosing a new target far removed from the most recent victim so that the opportunity to exchange experiences will not occur. Some women may uphold men who are abusers or sexual harassers within the movement because they are thankful that someone is articulating so strongly on behalf of animals. They recognize that women will not be heard in the way that the men or some men are. They accept, even at an unconscious level, that women are not going to be as successful, so they side with someone, even if that person has harmed them, who they think will succeed. In these ways, women are silenced so that animals can be helped. Who is the voiceless now?

Conclusion

In this essay, I have taken up the question of what it would mean for the movement on behalf of other animals to acknowledge women's inequality, and I have suggested that MacKinnon offers a necessary corrective to the limits of contemporary animal rights activism and critical theories of animal domination. What I have called the sex-species system keeps oppressions interlocking and interactive; indeed the sex-species system gains its strengths through its interlocking nature (see Adams 2007).[6] Yet, problematically, many *radical* animal activists and theorists continue to adopt a *liberal* perspective regarding sexuality, seeing it as essentially gender neutral. In doing so, they obscure one of the most important *bases* of animal domination, which is the sex hierarchy system.

If taken seriously, however, the problem of sexual inequality raises a host of quite vital and relevant questions for those who would liberate other species: Are the animal movement's theories of *why* animals are abused ignoring one of the primary reasons for that exploitation—patriarchy? Can nonhuman animals really be saved without also eradicating sexual inequality among human ones? Will animal activists also free the animals in pornography, in situations

---

[6]Crush videos are one example, in which women in stiletto heels are shown crushing small animals to death. (Crush videos also prove MacKinnon's point that "Nowhere are the powerless as powerful as in the imagination of those with real, not imaginary, power." [2007: 320])

where they are killed by batterers, killed by hunters, killed because they are female or equated with the female?

Does anyone really believe that that the animal movement because of its "pure" focus—on others who are unable to fight for themselves[7]—is inoculated from problems of dominance within its ranks? Gender reflects a hierarchy, a division of power that's expressed and acted out, primarily sexually. There are therefore in fact two realities at the minimum in current animal activism: men's and women's.[8] These realities are determined by the dominant culture in which animal activism is trying to intervene. Failure to acknowledge these conflicting realities and the sexual inequality that creates them does harm to women and sets the animal movement back. The problem for animal activism is that it not only faces and must change a speciesist world, but also it faces and must change a sexist world that expresses its sexism through speciesism and expresses its speciesism through sexism. For the feminist, animal activism's failure to confront the problems of sexual inequality is sad; but for animal activism, such a failure may be fatal. The animal movement is trying to eradicate the oppression of animals without addressing how sexual inequality structures species inequality. But it can't be done.

What would it mean, then, for the movement on behalf of other animals to acknowledge women's inequality? As I have argued, the animal movement benefits from women's inequality in its structure, its focus, its arguments, its use of women's efforts, and in the accessibility it provides to sexual exploiters. So long as the movement refuses to

---

[7]As it is often formulated; though evidence of animals' resistance to their exploitation and treatment continues to appear: cows running away from the slaughterhouse; pigs jumping out of trucks transporting them to the slaughterhouse, etc.

[8]In addition, the work of critical race theorists who address the issue of animal activism and veganism indicate two other realities: that of white activists and that of people of color. See the work of Harper.

acknowledge that it is a part of a dominant culture in which women's inequality still prevails, so long as it resists addressing the problem of this inequality, it will unconsciously undermine its own vision for a new kind of society, one based on genuinely universal equality, justice, and caring.

Tom Tyler is a lecturer in digital culture at Leeds University, UK. He has published widely on animals and anthropocentrism within philosophy, critical theory, and the history of ideas. He is the author of *CIFERAE: A Bestiary in Five Fingers* (Minneapolis: University of Minnesota Press, 2012), co-editor of *Animal Encounters* (Leiden: Brill, 2009), and editor of *Animal Beings* (Parallax #38, 12.1, 2006).

11

An animal manifesto: Gender, identity, and vegan-feminism in the twenty-first century interviewed by Tom Tyler

Tom Tyler: The theme of this issue of *parallax* is *Animal Beings*, and specifically an investigation into ways in which human beings can or should be considered animal beings. Do you consider this an appropriate approach to the question of animals and identity?

Well, first, hoorah! Any writings that explore and extend the discussion of our being animals, and our relationships to other animal beings, makes me hopeful. Of course, as you well know, the concept of the "animal" or "animal beings" usually exists in relationship to concepts of human beings in a dyadic dance of definition by negation. When we eliminate the negation that *animal* has meant to the human, the absence of the human (qualities) that being animal has meant, how does this also redefine, and perhaps dethrone "human"? A popular feminist button in the States asserts that "Feminism is the radical notion that women are human." I won't wear that button. I don't find that a radical notion; I find that a conformist notion even though I understand why it is so insistent on this point. While it goes without saying that "humans are animals" the way this insight has been used has been hierarchically, i.e., racial and sexual distinctions were used to equate people of color and women with other animals or to impute animal characteristics on those who were not white, propertied men. "Human" became a definition not only about humans versus (other) animals, but also defining who among *Homo sapiens* **would** have the power to act as "humans"—voting, holding property, making laws, committing violence with impunity. Human has always been a label that is tied to power. But for feminism to want firmly to establish women's "humanness" while upholding the boundary between humans and other animals, defeats what I believe to be the truly radical insight of feminism. Josie Donovan and I articulated what we saw as the radical insight of feminism in our introduction to *Animals and Women*: "We believe that feminism is a transformative philosophy that embraces the amelioration of life on earth for all life-forms, for all natural entities. We believe that all oppressions are interconnected: no one creature will be free until all are free—from abuse, degradation, exploitation, pollution, and commercialization" (1995: 3).

When we begin to explore what it means to be "animal beings," too, we often begin by acknowledging our commonalities: we bleed, we experience pain and express it, some of us females share the experience of pregnancy and lactation. I think such politics of identity can be both promising and limiting: while having lactated makes me sympathetic to the degradation and miserable experience of nursing pigs and cows under confinement situations, I would not want to imply that experience is required to cultivate sympathy for suffering. Yet, lactation is an example of continuity across species, and many such examples of experiencing continuity or commonality exist. Neal Barnard, founder of Physicians Committee for Responsible Medicine, traced his vegan awareness to participating in an autopsy in which human ribs were removed from the body. Then he went to lunch: "This day in the cafeteria, they were serving ribs for lunch. They looked so much like the human ribs that I couldn't eat them" (Barnard 2004). An anti-Vietnam war activist told me that she traced her vegetarianism to the day she stopped at a slaughterhouse to get blood to use for an anti-war protest, walked away with the blood in hand, sickened with the thought, "what's the difference?"

As you know, I had to postpone this interview because of a medical emergency. And it was in midst of this crisis that I was reminded of what it means to be an animal. A close friend had to have her right leg amputated to the knee. After the surgery they had a problem adequately medicating her for the pain. Apparently some amputees feel no pain. For her, this was not the case. She returned to the room after being in the recovery room, crying "my leg, my leg." That was horrifying, but I didn't have time even to feel that horror because the nurses summoned me in to hold her hand so that she would not have to have her hands bound to the bed. My partner was holding one hand and I the other as five nurses worked to settle her in. She was trying to grab at the bandage around the stump, and so the necessity of not letting go was urgent. When the pain medication finally took hold and we sort of slumped into chairs by her bed, all I could think was "and animals will bite off their own legs to escape a leg-hold trap!" (Trappers call this a "wring-off."[1]) Seeing the pain she endured from the amputation, I could only imagine the pain

---

[1] "In an agony of pain and confusion, the animal struggles in frenzy, often mutilating themselves, dislocating joints, breaking their teeth, chewing their leg or paw—in an attempt to break free. If they succeed, the traumatized animal has scant hope for survival in the wild; death will come surely by infection, by starvation or by the animal's being an easy prey to their predators." "Fur-trapping in the U.S."

that animals must endure in such a trap that they will self-amputate to escape it.

When I give an example such as this of trans-species commonalties, am I drawing an analogy, identifying grounds for empathy, acknowledging continuity? Or all three and something more as well? And do we have to have similarities established in order to stop harming animals? Do we perpetuate a biological approach to other animals? I admire Barbara Noske's proposal that we need an anthropology of other animals, not a zoology (Noske 1997: 161–70).

Gail Melson, the author of *Why the Wild Things Are: Animals in the Lives of Children*, examines the role of animals in the development of children. She suggests that children may see animals, including domesticated animals, as "interspecies peers." This sense of interrelatedness prompts moral questions such as "why are we mistreating/eating our peers?" Melson explains, "Precisely because children accept animals as other living beings, they raise issues of just, fair, right, and kind conduct" (2001: 97). Unfortunately, we socialize children to forget this recognition and accept utilitarian relationships with other animals. (By the way, if we saw ourselves as animals, I think a part of the antiabortion movement would lose its forcefulness, because it fetishizes the human embryo over the full term nonhuman animal.)

Once one becomes aware of two things—one's own animal body and what we are doing to other animals' bodies because of our claim of human superiority—once those two awareness's inform your thinking and being, how can you not want to write a manifesto, i.e., a sort of scream to the world, "What are you doing? And why are you still doing it?" But people, especially those in academia, are supposed to be measured and reasoned so you measure your words to find a way to get others to listen (and perhaps the result is an academic paper!). I realized half way through writing *The Sexual Politics of Meat* that if I sounded angry and the book felt like a rant people wouldn't read it; they would walk away. So I had to learn to hide the anger, or work with the anger, and massage it into prose that didn't betray the anger but arose from the motivation of anger.

You suggest that one might declare "I am a vegan because I am an animal," but it is also the case, I think I am right in saying, that you are a vegan because you are a feminist. Prompted by your work, I have long been struck by the fact that veganism, even more so that vegetarianism, is an explicitly feminist issue: it is female animals who are forced to produce milk and eggs, for instance. You mention a manifesto: do you envision this as a vegan-feminist manifesto perhaps? What would such a proposal look like?

Yes, one could envision a manifesto. With your prompting, it seems time to articulate at least four main vegan-feminist claims:

1 Flesh eating and veganism should properly be defined as relationships with other animals. Flesh eaters choose one relationship, one that in the Western world I would characterize as dominance and murder, and vegans choose another.[2] The reason I would like to establish that flesh eating is a relationship that humans chose among other choices in relating to other animals is that it helps to put debates between flesh eaters and vegans in perspective. It is never just two people debating the choice to eat dead animals. There is a third animal involved, one who has disappeared. That is what

---

[2] I choose the stronger word "murder" over the less emotive word "death," just as I chose the word "corpse" rather than "carcass" in *Neither Man nor Beast: Feminism and the Defense of Animals*. If we acknowledge human animal-nonhuman animal continuity then words that have been used to apply only to humans must be employed to refer to what happens to the other animals. In addition, I have been working on bringing back into print an eighteenth-century vegetarian pamphlet that never entered the vegetarian canon. In it, the author refers to flesh eating as "murdering animals." See Adams 2005.

activists point out with comments such as vegan activist Bruce Friedrich's "I can survive without greasy chicken wings—but the chicken can't."[3]

2   As your comments suggest, I would like to see reproductive freedom for all female animals, not just human females. What Barbara Noske has called "the animal industrial complex" requires the absolute exploitation of female animals. There would be no eating of domesticated animals if female animals weren't kept pregnant to produce the animals being consumed. There would be no milk, if cows weren't kept lactating; no eggs if chickens weren't kept ovulating. All flesh eaters benefit from the alienated labor of the bitches, chicks, (mad) cows, and sows whose own bodies represent their labor and whose names reveal a double enslavement—the

Figures 11.1 and 11.2

---

[3]Bruce Friedrich, personal correspondence, September 7, 2005.

literal reproduction forced upon them, and the metaphoric enslavement that conveys female denigration, so that we human females become animals through insults, we become the bitches, chicks, cows, and sows, terms in which our bodies or movements are placed within an interpretative climate in which female freedom is not to be envisioned.

3   No matter the multiplicity of selves we each might constitute, and the academic concern for totalizing theories that consume slippery, ambiguous meanings and possibilities, eating as an act is something that is locatable. When one eats, one eats with one mouth, uses one tongue, swallows with one throat, digests with one stomach (stapled or unstapled). I am always surprised during a conversation with poststructuralists and postmodernists that those who aren't vegan announce this to me. They seem to confirm that they are implicated by their implements: the fork they wield over a dead animal's body is not only a dead end for the animals but for theories that oppose totalizing epistemologies while participating in totalizing ontologies that leave farmed animals an undisturbed category.

4   I am a vegan-feminist because I am one animal among many, and I don't wish to impose a hierarchy of consumption upon this relationship. Let the worms eat me when I am dead, and let the worms eat the bodies of the animals usually destined for human mouths. When I say I am vegan-feminist because I am one animal among many, I am not articulating a manifesto based on otherness. If we begin by saying, "we are animals, we move in animal bodies, we are connected to and related to— kin and akin to animals"—then I don't think we see animals as *others*. What we are writing about, gesturing toward, is not a resituating of animals as "others."

Would it be accurate to describe this proposal as a "posthuman" vegan-feminist manifesto, dealing as it does with questions of gender and power hierarchies within the context of nonhuman identity and modes of being?

I'm not sure that I am the one to articulate a posthuman feminist-vegan stance, because I still locate myself within the radical feminist arena. First, my theories arise from my years of activism against battering and rape. Second, the information about the abuse of the reproductive systems of other animals prompts me to examine how this affects our inability to see them as individuals. I discuss this toward the end of *The Pornography of Meat*, and how this rebounds on women's status. In *The Pornography of Meat*, drawing on images from popular culture, I try to show how the gender that is associated with other species (women) and the species that are associated with the exploitation of femaleness (domesticated animals) become locked in interconnected oppressions. I think this is the work of a radical feminist.

Your proposed manifesto seems to raise questions of autobiography, which puts me in mind of Derrida's lecture "The Animal That Therefore I Am (More to Follow)." This piece is by far Derrida's longest discussion of animals currently available in English, and certainly the most radical from a vegan-activist perspective. It is, I think, a heartfelt piece: what Derrida has to say about his relationship with his cat, and his comparison of factory farms with the Holocaust (not in itself a new idea), for instance, demonstrate a genuine animal rights sensibility.

Around the time that Derrida's fascinating paper was being translated into English, I was in the UK at a conference called "Millennial Animals." Cary Wolfe and I were the keynoters. Cary was familiar with the content of the paper and explained what was in it. I remember a part of me simplifying it in my mind to "how Derrida's discovery of his body because of his cat, influenced and politicized Derrida's thought about other animals." Of the many feminists who were in the group listening, several began a discussion around the issue "why does it take Derrida's discovery, through his cat, of his body, to make this worthy of discussion? This is something women have known and said for years!" Cary agreed, but said, if I can paraphrase: "because it is Derrida who is now saying this, it is very important." And it is true, it is exciting that Derrida said it, but I also think the autobiographical aspect itself is pedagogical. Often, when I talk to flesh eaters I say, "tell me about your relationships with animals." I find this is a way "in" to their deepest feelings and sensibilities. Their reflections are not necessarily as profound as Derrida's insights, and yet within the process of reflecting there is always the potential for movement toward a less hierarchical relationship with other animal beings because of what they have experienced in and through a trans-species relationship.

Would your manifesto push Derrida's approach a little further: "The *Vegan* Animal That Therefore I Am" perhaps?

It would only have to be the littlest of a push because Derrida remarkably identifies the most egregious actions we as humans have taken against other animals (including subsuming them all under one name). Derrida has it all there, and when he speaks about what is happening to animals in contemporary society, you feel a heat in his words. A vegan manifesto, one might argue, is in the center of his paper, even though it is not precisely articulated. His citation of Genesis 1 ends just before the verse that establishes that the "dominion" introduced in Genesis 1:26 (no matter what the word "dominion" itself means in that verse) is delimited by existing within a vegan world (Gen. 1:29). I know he is moving toward his discussion of Genesis 2, and of what follows, yet veganism is implicit in the early chapters of Genesis. Another myth he returns to, the myth of Prometheus, has been associated with the introduction of meat eating to human beings as it is only through the intervention of fire that animals' dead bodies are consumed, notwithstanding oysters and sushi (Adams 2015: 100–01). But it is in his mode of discourse in the section when he talks about humans' treatment of animals, that one might feel one is reading a manifesto: "Everybody knows," he says, "Everybody knows what terrifying and intolerable pictures a realist painting could give to the industrial, mechanical, chemical, hormonal, and genetic violence to which man has been submitting animal life for the past two centuries." (I wonder if he ever saw the paintings of Sue Coe!) And, "Everybody knows what the production, breeding, transport, and slaughter of these animals has become" (2002: 395). He also says, "No one can deny the suffering, fear or panic, the terror or fright that humans witness in certain animals" (2002: 396). These are the rhetorical devices of a manifesto. They don't hesitate to be explicit, and they pose a question to the reader: would *you* deny? *Do* you know?

Donna Haraway has, of course, written two manifestos already: for cyborgs (1991) and for companion animals (2003). I know you have reservations about the latter: what are its limitations from the perspective of a vegan-feminist manifesto?

I think she is attempting something more profoundly personal here. But I found the final product, her small pamphlet, extremely disturbing. It feels uneven, as though it were cobbled together. And her voice is not so much ambiguous as inconsistent. Sometimes it feels downright petulant. It's the lacunae in Haraway that disturb.

Reading it against and with Derrida make what is left unsaid so damning. Derrida's feels to be a manifesto in all but name; Haraway's is a manifesto only in name, more an apologia. Discussing circuses, Derrida paints a picture of "an animal trainer having his sad subjects, bent low, file past" (2002: 407). Haraway, through a reference to Vicki Hearne's beliefs, defends "circus trainers," referring to animals in the circus as "the animals they work with." At this point, with all the information about circuses, why would someone alert to how words work, choose the euphemism "work with"? Derrida, as you point out, does not shy away from engaging the issue of the Holocaust and genocide when talking about what is happening to animals, while Haraway pauses to condemn "the outrageous equating of the killing of the Jews in Nazi Germany, the Holocaust, with the butcheries of the animal-industrial complex" (Haraway 2003: 51).

Regarding animal rights, Haraway is dismissive, calling us the "rights besotted" (48). Derrida, more generously, acknowledges "In response to the irresistible but unacknowledged unleashing and the organized disavowal of this torture, voices are raised—minority, weak, marginal voices, little assured of their discourse, of their right to discourse and the enchantment of their discourse within the law, as a declaration of rights—in order to protect, in order to appeal (we'll return to this) to what is still presented in such a problematic way as *animal rights*, in order to awaken us to our responsibilities and our obligations with respect to the living in general, and precisely to this fundamental compassion that, were we to take it seriously, would have to change even the very basis (and the basis is what I wish to discuss today) of the philosophical problematic of the animal" (Derrida 2002: 395).

Haraway's embrace of Vicki Hearne's position, a position left fixed by Hearne's death, results in an impatient, and I would argue, dated, dismissal of "animal rights." Haraway's aversion to animal rights doesn't seem to have mutated or adapted since Hearne's 1991 article against animal rights (1991: 59–64). I wish I could understand the categorical disparagement of animal rights that, with a broad sweep, includes even those animal advocates who challenge "rights language," a large majority of whom are women. For which companion species can we safely advocate if we wish to avoid her derision? Only dogs? I do not comprehend why a feminist concerned with relations between species decidedly ignores the many feminist scholars who have been writing and talking about this issue, some for at least twenty years. Haraway is interested in finding the "relational model of training," (2003: 54) making her disinterestedness in a relational model for veganism and other relationships with animals more shocking. Derrida says "no one can deny the *unprecedented* proportions of this subjection of the animal. . . . No one can deny seriously, or for very long, that men do all they can in order to dissimulate this cruelty or to hide it from themselves, in order to organize on a global scale the forgetting or misunderstanding of this violence that some would compare to the worst cases of genocide (there are also animal genocides: the number of species endangered because of man takes one's breath away)" (Derrida 2002: 394). Yet Haraway seems to.

And what of dogs? She is interested in "naturecultures"—the naturecultures of humans and canines, for instance, and "ethical relating, within or between species." She condemns "impulse buyers: of special breeds of dogs who then dump their dogs" (24), but the breeders for whom the "whole dog" is both a kind and an individual (perhaps the beginning of the problem), and who continue to produce these "purebreds," escape her critique in this part of the manifesto. Where do the impulse buyers get their dogs?

Can a manifesto compromise? Shouldn't a manifesto leap to the place where compromise—or half responses—are seen as what they are, a bargain with the established order against which your manifesto is standing? Like a manifesto for companion animals that uses purebreds as the referents? Why breed animals? Why claim for history more value than contemporary situations?

While Haraway acknowledges the "scandal of the meat-producing 'animal industrial complex,'" (43, quoting Noske), she only finds historical irony in the introduction of "Basque Pyrenean mountain dogs, who were nurtured in the purebred dog fancy, onto the ranches of the US west to protect Anglo ranchers' xenobiological cattle and sheep." Surely there is more than irony here. She seems so hesitant to address herself to the species with whom humans have the least ethical relation—the animals that people eat—indeed, referring to a stop at *Burger King* to get "burgers, coke, and fries" (40). Her book was published after *Burger King* started selling veggie burgers, but she fails to tell us what sort of burger she bought.

Haraway protects the dominance that ontologizes animals as edible just as the sheepdogs she celebrates protect the ontologized "livestock." She renders unto the renderers the bodies of animals. "Livestock" become the untouchable natureculture intersection and not because of the prions from rendered "mad" cows that cannot be destroyed, but because she cannot or will not acknowledge the possibility that livestock might also be companion species.

I know Haraway is not alone in viewing "animal rights" discourse as proscriptive and ideological, that some people believe a certain possibility of becoming is denied when one tells another what not to do, that we deprive another when we speak or make demands, that activists are dictating to others. But in any evolving natureculture, we should stipulate that flesh eating, unlike debates about it, involves more than human beings. Humans consume animal beings. In human-oriented arguments, the fact that others are dictating to animals by eating them disappears. If we agree to one of the points

I propose in the vegan-feminist manifesto, that at least three beings are involved in a discourse about flesh eating (the speaker, the hearer and the animal being eaten), then we see that there is an *a priori* deprivation within these critiques that needs to be acknowledged: the death of the animal.

How do you account for this persistent academic resistance to "animal rights" discourses?

Perhaps an academic finds ambivalences more acceptable than the activist, who desires something more tangible: non-ambivalent action. And perhaps it is an "easy out"—sweeping away difficult questions because it appears the answer, i.e., "rights language," is wrong.

Your most recent paper, "Post-meateating," considers animal rights as a modern movement in a postmodern age.

This may offer another explanation for the dismissal of animal rights discourses. In *The Sexual Politics of Meat*, I proposed that nonhumans used for meat were absent referents. In "Post-meateating," I explore the implications of Frederic Jameson's insight that in general we have passed from the modern period with nature still a referent, to a postmodern period with culture as the referent. His insight suggests that in a postmodern time the animals have been loosed completely from their status as absent referent—instead the referent will have a cultural context only.

When postmodernism supplanted the idea of the individual, autonomous subject with the idea of multiple selves and a fluid subject, Tom Regan's scholarly attempt to claim consciousness and biography for animals, *The Case for Animal Rights*, seemed to lose its relevance. (But why not attribute such multiple selves to other animals too?) The animal rights movement that traces itself to Regan or Peter Singer has the misfortune of articulating a modernist claim just as postmodernism absorbs and displaces modernist thinking. It appears dated, announcing in its activism (boycotts/placards/lobbying) its own supposed anachronism. It appears absolutist and serious in a time when irony and self-deprecation prevail. It is seen as too literal, too preachy. Trying to get culture to get back to the referent "animal" is seen as too boring, not playful.

This appears to be what PETA knows. They often deploy visual images but with cultural referents. They use supermodels. They use actors. They take any cultural idea that is circulating and appropriate it. Rather than producing for general consumption the "bleeding Jesus" pictures, as one Catholic friend calls them, of damaged, injured animals, PETA puts on Mickey Mouse masks to protest animal experimentation. They're ironic.

PETA seems to acknowledge that for many people the referent, animals, is gone. And they are trying to work with what is there, cultural consumption, by manipulating cultural images/issues. They are trying to get people to talk about veganism without having to address what has disappeared. It doesn't matter who they piss off. In fact, the more the better. Tastelessness is newsworthy; nonhuman farmed animals aren't. The strongest reminder for me of this is that people continue to eat "beef" after the news about mad cows.

One of the results when the cultural becomes the referent is not only that we forget we are animal beings, but we are allowed to forget that other animals are animal beings, too! Karen Davis says the human hand is the cruelest thing a chicken will know. The non-ambivalent action the activist wants is to stop that hand. I think I still cling to words like "integrity." What sort of referents are animals in scholarly discourse? Are they allowed to be embodied animal beings? Are they impaled by forks over scholarly dinners or not? What are the hands that are a part of our own animal bodies doing?

Figure 12.1 "Beefeater" was painted at the Skowhegan School, Skowhegan, Maine, in 1984. This oil on canvas portrait was done of David Hacker, a football player with the California 49ers. Hacker, himself an artist, kindly modeled for Tower while at Skowhegan. Cindy Tower's artwork was selected by the editors of *Heresies*, a feminist art magazine to accompany my early article on "The Sexual Politics of Meat" when it appeared there in 1984.

Cindy Tower, *Beefeater*, 84.

12

Post-meateating

In the early 1990s, activism against the methods used to catch tuna
fishes resulted in the Dolphin Protection Consumer Information
Act (DCPIA). The DCPIA was aimed at protecting dolphins so that
they would no longer be captured and die as a result of the nets used.
National Public Radio carried a report when Congress passed the
DCPIA. As a follow up to the story, Linda Wertheimer, then one of the
hosts of National Public Radio's news program "All Things Considered,"
conducted an interview. Did she conduct it with an activist against
the nets? A marine biologist? A trainer of dolphins in an aquarium?
None of these. She interviewed the creators of the award-winning play
"Greater Tuna," and asked them what their fictional characters from
the town of Tuna, Texas would say about the new regulations.

Or consider this: in the twentieth century, a hotel in Washington, took
lamb chops off their menu whenever the late puppeteer extraordinaire
Sheri Lewis and her puppet "Lamb Chops" were visiting.

In each of these instances, the issue, which might be seen as the
impact of human beings on other animals—tuna fishes, dolphins, and
lambs—becomes instead an impact on the cultural beings—actors
and puppets—who become the focus of attention. Sensibilities about

"Post-Meateating" first appeared in *Animal Encounters*, ed. Tom Tyler and Manuela Rossini
(Leiden and Boston: Brill, 2009), 47–72.

something *cultural* are being evoked, not sensibilities about something ostensibly "natural." The referent is cultural; actual dolphins, tuna fishes, and lambs are eclipsed by the cultural.

In *The Sexual Politics of Meat*, I proposed that nonhumans used for meat were absent referents. Behind every meal of meat is an absence: the death of the nonhuman animal whose place the meat takes. The "absent referent" is that which separates the meat eater from the other animal and that animal from the end product. Consider the *New Yorker* cartoon by Robert Mankoff called "The Birth of a Vegetarian": a man is sitting in front of a slab of meat, looking startled because the sound "moo" was emanating from the steak. Of course, the nonhuman's death is not in our face; only the postmortem state of a nonhuman's corpse is. We do not see our meat eating as contact with another animal because it has been renamed as contact with *food*. This is the function of the absent referent—to keep our "meat" separated from any idea that she or he was once a nonhuman animal, to keep the moo away from the meat, to keep some*thing* from being seen as having been *someone*. And if our references to animals in culture refer back to something else that is also cultural—the residents of Greater Tuna, or Lamb Chop—they do not have to be about someone else, that is, they do not have to ever land on nonhuman animals themselves. This point was made in the greatly entertaining but evanescent Pooh furor of 1998.

"Free the Pooh Five" demanded a chorus of British newspapers in early 1998. A British Member of Parliament had visited the New York Public Library where the original stuffed animals of Christopher Milne, those that inspired the stories about Winnie the Pooh, reside. It seems that M. P. Gwyneth Dunwoody detected that Pooh, Tigger, Eeyore, Owl and Kanga were unhappy there, as they were "incarcerated" in a glass case (in fact, a climate and light-controlled, bulletproof glass case). She insisted they needed to return to Britain. The *New York Times* jumped into the fray with a jocularity equal to the British papers

(Barry 1998). The *Times* carried photos of the stuffed animals on the front page. As a *Times* reporter once observed to me, a newspaper writer must know how to write well about nothing. But what provided some fun headlines for the newspapers and unbearable puns for the politicians confirmed the existence of the age of postmodern referent. Everyone knew that no stuffed bear was actually unhappy; no stuffed kangaroo was actually homesick. The "sympathy" evoked in the media stories damages real animals in several ways: in what it says about people who express care (such as those activists who worked to bring about protection of dolphins) and the ones for whom the care is expressed (dolphins). By substituting a cultural referent for the absent referent it displaces any sympathy we might have for the real suffering of real animals. Secondly, its humor undercuts our (meager) store of concern for animals. Finally, consumers of the images and stories may consider that they have an animal encounter when they encountered solely cultural beings.

During the year 2000, New York City hosted more than 500 life-sized fiberglass glass cows that had been decorated by artists. They were placed around the five boroughs of New York in a "CowParade." Among fanciful and colorful cows like a Rockette cow, a surfing cow, and a taxi cow, was filmmaker David Lynch's "Eat My Fear" cow. With forks and knives stuck into the cow's behind, the bloody disemboweled cow was displayed for only a couple of hours. During that time at least one small child, upon seeing it, started crying. Then it was banished to a warehouse and put under wraps (Friend 2000). While meat eating requires violence, the absent referent functions to put the violence under wraps: there is no "cow" whom we have to think about, there is no butchering, no feelings, and no fear, just the end product. (And David Lynch is correct: people eat animals' fear. Nonhumans who experience fear before death release adrenalin which can leave soft, mushy spots in their "meat," making their flesh tougher.) In the case of the banished cow, it was a cultural product—David Lynch's artistic representation of a slaughtered cow—that was offensive and removed.[1]

In modernism there was something to be alienated from. Modern humans were sensible of their distance from the "real." Indeed, there was a nostalgic sense that there existed a *real* to be alienated from. In postmodernism, there is nothing to be alienated from. There is only the system. We can never know the structure itself that we are in. Ontologically, the cultural becomes the "real." There isn't anything more real to someone than Lamb Chop the puppet or the play "Greater Tuna" or Pooh Bear. Such a change in perspective is a devastating one for it enables a further distancing from the fates of individual nonhuman animal beings. There is a great divide between those who love lambs and do not eat lamb chops and those who love Sheri Lewis's Lamb Chop. What we have now is an extreme distancing from the experience of most nonhuman animals at the same time that people express and act upon deep longings for connections with others, including nonhuman animals and the rest of "nature"—whatever that is. As the *appearance* of the "actual" displaces the actual experience of nonhuman animals as the referent for our relationships with other animals, feelings of alienation and separation for humans as well as a deep longing for connection intensify. (On this point see Berger 1980.) Frederic Jameson observes in *Postmodernism*:

> In modernism . . . some residual zones of "nature" or "being," of the old, the older, the archaic, still subsist; culture can still do something to that nature and work at transforming that "referent."

---

[1] In the United States, since the nineteenth century, slaughterhouses themselves have been banished from the marketplace through zoning laws that forbade their operation in certain sections of a city. In the first test of the Fourteenth Amendment in 1873, this zoning was upheld. See my discussion of the "Slaughterhouse Cases" (2015: 215, n 23.)

> Postmodernism is what you have when the modernization process is complete and nature is gone for good. It is a more fully human world than the older one, but one in which "culture" has become a veritable "second nature." (Jameson 1992: ix)

Jameson argues that in general we have passed from the modern period, with nature still a referent, to a postmodern period with culture as the referent. His insight suggests that in a postmodern time animals too will more frequently have cultural referents. The response to the Lynch-ed cow was not that David Lynch should become an animal rights activist (he admits that he eats meat), but that he should return to filmmaking—return to more acceptable cultural productions (Friend 2000: 62–63).

During the modern period actual animals were the referent, albeit often absent. Now our culture's *concept* of animals is the referent. The cultural referent is stuffed animals, puppets, fiberglass cows, and plays. In response to the Pooh furor, an ironic reminder of cultural consumption at its most literal was invoked. A *Times* editorial reminded its readers of Maurice Sendak's classic comment about great children's book: few first editions exist because they have been eaten ("Psychoanalyzing" 1998).

Modern versus postmodern animal encounters

If, as I suggest above, there has been a shift in relationship to animals and what prevails now is a cultural concept of animals, such a shift should be evident in a variety of cultural manifestations. In this section I identify some of the areas in which this change can be perceived. The shifts from modern to postmodern approaches are often telegraphed through a chart of binaries. David Harvey (1997), for instance, reproduces Ihab Hassan's (1985) thirty-two binaries that show schematic differences between modernism and postmodernism: purpose/play, design/chance, hierarchy/anarchy, presence/absence, centring/dispersal, paradigm/syntagm, metaphor/metonymy, master code/idiolect, symptom/desire, paranoia/schizophrenia, metaphysics/irony, determinancy/indeterminancy, et al. (Harvey 1990: 43; Hassan 1985: 123–24). As Harvey explains, "the 'real structure of feeling' in both the modern and postmodern periods, lies in the manner in which these stylistic oppositions are synthesized" (42).

Such an evocation of binaries can be helpful in demonstrating how human beings are encountering animal beings today. In Table 6, I identify some of the changes I perceive. A discussion of each of these dyads follows.

Table 6 Modern and late capitalist animal-related binaries

Modern	Late capitalist
• transforms the referent of nature	• transforms the referent of culture
• animals are absent referents	• "animals" as referents
• factories modeled on slaughterhouses	• farms modeled on factories
• farms owned by individuals	• factory farms owned by corporations
• zoos	• conservation that becomes p/reservation
• animals as machines, "beast machines"	• machines as animals, "gigapets"
• vivisection in universities	• Biomedical research by corporations
• *in vivo* research—uses the whole animal	• in *vitro* research—uses isolated animal parts
• "pollo-vegetarians"	• mock meat
• viruses	• prions
• animal rights	• animal rites
• product liability	• product "libel-ity"
• *Animal Farm*	• *Jurassic Park*

Factories modeled on slaughterhouses > Farms modeled on factories

In *The Sexual Politics of Meat* I described how the division of labor on factory assembly lines owes its inception to Henry Ford's visit to the disassembly line of the Chicago slaughterhouses (2015: 32–33). Ford credited the idea of the assembly line to the fragmented activities of animal slaughtering: "The idea came in a general way from the overhead trolley that the Chicago packers use in dressing beef" (Ford 1922: 81). One book on meat production (financed by a meat-packing company) describes the process: "The slaughtered animals, suspended head downward from a moving chain, or conveyor, pass from workman to workman, each of whom performs some particular step in the process." The authors proudly add: "So efficient has this procedure proved to be that it has been adopted by many other industries, as for example in the assembling of automobiles" (Hinman and Harris 1939: 64–5).

Although Ford reversed the outcome of the process of slaughtering in that a product is created rather than fragmented on the assembly line, he contributed at the same time to the larger fragmentation of the individual's work and productivity. The dismemberment of the human body is not so much a construct of modern capitalism as modern capitalism is a construct built on dismemberment and fragmentation. As James Barrett observes, "Historians have deprived the [meat]packers of their rightful title of mass-production pioneers, for it was not Henry Ford but Gustavus Swift and Philip Armour who developed the assembly-line technique that continues to symbolize the rationalized organization of work" (1987: 20).

The introduction of the assembly line in the auto industry—called "Fordism" by David Harvey in *The Condition of Postmodernity*—had a quick and unsettling effect on the workers. Standardization of work and separation from the final product became fundamental to the laborers' experience. The result was to increase worker's alienation from the product they produced. Automation severed workers from a sense of accomplishment through the fragmentation of their jobs. In *Labor and Monopoly Capital: The Degradation of Work in the Twentieth Century,* Harry Braverman explains the initial results of the introduction of the assembly line: "Craftsmanship gave way to a repeated detail operation, and wage rates were standardized at uniform levels." Working men left Ford in large numbers after the introduction of the assembly line. Braverman observes: "In this initial reaction to the assembly line we see the natural revulsion of the worker against the new kind of work" (1974: 148–49). Ford dismembered the meaning of work, introducing productivity without the sense of being productive. Fragmentation of the human body in late capitalism allows the dismembered part to represent the whole. Fordism created mass consumers as well as mass producers, insuring a plentiful supply of consumers for, among other things, those slaughterhouse products.

David Harvey's *Condition of Postmodernity* traces the architectural changes from modern to postmodern, from a time when space was shaped for aesthetic purposes to a time when "timeless and 'disinterested' beauty" was an objective in itself (1997: 67). In the reversal of the reversal—from disassembly line to assembly line—factories provide the architectural template for the new production methods applied to nonhumans. The attitude advised for pig farmers—"Forget the pig is an animal," but see him or her instead as "a machine in a factory" (Byrnes in Mason and Singer 1980: 1)—required an architecture of disinterest, of mass production, of factories. Architecture, which in many ways had failed to respond to the human shape, errs even more so with farmed animals. Thus, animals kept warehoused are crowded, unable to move or stretch. It is not surprising that they engage in antisocial behavior. The architectural change has enabled cannibalism. Rather than ameliorate the situation by changing the architecture, the response was to change the animal, for instance by removing the beaks of chickens and turkeys or the pigs' tails.[2]

Harvey cites the analysis of "symbolic capital" proposed by Bourdieu: product differentiation in urban design has become more and more important in the "pursuit of the consumption dollars of the rich." Luxury goods manifest this symbolic capital, whose purpose is to "conceal the fact that it originates in 'material' forms of capital" (1997: 77). Meat, once only available for the consumption of the rich in Europe during the early modern period, became "democratized" in the United States during the nineteenth century—a food that was available to all classes. It became one of the commodities that lessened the injury of class. Drawing on Bourdieu, Harvey explains the function of symbolic capital: since "the most successful ideological effects are those which have no words, and ask no more than complicitous silence," the production of symbolic capital serves ideological functions because the mechanisms through which it contributes "to the reproduction of the established order and the perpetuation of domination remain hidden" (78–79). Ideological effects are found too in the architecture of factory farms. They, too, required no more than a complicitous silence, enacted by the verbal silence of the nonhumans within and by the restriction on access to their inner spaces. In order to control the means of cultural production, it is illegal in many states to take photos or make videotapes of the conditions that prevail. These "ag-gag" laws are being challenged, and slowly overthrown.

---

[2]Sunuara Taylor shows how contemporary agriculture actively disables farmed animals in *Beasts of Burden* (2016).

Farms owned by individuals > Factory farms owned by corporations

After World War II this new way of "producing" nonhuman animals for human consumption also meant a change for the individual farmers. Farmers became contract laborers who grow the nonhumans at the corporations' behest, and the family farm disappears. This is a radical transformation: it changes the way some people can earn money; it changes the "countryside" as huge farms appear and produce, among other things, immense piles of manure; it changes the relationship between farmer and farmed; and it changes the very lifecycles of the farmed animals, e.g., the early removal of calves from their mothers, the killing of male chicks who have no economic value to the farmer.

Zoos > Conservation that becomes p/reservation.

According to Randy Malamud, the zoo is a model of empire and also imperial confiscation. The zoo "is the analogue, in popular culture, to the colonialist text in literary culture" (1998: 58). Zoos present a restricted, imperialistic, supremacist view of the natural world. Zoos are cruel to the animal beings who reside there. They inflict pain. Zoos steal not only the physical animals but also "their more metaphysical essence and integrity" (325). Zoos are not, despite their claims, mimetic of a larger macrocosm. Animal captivity therefore is harmful to the captive animal and to the human spectator. "People imprison animals, and pretend that they are bettering themselves by such actions" (27). Zoos want us to misread them as they inculcate in us a spectatorship of voyeurism.

Under attack for the conditions of nonhumans under their care, zoos in the late twentieth century discovered a new raison d'etre besides exhibiting the otherness of the other animals: *saving* them. While failing to acknowledge that the existence of one's species is of no relevance to an individual tiger or elephant, under the umbrella of preventing extinction zoos have become sites of preservation, "reservations" for those whose otherness is deemed worthy of perpetuating for human spectatorship. This leads to incongruous alliances. For instance, the Dallas Zoo and Exxon Corporation together created a $4.5 million tiger exhibit and breeding facility. Called "Exxon Endangered Tiger Exhibit," it is funded by city bonds, a $765,000 grant from Exxon, and the National Fish and Wildlife foundation's "Save the Tiger Fund." The Exxon exhibit was planned to house as many as ten Sumatran and Indochinese tigers and to include a facility where tigers could be bred every four to five years. Also included would be air-conditioned indoor holding areas with sleeping shelves and skylights, an outdoor exercise yard and two maternity dens.

Explaining why an oil company was undertaking this venture, Ed Ahnert, president of the Exxon Education foundation and manager of contributions for Exxon Corp explained, "We are the company that puts a tiger in your tank." The cultural referent is *Tony the Tiger.* A cultural tiger is concerned about "real" tigers. Whether a tiger in tank or a tiger in zoo, the idea of "tiger," like the idea of "the wild" is undergoing massive change. Since extinction doesn't matter to the individual (see Kappeler 1995), but to the group, a humanocentric concern is being imposed to create a unitary perspective. Further, the conditions of poverty, colonialism, and hunting that threaten the "tiger" are not identified. The political context is not a referent, only the cultural; "the zoo"—whose existence is traced to the human need to reaffirm human superiority over the other animals—becomes the referent for (and saver of!) the tiger. The logical extension of this is that one day there will be one or two animals of each species left—but they will be available to all of us, perhaps via the Internet. Whenever we want to "see" an animal, we can just log in to the virtual zoo, or "pet" store, or rain forest.

Animals as machines > Machines are beasts

Tom Regan's scholarly attempt to claim consciousness and biography for animals, *The Case for Animal Rights*—a valuable effort at recognizing the individuality of nonhumans—is notable, for our purposes, for two things. First, it was practically dated, even before its appearance, by postmodernism's replacement of the idea of the individual, autonomous subject with the idea of multiple selves and a fluid subject. Secondly, however, Regan's attempt as a "modern" project, of repudiating once and for all Descartes's definition of animals as machines, was an important development. Others, especially Steve Wise have followed in his footsteps (Wise 2001).[3]

While farmed animals become treated more and more like machines in factory farms when alive, the idea of machines as animals proliferates. I proposed earlier that one aspect of the postmodern relationship to the "cultural" animal is reflected ontologically: there is only "the system." Ontologically, the virtual becomes the real and this is effectively demonstrated in the development of the virtual pet, a digital toy that is treated as a pet. The "Tamagotchi" is one of the most well-known brands. One consumer describes the Tamagotchi:

> The object is to see how long you can get your tamagotchi to live and how well you care for it. Nothing complicated about it, which means no breeding, no nothing. With great care the tamagotchi can live 30 years (days). If you neglect [it] might only live about 6–9 years (days). It's up to you how you want your tamagotchi to be. (Lisa "insane" 2005)

---

[3] See also *Unlocking the Cage*, the documentary directed by Chris Hegedus and D. A. Pennebaker about Steven Wise's challenge to break down the legal wall that separates animals from humans. http://www.unlockingthecagethefilm.com/.

Another explains just how to keep your "pet" alive:

> You feed the pet, care for it, clean up after it, and teach it to behave. The second model has a sensor on top that lets your pet interact with other version 2 pets to play or even mate to make the next generation of Tamagotchis. The third model is able to use codes . . . to give your pet gifts, special food treats, and toys. (Miss Kitty "Toy Diva" 2006)

Giga Farms and Giga Circuses have also appeared. The majority of the first round of virtual pets was sold to girls. Manufacturers—to tap into the "boy" market—decided to forget about pets that need to be nurtured and decided to market virtual pets that fight. Computer game playing involving killing and blasting things fetishizes death in such a way to remove the concept of death. But with virtual pets, "dying" takes on another meaning: the playing is over. In order to understand the concept of meat eating, much less the "fact" of it, you have to comprehend the dying involved. In the computer-mediated world of virtual pets death involves mere disposability and replaceability.

The mediated realm of the computer-influenced age involves never seeing the actual animal and yet experiencing the animal as virtual pet. Elaborate mourning procedures can occur when a virtual pet died. Needless to say, however, a relationship with a virtual pet is not an encounter with an animal being.

Vivisection > Biomedical research; *In Vivo > In Vitro* research

"Vivisection" sounds so quaint; "biomedical research" has replaced it. The latter term works by association: biomedical research is research on animals. Where "vivisection" sounds perhaps unsavory and invasive, "biomedical research" sounds important and necessary. Thus, negative connotations accrue to those opposed to experimentation on animals: if one is not experimenting on animals one is not doing biomedical research. University research has spawned spin off for-profit companies. Research no longer focuses on how the nonhuman animal as an entity experiences something (*in vivo* research) but instead on how isolated animal parts experience being experimented upon (*in vitro* research). Ironically, the postmodern state has seen the proliferation of experimentation on nonhumans at the behest of the government at the same time that the possibilities for replacing such experimentation come into existence.

The bureaucratic state has reinforced the use of the nonhuman through a Byzantine regulatory process that insures that questionable animal studies are performed instead of quicker, less expensive non-animal ones. If relevant information from the experience of humans exists, it may be disregarded for questionable data from animals because of these regulations. Tests on nonhuman animals introduce variables that are not predictable and not necessarily reproducible.[4] Yet, because they are required by regulations, they continue.

Consider, for instance, one of the most popular nonhumans for animal experiments: rats. Rats cannot vomit toxins; humans can. Rodents are nose breathers; humans breathe through both the nose and the mouth, enabling us to ingest toxins simultaneously through both routes. Rats can synthesize Vitamin C in their bodies; humans do not. Excess fat accumulates in rat's liver; in humans it accumulates in the coronary arteries. Rats have no gall bladder; humans do. Animals are exposed to high doses of materials being tested; humans are exposed to low doses. Arsenic, to take one example, is not

---

[4]See, for instance, the infamous effects of thalidomide, taken by pregnant women in the 1950s and the 1960s. In the twenty-first century, it has been found to be efficacious in some cancers and other diseases.

carcinogenic in rodents; it is in humans. Because of this and numerous other differences that Alix Fano enumerates,

> the toxic effects observed in rodents may be completely irrelevant to those observed in humans because the organs that are affected, the types of cancers that are produced, the way in which they metastasize, and the rates at which they manifest themselves, are vastly different. (1997: 53)

At the same time that the postmodern state requires use of nonhuman animals, technological advances have created alternative, non-animal methods, including "computerized modeling and predication systems . . ., genetically engineered cell lines, X-ray assays, batteries of human skin and tissue cultures, epidemiological studies of populations, and carefully controlled clinical trials" (Fano 1997: 136). Most of these are fast, less costly, reproducible, and importantly, more accurate. Some companies have begun to use these alternatives. But regulations imposed by governmental bodies have created a double standard, requiring that non-animal methods be validated before they can be used, even though, as Fano explains, "it has never been scientifically shown that animal tests could be used to establish qualitative or quantitative carcinogenic risk for humans" (69).

The latest foray is xenotransplantation: because humans beings fail to designate their organs for use by others after their death, transplants from nonhuman animals whose consent is not necessary is being developed.

Pollo vegetarians > Mock meat

A response that weakened the concept of vegetarianism was its modification through terms such as "pollo-vegetarian" or "pesco-vegetarian." Individuals using such (mis)nomenclatures for themselves are actually omnivores who omit only dead four-legged beings or land animals from their diet. One might argue that the "pollo's" and the "pesco's" were hijacking vegetarianism back within a dominant modernist framework: the radical critique by vegetarianism of the consumption of dead bodies was eviscerated. Clearly, meat eaters who did not eat dead cows thought they could be classified as vegetarian because they did not eat "red meat." Chickens and fishes continued to be absent referents.

In contrast to meat eaters who believed themselves to be vegetarians has been the appearance of vegetarians who eat "meat." Prior to its contemporary manifestation, the use of substitutes that resemble the texture of meat could be found in many cultures. Now, however, mock meat is much more widely available, giving a new meaning to "mock turtle soup." Chinese cuisine pioneered the use of flavored gluten as a meat substitute. Buddhist vegetarians could dine on sweet and sour "shrimp," Chinese "duck," and kung pao "chicken." Chinese vegetarian restaurants whose entire menu comprises meat substitutes can be found in major cities throughout the United States. Meanwhile, mock meat suppliers of "tofuturkey," veggie "hot dogs," veggie "burgers" and even Canadian "bacon" have made inroads into traditional supermarkets. In the second decade of the twenty-first century, vegan "butcher" shops opened in Germany and the United States.

Here, quotation marks allow for the substitution of a cultural referent for the absent referent without any harm befalling animals. Ersatz meat is meat without the animal. There is no absent referent. Rather than meat eaters believing themselves to be vegetarians (pesco or pollo), the postmodern period has allowed for veg*ns to eat "meat." Moreover, it means that meat eaters may be eating veg*n meals without even knowing it.[5] Thus, post-meateating. Does a meal still

---

[5]In *Living Among Meat Eaters*, I argue that "Nonvegetarians are perfectly happy eating a vegan meal, as long as they are not aware they are doing so" (2009: 208).

require an ending, a closure? The modernist's ending was that a meal required meat. Perhaps, in fact, the idea of meat in a meal is a legacy of modernism. Postmodernism may liberate the absent referent from the meal without the consumer experiencing a perception of lack, of deprivation. The referent of tofuturkey can be unconsumed.

Viruses and antibodies > Prions

Viruses, such as HIV, influenza, and Ebola are modern diseases. Though they may have been around for centuries, especially influenza, they were only "discovered" during modern times. Viruses contain genetic material and require an animal host. A virus, by virtue of being a virus infects cells. The metaphor for describing the working of a virus is *invasion:*

> When a virus successfully invades a cell, it inserts its own genes into the cell's genome, and the viral genes seize control from the cell's own genes. The cell's internal machinery then begins producing what the viral genes demand instead of what the cell needs for itself. (Barry 2004: 100)

The influenza pandemic of the early twentieth century and the threat of another one share a common source—birds. Indeed, "evidence now suggests that *all* pandemic influenza viruses—in fact all human and mammalian flu viruses in general—owe their origins to avian influenza" (Greger 2006: 13).

One of the diseases that represents postmodern times is so-called "mad cow disease," a transmissible spongiform encephalopathy (see Chapter 6). Like viruses, this disease jumps species. Unlike viruses, it is believed that the agent that causes mad cow disease—prions—has no genetic material. As with the avian flu virus, mad cow disease signals the return of the referent as the prions leap from cows to human beings causing Creutzfeldt-Jakob Disease, the fatal human equivalent of mad cow disease.

> In 1984, Dr. Stanley B. Prusiner proposed that TSEs were caused by rogue proteins known as prions that are thought to be abnormal variants of the prion protein normally present on the surface of nerve cells.... Prions lack the DNA and RNA that are the hereditary material of other transmissible agents. (Altman 1996b)

Dr. Prusiner's studies, for which he won the Nobel Prize, were at first "regarded as heretical because they invoked a bizarre concept that infections could be caused by an agent without genetic material" (Altman 1996b). This idea of infectious proteins that cause disease was heretical because, as Laura Beil put it, "to science, that's a bit like announcing that after some research, it turns out that computers can crunch numbers perfectly fine without software" (Beil 1996: 8D).

TSE's appear invulnerable: cooking, canning, freezing, bleaching, and sterilizing cannot destroy them. They have been called "the smallest . . . most lethal self-perpetuating biological entities in the world" (Greger 1996). It is difficult to "make science" when a disease has no genetic material, a long incubation period, and cannot be precisely identified until after death. These leave laypeople, who are often acculturated to a science that works as a fact delivery system, uneasy. What makes it the representative postmodern disease is that it has no genetic materiality for it to refer back to.

Animal rights > Animal rites

After an incredible flourishing in the 1970s the animal rights movement has undergone some difficult times. First, many people seem concerned about animal welfare, but not quite as many are willing to go vegan or stop going to zoos. Secondly, because it has been best known as a "rights" movement, anyone who does not feel "rights" is the appropriate language because of its liberal assumptions (from environmentalists to postmodernists), disassociate themselves from the intent of the movement as well.[6]

In the narrative that imposes cause and effect on radical movements, the animal rights movement is traced to Peter Singer's *Animal Liberation* (1975), which doesn't actually advocate rights per se. More probably the awareness of the oppression of nonhumans that erupted in the 1970s was a result of a confluence of forces, including the extension of the anti-Vietnam war and anti-violence activism of the late 1960s and early 1970s to concern for nonhumans, the evolution of Earth Day from 1970 onward, and the extension of feminist insights to beings other than humans.

The animal rights movement has the misfortune of articulating a modernist claim just as postmodernism absorbs and displaces modernist thinking. It appears dated, announcing in its activism— boycotts, placards, lobbying—its own anachronism. It appears absolutist and serious in a time when irony and self-deprecation prevail. It is seen as too serious, too literal, too preachy. Trying to get culture to get back to the referent "animal" is seen as too boring, not playful. Peter Singer and Tom Regan, major theorists about nonhuman animals, are dismissed in a postmodern response that rejects their basic assumption that a modern, autonomous subject exists from which to extend their rights to nonhuman animals. For postmodernism, multiple, evolving selves exist, not a fixed unity.

This appears to be what PETA acknowledges. They don't spend too much time in their public campaigns saying, "care about the animals." Instead, they shock. They use visual images but with cultural referents, not animals. They're ironic. "Got Beer?" they ask in their

---

[6]Another way exists, as Josephine Donovan and I have sought to establish (2007).

attempt to point out that it "safer" to drink beer than milk, infuriating anti-drinking activists. "Got prostate cancer?" they asked when Rudi Giuliani—who indeed, did—was Mayor of New York City. (They were pointing out the connection between drinking cow's milk and prostrate cancer.) PETA has recognized that the referent, animals, is gone. And they are trying to work with what is there, cultural consumption, by manipulating cultural images and issues as I point out in the *parallax* interview (pp. 331–345).

David Harvey suggests that another aspect of the condition of postmodernity is that "widespread insecurity in labour markets, in technological mixes, credit systems, and the like" prompts a preoccupation with identity, with heritage, with entertainment (1997: 87). We all carry around with us, according to Jencks, a "*musee imaginaire* in our minds" (cited in Harvey 1990: 87). Animal rites become a postmodern project, in which members of the dominant culture claim identification with Native practices such as hunting while they continue to get their meals of dead animals from dominant practices such as factory farming or "organic" farming. Animal rites as heritage or New Age expression—the use of eagle feathers, drumming with leather drums, et al.—supersedes animal rights.

Animal rites might also entail the desire to affect the trappings of primitive cultures via scarification, tattoos, piercing, and following diets like the "Paleolithic" Diet. Trying to recapture one's primitive roots through body modification and false rituals that offer a "mystical experience," from sweat lodges to hunting, becomes a cultural idea of the primitive.

Similarly, the referent for faux fur is cultural. As Diana York Blaine observes, the insistence by producers and promoters of "faux fur" that it is not "real" seems strange, "perhaps for a more postmodern reason than merely avoiding the politics of fur, especially when it's bizarre in color or form. No animal bears fur like that, so it's in effect 'virtual fur', divorced from any living being. If, in modernism there's something to be alienated *from*, postmodern faux fur has no relationship to an actual animal—so why wear it? *Perhaps the engineered is now the Real.*"[7]

Product liability > Product "libel-ity"

Commodification is a process that produces consumers as well as meat. If product *liability* was the concern of the modern reform movement seeking to protect consumers from the product, product *libel-ity* is the postmodern response, designed to protect the product from consumers advocates.

During modern times, advocates attempted to protect consumers from dangerously manufactured products. Ralph Nader's famous *Unsafe at Any Speed* (1965), outlining car manufacturers' reluctance to introduce safety features, originated in this time period. In postmodern times, product libel-ity predominates, whereby products are protected from the consumers, specifically from activists speaking out on behalf of consumers. In many cases the products being "protected" are consumable dead bodies. In Great Britain, *McDonald's* sued activists Helen Steel and Davis Morris in the infamous "McLibel" case (Vidal 1997). In Texas, the National Cattleman's Beef Association sued Oprah Winfrey and anti-meat eating activist Howard Lyman after Lyman had commented on Oprah's show that ranchers were feeding dead cows to their herds (Lyman no date).

Product "libel-ity" becomes the vehicle for corporations to protect the commodification of the product and of the consumer.

---

[7]Diana York Blaine, personal communication. February 8, 1998.

No particular relief

I am not claiming that the modern period was a "better" time for nonhuman animals; it was not. Exploitation was their fate then, too. Nor do I see a break, some definitive moment when the modern ended, for I am not examining a linear process, but one with both continuities and discontinuities. In many instances, *how* the nonhumans are exploited remain the same—they are eaten, experimented upon, are the captive entertainment at circuses and zoos. What seems to be different is how humans receive this information. I quoted Harvey's suggestion earlier that "the real 'structure of feeling' in both the modern and postmodern periods, like in the manner in which these stylistic oppositions are synthesized" (1997: 42). For instance, Hassan and Harvey identify a movement away from metaphysics toward irony. Such a movement enables the "ironizing" of animals' situation and of how humans encounter them.

Those caring for animals face another layer of denial that they must break through: not that people do not care, but that people are bored by it. Thus, we are more likely to encounter the (absent) animal referent in the Business section of the *New York Times* than in the News section. For instance, before the Thanksgiving holiday, celebrated in the United States on the fourth Thursday of November, regular newspaper articles will feature the silly (the President "pardons" one turkey), and the dead (how to cook the unpardoned ones). Meanwhile, in the Business section, the Patents column announced in 1997, "New techniques for raising and killing turkeys arrive just in time for Thanksgiving" (Riordan 1997). Because patents have to be very specific in their description, the *Times* had to be very specific in explaining them and why they were needed.

The patents were for the development of antibodies to counteract a hen's unhappiness when her eggs are removed, to insure she will continue to lay more eggs; radiating the upper beak to cause it to fall off; a turkey call on a shotgun; and a suffocation process for killing turkeys by placing them in a chamber with carbon dioxide, argon, and little oxygen. The specificity of description of *why* the patents were needed was fascinating, touching on reproduction, the turkey's role as producer, and the transformation of live into dead—all topics that require describing what happens to the absent referent:

- Reproduction: Though turkey hens "like to lay a clutch of eggs and then sit on them until they hatch," the turkey farmer removes the eggs to hatch elsewhere. Yet, the *Times* acknowledges, the turkey hens are "upset" and "unhappy over the absence of their progeny."

- The turkey's role as producer of their own flesh: because turkeys live "in close proximity"—recall that farm architecture has changed, enabling cannibalism—the "tips of their beaks often are either cut off or cauterized to prevent the birds from injuring one another."

- During slaughtering, poultry workers must shackle a turkey's legs, hanging them upside down so that their head is immersed in water. The bird is stunned by an electrical current passing through the water. We are told that for the turkeys, "Their wings are flapping and they're very unhappy." *Then* their throats are slit.

The newly registered patents were attempts to ameliorate the situation for the farmer and the consumer, not the "unhappy" turkey, who still faces loss of progeny, beak, and life.

Just as the banning of the cow from the CowParade suggests a rather definite substantiality to the referent, so too does the acknowledgment of slaughter in the *New York Times*' Business section. This is what complicates the postmodern response to activism on behalf of other animals. How does the absent referent become restored, made present? How is the very real animal body encountered? In contrast to activist efforts to undo reification, the postmodern cultural referent may only further objectify, and thus complicate, the attempt at restoration. Even if there were agreement that someone *is* there, who is it?

Playboar—the Pig Farmer's Playboy offers one answer. *Playboar's* function is to create a playful male identity. I was sent my first copy of *Playboar* shortly after the 1990 publication of *The Sexual Politics of Meat.* At first *Playboar* seemed to me a dated—modern—example of sexist humor. Its cover announced this, as it featured an homage to the 1960's movie version of *Lolita.* The movie advertisement for *Lolita* depicted heart-shaped sunglasses being worn by Lolita; with *Playboar,* a piglet wears heart-shaped sunglasses. In the many years of its existence, *Playboar* has felt the need to update itself only minimally. It did so with one aspect of its centerfold (reproduced on p. 232). I had described the centerfold that appeared in *Playboar* in *The Sexual Politics of Meat* (2015: 20). At that time, I did not know that the image I was describing was from this magazine. I had encountered it in the pages of *The Beast,* a British animal activist magazine, in the early 1980s. (The history of that image can be found on pp. 233–236.)

At the time that I first encountered this seductive pig, she was called "Ursula Hamdress"—a reference to Ursula Andress, the buxom movie star of the 1960s. But in the copy of *Playboar* sent to me by an activist in the 1990s, this "Littermate of the Year" had been renamed: "Taffy Lovely." Sensing that some cultural referent had gone out of style, *Playboar* updated itself. But regarding the animals themselves, nothing had to be changed.

In Chapter 3 of *The Conditions of Postmodernity,* Harvey provides a discussion of the postmodern binaries referred to in part two of this essay. He observes "the evaporation of any sense of historical continuity and memory, and the rejection of meta-narratives" (55). One of the manifestations of postmodernity is that, "The immediacy of events, the sensationalism of the spectacle (political, scientific, military, as well as those of entertainment), become the stuff of which consciousness is formed" (54). Running parallel to the text in that chapter are the images of naked women that I discussed in Chapter 7. If he had encountered "Ursula" or "Taffy" in his research he might have included her as well for she, too, like Manet's *Olympia*, is posed in a reworking of the ideas of Titian.

The question to be asked of both of them is are they masturbating? Those who manipulated the pig offer the answer that at first art historians hesitated to admit about the *Venus D'Urbino*: her genitalia are not being *covered*, they are being *stimulated*. The major difference between them is the gaze: Venus beholds us directly, but would, or could, the pig? Is the pig even alive?

Harvey acknowledges "that the subordination of women, one of many 'troublesome contradictions' in bourgeois Enlightenment practices, can expect no particular relief by appeal to postmodernism" (Harvey 1990: 65). Recently I came upon *Playboar* for sale at the bookstore at one of *the* most upscale of Dallas's upscale malls, where symbolic capital is their stock-in-trade. *Playboar* was placed immediately in front of the check-out counter.

"Out of curiosity," I said to the clerk, "I am wondering why are you carrying this?"

"We can't keep it in stock!" the man behind the counter responded.

Playboar confirms Harvey's claim that some things do not change and there are some things that postmodernism has not relieved.

Clearly gendered, the pig is either drugged or dead to be posed in this position. Her eventual fate is represented there: dead, consumable female flesh.

Which will prove harder to change, the menu with pig, cow, chicken and other flesh still central to it, or the subordination of women? It depends in part upon whether butchery truly animates an aspect of women's consumability and whether women's subordination creates the environment for the absent referent status of nonhumans (see Adams 2003a).

Playboar conveys a message to those injured by class, a message that meat eating once was able to sustain on its own: not only, "I can't be wealthy, but I can eat meat," but also, "I can't be wealthy, but I can own a woman, I can eat meat, and I can enjoy the comic degradation of women and animals."

With the absent referent, we do not have to see meat eating as contact with a once-living *animal* because it has been renamed as contact with *food*. We do not have to think, "This is an encounter with an animal, an animal whom I required be violently killed and dismembered." Whether or not that nonhuman is able to be experienced more fully because of the slippery nature of the subject as ushered in by postmodernism, it remains the case that whatever subject status nonhumans might gain from postmodernism, they have yet to gain it at the supper table.

When I meet postmodern theorists whose work I value and we discuss the status of nonhuman animals something peculiar happens. I think that we are discussing the cultural referent when suddenly a defensive acknowledge is made. I am not told, "I think the referent is even more slippery or culturally-mediated than you discuss in your book." Instead, I am informed, "You need to know, I'm not a veg*n." I am always surprised that they feel compelled to tell me this, as in those situations I usually follow a "don't ask, don't tell" rule.[8] Sometimes, precisely which nonhumans the theorist consumes are identified ("I still eat fish," "chicken," etc.). The autonomous, unitary human fades in the presence of postmodernism, *except* at a meal. At that time, there is only one mouth, one stomach, one tongue performing the act of feeding one body.

---

[8] On the dynamics of discussions between veg*ns and meat eaters, see my *Living Among Meat Eaters* (2009), especially 91–122.

If George Orwell's *Animal Farm* is the representative modern novel, in both its theme and depiction of a time when animals are owned by individual farmers, Michael Crichton's *Jurassic Park* is perhaps the postmodern equivalent: animals produced by science, especially the computer, and then computer graphics bring the animals to "life" at the movies. In *Animal Farm* one of the first things the liberated pigs do is to throw away the implements of their oppression. In *Jurassic Park*, a meat eater's nightmare is depicted, as carnivorous dinosaurs attempt to do to people what people do to nonhuman animals, i.e., eat them. From a farm to a park, from politics to play, from animals representing the working laborers overthrowing the moneyed class, to the consumption of leisure and entertainment for that moneyed class. The individual who saves the human from the nonhumans in *Jurassic Park* is the sole vegetarian in the movie. She does so not through battling the foe in hand to claw combat, but by breaking the computer's password that enables certain doors to close and stop the carnivores.

Ursula Nordstrom, the famous Harper & Row children's editor, who worked with almost every luminary of children's literature—Margaret Wise Brown, Maurice Sendak, Laura Ingalls Wilder, and E. B. White among them—tells an interesting story. She was once offered a meal with a dead rabbit as the main course. She demurred, explaining "I publish rabbits" (Marcus 1998: xxxi). The referent was cultural.

Not a break, not a dichotomy, but something continuous from *Animal Farm* onward remains in the present. It the difference between eating one's childhood copy of a children's classic and eating a rabbit or a cow.

Figure 12.2

Matteo Gilebbi is a senior lecturing fellow and cultural advisor in the Romance Studies Department at Duke University. His primary area of research is the interaction between literature, philosophy, and digital media in modern and contemporary culture, with a particular interest in animal studies. His recent publications take an eco-critical approach to Italian contemporary poetry and cinema, examining poets such as Ungaretti, Luzi, Volponi, and Ferrari, and filmmakers such as Sorrentino, Garrone, Crialese, and Rohrwacher.

13

Ecofeminism, anti-speciesism, and eco-activism: An interview with Carol J. Adams by Matteo Gilebbi

Matteo Gilebbi: You have just co-edited and published a new book entitled *Ecofeminism: Feminist Interactions With Other Animals and the Earth*. In the first chapter, "Groundwork," together with Lori Gruen and other authors, you delineate a sort of history of ecofeminism. In light of this history, could you talk about the struggles and successes of an ecofeminist approach to anti-speciesism and eco-activism?

The word "ecofeminism" first appeared in the early 1970s as part of the radical feminist movement that was appearing around the world to challenge patriarchal power. Out of that movement of the early

"Eco-Feminism, Anti-Speciesism and Eco-Activism. An Interview with Carol J. Adams" by Matteo Gilebbi was first published in 2016 in a special issue on "Animal Studies," in the journal *Rivista italiana di antispecismo, Novalogos, Aprilia*, edited by Alessandra Pigliaru and Eleonora Adorni. Used by permission.

seventies came the domestic violence movement—the exposure of how much violence happened in the home. The radical feminist movement at that time also identified date rape and marital rape as more frequent forms of sexual violence than stranger rape. Sexual harassment became defined at that time. So at a time when underlying violent institutions were identified as part of patriarchal power, ecofeminism appeared. It said, "You can't understand environmental problems without a feminist perspective. And you can't understand feminist issues without an environmental perspective." From that dialogue between environmentalism and feminism became the activism and scholarship known as ecofeminism.

In the early nineties, ecofeminism became the focus of much scholarly work—including a special edition of *Hypatia*. Several anthologies appeared. Ecofeminist philosophy was being engaged with by other disciplines. At that point, one aspect of ecofeminism challenged the idea that you could talk about the environment and consider yourself an environmentalist without addressing the fact that people were eating animals and dairy products and eggs. This strand of ecofeminism became known as "animal ecofeminism" in some quarters.[1]

And then the backlash occurred. It occurred on several levels. First, ecofeminists were described as being essentialists, i.e., that we were saying that there was something unique or distinct about being a woman that made us more pacifist or less violent, that we were somehow holding an essentialist position that upheld the gender binary. Lori and I felt it was important to respond to this explicitly in the new anthology. We say, "Exposing dualistic frameworks operating in oppressive situations did not mean that ecofeminists valorized the

---

[1]For bibliographies and discussions of the writings generated, see Adams and Donovan (1995), Donovan and Adams (2007), and Adams and Gruen (2014).

non-dominant parts of the dualism nor viewed the characteristics of the non-dominant part as 'natural.' In arguing relationally and developing a care tradition in animal ethics, ecofeminists were challenging, not accepting the essentializing structure of the division between men as rational and women as emotional" (Adams and Gruen 2014: 30).

The second reaction was that ecofeminism became equated with a sort of second wave of feminism that posthumanism distrusted. And I think one reason posthumanists distrusted this second wave feminism is that after twenty years the perception of what had been achieved and what had been envisioned had eroded or been diluted (for instance, what had been accomplished in naming and challenging intimate violence). And so a stock character "second wave radical feminism" was being dismissed rather than an engagement with what the radical feminism of the early 1970s had been characterized by— including an intersectional approach to oppression. Third, animal rights and animal liberation, which are part of a mainstream analytic philosophy were becoming the predominant ways we were talking about the animals, and it trumped ecofeminism, which was becoming less and less well understood. That is one reason Lori and I began the new *Ecofeminist* anthology with a chapter on "Groundwork" to establish that "Analyzing mutually reinforcing logics of domination and drawing connections between practical implications of power relations has been a core project of ecofeminism, even before the word 'ecofeminism' was coined" (7).

The early 1990s was a very fertile time for the development of new disciplines: critical animal studies, animal studies, ecocriticism. They all started emerging around that time and they all have their roots at least partially or more fully in ecofeminism and yet fail to recognize that or acknowledge that. This, too, is a point we felt it was important to make: "In addition to this continuing misreading [of ecofeminism as essentialist], another problem became obvious, enabled in part by the misreading: the failure to credit ecofeminism's influence. The emerging field of Animal Studies grows out of, at least in part, feminist and ecofeminist theory. But this groundwork and history is often ignored or distorted in many discussions of animal studies. The result is not only the disappearance of ecofeminism, but the appropriation of ecofeminist ideas in which embodied authorship disappears." Greta Gaard's "New Directions for Ecofeminism: Toward a More Feminist Ecocriticism" (2010) and Susan Fraiman's important critique of the gendered omissions and distortions in the story of the beginnings of critical animal studies ("Pussy Panic versus Liking Animals: Tracking Gender in Animal Studies" [2012]) have helped to point out this problem of an inspiration that fails to be acknowledged.

I can't tell you how many graduate students of the early nineties told me *The Sexual Politics of Meat* gave them permission to write about animals. But if you look at the work that got published, you don't see that trail, you don't find the footprint of ecofeminism in the writing. And so suddenly you've got these disciplines, critical animal studies and ecocriticism that ten years after we were saying things are suddenly saying it, as though they have discovered it. And by the time we get to 2008–09, ecofeminists had realized that our history has been in a sense betrayed or denied and the radical and important creative ideas that we had postulated were being responded to in a new way now without anybody having a grasp of how long these ideas had actually been out there or that they had been developed and articulated by ecofeminists.

So, with "Groundwork" we were trying to say, "Look—these ideas, these *ecofeminist* ideas, this is not new, this is not recent; we have been intersectional and we have been engaging around these ideas for a long time and it is important for us to recognize it." So why is it important? One thing is, when you look at the philosophical description or history of animal activism it's traced only to the mid-1970s, and we have a *father*; Peter Singer is called the *father* of the Animal Liberation Movement, and what that does is completely cut out more than ten years in which women were the first ones writing about it: Ruth Harrison in 1964 in *Animal Machines* and Brigid Brophy in 1965 in her "On the Rights of Animals" in the London *Sunday Times*. Searching for a "father" also eliminates the role of radical feminism in the early seventies in identifying that the treatment of animals is a patriarchal issue and as being the source for ecofeminist theory and activism.

By eliminating the earlier history and looking to *fathers*, we end up with a very rational philosophical approach to animals that ignores the major reason many people have for becoming involved: they care about animals, they respond to animals because they *care*. It eliminates the radical feminist critique of violence, of interconnected violence that ends up with images like "Ursula Hamdress." And it fails to acknowledge the influence of women who wrote in the 1960s. After all, Peter Singer's first writing on the subject was a response to an anthology, an anthology that included work by Ruth Harrison, the woman who wrote in 1964. So we've ended up with a truncated history, an incomplete history, and a history that does not register the problem of interconnected violence. And when we don't register interconnected violence we're not going to see the problem that patriarchal solutions (like PETA's) to animal oppression can't succeed because they are not cutting at the root of oppression. Rather than postulating a teleological understanding of the evolution of movements (per *Animal Liberation*), to wit: first there was Gay Liberation, then there was Black Liberation, then Women's Liberation and now Animal Liberation, ecofeminism says, "these liberations movements are connected and understanding how and why is important." Otherwise, we encounter embarrassing examples of using feminism and anti-racist insights to argue for animal liberation without ever acknowledging how animal liberation activism may appear sexist or racist.

According to the findings of some very recent studies our planet is on the verge of several ecological disasters (I am referring to the 2004 updated version of *The Limits of Growth, the 5th Intergovernmental Panel on Climate Change* report, and the NASA/ UC-Irvine study on Antarctica). In light of these reports, what does it mean to be an ecofeminist, a vegan, and an environmental activist today, in the era of the Anthropocene that is moving toward the post-human?

First it means we are trying to offer not a solution, but a remedy to the culture that has created the ecological crisis. I think an ecofeminist like me says "How did this crisis originate?," and that one of the ways it originates is through the postulation of the "autonomous" subject, the enlightenment, ontological rights-bearing subject, who comes to believe that what they've achieved has been achieved on their own. Even the animal rights movement holds to the idea that it's autonomous subjects who are the actors. (And then what we find is debates about whether Regan or Singer or Francione are "correct" when in fact they all presuppose the enlightenment subject, who is seen as separate from others).

One question ecofeminism asks is, "What's the origin of this crisis?"; and one of the answers is "the origin of this crisis is patriarchal ideas of separation and autonomy." In *The Pornography of Meat*, I argue that political privilege creates pleasure and then the privilege disappears and all that people experience is the pleasure. They never question, "Where did my privilege come from?" "Why do I assume I have emerged as an autonomous subject with this privilege?" "Where did my privilege to be eating dead animals come from?"

Because the privilege hides behind the pleasure, and the "pleasure" is depoliticized, experienced as apolitical—having no relevance to politics, when we come along and critique the situation we are seen to be challenging someone's *pleasure* rather than someone's *privilege*. To be a vegan in this culture, in Western culture, we're seen as taking away someone else's pleasure, just like radical feminists were thought to be taking away the pleasure of sexuality when all we were saying is that we were against inequality. Vegans say inequality has been made tasty; radical feminists say that inequality has been made sexy. The average person experiences the "tastiness" and "sexiness" of these different forms of inequality without recognizing the structures of oppression that enable "tastiness" and "sexiness" at the expense of others' bodies and lives.

So I think we have to begin with the ecofeminist analysis of where did the alienation from the rest of the world come from? And where did the privilege that creates the pleasure that causes the privilege to disappear come from? Privilege structures pleasure so that people fail to look beyond their own actions in what they are eating and connect it with carbon dioxide emissions that result from eating meat; they don't connect their pleasure as having immense effects, with having a carbon footprint, or a carbon hoofprint.

Another aspect of the ecofeminist response is that we are interconnected, that care is part of how we relate to the other, and that the "other" isn't just another so-called "human being," "homo sapien" or whatever, but that the other is potentially any part of this planet. I was working on a memoir of caregiving, and I was looking back at Martin Buber's *I and Thou*, which I'm sure many view as clearly a humanist work, but Buber is talking about how we relate to others—and "thou" would be the incorrect translation now, I think it would be "I and you." Buber explores what does it mean when I relate to another? And how do we describe this closeness in which there's a sort of fulfillment, a depth, a disappearance of each singular being into a connection? Buber recognizes that this experience that occurs in relationships also can happen with a tree. It's not something confined to these limited notions of our subjectivity. That's just an example because I've been thinking about the I-Thou relationship in caregiving, and the importance of the hyphen in connecting the caregiver and the care receiver.[2]

For an ecofeminist to talk about *care*—care is a radical, political way of situating ourselves. I think many people characterize it as conservative and reformist. But "care" is a radical political situating of ourselves in relationships to others. We all know that non-verbal expressions of pain are the most acute expressions of pain. And that even people who can use words lose their ability to articulate words when they experience extreme pain. (Elaine Scarry's *The Problem of Pain: The Making and Unmaking of the World* has shown this.) I know that a cow experiences extreme sadness and laments the separation from her calf. And if I know that this is true for the one cow and the one calf who were in a pasture in upstate New York, I can generalize from that and say something about all lactating cows, all cows who've given birth whose children are taken from them within two days. I care that they are suffering. I hear the note of lament and feel that we are called to stop it.

The radical feminist movement recognized that something was diluted in the radical critique of violence when we went from saying, "You have a foot on your neck, let me help you get it off," to "You have a foot on your neck, how does it feel?" The kind of ethic of care I'm talking about (and see *The Feminist Care Tradition in Animal Ethics: A Reader* for a fuller discussion), says: "Because I know how

---

[2] In *The Aesthetics of Care*, Josephine Donovan also considers Buber's I-Thou as applicable to the rest of nature (2016: 81–83).

you feel, I will remove my foot from your neck." Those who eat flesh and dairy have their foot on the necks of cows and calves, and all the other nonhuman animals they wish to eat. And the response has been this retrograde one of "humane slaughter" and the "locavore movement": "Oh, yes, I do indeed have my foot on your neck, but I can tell you aren't really suffering as badly as those other factory farmed cows, and when I kill you, my knife on your neck will be very fast."

The ecofeminist articulation of "care" becomes both a radical critique of patriarchal privilege as it has been depoliticized and becomes a remedy for responding to the crisis. So from a vegan ecofeminist position in this Anthropocene time when the world is so threatened, we're saying the response has to be, "It is not about *my* privilege to have this protected pleasure. My privilege is something that I've been granted because of the political structures that have allowed me to have it; a privilege over some other human beings, a privilege over all nonhuman beings, and a privilege over the earth. And because the consequences of this privilege have disappeared (the suffering and death of nonhuman animals and the destruction of the habitat, and the threat to the Earth), my job is to help people see both how the privilege was constructed and what those consequences are."

But also we need to challenge the idea that a vegan diet is about deprivation and lack of pleasure. What if the radical truth were: people can be perfectly happy as vegans but the dominant culture can't or won't acknowledge this? We aren't talking about creating a world in which everyone is deprived. Being vegan is not a diet of deprivation that we are undergoing just to save the planet. Being vegan is an exciting, wonderful culinary experience and we probably don't even know what's possible because it's still so new. So vegan, or animal, ecofeminism is an intervention that critiques and is visionary; that looks at individuals and at social structures, that deconstructs but also offers solutions.

I am particularly interested in eco-criticism and environmental humanities, that is the study and interpretation of texts focusing on the subject of nature, human-nature interaction, and environmental issues. With the ecological emergencies that this planet is facing, I consider eco-criticism the quintessential "political" form of criticism and what I like to call a "necessary hermeneutics."

In your opinion, in which ways can an eco-critical approach to art, literature, cinema, etc. have the potential to enrich the philosophical and ethical debate on anti-speciesism in general and ecofeminism in particular? And would you suggest any work of art or artist in particular that has the potential of educating the audience about environmental issues and ecofeminism?

I think that there is a huge potential for that—not that art has to prove the potential to be pedagogical, but that art is transformative. Art opens us to seeing in new ways. Look at *Guernica*. It could not even travel to Spain while Spain existed under a dictator. Here was a homeless piece of art invested with the hope and vision of a return, a vision that the artwork could not itself contain. When did it finally go back to Spain? 1981. Here is this profound statement of both grief and anger about war. I think poetry is revolutionary, too. I was looking at a poem this morning "On Being Asked To Write A Poem Against The War In Vietnam" by Hayden Carruth, and—I don't know the poem by heart but he says something like "I have to write a poem against Vietnam, and of course I will. I wrote it against Korea, and I wrote it against the war I served in, and I wrote it as a teenager against the war in Spain and Abyssinia, and war is so happy I do it because every once in a while it notices, it glances over and realizes here I am, once again, writing against it," and sort of implying a certain "I've been impotent against this huge thing called war" (Carruth 1992). But there is something subversive there, too.

I think that art changes lives and I don't know that our world allows us to experience it as much as we used to be of being exposed to transformative visions. I was at *Minding Animals* in 2009 in Australia, and every day there was a different art gallery opening, and one night Peter Singer was the speaker and one night I was the speaker. And Peter talked about how expensive art is and how people around the world are dying from hunger and he talked about his most recent book (*The Life You Can Save*) and I thought, well it is true, but why would we not want artists to make statements about this world? And the next night—I didn't know what I would be introducing—but I went to the art gallery early so I could walk around, and one of the pieces an artist had created was about endangered species. There were many small little ceramic pieces, and they represented all the endangered animals of the world that were close to extinction. And to experience the art you walked upon it, destroying it. And there was something visceral as you stepped on them, knowing this is what's truly happening.

And I think of a more recent example. Kathryn Eddy created an installation in which she left several paintings outside so that the weather—wind, rain, sun—would distort and eventually destroy the paintings. Many people became upset at this; and she responded by pointing out, "Why is it that you are more upset about these paintings being destroyed than you are about what is happening to animals?" We include her painting "Pig Blindness" in our *Ecofeminism* anthology because we address this issue of representation in the chapter on "Groundwork." There we say, "Issues of representation are urgent for oppressed groups because representations act as propaganda for dominance; transforming and resisting oppressive representations is part of the struggle toward liberation" (Adams and Gruen 2014: 25).

Figure 13.1

Figure 13.2

Figures 13.1 and 13.2 Artist's Statement: In my installation, *The Problematic Nature of Flatness*, 2012, I explored absence, an ongoing concern. It was an immersive installation in two parts, including a sound installation of farmed animal voices inside the gallery, while outside, in the middle of a field, stood a simple wooden structure, a human-sized cage approximately seven feet high, seven feet long, and five feet wide. Solar-powered spotlights shined from the slatted roof and highlighted the structure at night, while inside the space and open to the elements were hung two paintings of toy, plastic farm animals. By painting the plastic farm animals, as opposed to painting the animals themselves, I highlighted how we use idealized toys as a way to further separate ourselves from the suffering of real animals.

The idea was that this structure and the paintings would be forgotten and left outside, just as animals are absent from our everyday lives. The inconvenienced viewer walked out into the field and into a crowded and confined space to view the paintings, thus creating an immersive and performative space that mirrored the often forgotten confinement of the animals. Many expressed concern for the paintings being left out in the rain for the duration of the exhibition, which served to amplify the lack of concern for the actual animals that suffer within the unseen industrial agricultural complex.

Kathryn Eddy, *The Problematic Nature of Flatness*, Outdoor Installation, 2012.
The Problematic Nature of Flatness, Outdoor Installation, Paintings on Canvas, Wood, 2012. Photograph by Patricia McInroy.
The Problematic Nature of Flatness, Outdoor Installation at Night, Paintings on Canvas, Wood, 2012. Photograph by Patricia McInroy.

Since the publication of *The Sexual Politics of Meat*, artists have written to me to share their work with me. I have tried to include artists' works in subsequent books like *Neither Man nor Beast* and *The Pornography of Meat*. I believe there are some remarkable artists who are helping us challenge dominant viewpoints. And this gives me lots of hope. Art returns us to the issue of patriarchal methodologies. The patriarchal methodology has often been that even as we reject something like war, we protest it in ways that fit into a patriarchal methodology. How do we ever break out of it and create a sort of more right-brain, or creative way to change consciousness? Why do we think that winning a conversation, an argument, is the way to change somebody's mind? Why not cherish incubation? Why not recognize that people can grow and that change doesn't just happen by winning an argument? I saw an interesting example on Facebook: "Have you seen this animal?" It was modeled on those flyers that are posted that say, for instance, "Have you seen Rosie the cocker spaniel? She disappeared on this day, please call." But the stickers were of chickens and they were placed on the dead bodies of chickens being sold at the grocery store. "Have you seen this chicken?" It prompted the idea that the chicken had once been alive; it challenged the structure of the absent referent that enables meat eating. It both captured and challenged the absent referent by asking, "Have you seen Rosie the chicken? Please call."

Art that causes a disjunction between what we think we know and what we do know opens up an epistemological space that wasn't there, challenging the ontological that we've accepted and catalyzing us to throw off the shackles of the privilege we've left unexamined, and the pleasure we've benefitted from.

One of the amazing things of being the author of *The Sexual Politics of Meat*—which I could never have anticipated would be such an amazing experience and truly has been since the moment the book was published—is that there will be an art exhibit by fourteen women artists on how their artwork was influenced by reading *The Sexual Politics of Meat.* It is called *The Art of the Animal*, it is going to be a visually stunning and intellectually stirring investigation of the female and animal body from a multitude of perspectives. Each artist reflects on her work, placing it within the context of their experiences as women, activists, and embodied beings. The artists include Nava Atlas, Sunaura Taylor, Hester Jones, Patricia Denys, Suzy Gonzalez, Maria Lux, Olaitan Callender-Scott, Renee Lauzon, Angela Singer, Lynn Mowson, Yvette Watt, L. A. Watson, Janell O'Rourke, and Kathryn Eddy. It will be both an art exhibit at the National Museum of Animals and Society, and an exhibit book (Eddy et al. 2015. For more information see p. 100, note 3). To me this is remarkable, that my critical theory is a catalyst for artists; it's a beautiful gift.

Cowspiracy, a 2014 documentary denouncing the disastrous impacts of industrial livestock production and the invisibility of carnivore-normativity, faced challenges in filming and distribution and even received threats. What are your thoughts on the relationship between economy, animal-farming, and carnivore-normativity, and people's ability to communicate about it?

The question is: how do people think their way out of their worldview? Way back when, somebody said to me, "You can't argue with a country's or a person's mythology." And yet that's what I'm trying to do, that's what we're trying to do as vegans, as ecofeminists, and as vegan-feminists, we are really arguing with a mythology. So how do you do that? I think we've got to assume that sometimes arguments work, sometimes you and I can go around and around about this for thirty minutes and you say "Oh now I see. I'm going to stop today." And some vegan activists tell me they're very successful. Often the vegan activists that tell me that are men. I wrote *Living Among Meat*

Eaters to argue that we should view meat eaters as blocked veg*ns, and that in their response to us they are telling us why they are blocked. And if we look at them as being blocked vegans, then we'd realize that the question is not "Why did I become a vegan?" but "What's keeping them from being a vegan?" And if we approach it that way then perhaps we could sort of destabilize the conditions to open up the possibilities.

I suggest that we fix great vegan meals and not even remind people they are eating vegan because they know it at some level and then they get to incubate it and realize it and respond to it from their own experience. I'm always torn because there is a part of me that wants to be so damn confrontative, and say "God! Don't you know what you're doing?! What the hell! It's 2014 and you're eating barbecue?! Really?" But, you know what? I did that for twenty years. I've been a vegetarian for forty years and I've been a vegan for more than twenty years, and for the first twenty years I did it wrong, I answered every argument and what I learned was that because I had more answers than people had questions I was the one considered strident, I was the one considered intolerant. I was never granted the debate win because I had won; I was instead the confrontational, problematic, unhappy person. So, then I started thinking "All right, maybe there's a different way to do this; and that's when I started to try to take the position that I don't need to move and I don't need to defend myself. Let me throw off carnivore-normativity by requiring them to come to me. Instead of allowing the defensiveness to grow, what if I didn't take on that defensiveness, what if I try to see through it, what if I said "Well, what happens when you eat animals if you know that that's what you're doing?" or "Tell me about how you felt when your dog died? What were those feelings?" I believe that models for social change are stuck within the framework of the world we're trying to change. And I'm looking for models that break out of those normative assumptions.

And that's why vegan meals, creative responses, and puppets, and marches, but also songs and films and anything that sort of dislodges the autonomous individual's sense of having to hold onto whatever their notion of themselves is and instead opens up enough of a space that it can begin to take root. Now, with the kind of climate crisis we have, this process takes longer than we might have. So I'll also say that we can change the world if the United States government, for one, stopped subsidizing animal agriculture, stopped holding milk prices low, started charging for the water that is used by animal agriculture. Just removing federal subsidies would cause the price of meat to go up. And suddenly the free market would prevail for veganism. We don't actually have a free market economy for dairy, eggs and meat. We have a much more subsidized economy and I'm not even talking about the federal government subsiding the healthy diet, or subsidizing the environmentally more appropriate diet. All I'm saying is if the federal government removes the subsidies for the disastrous diet. . . .

Thank you Carol for this illuminating conversation. Is there anything you would like to add to what we have covered in this interview?

I have a lot of hope. After having worked around this issue for forty years, I think one of the things I'm happy about is how many people take ecofeminist ideas for granted now. That there are people on Twitter saying "I am a vegan," "I am a feminist," "I am a vegan feminist." Forty years ago when I started talking about this idea people truly thought I was crazy. What could possibly be the connection between vegetarianism and feminism? So whenever I see a vegan-feminist it's like "Yes! The world moves forward!" and I feel lucky to be a part of that.

Figure 14.1 *This is a collective statement created by the feminist artists participating in the* Point of Reference *art exhibit on May 28–July 18, 2015 at Watkins College of Art, Nashville Tennessee. They explain "each member of our group sat down and wrote for ten minutes about what feminism meant to them. Two writers of the group then composed this poem from each of the writings, so this piece truly is a collective work. Together, we created a stencil from 'butcher-paper', fastened the stencil to the wall, and applied spray paint to the stencil. The piece is approximately 10′ by 10′."*

Exhibition statement: *Feminist ideologies are easily misinterpreted throughout history; our departure will constitute our own point of reference. This exhibition explores the ideals of feminism historically pre-defined. No longer passively accepting all knowledge as truth, we are actively approaching our individual experiences, and have formed a group to create our dialogue with stories untold. The purpose of this group is to learn and share the knowledge and experiences of feminist artists living within the contemporary world.*

Manifesto statement: *In this defining manifesto, we focus more on our individuality, our mode of thought and philosophy, and our explicit wishes starting to turn to action more than a rigid call to action requested of the public. It is a thought-imbued blueprint, positioning as an upbeat and positive threshold to the road of our futures, and fuel and inspiration for battling obstacles of patriarchy, or perhaps, our own fears. Its gentle nature inversely and forcefully reminds us, that yes, our cause is worth it, we are worth it, and that feminism is important.*

Manifesto. "Nashville Feminist Art Collective," spray paint on stenciled "butcher-paper," 10′ by 10′. *Point of Reference* was organized by Jill Schumann and originally shown in Kent State University's Main Hall Art Gallery, March 10 to April 6.

Afterword: Manifesto

EVERYONE.
I WANT TO BE EVERYONE.
MY SUFFERING IS NOT MY OWN.
WE ARE SO TIRED OF BEING SMALL
WE WANT TO BE EXPANSIVE.
ARE WE CAPABLE
OF TRANSCENDING OPPRESSION?
I THINK I CAN.
I KNOW WE CAN.

WE SHALL SHOW YOU WAYS IN WHICH
WE CHOOSE TO TRANSCEND.
DO NOT FEAR YOUR EXPERIENCES
AS WE DO NOT FEAR OURS
MEANING IS USE.
EVERYONE WE KNOW.
EVERYTHING WE KNOW
TRANSFORMS US AGAIN & AGAIN.
TAKE THE LIBERTY TO DEFINE YOURSELF

WHEN WE MOVE IT IS A MOVEMENT.
WE ARE ALL ON THIS JOURNEY TOGETHER!

Figure 14.1

Artists' biographies

Robert Dunn was the editorial cartoonist for the (now defunct) *Buffalo Courier Express* for thirty years, from 1952 until it closed in 1982.

Kathryn Eddy is an interdisciplinary artist who uses painting, drawing, collage, photography, sculpture, writing, and immersive sound installation to explore the complexities of the animal/ human–animal relationship. As an activist against racism, domestic violence, and animal abuse, her current work comments on these issues and examines the patriarchal power structure that perpetuates them. Recognizing that speciesism, racism, and sexism are linked oppressions, she continues to question the political and social ramifications of living in a world where animals and women are mere objects for consumption. Eddy has exhibited her work in galleries and museums throughout the United States, most recently at the National Museum of Animals and Society in Los Angeles, California (http://kathryneddy.com/home.html).

Suzy González received her BFA in painting from Texas State University and earned her MFA in painting at the Rhode Island School of Design. She has attended residencies at Vermont Studio Center, Roger Williams National Memorial Park, and the Trelex Residency at the Tambopata Research Center in Peru. Recent exhibitions include

Sub-Scheme at Western Exhibitions in Chicago, the fifteenth Annual Alumni Invitational at Texas State University, and Young Latina Artists: *Y Que?* at the Mexic-Arte Museum in Austin, Texas. Book publications include *The Art of the Animal: Fourteen Women Artists Explore the Sexual Politics of Meat* and *Widening the Cycle: Menstrual Cycles and Reproductive Justice* (www.suzygonzalez.com).

Kathryn Kirkpatrick is a professor of English at Appalachian State University where she also serves as editor of *Cold Mountain Review*. She is the author of six collections of poetry, most recently two recipients of the NC Poetry Society's Brockman-Campbell award, *Our Held Animal Breath* (2012), and *Her Small Hands Were Not Beautiful* (2014). As a literary scholar in Irish studies and the environmental humanities, she has published essays on class trauma, eco-feminist poetics, and animal studies.

Vance Lehmkuhl is the vegan columnist for the *Philadelphia Daily News*, covering the city's plant-based food scene in his print column "V for Veg" and philly.com blog "V for Vegan." He is also the founder of the eco-pop band Green Beings, known primarily for the patter song "Leftovers" listing all the variety of food available without meat and dairy. For the first eight years of *VegNews*, he drew the magazine's editorial cartoon, Edgy Veggies, and in 1997, he published a collection of vegetarian cartoons, *The Joy of Soy*. He has often been known to draw humorous caricatures intended merely for friends' enjoyment.

Jo-Anne McArthur is an award-winning photojournalist, author, and activist who has been documenting the plight of animals around the globe for over a decade. She is the founder of *We Animals*, an internationally celebrated archive (http://weanimals.org/). Over one hundred animal organizations have benefited from her photography, many of which continue to work closely with Jo-Anne on stories, investigations, campaigns, and humane education. Jo-Anne is the subject of Canadian filmmaker Liz Marshall's acclaimed documentary *The Ghosts in Our Machine*, and her first book, *We Animals*, was published by Lantern Books in 2013. With Keri Cronin, she started *The Unbound Project*, to celebrate the inspiring women around the globe who are changing the world for animals (http://www. unboundproject.org/).

Pamela Nelson is an artist living in Dallas, working in painting, mixed media, and public art installations. Pamela has exhibited in over 100 national venues, including the Dallas Museum of Art, Austin Museum of Art, Arkansas Art Center in Little Rock, Beaumont Museum of Art, Texas, National Museum of Women in the Arts in Washington DC, and the National Arts Club in New York City. Public artworks by Nelson include designing four Dallas Area Rapid Transit (DART) light rail stations, designing twenty-four stained glass windows for a Richardson church, creating a terrazzo floor medallion at DFW Airport, and installing a color theory project at NorthPark Center in Dallas. She received her BFA in 1974 from Southern Methodist University. She served for ten years as vice chair of the U. S. Commission of Fine Arts in Washington DC, a monthly review panel for public art and architecture in Washington. Her gallery representation is Craighead Green Gallery, Dallas (www. pamelahnelson.com).

Janell O'Rourke is a multidisciplinary artist who lives and works in Queens New York. Janell has a BFA from Colorado State University, an MFA from Vermont College of Fine Arts, and has done postgraduate studies at New York University. Her recent work has been exhibited at the National Museum of Animals & Society (NMAS) in Los Angeles,

California, Kentler International Drawing Space in Brooklyn, New York, and St. Joseph's College in Patchogue, New York. She has received a number of awards, including the Merit Award, Vermont College of Fine Arts (2011); the Soaring Gardens Artists' Retreat, Pennsylvania (2010); and the Individual Artist Initiative from Queens Council for the Arts (2009). She is a founding member of the collective ArtAnimalAffect (http://janellorourke.com/).

Dan Piraro is the creator of the critically acclaimed, syndicated comic *Bizarro* and the author of numerous collections of his comics. He is an animal rights activist, atheist, NRA hating, ex-husband, father, stand-up comedian, painter, former host of FOX TV's "Utopia," philosophizing cartoonist who makes his living writing and drawing a new cartoon every day, 365 days a year. He has won several awards from the National Cartoonist Society for his comics, and in 2010 was named their Outstanding Cartoonist of the Year (http://bizarro.com/).

Darrell Plunkett was born in Dallas and grew up in Lewisville, Texas. He has been using acrylic paint, but has recently been experimenting with chalk pastels. He has been in The Stewpot Art Program since 2010 (http://thestewpot.org/art-program).

Melissa Potter's work has been exhibited at venues nationally and internationally. Grants for this work include three Fulbright awards to Serbia and Bosnia and Herzegovina, ArtsLink, the Soros Fund for Arts and Culture, and the Trust for Mutual Understanding. Her curatorial work has been funded by the Ellen Stone Belic Institute, the Crafts Research Fund, and the Clinton Hill Foundation, among others. She is currently an associate professor and director of the Book & Paper Program in the Art & Art History Department of Columbia College Chicago (http://www.melpotter.com/).

Eric Reinders is an associate professor of East Asian religions at Emory University. His most recent book is *Buddhist and Christian Responses to the Kowtow Problem in China* (2015). He provided the illustrations for *Fun With Chinese Grammar* (2014).

Angela Singer has explored the human-animal relationship since the mid-1990s. Her practice explores the ethical and epistemological consequences of humans using nonhuman life. Combining mixed-media with "recycled" vintage discarded taxidermy she aims to turn taxidermic meaning. Recent exhibitions include: 2016, *Dead Animals*, or the curious occurrence of taxidermy in contemporary art. David Winton Bell Gallery, Brown University, Providence, Rhode Island, USA; and 2014, *Points de vue d'artistes*. Universcience Cité des sciences et de l'industrie, Paris, France; and *Ecce animalia. Museum of Contemporary Sculpture*, Poland. (http:// www.angelasinger.com/).

Cindy Tower, daughter of a weapons test pilot, was born at Hollowman air force base next to the trinity test bomb site in Alamogordo, New Mexico. She moved to New York upon graduating from Cornell and went to graduate school at University of California, San Diego, to study with Allan Kaprow, a sixties conceptualist inventor of happenings. Tower lived in Brooklyn, New York, for thirty years before moving to San Antonio, Texas, where she is teaching.

L. A. Watson is an interdisciplinary artist and writer working in the field of human-animal studies. Watson holds an MFA from Vermont College of Fine Arts and has a BA in Gender and Women's Studies from the University of Kentucky. Her work has been exhibited both nationally and internationally, including the Mary H. Dana Women Artist Series at Rutgers University, and is in the permanent collection of The NMAS. She is a founding member of the artist coalition

ArtAnimalAffect; a cocurator for the Uncooped exhibition at NMAS; a coeditor of *The Art of the Animal*; and has recently contributed a chapter on the subject of "road kill" to *Economies of Death*. Watson currently works in her studio on Elk Hill farm in Frankfort, Kentucky (www.lawatsonart.com).

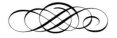

References

Adams, Carol J. 1975. 1990/2015 *The Sexual Politics of Meat: A Feminist-Vegetarian Critical Theory*. New York and London: Bloomsbury.

Adams, Carol J. 1991. "Ecofeminism and the Eating of Animals." *Hypatia* 6 (1): 125–45. Reprinted in *Neither Man nor Beast* (1994b/2015).

Adams, Carol J. 1994a. "Bringing Peace Home: A Feminist Philosophical Perspective on the Abuse of Women, Children, and Pet Animals." *Hypatia: A Journal of Feminist Philosophy* 9 (2). Reprinted in *Neither Man nor Beast* (1994b/2015).

Adams, Carol J. 1994b. (2015) *Neither Man nor Beast: Feminism and the Defense of Animals*. New York: Continuum International. Lantern Books Reprint.

Adams, Carol J. 1994c. "Sheltering the Companion Animals of Battered Women." *Feminists for Animal Rights Newsletter* 8, nos. 1–2 (Spring–Summer): 1, 8.

Adams, Carol J. 1994d. *Woman-Battering*. Minneapolis, MN: Fortress Press.

Adams, Carol J. 2001. (2008) *Living Among Meat Eaters: The Vegetarian's Survival Guide*. New York: Three Rivers Press. Lantern Books Reprint.

Adams, Carol J. 2003a (2015). *The Pornography of Meat*. New York: Continuum International. Lantern Books Reprint.

Adams, Carol J. 2003b. "Introduction to the Illinois Edition: Challenging Kreophagy and 'Meat-and-Potatoes' History." In *The Ethics of Diet: A Catena of Authorities Deprecatory of the Practice of Flesh-Eating*, edited by Howard Williams, ix–xxiv. Urbana and Chicago: University of Illinois Press.

Adams, Carol J. 2005. "Robert Morris and a Lost 18th-Century Book: An Introduction to Morris's *A Reasonable Plea for the Animal Creation*." *Organization and Environment* 18 (4) (December): 458–76.

Adams, Carol J. and Josephine Donovan, eds. 1995. *Animals and Women: Feminist Theoretical Explorations*. Durham: Duke University Press.

Adams, Carol J. and Patti Breitman. 2008. *How to Eat Like a Vegetarian Even if You Never Want to Be One*. New York: Lantern Books.

Adams, Carol J. and Lori Gruen. 2014. *Ecofeminism: Feminist Intersections with Other Animals and the Earth*. New York and London: Bloomsbury.

Altman, Lawrence K. 1996a. "W.H.O. Seeks Barriers Against Cow Disease." The *New York Times*. April 4: A4.

Altman, Lawrence K. 1996b. "Mad Cow Epidemic Puts Spotlight on Puzzling Human Brain Diseases." The *New York Times*. April 2.

Altman, Lawrence K. 1996c. "U.S. Confident on Mad Cow Disease." The *New York Times*. March 27: A8.

Altman, Lawrence K. 1996d. "Voluntary Rules on Feed After Cow Disease." The *New York Times*. March 30: 9.

Arendt, Hannah. 1970. *On Violence*. New York: Harcourt, Brace & World.

Attridge, Derek, ed. 1992. *Acts of Literature*. London: Routledge.

Avery, Byllye. 1990. "A Question of Survival/A Conspiracy of Silence: Abortion and Black Women's Health." In *From Reproduction to Reproductive Freedom: Transforming a Movement*, edited by Marlene Gerber-Fried, 75–82. Boston: South End Press.

Baker, Steve. 1993. *Picturing the Beast: Animals, Identity and Representation*. Manchester and New York: Manchester University Press.

Barnard, Neal D. 1996. "Mad Cow: The Risks of Meat Diet." The *Hartford Courant*. March 31.

Barnard, Neal D. 2004. "First Person Singular." *Washington Post*. 5 December, W05, http://www.washingtonpost.com/wp-dyn/articles/A28550-2004Dec2.html.

Barrett, James. 1987. *Work and Community in the Jungle: Chicago's Packinghouse Workers, 1894-1922*. Urbana and Chicago: University of Illinois Press.

Barry, Dan. 1998. "Back Home to Pooh Corner? Forget It, New York Says." The *New York Times*, February 5: 1 and A20.

Barry, John M. 2004. *The Great Influenza: The Epic Story of the Deadliest Plague in History*. New York: Viking.

Bartlett, Katharine T. 1987. "MacKinnon's Feminism: Power on Whose Terms?" *California Law Review* 75: 1559–70.

Bastian, Frank O., ed. 1991. *Creutzfeldt-Jakob Disease and Other Transmissable Spongiform Encephalopathies*. St. Louis: Mosby Year Book.

Beard, George M. 1898, 1972. *Sexual Neurasthenia [Nervous Exhaustion]: Its Hygiene, Causes, Symptoms and Treatment with a Chapter on Diet for the Nervous*. New York: Arno Press.

Beil, Laura. 1996. "What's the Beef? Unusual Type of Infectious Agent is Likely Suspect in 'mad cow' Disease." The *Dallas Morning News*. April 15: 8D, 9D.

Benton, Ted. 1988. "Humanism=Speciesism. Marx on Humans and Animals." *Radical Philosophy* 50: 4–18.

Benton, Ted. 1993. *Natural Relations: Ecology, Animal Rights, and Social Justice*. London and New York: Verso.

Berger, John. 1980. "Why Look at Animals?" In *About Looking*, 3–28. New York: Pantheon Books.

Bewes, Timothy. 2002. *Reification or The Anxiety of Late Capitalism*. London and New York: Verso.

Blakeslee, Sandra. 1994. "New Understanding of How a Protein Runs Amok." *The New York Times*. August 16: B8.

Blanchard, Dallas, and Terry J. Prewitt. 1993. *Religious Violence and Abortion: The Gideon Project*. Gainesville: University Press of Florida.

Blanchot, Maurice. 1995. *The Writing of the Disaster*. Translated by Ann Smock. Lincoln and London: University of Nebraska Press.

Bogle, Donald. 2001. *Toms, Coons, Mulattoes, Mammies, and Bucks: An Interpretive History of Blacks in American Films*. New York and London: Continuum.

Bradley, R. and J. W. Wilesmith. 1993. "Epidemiology and Control of Bovine Spongiform Encephalopathy (BSE)." In *Spongiform Encephalopathies*, edited by I V Allen, 932–59. Edinburgh: Churchill Livingstone.

Braverman, Harry. 1974. *Labor and Monopoly Capital: The Degradation of Work in the Twentieth Century*. New York and London: Monthly Review Press.

Brophy, Brigid. 1966. "The Rights of Animals." In *Don't Never Forget: Collected Views and Reviews*, 15–21. New York: Holt, Rinehart and Winston. (First published in the *Sunday Times,* October 1965.)

Brown, Wendy. 2002. *Manhood and Politics: A Feminist Reading in Political Thought*. Lanham, MD: Rowman and Littlefield.

Browne, Angela. 1987. *When Battered Women Kill*. New York: Free Press.

Bunster-Bunalto, Ximena. 1993. "Surviving Beyond Fear: Women and Torture in Latin America." In *Feminist Frameworks*, 3d ed., edited by Alison M. Jaggar and Paula S. Rothenberg, 252–61. New York: McGraw Hill.

Calarco, Matthew. 2004. "Deconstruction Is not Vegetarianism: Humanism, Subjectivity, and Animal Ethics." *Continental Philosophy Review* 37: 175–201.

Canedy, Dana. 1998. "Craze for Beanie Babies Helped Surge in '97 Toy Sales." *The New York Times*. February 10: C5.

Carby, Hazel V. 1987. *Reconstructing Womanhood: The Emergence of the Afro-American Woman Novelist*. New York: Oxford.

Carlin, Kathleen. n.d. *Defusing Violence: Helping Men Who Battered*. Atlanta, Georgia: Men Stopping Violence.

Carruth, Haydn. 1992. *Collected Shorter Poems, 1946-1991*. Port Townsend, Washington: Copper Canyon Press.

Caruth, Cathy. 1995. *Trauma: Exploration in Memory*. Baltimore: Johns Hopkins University Press.

Catoctin Broadcasting Corp., 2 FCC Rcd 2126 (Rev. Bd. 1987).

Cavalieri, Paola. 2009. *The Death of the Animal: A Dialogue*. New York: Columbia University Press.

Chadwick, Whitney. (1990) 1996. *Women, Art, and Society*. London: Thames and Hudson.

Chazot, G., E. Broussolle, C. I. Lapras, T. Blättler, A. Aguzzi, and N. Kopp. 1996. "Letters to the Editor: New Variant of Creutsfeldt-Jakob Disease in a 26-year-old French man." *The Lancet*. April 27: 1181.

Clark, Kate. 1998. "The Linquistics of Blame: Representations of Women in the *Sun's* Reporting of Crimes of Sexual Violence." In *The Feminist Critique of Language*, edited by Deborah Cameron, 183–97. London and New York: Routledge.

Coetzee, J. M. 1999. *The Lives of Animals*. Princeton, NJ: Princeton University Press.

Cohen, Lizbeth. 2003. *A Consumer's Republic: The Politics of Mass Consumption in Postwar America*. New York: Knopf.

Collins, Patricia Hill. 1990. *Black Feminist Thought: Knowledge, Consciousness, and the Politics of Empowerment*. Boston: Unwin Hyman.

Cowell, Alan. 1996. "Britain Asks Europe to Pay Most of Cost of Killing Cows." The *New York Times*. April 2: A3.

Cox, Peter. 1992. *The New Why You Don't Need Meat*. London: Bloomsbury.

Crenshaw, Kimberlé. 1991. "Demarginalizing the Intersection of Race and Sex: A Black Feminist Critique of Antidiscrimination Doctrine, Feminist Theory, and Antiracist Politics." In *Feminist Legal Theory: Readings in Law and Gender*, edited by Katharine T. Bartlett and Rosanne Kennedy, 57–80. Boulder: Westview Press.

Crenshaw, Kimberlé. 1992. "Whose Story Is It Anyway? Feminist and Antiracist Appropriations of Anita Hill." In *Race-ing Justice, Engendering Power: Essays on Anita Hill, Clarence Thomas, and the Construction of Social Reality*, edited by Toni Morrison, 402–40. New York: Pantheon Books.

Darnton, John. 1996a. "British Beef Sales Plunge as Germany and Italy Join Import Ban." The *New York Times*. March 23: 3.

Darnton, John. 1996b. "France and Belgium Ban British Beef over Cow Disease." The *New York Times*. March 22: A3.

Darnton, John. 1996c. "The Logic of the 'Mad Cow' Scare." The *New York Times*. March 31. The Week in Review: 1, 5.

Darnton, John. 1996d. "Europe Imposes an Export Ban On British Beef and Byproducts." The *New York Times*. March 28: A1.

Darnton, John. 1996e. "London Adamant as European Union Bans British Beef." The *New York Times*. March 26: A3.

Davanipour, Z., M. Alter, E. Sobel, and M. Callahan. 1985. "Sheep Consumption: A Possible Source of Spongiform Encephalopathy in Humans." *Neuroepidemiology* 4 (4): 240–49.

Davis, Angela Y. 1981. *Women, Race, and Class*. New York: Vintage Books.

Davis, Karen. 1988. "Farm Animals and the Feminine Connection." *The Animals' Agenda* January/February: 38–39

Davis, Karen. 1995. "Thinking Like a Chicken: Farm Animals and the Feminine Connection." In *Animals and Women: Feminist Theoretical Explorations*, edited by Carol J. Adams and Josephine Donovan, 192–212. Durham, NC: Duke University Press.

Davis, Karen. 1996/2009. *Prisoned Chickens, Poisoned Eggs: An Inside Look at the Modern Poultry Industry.* Summertown, TN: The Book Publishing Company.

Davis, Karen. 2001. *More than a Meal: The Turkey in History, Myth, Ritual, and Reality.* New York: Lantern Books.

Davis, Karen. 2005. *The Holocaust and the Henmaid's Tale: A Case for Comparing Atrocities.* New York: Lantern Books.

Davis, Kara and Wendy Lee. 2013. *Defiant Daughters: 21 Women on Art, Activism, Animals and The Sexual Politics of Meat.* New York: Lantern Books.

Davis, Susan and Margo DeMello. 2003. *Stories Rabbits Tell.* New York: Lantern.

Dealler, Stephen and Richard Lacey. 1991. "Beef and Bovine Spongiform Encephalopathy: The Risk Persists." *Nutrition and Health* 7: 117–33.

Deckha, Maneesha. 2006. "The Salience of Species Difference for Feminist Theory." *Hastings Women's Law Journal* 17 (1): 1–38.

De Angelis, Richard. 2005. "Of Mice and Vermin: Animals as Absent Referent in Art Spiegelman's *Maus.*" *International Journal of Comic Art* 7 (1): 230–49.

Derrida, Jacques. 1976. *Of Grammatology.* Baltimore: Johns Hopkins University.

Derrida, Jacques. 1991. "'Eating Well', or the Calculation of the Subject: An Interview with Jacques Derrida." In *Who Comes After the Subject?* edited by Eduardo Cadava, Peter Connor, and Jean-Luc Nancy, 96–119. London: Routledge.

Derrida, Jacques. 1992. "'This Strange Institution Called Literature': An Interview with Jacques Derrida." In *Acts of Literature*, edited by Derek Attridge, 33–75. London: Routledge.

Derrida, Jacques. 2002. "The Animal that Therefore I Am (More to Follow)." Translated by David Wills. *Critical Inquiry* 28: 369–418.

Derrida, Jacques. 2009. *The Beast & the Sovereign, volume 1.* Edited by Michel Lisse, Marie-Louise Mallet, and Ginette Michaud. Chicago and London: The University of Chicago Press.

DeWaal, Caroline Smith. 1996. *Playing Chicken: The Human Cost of Inadequate Regulation of the Poultry Industry.* Washington: Center for Science in the Public Interest.

Dill, Bill. 1989. "Serafin to Appeal FCC Ruling on WBUZ License Renewal." *Dunkirk Observer,* February 24.

Donovan, Josephine. (1990) 2007. "Animal Rights and Feminist Theory." *Signs: Journal of Women in Culture and Society* 15 (2). Reprinted in *The Feminist Care Tradition in Animal Ethics: A Reader*, edited by Josephine Donovan and Carol J. Adams. New York and London: Columbia University Press.

Donovan, Josephine. 2016. *The Aesthetics of Care.* New York and London: Bloomsbury.

Donovan, Josephine and Carol J. Adams. 2007. *The Feminist Care Tradition in Animal Ethics: A Reader*. New York and London: Columbia University Press.

Douglas, Susan J. (1994) *Where the Girls Are: Growing Up Female with the Mass Media*. New York: Random House.

Dunayer, Joan. 1995. "Sexist Words, Speciesist Roots." In *Animals and Women: Feminist Theoretical Explorations*, edited by Carol J. Adams and Josephine Donovan, 11–31. Durham, NC: Duke University Press.

Dunayer, Joan. 2001. *Animal Equality: Language and Liberation*. Derwood, MD: Ryce.

Durning, Alan Thein and Holly B. Brough. 1992. "Reforming the Livestock Economy." In *State of the World: A Worldwatch Institute Report on Progress Toward a Sustainable Society*, edited by Lester R. Brown, 66–82. New York: Norton and Co.

Dutton, Mary Ann. 1992. *Empowering and Healing the Battered Woman: A Model for Assessment and Intervention*. New York: Springer.

Dworkin, Andrea. 1983. *Right Wing Women*. New York: Perigree.

Dwyer, Johanna and Franklin M. Loew. 1994. "Nutritional Risks of Vegan Diets to Women and Children: Are they Preventable?" *Journal of Agricultural and Environmental Ethics* 7 (1): 87–110.

Eddy, Kathryn, L. A. Watson and Janell O'Rourke. 2015. *The Art of the Animal: Fourteen Women Artists Explore The Sexual Politics of Meat*. New York: Lantern Books.

EG Smith Collective. 1997. *Animal Ingredients A to Z*. 3rd ed. Oakland, CA: AK Press.

Estrich, Susan. 1987. *Real Rape*. Cambridge, MA: Harvard University Press.

Faludi, Susan. 1994. "The Naked Citadel." *The New Yorker*. 5 September.

Faludi, Susan. 2007. *The Terror Dream: Fear and Fantasy in Post-9/11 America*. New York: Henry Holt.

Fano, Alix. 1997. *Lethal Laws: Animal Testing, Human Health and Environmental Policy*. London and New York: Zed Books. Distributed in the United States by St. Martin's Press.

Fein, Esther B. 1986. "Fredonia Radio Station is Denied License Renewal; Bias is Charged." The *New York Times*, August 23: 41.

Ford, Henry, in colloboration with Samuel Crowther. 1922. *My Life and Work*. Garden City, N. Y.: Doubleday & Co.

Fraiman, Susan. 2012. "Pussy Panic versus Liking Animals: Tracking Gender in Animal Studies." *Critical Inquiry* 39 (1): 89–115.

Frankel, Glenn. 1990. "British Beef about Risk of Brain Illness." *Buffalo Evening News* May 20.

Fraser, Nancy. 1989. *Unruly Practices: Power, Discourse and Gender in Contemporary Social Theory*. Minneapolis: University of Minnesota Press.

Fredrickson, George M. 1971. *The Black Image in the White Mind: The Debate on Afro-American Character and Destiny, 1817-1914*. New York: Harper & Row.

Friend, Tad. 1993. "(Still) Looking for America." *The New Yorker*. October 11: 43–44.

Friend, Tad. 2000. "The Artistic Life: Kidnapped? A Painted Cow Goes Missing." *The New Yorker*. August 21 and 28: 62–63.

Frith, Katherine T. 1997. "Undressing the Ad: Reading Culture in Advertising." In *Undressing the Ad: Reading Culture in Advertising*, edited by Katherine T. Frith, 1–14. New York: Peter Lang.

Fur-Trapping in the U.S. n.d. http://www.antifursociety.org/Bloodsport_in_the_United_States.html (accessed February 8, 2016).

Gaard, Greta. 2010. "New Directions for Ecofeminism: Toward a More Feminist Ecocriticism." *Interdisciplinary Studies in Literature and Environment* 17 (4): 643–65.

Gaarder, Emily. 2011. *Women and the Animal Rights Movement*. New Brunswick, NJ: Rutgers University Press.

Ganley, Anne L. 1985. *Court-mandated Counseling for Men Who Batter: A Three-Day Workshop for Mental Health Professionals*. Washington, DC: Center for Women Policy Studies. Originally published 1981.

Ganley, Anne L. 1989. "Integrating Feminist and Social Learning Analyses of Aggression: Creating Multiple Models for Intervention with Men Who Batter." In *Treating Men Who Batter: Theory, Practice, and Programs*, edited by P. Lynn Caesar and L. Kevin Hamberger, 196–235. New York: Springer Publishing.

Garland-Thomson, Rosemarie. 2009. *Staring How We Look*. New York: Oxford University Press.

Garrett, Laurie. 1994. *The Coming Plague: Newly Emerging Diseases in a World out of Balance*. New York: Penguin Books.

Gilbert, Sandra M. and Susan Gubar. 1979. *The Madwoman in the Attic: The Woman Writer and the Nineteenth-Century Literary Imagination*. New Haven and London: Yale University Press.

Glaspell, Susan. 1927. *A Jury of Her Peers*. London: Ernest Benn.

Golden, Stephanie. 1992. *The Women Outside: Meaning and Myths of Homelessness*. Berkeley, CA: University of California Press.

Gonzales-Foerster, Dominque. 2008. "Essay." http://www.tate.org.uk/modern/exhibitions/dominiquegonzalezfoerster/essay.shtm.

Goodeve, Thyrza Nichols. 2008. "Meat is the No Body." In *Meat after Meat Joy*, edited by Heide Hatry, 10–17. Cambridge: Pierre Menard Gallery and New York: Daneyal Mahmood Gallery.

Gordon, Michael R. 1996. "U.S. Chicken in Every Pot? Nyet! Russians Cry Foul." The *New York Times*. 17.

Gordon-Reid, Annette. 2008. *The Hemingses of Monticello: An American Family*. New York and London: W. W. Norton & Co.

Gourevitch, Philip. 1998. *We Wish to Inform You that Tomorrow We Will Be Killed with Our Families: Stories from Rwanda.* New York: Farrar, Straus and Giroux.

Gray, Elizabeth Dodson. 1982. *Patriarchy as a Conceptual Trap.* Wellesley, MA: Roundtable Press.

Greger, Michael. 1996. "The Public Health Implications of Mad Cow Disease." *32nd World Vegetarian Congress.* http://www.ivu.org/congress/wvc96/madcow.html (accessed 11 September 2007).

Greger, Michael. 2006. *Bird Flu: A Virus of Our Own Hatching.* New York: Lantern Books.

Gruen, Lori. 2011. *Ethics and Animals: An Introduction.* Cambridge: Cambridge University Press.

Gruen, Lori and Greta Gaard. 1995. "Comment on Kathryn Paxton George's 'Should Feminists be Vegetarians?'" *Signs: Journal of Women in Culture and Society* 21 (1): 230–41.

Gustafson, Mickie. 1992. *Losing Your Dog: Coping with Grief when a Pet Dies.* Translated by Kersti Board. New York: Bergh Publishing.

Haddad, Charles. 1980. "Red-Hot Housing Debate is Costing Dunkirk Millions." *Buffalo Courier-Express* June 29: 1, D–13.

Hager, Mary and Mark Hosenball. 1996. "'Mad Cow Disease' in the U.S.?" *Newsweek* April 8: 58–59.

Hale, Grace Elizabeth. 1998. *Making Whiteness: The Culture of Segregation in the South: 1890-1940.* New York: Vintage Books.

Haraway, Donna. 1988. "Situated Knowledges: The Science Question in Feminism and the Privilege of Partial Perspective." *Feminist Studies* 14 (3): 575–99.

Haraway, Donna., ed. 1991. "A Cyborg Manifesto: Science, Technology and Socialist-Feminism in the Late Twentieth Century." In *Simians, Cyborgs, and Women: The Reinvention of Nature*, 149–81. London: Free Association.

Haraway, Donna. 2003. *The Companion Species Manifesto: Dogs, People, and Significant Otherness.* Chicago: Prickly Paradigm Press.

Harding, Sandra. 1983. "Is Gender a Variable in Conceptions of Rationality?" In *Beyond Domination: New Perspectives on Women and Philosophy*, edited by Carol Gould, 43–60. Totowa, NJ: Rowman and Allanheld.

Harding, Sandra. 1991. *Whose Science? Whose Knowledge? Thinking from Women's Lives.* Ithaca: Cornell University Press.

Harlow, Caroline Wolf. 1991. "Female Victims of Violent Crime." *Bureau of Justice Statistics* 5 (January).

Harper, Breeze A., ed. 2010. *Sistah Vegan: Black Female Vegans Speak on Food, Identity, Health and Society.* New York: Lantern Books.

Harris, Angela P. 1991. "Race and Essentialism in Feminist Legal Theory." In *Feminist Legal Theory: Readings in Law and Gender*, edited by Katharine T. Bartlett and Rosanne Kennedy, 253–66. Boulder: Westview Press.

Harris, Michael D. 2003. *Colored Pictures: Race and Visual Representation.* Chapel Hill and London: The University of North Carolina Press.

Harrison, Beverly Wildung. 1983. *Our Right to Choose:Toward a New Ethics of Abortion.* Boston: Beacon Press.

Harrison, Robert Pogue. 2005. *The Dominion of the Dead.* Chicago: University of Chicago Press.

Harrison, Ruth. 1964. *Animal Machines: The New Factory Farming Industry.* London: Vincent Stuart Publishers.

Hart, Barbara. 1986. "Lesbian Battering: An Examination." In *Naming the Violence: Speaking Out About Lesbian Battering,* edited by Kerry Lobel, 173–89. Seattle, WA: Seal Press.

Hartsock, Nancy C. M. 1983. *Money, Sex and Power: Toward a Feminist Historical Materialism.* New York: Longman.

Harvey, David. (1990) 1997. *The Condition of Postmodernity.* Cambridge, MA and Oxford: Blackwell.

Hassan, Ihab. 1985. "The Culture of Postmodernism." *Theory, Culture, and Society* 2 (3): 119–32.

Hearne, Vicki. 1991. "What's Wrong with Animal Rights." *Harpers.* September: 59–64.

Herman, Judith. 1992. *Trauma and Recovery.* New York: Basic Books.

Hine, Darlene Clark. 1989. "Rape and the Inner Lives of Black Women in the Middle West: Preliminary Thoughts on the Culture of Dissemblance." *Signs: Journal of Women in Culture and Society* 14 (4): 912–20.

Hinman, Robert B. and Robert B. Harris. 1939. *The Story of Meat.* Chicago: Swift & Co.

Hoagland, Sarah Lucia. 1988. *Lesbian Ethics: Toward New Values.* Palo Alto: Institute for Lesbian Studies.

Hochswender, Woody. 1990. "Clothes Make the Party, as Well." The *New York Times.* August 29: B2.

Hock, Paul. 1979. *White Hero, Black Beast: Racism, Sexism and the Mask of Masculinity.* London: Pluto Press.

Homans, Margaret. 1986. *Bearing the Word: Language and Female Experience in Nineteenth-Century Women's Writing.* Chicago: University of Chicago Press, 1986.

Homeless Women's Rights Network. 1989. Victims Again: Homeless Women in the New York City Shelter System.

Horyn, Cathy. 2004. "A Shelf Life So Short It Takes the Breath Away." The *New York Times.* November 16.

Hotchner, A. E. 2013. "Steak Shows Its Muscle." *Vanity Fair* (May). http://www.vanityfair.com/culture/2013/05/aa-gill-bull-blood-steak (accessed January 31, 2015).

Hughes, Robert. 1980. *The Shock of the New: Modern Art, Its Rise, Its Dazzling Achievement, Its Fall*. New York: Alfred A. Knopf.

Ingold, Tim. 1983. "The Architect and the Bee: Reflections on the Work of Animals and Men." *Man* 18: 1–20.

Jaggar, Alison M. 1988. *Feminist Politics and Human Nature*. Totowa, NJ: Rowman & Littlefield.

Jameson, Fredric. 1992. *Postmodernism or, The Cultural Logic of Late Capitalism*. Durham: Duke University Press.

Jeffrey, Sheila. 2008. *The Industrial Vagina*. New York: Routledge.

Jones, Ann. 1980. *Women Who Kill*. New York: Holt, Rinehart and Winston.

Jones, Ann. 1994. *Next Time, She'll Be Dead: Battering and How to Stop It*. Boston: Beacon Press.

Jones, Ann, and Susan Schechter. 1992. *When Love Goes Wrong: What to Do When Your Can't Do Anything Right. Strategies for Women with Controlling Partners*. New York: HarperCollins.

Jones, Maggie. 2008. "The Barnyard Strategist." *The New York Times Magazine*. October 24.

Jones, Patrice. 2007. *Aftershock: Confronting Trauma in a Violent World: A Guide for Activists and Their Allies*. New York: Lantern Books.

Jordan, Winthrop D. 1969. *White Over Black: American Attitudes Toward the Negro: 1550-1812*. Baltimore: Penguin Books.

Joy, Melanie. 2010. *Why We Love Dogs, Eat Pigs, and Wear Cows: An Introduction to Carnism*. Newburyport, MA: Conari Press.

Judge warns attorneys in Oprah trial. *The Dallas Morning News*, Associated Press report. February 7, 1998, 30A.

Kalechofsky, Roberta. 1987. "Metaphors of Nature: Vivisection and Pornography—The Manichean Machine." *Between the Species* 4 (3): 179–85.

Kappeler, Suzanne. 1986. *The Pornography of Representation*. Minneapolis: The University of Minnesota Press.

Kappeler, Suzanne. 1995. "Speciesism, Racism, Nationalism . . . or the Power of Scientific Subjectivity." In *Animals and Women: Feminist Theoretical Explorations,* edited by Carol J. Adams and Josephine Donovan, 320–52. Durham, NC: Duke University Press.

Katz, Gregory. 1996. "Anger, fright grow in British beef crisis." *The Dallas Morning News*. March 26: A1, A12.

Kelly, Liz. 1988. *Surviving Sexual Violence*. Minneapolis: University of Minnesota Press.

Kemmerer, Lisa, ed. 2011a. *Sister Species: Women, Animals and Social Justice*. Champlain and Chicago: University of Illinois.

Kemmerer, Lisa, ed. 2011b. *Speaking Up for Animals: An Anthology of Women's Voices*. Boulder and London: Paradigm Press.

Kheel, Marti. 2007. *Nature Ethics An Ecofeminist Perspective.* Lanham, MD: Rowman and Littlefield.

King, Ynestra. 1989. "Healing the Wounds: Feminism, Ecology, and Nature/ Culture Dualism." In *Gender/Body/Knowledge: Feminist Reconstruction of Being and Knowing,* edited by Alison M. Jaggar and Susan R. Bordo, 115–41. New Brunswick, NJ: Rutgers University Press.

Kleinman, Dana. 1985. "Debate on Abortion Focuses on Graphic Film." *Conscience* 6 (2): 11–12 (March/April).

Kovel, Joel. 1971. *White Racism: A Psychohistory.* New York: Vintage Books.

Kristof, Nicholas and Sheryl WuDunn. 2010. *Half the Sky: Turning Oppression into Opportunity Worldwide.* New York: Vintage.

Kuper, Leo. 1983. *Genocide: Its Political Use in the Twentieth Century.* New Haven, CT: Yale University Press.

Lacey, Richard W. and Stephen R. Dealler. 1991. "The BSE Time-Bomb? The Causes, the Risks, and the Solutions to the BSE Epidemic." *Ecologist* 21 (3): 117–22.

Lacey, Richard W. and Stephen R. Dealler. 1994. "The Transmission of Prion Disease. Vertical Transfer of Prion Disease." *Human Reproduction* 9 (10): 1792–96.

Langley, Gill, ed. 1989. *Animal Experimentation: The Consensus Changes.* New York: Chapman and Hall.

Lansbury, Coral. 1985. *The Old Brown Dog: Women, Workers and Vivisection in Edwardian England.* Madison: University of Wisconsin Press.

Lappé, Frances Moore. 1982. *Diet for a Small Planet.* New York: Ballantine Books.

Lardner, George, Jr. 1992. "The Stalking of Kristin: The Law Made It Easy for My Daughter's Killer." *The Washington Post.* https://www.washingtonpost.com/archive/opinions/1992/11/22/the-stalking-of-kristin/a569041c-6f52-4d44-b9b3-82b7f8cdda6d/ (accessed February 19, 2016).

Lisa "insane." 2005. "A Review on the Original Tamagotchi." *Amazon Customer Review.* June 12. http://www.amazon.com/review/R11K6BZTYVAPIZ/ref=cm_cr_rdp_perm (accessed 8 February 2008).

Lloyd, Genevieve. 1986. *The Man of Reason: Male and Female in Western Philosophy.* New York: Routledge.

Lorenz, Konrad. 1955. *Man Meets Dog.* Translated by M. K. Wilson. Cambridge, MA: Riverside Press.

"Lovelace," Linda [Linda Marchiano], with Mike McGrady. 1980. *Ordeal.* New York: Berkley Books.

Luke, Brian. 1992. "Justice, Caring, and Animal Liberation." *Between the Species* 8 (2): 100–08. Reprinted in *The Feminist Care Tradition in Animal Ethics: A Reader,* edited by Josephine Donovan and Carol J. Adams. New York: Columbia, 2005.

Luke, Brian. 1995. "Taming Ourselves or Going Feral? Toward a Nonpatriarchal Metaethic for Animal Liberation." In *Animals and Women: Feminist Theoretical Explorations*, edited by Carol J. Adams and Josephine Donovan, 290–319. Durham: Duke University Press.

Luke, Brian. 2007. *Brutal: Manhood and the Exploitation of Animals.* Champagne-Urbana, IL: University of Illinois Press.

Lutz, Ted. 1980a. "Council Hears Supporters, Opponents of Public Housing." *Dunkirk Evening Observer* March 5: 1, 4.

Lutz, Ted. 1980b. "City's Blacks, Whites Exchange Barbs Over Public Housing Issue." *Dunkirk Evening Observer* March 8: 1, 4.

Lyall, Sarah. 1996. "Britain's Daunting Prospect: Killing 15,000 Cows a Week." The *New York Times*. April 3: A1, A5.

Lyman, Howard (no date). *Mad Cowboy.* http://www.madcowboy.com/ (accessed February 11, 2008).

Lyons, Richards. 1981. "Mistrust Embroiling 2 Upstate Towns." The *New York Times*, December 20: 61.

MacKinnon, Catharine. 1983. "The Male Ideology of Privacy: A Feminist Perspective on the Right to Abortion." *Radical America* 17 (July-August): 22–35.

MacKinnon, Catharine. 1987a. *Feminism Unmodified: Discourses on Life and Law.* Cambridge, MA and London: Harvard University Press.

MacKinnon, Catharine. 1987b. "Reply by MacKinnon." *Radical America.* 69–70.

MacKinnon, Catharine.1989. *Toward a Feminist Theory of State.* Cambridge, MA and London: Harvard University Press.

MacKinnon, Catharine. 1990. "Liberalism and the Death of Feminism." In *The Sexual Liberals and the Attack on Feminism,* edited by Dorchen Leidholdt and Janice G. Raymond, 3–13. New York: Teachers College Press.

MacKinnon, Catharine.1991. "The Palm Beach Hanging." The *New York Times.* December 15.

MacKinnon, Catharine. 1993. *Only Words.* Cambridge, MA: Harvard University Press.

MacKinnon, Catharine. 1996. "From Practice to Theory, or What is a White Woman Anyway?" In *Radically Speaking: Feminism Reclaimed*, edited by Diane Bell and Renate Klein, 45–55. North Melbourne, VIC: Spinifex.

MacKinnon, Catharine. 2001. *Sex Equality.* New York: Foundation Press.

MacKinnon, Catharine. 2005. *Women's Lives, Men's Laws.* Cambridge, MA and London: Harvard University Press.

MacKinnon, Catharine. 2006. *Are Women Human? And Other International Dialogues.* Cambridge, MA and London: Harvard University Press.

MacKinnon, Catharine. 2008. "Of Mice and Men." In *The Feminist Care Tradition in Animal Ethics: A Reader,* edited by Josephine Donovan and Carol J. Adams, 316–32. New York and London: Columbia University Press.

Mahoney, Martha R. 1991. "Legal Images of Battered Women: Redefining the Issue of Separation." *Michigan Law Review* 90: 1–94.

Malamud, Randy. 1998. *Reading Zoos: Representations of Animals and Captivity.* New York: New York University Press.

Mangels, Ann Reed and Suzanne Havala. 1994. "Vegan Diets for Women, Infants, and Children." *Journal of Agricultural and Environmental Ethics* 7 (1): 111–22.

Marcus, Leonard S., ed. 1998. *Dear Genius: The Letters of Ursula Nordstrum.* New York: HarperCollins.

Mason, Jim. 1981. "Fear and Loathing on the Hog Farmer Trail: Jim Mason Takes a Poke at the 1981 American Pork Congress." *Vegetarian Times* (June) 47: 66–68.

Mason, Jim. 1993. *An Unnatural Order: Why We Are Destroying the Planet and Each Other.* New York: Simon and Schuster.

Mason, Jim, and Peter Singer. 1980. *Animal Factories.* New York: Crown Publishers.

Massey, D. 1991. "Flexible Sexism." *Environment and Planning* 9: 31–57.

Matsuda, Mari J., ed. 1993. "Public Response to Racist Speech: Considering the Victim's Story." In *Words That Wound: Critical Race Theory, Assaultive Speech, and the First Amendment.* Boulder: Westview Press.

McCarthy, Colman. 1996. "Eating Cows is the Real Madness." *The Washington Post.* April 9.

McLibel Support Campaign. 1996. Shareholders' Meeting of McDonald's Corporation Marred by Difficult Questioning and Protest. May 23. Press release, via Internet from the McLibel Support Group.

The McLibel Trial (no date). *McSpotlight.* http://www.mcspotlight.org/case/ (accessed February 11, 2008).

McShane, Claudette. 1988. *Warning: Dating May Be Hazardous to Your Health!* Racine, WI: Mother Courage Press.

Melson, Gail F. 2001. *Why the Wild Things Are: Animals in the Lives of Children.* Cambridge, MA: Harvard University Press.

Miller, Jean Baker. 1976. *Toward a New Psychology of Women.* Boston: Beacon Press.

Minkowski, Donna. 1994. "Missouri is Burning." *The Village Voice*, 8 February.

Miss Kitty "Toy Diva." 2006. Tamagotchi 1, 2, and 3. Amazon Customer Review. 22 June. http://www.amazon.com/review/R173PNY4320FJQ/ref=cm_cr_ rdp_perm/ (accessed February 8, 2008).

Mizelle, Brett. 2011. *Pig.* London: Reaktion.

Morrison, Toni. 1992. *Playing in the Dark: Whiteness and the Literary Imagination.* New York: Random House.

Moshenberg, Daniel. 2006. "Letter" to The *New York Times.* October 5.

Nader, Ralph. 1965. *Unsafe at Any Speed: The Designed-In Dangers of The American Automobile.* New York: Grossman.

Nevins, Allan. 1954. *Ford: The Times, The Man, The Company.* New York: Charles Scribner's Sons.

New York Times. May 7, 2009. Carole C. Noon obituary. http://www.nytimes.com/2009/05/07/science/07noon.html?_r=2&ref=obituaries.

Noske, Barbara. 1989/1997. *Humans and Other Animals: Beyond the Boundaries of Anthropology.* London: Pluto Press. Reprinted 1997 as *Beyond Boundaries: Humans and Animals.* Montreal, New York and London: Black Rose Books.

Olsen, Tillie. 1974. *Yonnondio: From the Thirties.* New York: Dell.

Olson, Joel. 2004. *The Abolition of White Democracy.* Minneapolis: The University of Minnesota.

Onions, C. T., ed. 1966. *The Oxford Dictionary of English Etymology.* Oxford: Clarendon Press.

Paczensky, Susanne von. 1990. "In a Semantic Fog: How to Confront the Accusation that Abortion Equals Killings." *Women's Studies International Forum* 13 (3): 177–84.

Painter, Nell Irvin. 2010. *The History of White People.* New York: Norton.

Parry, Jovian. 2010. "Gender and Slaughter in Popular Gastronomy." *Feminism & Psychology* 20 (3): 381–96.

"Patents" column. The *New York Times*, November 24, 1997: C2.

Patterson, Charles. 2002. *Eternal Treblinka: Our Treatment of Animals and the Holocaust.* New York: Lantern Books.

Physicians Committee for Responsible Medicine (PCRM). 1996. *Mad Cow Disease: The Risk to the U.S.* Obtain from PCRM, 5100 Wisconsin Avenue, NW Suite 404, Washington, DC. 20016.

Pluhar, Evelyn. 1992. "Who Can be Morally Obligated to be a Vegetarian?" *Journal of Agricultural and Environmental Ethics* 5, no. 1: 189–215.

Plumwood, Val. 1993. *Feminism and the Mastery of Nature.* London and New York: Routledge.

Plutarch. 2003. "Essay on Flesh Eating." In *The Ethics of Diet: A Catena of Authorities Deprecatory of the Practice of Flesh-Eating,* edited by Howard Williams. Reprint Urbana and Chicago: University of Illinois Press, with an introduction by Carol J. Adams.

Pornography and Sexual Violence: Evidence of the Link. The Complete Transcript of Public Hearings on Ordinances to Add Pornography as Discrimination Against Women, Minneapolis City Council, Government Operations Committee. Dec. 12 and 13, 1987. 1988. Minneapolis, MN: Minneapolis City Council.

Potts, Annie. 2012. "Meat Chicks and Egg Machines" in *Chicken.* London: Reaktion Books.

Power, Samantha. 2002. "*A Problem from Hell*": America and the Age of Genocide. New York: HarperPerennial.

References415

Psychoanalyzing Winnie-the-Pooh. 1998. "Editorial." The *New York Times*. 6 February.

Purdum, Todd S. 1996. "Clinton Aids Beef Industry in a Season of Low Prices." The *New York Times*. May 1: A9.

Quine, Willard Van Orman. 1960. *Word and Object*. Cambridge, MA: MIT Press.

Regan, Tom. 1983. *The Case for Animal Rights*. Berkeley and Los Angeles: University of California Press.

Reiheld, Alison. 2015. "Just Caring for Caregivers: What Society and the State Owe to Those Who Render Care." *Feminist Philosophical Quarterly* 1: 2, Article 1.

Renzetti, Claire M. 1992. *Violent Betrayal: Partner Abuse in Lesbian Relationships*. Newbury Park, CA: Sage.

Research Links Cancer Risk. 1996. The *New York Times*. C19.

Reuters North America via Internet. 1996. British teens stop eating beef, survey finds. May 28.

Rifkin, Jeremy. 1992. *Beyond Beef: The Rise and Fall of the Cattle Culture*. New York: Dutton.

Riordan, Teresa. 1997. "Patents." The *New York Times*. 24 November: C2.

Robbins, John. 1987. *Diet for a New America*. Walpole: Stillpoint.

Robinson, Mark M.,William J. Hadlow, Tami P. Huff, Gerald A. H. Wells, Michael Dawson, Richard F. Marsh, and John R. Gorham. 1994. "Experimental Infection of Mink with Bovine Spongiform Encephalopathy." *Journal of General Virology* 75: 2151–55.

Roediger, David R. 2008. *How Race Survived U.S. History: From Settlement and Slavery to the Obama Phenomenon*. London and New York: Verso.

Rubin, James H. 1994. *Manet's Silence and the Poetics of Bouquets*. London: Reaktion Books.

Ruether, Rosemary R. 1991. *Gaia and God*. San Francisco: HarperSan Francisco.

Russell, Diana E. H. (1982) 1990. *Rape in Marriage*, rev. ed. Bloomington: Indiana University Press.

Russell, Diana E. H. 1984. *Sexual Exploitation: Rape, Child Sexual Abuse, and Workplace Harassment*. Newbury Park, CA: Sage Publications.

Santa Ana, Otto. 2002. *Brown Tide Rising: Metaphors of Latinos in Contemporary American Public Discourse*. Austin: University of Texas Press.

Sax, Boria. 2000. *Animals in the Third Reich: Pets, Scapgoats, and the Holocaust*. New York: Continuum.

Scarry, Elaine. 1987. *The Body in Pain: The Making and Unmaking of the World*. New York and Oxford: Oxford University Press.

Schama, Simon. 1996. "Mad Cows and Englishmen." *The New Yorker*. April 8: 61–62.

Schmidt, Alfred. 1971. *The Concept of Nature in Marx*. Translated by Ben Fowkes. London: NLB.

Scholtmeijer, Marian. 1993. *Animal Victims in Modern Fiction: From Sanctity to Sacrifice*. Toronto, Buffalo, and London: University of Toronto Press.

Seager, Joni. 1993. *Earth Follies: Coming to Terms with the Global Environmental Crisis*. New York: Routledge.

Sedgwick, Eve Kosofsky. 1990. *Epistemology of the Closet*. Berkeley and Los Angeles: University of California Press.

Serpell, James. 1986. *In the Company of Animals: A Study of Human Animal Relationships*. New York: Basil Blackwell.

Sheraton, Mimi. 1996. "Love, Sex, and Flank Steak." *New Woman*. March.

Simonsen, Rasmus Rahbek. 2012. "A Queer Vegan Manifesto." *Critical Animal Studies* 10 (3): 51–80.

Singer, Jasmin. 2007. "Coming Out for Animal Rights: LGBTQ Animal Advocates Make the Connection." *Satya Magazine*. http://www.satyamag. com/mar07/singer.html (accessed February 8, 2016).

Singer, Jasmin. 2011. Our Hen House Launches "The Gay Animal Series," Featuring Nathan Runkle. http://www.ourhenhouse.org/2011/03/our-hen-house-launches-the-gay-animal-series-featuring-nathan-runkle/ (accessed February 8, 2016).

Singer, Peter. 1975. 1990. *Animal Liberation*. New York: New York Review Press.

Singer, Peter. 2009. *The Life You Can Save: How to Do Your Part to End World Poverty*. New York: Random House.

Slicer, Deborah. 1991. "Your Daughter or Your Dog?" *Hypatia: A Journal of Feminist Philosophy*, Special Issue on Ecological Feminism 6 (1): 108–24.

Smith, Bonnie G. 1998. *The Gender of History: Men, Women, and Historical Practice*. Cambridge, MA and London: Harvard University Press.

Spencer, Colin. 1996. "The Beef That Built an Empire." The *New York Times*. March 30: 19.

Spencer, Daniel. 1996. *Gay and Gaia: Ethics, Ecology, and the Erotic*. Cleveland, OH: Pilgrim Press.

Spender, Dale. 1980. *Man Made Language*. London, Boston, and Henley: Routledge and Kegan Paul.

Spiegelman, Art. 1986. *Maus: A Survivor's Tale*. Book 1, *My Father Bleeds History*. New York: Pantheon.

Stănescu, Vasile. 2011. "'Green' Eggs and Ham? The Myth of Sustainable Meat and the Danger of the Local in the Works of Michael Pollan, Barbara Kingsolver and Joel Salatin." In *Critical Theory and Animal Liberation*, edited by John Sanbonmatsu, 239–56. Lanham: Rowman & Littlefield.

Stevenson, Seth. 2006. "Original SUVs for Hippies? Hummer Courts the Tofu Set." *Slate*. August 14. http://www.slate.com/articles/business/ad_report_card/2006/08/suvs_for_hippies.html (accessed June 13, 2015).

Stoltenberg, John. 2000. *Refusing to be a Man: Essays on Sex and Justice*. New York, NY: Routledge.

Stordeur, Richard A., and Richard Stille. 1989. *Ending Men's Violence Against Their Partners: One Road to Peace*. Newbury Park, CA: Sage.

Stout, David. 1996. "Gingrich a Vegetarian? So Says a Prankster." *The New York Times*. April 2: A10.

Straus, Murray, 1977. "A Sociological Perspective on the Prevention and Treatment of Wifebeating." In *Battered Women: A Psychological Study of Domestic Violence*, edited by Maria Roy, 194–239. New York: Van Nostrand Reinhold Company.

Strom, Stephanie. 1996. "Wary Britons Turning Backs on Beef." *The New York Times*. March 29: A3.

Study to Examine Downside of Erath's Dairy Business. 1991. *Dallas Times Herald*. October 23: A16.

Taylor, Sunuara. 2016. *Beasts of Burden: Animal and Disability Liberation*. New York: The New Press.

Thomas, Keith. 1983. *Man and the Natural World*. New York: Pantheon.

Tuan, Yi-Fu. 1984. *Dominance and Affection: The Making of Pets*. New Haven: Yale University Press.

Turner, Douglas. 1986. "Official Cites Racial Bias in Lifting Radio License." *The Buffalo News*, August 23: C–4.

Varner, Gary. 1994a. "In Defense of the Vegan Ideal: Rhetoric and Bias in the Nutrition Literature." *Journal of Agricultural and Environmental Ethics* 7 (1): 29–40.

Varner, Gary. 1994b. "Rejoinder to Kathryn Paxton George." *Journal of Agricultural and Environmental Ethics* 7 (1): 19–28.

Vidal, John. 1997. *McLibel: Burger Culture on Trial*. New York: The New Press.

Walker, Lenore, 1979. *The Battered Woman*. New York: Harper and Row.

Warren, Karen J. 1987. "Feminism and Ecology: Making Connections." *Environmental Ethics* 9 (1): 3–20.

Warren, Karen J. 1990. "The Power and the Promise of Ecological Feminism." *Environmental Ethics* 12 (2): 125–46.

Watson, L. A., and Abbie Rogers. 2014. *Uncooped: An Exhibition for the National Museum of Animals & Society*. Los Angeles: The National Museum of Animals & Society.

Will, R.G., J.W. Ironside, M. Zeidler, S.N. Cousens, K. Estibeiro, A. Alperovitch, S. Poser, M. Pocchiari, A. Hofman, and P. G. Smith. 1996. "A New Variant of Creutzfeldt-Jakob Disease in the UK." *The Lancet* April 6: 921–25.

Wise, Steve. 2001. *Rattling the Cage: Toward Legal Rights for Animals*. New York: Perseus.

Wolfe, Cary (2003) *Animal Rites: American Culture, the Discourse of Species, and Posthumanist Theory*. Chicago and London: University of Chicago Press.

Women and Violence: Hearings Before The Senate Committee on the Judiciary. 1990. 101st Congress. 2d Session 117 [testimony of Angela Browne, Ph.D.).

Wronoski, John. 2008. "Introduction." *Meat after Meat Joy,* edited by Heide Hatry, p. 7. Cambridge: Pierre Menard Gallery and New York: Daneyal Mahmood Gallery.

Index

Note: page locators followed by "n" indicate notes section.